The Pruning of
Trees, Shrubs and Conifers

THE PRUNING OF TREES, SHRUBS AND CONIFERS

by

George E. Brown

with a new Foreword by
John E. Bryan

and a
Nomenclatural Update

Timber Press
Portland, Oregon

First published in 1972 by Faber and Faber Limited

Timber Press, Inc.
The Haseltine Building
133 S.W. Second Avenue, Suite 450
Portland, Oregon 97204, U.S.A.

Printed in Hong Kong

Library of Congress Cataloging-in-Publication Data

Brown, George Ernest.
    The pruning of trees, shrubs, and conifers / by George E. Brown :
with a new foreword by John E. Bryan, and a nomenclatural update.
       p.   cm.
    Orginally published: London : Faber, 1972.
    Includes index.
    ISBN 0-88192-319-2
    1. Pruning. I. Title.
SB125.B76 1995
635.9'77—dc20

94-46985
CIP

This book is dedicated to my Wife

Acknowledgements

Miss Audrey Barton for her work on the diagrams with the exception of Figs. 4, 52, 53 and 54 which were drawn by Mr Peter Styles.

Dr D. M. Dring for his advice on Chapter 5.

For the Photography:
  Mr R. Zabeau – Plates 1, 2, 3, 7, 10, 11, 37, 59 and 84a
  Mr A. Gilpin – Plates 69 and 72
  Mr J. Harley – Plates 50 and 51
  Mr A. Carpenter for the remainder with the exception of Plates 25, 26, 31, 32, 33, 36, 47, 77 and 81, which were taken by the Author. With the exception also of Plates 79, 84b and 85, which were reproduced by the kind permission of Messrs. Wilkinson Sword (Colnbrook) Ltd.

For the illustrations of tools and equipment in the plate photographs:
  Messrs. Wilkinson Sword (Colnbrook) Ltd. – Plates 79, 84b and 85
  Messrs. Hayters Ltd. – Plate 66
  Messrs. Ransomes, Sims & Jefferies Ltd. – Plate 63
  Messrs. Burton McCall & Co. – Plates 30, 40, 48, 61 and 62 (Felco Secateurs), also Fig. 52 (Tina Knife)
  Messrs. Spearwell Tools Ltd., Plate 44
  Messrs. Ramsay Ladders, Plate 60
  Messrs. S. H. Rainbow Ltd., Plates 15 and 19
  Permission to photograph for reproduction – Mr J. Gilbert – Plate 84a
  Mr E. Brown – Plate 50 and 51

Foreword

It is an honor to write the foreword to this edition of *The Pruning of Trees, Shrubs and Conifers* by George E. Brown. The magnificent collections of shrubs and trees at the Royal Botanic Gardens, Kew, are testimony to the author's skill, for they were in his charge while he was Assistant Curator there. Many specimens at Kew have their classic form because he knew exactly how, when and where to prune. This knowledge was based on keen and thoughtful observation of one of the most extensive collections of plants in the world. This wealth of experience is beyond value yet is available to all who read this book.

When Mr. Brown's book was first published, Frank Knight, Director of the Royal Horticultural Society's garden at Wisley said, "practising arboriculturists, professional and amateur gardeners or landscape architects have been provided with a text book which is certain to be a standard work for the foreseeable future." This is still the case. Nothing has been published since the book first appeared which rivals it for in-depth, plant-by-plant coverage of the pruning practices for nearly 450 genera. Readers will also obtain an idea of the form, habit, color and texture of the plants discussed and become acquainted with shrubs and trees that are not demanding of maintenance.

Techniques change. It is no longer the general practice to coat wounds or pruning cuts. Some authorities continue to debate this question. George Brown was perhaps thinking ahead, as he writes, "The healing power of the cut varies, for much depends upon the size of the wound, upon the age, health and vigour of the shrub or tree and upon the actual species or type." His subsequent discussion of the different healing properties of various species points to the unique value of this book. The practice may have changed, but the wisdom endures.

George Brown hinted that just where to make a cut depends on various factors. He anticipated much of the current thinking of arborists who prefer to cut at the "collar" of the branch by noting, "The point to remember is that while the general aim is to make the cut close to the stem, the need to keep the wound as small as possible is also important." Readers should consult the accompanying illustration here for the proper cut as suggested by today's authorities.

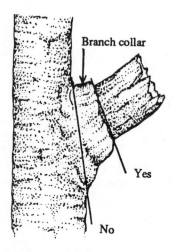

Correct and incorrect cuts (reprinted with permission from *The Oregon Master Gardener Handbook*, courtesy of Oregon State University Extension Service).

Any book which leads the reader through the "whys and wherefores" that justify recommended procedures is useful. I have found in my many years in horticulture that knowing why actions should be taken is as important as knowing how. This understanding provides a solid foundation upon which to build—using the "bricks" of up-to-date information as they are acquired. The knowledge obtained from *The Pruning of Trees, Shrubs and Conifers* allows a reasoned and thorough evaluation of newer techniques.

Hailed as a masterpiece when it was first published, it remains one today and should be read by all who undertake pruning, and all landscape architects and nurserymen. Anthony Huxley wrote that this was "probably the most comprehensive and thorough-going textbook on pruning ever written." One word needs to "pruned" from this statement—the word "probably"! No other book describes in such detail the pruning needs of so many shrubs, trees and conifers, information as invaluable today as the day it was written.

JOHN E. BRYAN
Fellow, Institute of Horticulture

Preface

The subject of this opus, the pruning and training of trees and shrubs is a surprisingly wide one and the methods which are used are so diverse, that no attempt has been made to deal with these in detail. In many cases there is a considerable overlapping with cultural methods generally, but in a book of this nature it has been found necessary to define boundaries where in actual fact none really exist.

As an example, no attempt has been made to explain the advanced and skilled techniques which are involved with the profession and art which is widely known as tree surgery. This is more a subject for a companion book, wherein the various operations involving the use of specialised equipment and often work at considerable heights, can be explained in detail. In the hands of the unskilled person there is a considerable element of danger in heavy tree work, and it is a subject which cannot be taken lightly.

Having thus defined the limit in this direction, it should be emphasised that the work does explain principles of tree pruning in detail, and the reader is taken to the point where he knows what is needed and why.

The same is true also of other related subjects, for example with pests and diseases. The reader will find a chapter which deals with the subject in a very practical way, but only in so far as their control relates to pruning.

In order to be practical the metric measurements (in m. and mm.) are approximate only.

Admittedly the overlapping is rather involved and complex and the diagram represents an attempt to explain this diagrammatically.

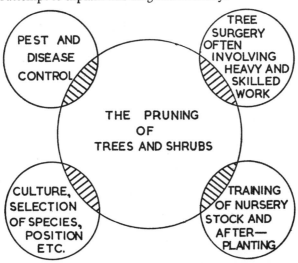

G. E. B.

Contents

Part One

CHAPTER ONE   THE GENERAL PRINCIPLES OF PRUNING

CHAPTER TWO   THE PRUNING OF TREES AND CONIFERS

CHAPTER THREE   THE PRUNING OF SHRUBS AND CLIMBERS

List of Plates

List of Figures

(With the exception of those in Appendix II Saw Sharpening and Maintenance.)

A

CHAPTER ONE

The General Principles of Pruning

The need for pruning – Some basic principles – The natural response to a cut or wound – Selecting the position of the cut – The angle of the cut – Avoidance of tearing – The protective dressing – The healing power of the cut – Cavities – Surface wounds – Causes of injury – Development of cavities – Work in the neighbourhood of roots – The effects of pruning roots – Dealing with damaged roots – Girdling roots – Importance of early training – Importance of good propagating material

INTRODUCTION

Pruning is an operation which regulates and controls growth, flowering and fruiting, and with its aid the form of a tree or bush is determined, often in its early years while still in the nursery.

The Need for Pruning

It is often asked why pruning should be needed as it does not occur in nature. Apart from this not being absolutely correct, for twig-shedding is found under natural conditions, there are several answers to this question.

In nature, the tree or bush which is produced is not always a good shape. Growth may be typical of the species, but under natural conditions plants are often found in ecological communities and in direct competition with other plants which may be larger. The larger plants frequently overpower the weaker, which will die unless they adapt to these conditions. This is not so in the garden, where the weaker ones may be protected by pruning the stronger subjects, be they trees or shrubs.

Trees and shrubs are commonly planted by paths or roads, as hedges or screens, on boundaries and against walls. If not pruned, they may well outgrow their positions or impede traffic.

Development often involves farmland, natural woodland and even gardens, large and small. The trees and shrubs which are preserved and allowed to remain are left under an entirely different set of conditions. They are also likely to come very much under the public eye and are often in enclosed positions. To help them to conform to their new environment it may be necessary to correct their shape and control their growth by pruning.

Many trees and shrubs, as they develop towards maturity, accumulate a number of dead twigs and branches, which should be removed as they are unsightly and may hinder development or harbour pests and diseases. Diseased wood should also be cut out.

Most plantings are made with a definite type of tree or bush, which from experience, is considered the most suitable form of the particular species or variety. Their training to these forms often involves the adoption of a pruning system which may take several years to complete. The need for these forms has been universally recognised for generations and British Standards publications lay down very definite sizes and types for the nursery stock of many common species and varieties.

A number of shrubs are grown for their displays of flowers and in many cases they are special varieties which have flowers larger than usual and which do not occur under natural conditions. Pruning is a necessary part of their cultivation if the required standards of growth and blossoming are to be maintained. Without it and a complementary feeding programme, growth may be weak and the flowers small, though in some cases all that is needed is the systematic removal of seed heads or fruits.

Only with good pruning and training can the grace and beauty of trees and shrubs in summer and winter be fully realised. Good training and growth in particular, show up very plainly with deciduous subjects in winter. A well-balanced plant improves most surroundings and helps to provide a restful scene for mind and eye but a mutilated tree or shrub is depressing and, in a modern urban setting, may be seen by thousands.

Some Basic Principles and Preconditions

It must not be assumed, however, that constant pruning is a necessity. Good nursery techniques require the provision of the best growing conditions in addition to correct pruning. Once a good plant has been produced and has been planted correctly in its final position with due regard for its particular needs, good growth will follow, provided of course that there is freedom from diseases and pests. Pruning is then often reduced to a minimum once the initial head or framework has been formed.

There are, of course, exceptions to this. Many shrubs are pruned annually for a particular reason, such as improved flowering, better foliage, etc. As a general rule, however, ornamental trees and shrubs, left to develop naturally in a suitable locality and environment, flower and fruit without regular pruning. Only a small proportion require the sort of attention normally necessary for economic crops, such as the apple.

It is most important that the pruner should know exactly what he is pruning for. He must have a thorough knowledge of the growth and flowering habits of the subject he is pruning and of the effects likely to be produced by his operations. Good judgement, skill and care are always needed, and conscientiousness and a love for trees and shrubs are essential. The care of tall trees in particular requires considerable experience as it may involve a large outlay on heavy equipment.

It is important that the general public should learn to love and appreciate trees and have a broad understanding of the work and problems connected with them. Good trees and public safety go hand in hand, and the latter should always be an overriding factor in any decision involving trees.

PRUNING CUTS AND HEALING

The Natural Response to a Cut or Wound

Any wound made on a woody stem which is growing actively and is healthy brings about a response in healing. This is the result of a reaction to the wounding by the meristematic cells, which then divide very rapidly, especially during the growing season. These cells, which form a tissue referred to as *cambium*, are in a continuous cylinder just beneath the bark. By rapid division they form a circle of raised tissue and by continuous growth and division on the inside of the circle the healing growth or *callus* moves over the bare face of the wound which, as a result, gradually becomes smaller, *see* Plate 8. Thus healing is a gradual process, the rate being directly related to the growth and health of the tree or shrub. It will be seen at once that if this wound is untidy or jagged the cambium may not be in a continuous circle and healing will thus take longer, for the various sections must first of all join, *see* Plates 3, 5 and 64.

As healing continues, the outermost layer of cambium forms a protective tissue or cork, a change which is brought about by the accumulation of a fatty substance called *suberin* on the walls of these cells. This layer of cork functions in exactly the same way as the surrounding bark but the healing tissue will always remain distinct throughout the life of the tree or shrub, *see* Plates 4 and 6.

Sometimes when a branch is removed, a number of shoots proliferate from the cut surface. These may need thinning out or may be removed entirely as often as is necessary at a later stage. They are referred to as *epicormic* shoots.

Selecting the Position of the Cut

Fig. 1. A Beech twig showing the ideal positions of cuts to remove snags (at a and b). However it might be better, in view of the unhealthy condition of the growth to make a cut at c. The lower growth appears to be healthier.

The position of the cut should be selected very carefully. It is important to ensure that the living tissue is maintained in the region of the cut by present and future growth and that the general appearance of the tree or shrub is not spoilt by the pruning. The choice is governed by the following considerations.

(i) If dead wood is being pruned away the cut must be made back to sound living tissue, as good callus formation and healing is only possible from sound wood, *see* Figs. 1 and 2.

(ii) It is essential that the cut is made at a point close to a branch or bud. Careless pruning often results in a length of stem being left projecting beyond this point. This piece of stem, which is called a snag, *see* Fig. 3a, Plates 5 and 7, will in the course of a few months die back to the tissue in the region of the nearest bud or branch. Thus healing over the cut is at the best delayed, but more often it is never completed because of the length of the snag. In due course, air and moisture combine to bring about the decay of this snag, but by this time the process has extended into the heartwood and a cavity is formed which may shorten the life of the tree or shrub. The subject is dealt with in greater detail under the heading 'Cavities and Wounds' on page 9.

It is noticeable, however, that those shrubs which regenerate freely, often from the base, can safely be cut back to older wood despite the fact that no buds may be visible. Should a snag be evident at a later date after new growth has broken out, it can be removed before extensive rotting occurs. It may even break off. As a general rule, snags are more likely to lead to trouble if they occur on trees and shrubs which have a permanent framework, rather than on those which grow quickly and regenerate freely. Often the latter, e.g. *Rubus*, produce canes from ground level which have only a life of two seasons, and the snags which are left after the old canes are cut off are not a real danger as they die off naturally.

(iii) The removal of diseased wood calls for extra care, for the infection may have progressed well beyond the portion which is completely dead or shows some form of fungal fructification. A good example of this is Fire Blight (*Erwinia amylovora*), where infection often extends for several feet through the stem or branch beyond the first visible signs of die-back.

(iv) It is essential to relate the position of the cut to the branch system as a whole. The tree or bush should, after pruning is completed, have a balanced and natural appearance. The position of the cut should not only be just above a bud or branch, but the most suitable one should be selected. To do this properly, a full knowledge of the natural habit of growth of the tree or shrub is essential.

Fig. 2. Heading back or dead-wooding. This is necessary with stag-headed trees or where die-back needs to be corrected on a large or small scale.
Cut 1. A very bad cut and one which will leave a snag of dead wood.
Cut 2. Well positioned to a selected limb, but this is in poor health and has no future.
Cut 3. Well positioned to a branch which is in good health.

The Angle of the Cut

When a complete branch is being removed a cut which is flush with the parent stem sheds water readily and there is less chance of its gaining access to the wood, especially if the wound is painted over with waterproofing material and the surface maintained, if necessary, by subsequent dressings at regular intervals, *see* Fig. 3b and c.

The angle of the cut also depends upon the nature, thickness and mechanics of the main stem. The point to remember is that while the general aim is to make the cut close to the stem, the need to keep the wound as small as possible is also important. At the same time the position of the strengthening tissues or wood should be considered. A cut in line with the main trunk or branch may cut through some of the tissues supporting the wood which is to remain, with a weakening effect. This would be a mistake, and an angle for the cut should be taken which avoids this, *see* Fig. 3c.

Some of the points and considerations given above may prove to be mutually conflicting, but with actual practice and experience there should be little difficulty in deciding where and how to make the cut in each particular case.

Avoidance of Tearing

Just as it is important to cut at the best angle, close to or flush with the stem, it is equally so to avoid tearing the bark on the trunk or part of the tree from which the branch is to be removed. Plate 5 illustrates the advantages of a clean wound as opposed to a torn one.

The effects which follow from a bad tear as a result of removing a limb can be enumerated as follows.

(i) A larger area is exposed and therefore the danger of pests and other harmful organisms entering the wound is increased.

(ii) The circle of cambium which surrounds a clean wound is broken in the region of the tear. Therefore the healing process is slowed down, *see* Plate 3.

(iii) With a bad tear it is possible that a portion of the heartwood will also be torn out, *see* Plate 60. This often leaves the base of the tear in a very untidy condition. Thus more work is involved in the task of cleaning the wound, for a pocket or sharply uneven surface should never be left where moisture can collect.

(iv) A bad tear as a result of a cut, even after cleaning and dressing, will be evidence of bad workmanship and this is undesirable. Pride in the work and in the finished appearance is important.

It is sometimes said that the surface of wounds should be pared smooth before the protective dressing is applied. This is true of the smaller cuts where the outer tissue and the wood itself may be ragged and untidy. With the larger wounds, however, only the edges and outer tissues need be pared. The large area of inner wood need not be touched as long as it is in a reasonable condition, for the protective substances usually used are tacky and are more effectively applied to a slightly roughened surface, *see* 'The Protective Dressing' *below*.

Method of Removing a Branch

With a light branch it is an easy matter to take the weight with the free hand as the cut is made, but this is not possible with heavier branches. Indeed, it might be unsafe even with lighter wood in high and difficult positions. It is possible, however, to cut off a very heavy branch by removing it gradually section by section. With large heavy branches this may involve several cuts and the use of slinging with ropes, in order that the pieces may be lowered gently.

As each cut is made it is important to undercut at least 1/6th of the diameter or until the cut closes, before cutting through the limb from above. This is made just beyond the undercut, *see* Fig. 3d and e.

Once the weight has been taken off, the final cut at the stub end should be from top to bottom in order to ensure that the surface of the wound is neat and

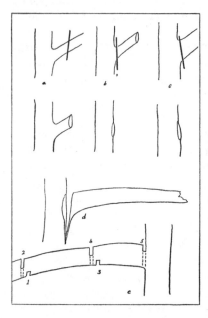

Fig. 3. Diagrams which illustrate good and bad cuts.

(a) The final cut has been poorly positioned leaving a bad snag.

(b) A good final cut which has been made close to the stem.

(c) The final cut made flush to the stem is sloping to allow for an increased girth of the parent branch or stem, through and below the junction in this region.

(d) A bad method of removing a limb. The only cut has been made without lightening the limb in any way with the result that the weight, as the limb has fallen, has taken the bark away for a considerable length.

(e) The branch has been removed in sections, the sequence of the cuts being 1 and 2, 3 and 4, to finish with a stub end the fall of which can be controlled as it is cut off at 5.

on one plane. Also, by this method the cut may be directed to be flush with the stem or at the desired angle. With a small limb the free hand can be used to take the weight, but with a heavier limb, even though it has been reduced to a stump, it may be necessary to use a rope and sling-piece before the cut is made in order to take the weight, *see* Appendix III, 'Slinging'.

The Protective Dressing

When a cut is made, a considerable amount of heartwood is exposed which, in the case of the larger stems and branches, has become salignified or hardened to give mechanical strength. This remains healthy and perfectly preserved, provided it is protected from air and water, pests and other harmful organisms and the tree is in a healthy condition. The cut immediately exposes this wood and it is vital, therefore, to protect it as speedily as possible before the destructive agents begin their work. It will be apparent how quickly a sealant must be applied, when it is realised that the air is full of spores of all kinds which may alight on the cut surface at any time. There is also the point that if it is left until later it is quite easily forgotten or overlooked, and in going back over the work extra effort is involved. All cuts over 25 mm. (1 inch) in diameter should be treated, although with young specimens even smaller wounds should be dressed.

The material used must be waterproof. It should retain its pliable nature for a long period without cracking. It should not be favourable to the development of diseases or pests – in fact the ideal dressing would have an active and lasting fungicidal property.

At present, the specially prepared bituminous products are most widely favoured for they are reasonably easy to apply and remain pliable for very long periods. Even these preparations, however, eventually dry and deteriorate to expose the wood, unless the healing has been completed, *see* Plate 33. It is therefore necessary to look over the wounds at least annually and, if necessary, make further applications, although a six-monthly inspection of every tree is in any case advisable, and it would be natural to inspect wounds at the same time. Often, radial cracks appear in the heartwood on the surface of a large wound as it dries out. These need to be filled in as they open and the surface covered with further applications of a wound dressing.

Undoubtedly, improved forms of wound dressings will be available in the future; for instance, the addition of a fungicide is an interesting development which has taken place within recent years. Up-to-date information should be sought from time to time in the Ministry of Agriculture, Fisheries and Food list of Approved Products.

Woods vary considerably in their resistance to decay and age is also an important factor. This will become very evident as experience is gained with a collection and it will soon be realised which trees require the most attention.

The Healing Power of the Cut

The healing power of the cut varies, for much depends upon the size of the wound, upon the age, health and vigour of the shrub or tree and upon the actual species or type. Some wounds will be too large, or the tree too old to heal completely, *see* Plate 8.

Dealing with size first, the small cuts, especially those on young trees, heal very quickly. Part of the reason for this is that the increase in girth is so rapid in a fast-growing tree that the area is soon engulfed by the developing tissue. Wounds of a similar size on older trees may take several years. The old, weak tree which is declining may never form more than a callus on the outer edge of the wound and even this may not be in a complete circle.

Often, there is a marked variation in the healing power of the cambium tissue round the sides of a wound. Any weakness or reluctance for the cambium to form is usually found on the vertical axis of a wound. Generally speaking the tissue on the sides is more freely formed and develops at a faster rate, *see* Plates 6 and 8. It is for this reason that the practice of cutting or forming an oval shape to a wound has been advocated. It is not altogether popular, for extra time is involved in the first shaping.

As stated earlier, the species or type needs to be taken into account. As an example, the Common Oak (*Quercus robur*), will heal over much faster than the Californian Horse-chestnut (*Aesculus californica*), which is often slow and uncertain and whose wood may rot in the meantime, despite an adequate dressing.

With shrubs that renew themselves readily from ground level and have a cane growth, for example Blackberry (*Rubus*), healing above ground level where the wood has a pith centre does not take place. This is not important, however, for the natural habit of these plants is to lose their wood after it is a few years old, and by that time the root stock has either sealed over the point of connection with the old stem and has thus healed itself completely, or the root is a creeping one and has moved on to fresh ground, leaving the older parts of the plant to die.

Healing is very important with those shrubs which do not readily renew their wood with a cane habit of growth, but keep their framework throughout their life, for example the shrubby Magnolias.

BLEEDING FROM A WOUND OR CUT SURFACE

A number of subjects, particularly deciduous ones, bleed if wounds (or pruning cuts) occur in the late winter or early spring. This is caused by the flow of sap, which is commencing to 'rise' or become active during this period, in preparation for bud development and growth, which takes place in the early part of the year.

Once bleeding has started from a wound, it is difficult, if not almost impossible, to stop until the subject breaks into leaf, when the flow which is being lost, is taken by the developing growth. With this difficulty in mind, it is important to avoid cutting live branches of deciduous trees during the weeks before budbreak, especially in those subjects which bleed badly, e.g. the Birches. (The genera which are especially prone to bleeding are mentioned in Part II.)

It is unusual for a subject to be killed by excessive bleeding, but in severe cases it may cause considerable die-back. The edible Vine is often quoted as an example of a subject which bleeds badly if it is pruned too late in the dormant period. It is a good choice, for the vine is spurred back annually to the main rod system and December is the best time for this. Should bleeding occur through late pruning, the loss may be reduced by lowering the vine to the horizontal, until the buds break. Lowering the rods in the spring is accepted as standard practice to encourage them to break evenly.

With a small wound it is possible to reduce the flow by a very tight binding. First the surrounds and then the wound itself are cleansed and dried as thoroughly as possible; this is important, especially if adhesive tape is used, for it will not adhere to a wet surface. It may be possible to hasten drying by the use of an electric hair-dryer, or a compressed air unit, but this is a question of availability at the point required. Hand bellows are of course useful and also absorbent paper.

When the surrounds are perfectly dry, cotton wool is placed over the wound itself, in order to soak up the oozing sap as the binding is made. As mentioned earlier, strong adhesive tape is usually used for the first binding and the layers are wound round really tightly, overlapping enough to give the maximum holding power. It is advisable to bind a length of stem above and below the wound, so that there is an adequate overlap. Finally the whole area should be bound over with a strip of strong canvas, which should be coated with a bituminous tree dressing as the binding proceeds. Again, a tight binding is essential and with the bituminous covering being bound in with each layer, it is a two-man task. Finally this covering should be tied in with strong cord, to prevent loosening and slipping.

At a later stage, when the growth is full and the danger of bleeding is past, the binding should be removed, otherwise restriction will take place in this area, as the stem swells.

CAVITIES AND WOUNDS

The reader would be excused for thinking that this subject is outside the scope of this work and yet good pruning and attention to the protection of cuts will reduce the chances of a cavity forming and some account must be given of their development.

The core of salignified tissue which extends through the trunk and branch system and most of the roots has already been mentioned and it is important to remember that the strength of the entire branch system of a tree depends partly on the condition of this tissue. It readily breaks down under the influence of bacteria and other organisms which, however, are only active when suitable conditions are present, including sufficient air and moisture. It should also be remembered that in a perfectly healthy tree this salignified tissue is protected from these agencies and from the associated diseases by the outer sleeve of living tissue. It will remain healthy provided this protective coat is intact and in good condition. The latter point is important, for the surface tissues on a tree which is in poor condition may not function properly and thus leave the heart-wood unprotected. At this stage it is necessary to differentiate between a cavity and a surface wound.

Cavities

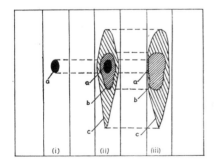

Fig. 4. A typical cavity in diagrammatic form.
(i) Opening to the cavity visible at (a).
(ii) A plan view from the same position as at (i) showing (a) the opening to the cavity, (b) the size of the cavity within the stem and (c), the area of degenerated tissue.
(iii) A sectional view of the stem taken from the side showing (a) the opening to the cavity,
(b) the actual cavity within the stem and (c) the area of degenerated tissue.

These often penetrate deeply into the branch or trunk. There is evidence to show that degenerative processes which are initiated on stubs or snags, often spread quickly into the parent branch or trunk by the old conducting tissue. As the breakdown continues the whole snag becomes rotten and may hold considerable moisture which encourages further spread. A lengthy snag prevents complete healing and the resultant callus forms a cup-shaped lip which collects moisture as the snag rots away completely. When this happens the moisture or standing water often remains permanently, and this encourages further decay into the centre of the trunk or branch. *See* Plates 7 and 10.

Surface Wounds

As implied, these are formed by injury to the bark, often leaving the salignified tissues intact. The old conducting strands are thus unaffected and do not have open ends for the destructive agencies to gain a ready access. It should not be inferred that a cavity never forms from this type of wound, but usually, if it happens at all, it is a slower process, especially in the earlier stages, and this gives a longer time for healing. Often too, such surface wounds remain dry, for unlike snags they do not present a receptive surface to rain. Such exposed areas of dry, undamaged heartwood are more likely to be broken down by wood worm attack, *see* Plate 9.

Causes of Injury

It has been mentioned that an injury to a limb readily leads to the development of a cavity in the parent branch or trunk unless corrected. This injury can be caused in a variety of ways. Wind, for example, sometimes accompanied by driving rain, may either snap branches and leave snags, or by taking them off at the main junctions leave bad tears on the main trunk, *see* Plate 59. Ice forming on the branch system during a glazed frost results in a considerable increase of weight and, with the wood in a brittle condition through the cold, a break or tear is likely. Snow has the same effect, conifers and evergreens suffering particularly, *see* Plate 60. Die-back through disease, ill-health or lack of light will also cause snags as dead limbs break off at the weakest point. Only rarely, however, does a direct tear on the main trunk occur as a result of die-back.

These are some of the main causes of snag-producing injuries and it should be noted that such damage is more likely to occur on a weak, badly-shaped tree. A well-trained tree with a good central lead is better equipped to withstand unusual stresses than, for instance, a tree with multiple leads. Such a tree tends to be weak because of the uneven distribution of weight and the narrowness of its crotches and is, consequently, more likely to suffer severe damage. Such weakness, however, does not always result in an obviously dangerous tear or break. The injury is sometimes only a small crack which may go undetected for years – a disastrous period when air and moisture with the accompanying decay are channelled into the very heartwood in the crown or head of the trunk, *see* Plate 60 and Fig. 10.

Development of Cavities

It must be recognised that however small a cavity is, once it has formed it is serious and in time, if allowed to develop, may weaken the tree and shorten its life. This may even be making light of the situation, for the wood deteriorates far in advance of the actual cavity and decay is often more extensive below the opening than above, *see* Fig. 4. The decay is usually most rapid in the softer-wooded trees such as Poplar. The more extensive rotting below the cavity is of course natural, for water often collects in the hollow, either as a result of rain or because of the seepage of sap from neighbouring living tissues. Once moisture does collect, putrefaction sets in and the effect is a progressive increase in the activity of the organisms causing the breakdown. This takes place very rapidly if there are other snags nearby, for the areas of degenerated and diseased wood quickly join up with each other and eventually the inner core of an entire trunk or branch will decompose to leave a hollow shell, *see* Plate 10. The danger at this stage is from any large branches which are adjacent to the area of decay, as their junctions are weakened. Eventually they are shed and the hollow trunk is left standing.

Thus the story is one of progressive decay which must, if left unattended, lead to a drastic shortening of the life of a tree. The rate of decay will speed up as the condition and health of the tree deteriorates, large limbs are lost and the root system suffers.

PRUNING AND THE ROOT SYSTEM

Workings in the Neighbourhood of Roots

In this age of rapid change and development it frequently becomes necessary to work near or among the root systems of trees. The safety margin beyond which there is a risk to the well-being and perhaps life of the tree varies considerably and is dependent upon several factors, but it is outside the scope of this book to deal with these in detail. One of the more important factors, however, concerns the amount of care the operators are prepared to take, both to avoid injury to the system and in making cuts and treating wounds properly, *see* Plates 12 and 13. Again, this is not the place in which to deal with general methods of minimising damage to root systems, but an account of the sort of root pruning which is frequently necessary must obviously be included.

The Effects of Pruning Roots

A reduction of, or injury to a root system affects growth to an extent which is directly proportional to the amount of damage incurred. Root pruning as a deliberate means of reducing growth is seldom used with ornamental subjects. Rightly, it is generally accepted that a careful selection should be made in the first place, when the ultimate size and habit are major factors to take into consideration.

In former days, root pruning was an established practice, with apple trees in particular, in order to bring over-vigorous trees into bearing. But nowadays, as a result of the wide range of selected rootstocks available, which provide an effective means of controlling size, vigour and fruiting, there is little need for such a drastic and expensive method and it has fallen into disuse. (But *see* 'The Pruning and Training of Semi-mature Transplants' on page 24.)

Dealing with Damaged Roots

Roots should, if possible, be cut off cleanly in the first instance, but any torn and jagged wounds must be trimmed up, cutting them back to sound wood with clean, pared cuts. The root should be cleared of soil sufficiently for the cut to be made, wiping it clean to avoid damage to the cutting tools. With large roots, the cuts may be made with a saw and the surface pared smooth. A hatchet or axe may be used for the severance, but unless it is in the hands of a skilled person, the results may be very poor indeed. Often, it is advisable to sever the root beyond the position of the intended cut, as in this way the final cut may be made without the surfaces closing to jam the saw. It is also easier to remove soil from beneath the stub-end of the root before cutting. Lastly, as soon as possible after the final cuts have been made the surface should be given an adequate covering of an approved dressing.

Sufficient time and labour should be allowed for this work as it is sometimes worthwhile to expose more root and to cut back cleanly to a branch root, even though it may be a minor one, without leaving a stub-end, for the same rules and dangers apply to roots as to branches. Snags will die back, giving a means of entry for diseases.

Great care should always be taken to avoid accidents, which are more likely when work is undertaken in cramped conditions. It should also be remembered that cuts and abrasions must be dressed immediately in order to keep them free from soil particles.

Girdling Roots

This term is applied to roots which develop over the main buttress or surface roots in a partial circle near the base of the trunk, see Plate 11. The effect is to arrest or impede the development of the main roots, but the extent to which this is harmful depends upon several factors. There may be scope for growth and increase in thickness in the root system as a whole if only one or two are affected. Again, the girdling root itself may not be very strong and may either be forced out of position or give way under increasing strain and pressure as the buttress roots swell. The first impulse is to cut through the offending root, and this is the best course if it can be done cleanly, but often the buttress or main roots have grown partly over the offending root and this would be difficult. The fact, also, that there must necessarily be two cuts and that the roots beyond the girdling position will die and rot, increases the risk of infection.

The matter must therefore be weighed very carefully. Obviously there is seldom any justification in cutting through the offending root if it entails making an excavation and leaving a wound in a position where it is likely to be damp and moist for a long period. It is generally more important to correct this condition on a growing tree than on one which has reached maturity and is past the period of rapid growth.

With young trees, it is possible to reduce the chances of these roots forming by careful training and planting. By cramming the roots into a small hole, either when planting in the nursery or at the final planting, this is more likely to happen, for the roots in part of the system may be twisted or looped together to bring about trouble later. The correct method of planting involves a large enough hole to allow the main roots to be straightened out.

There is also the same risk in planting trees and shrubs from pots or containers, especially when the roots have developed round the sides of the ball through restriction. It is, of course, necessary to raise certain trees and shrubs in pots, but they should not be left in these too long, as the root system may become seriously pot-bound.

PROPAGATION AND TRAINING

The good nurseryman and propagator takes a pride in his work and in the trees and shrubs under his charge. He must often wonder about the ultimate fate of the stock which he produces, but in present conditions of planting and development, a place will always be found for good, well trained material, for which there is a very great demand.

Most nurserymen are ready to advise on the plants which they raise and, just as the planner and planter have much to learn from them, so they in turn should keep in touch with the conditions under which their young nursery stock has ultimately to be established. There must be a two-way flow of ideas and information.

The Importance of Early Training

The future shape of a tree or shrub depends upon the nature of the training which is carried out in the early years after germination or rooting. A badly placed shoot or even a developing bud is quite easily removed when young, but if it is left until the specimen has reached maturity, not only does correction become a major operation but, even if this is possible, the effects may be seen for many years or may even be permanent. This is also true of the many shrubs which retain their branch system and build on this from year to year. As an example we may take *Magnolia × soulangeana* for with this subject much of the permanent branch system is formed in the first few years. *Forsythia × intermedia* 'Spectabilis' has a stool-like habit, with the branches springing from ground level, *see* Plates 38 and 39. In a healthy specimen, fresh growths will appear, to make up any gaps or to renew any of the older branches which often become weak and straggly with age. Such shrubs can make good a start from a poor one by the production of strong basal shoots which quickly outgrow the inferior ones, though in no way should this be used as an excuse for bad culture and methods of training.

The Importance of good Propagating Material

Poor seed or inferior propagating material often results in a bad start and a weakly, misshapen plant. The soundest policy, therefore, is to select the most suitable material for propagation and provide the best conditions possible for rooting and for subsequent growth during the training period. The following paragraphs give some of the factors which need to be taken into consideration.

Selection of material with Conifers. Where the propagation of Conifers is concerned it is sometimes necessary to use leading shoot material for propagation. The Monkey Puzzle (*Araucaria araucana*) is an example, for material propagated from lateral branches will not form shapely trees. Instead, they become no more than living branches with a unilateral habit. It is essential that the propagator should be acquainted with the growth and habits of the subject under his charge, so that he is able to adopt methods of training which are likely to give the best results.

The juvenile stage with some species. This may need to be taken into account, for the seedlings of some species pass through a juvenile stage when the growth may be entirely out of character with that of a mature plant. A well-

c

known example of this is with the Ivy (*Hedera helix*). The juvenile stage is the creeping form, when the growth extends along the ground and up trees or other supports. It is at a later stage that the mature branching develops which produces flowers and fruit. If the mature form is propagated it will not revert extensively to the creeping habit.

The balance of growth and flowering.   In the early years in the life of a tree or shrub there is a natural tendency for growth rather than flowering and subsequently fruiting. This is carried to the extreme with *Magnolia campbellii* which may take up to 20 years to flower from seed, while *Sophora japonica* may take up to 40 years.

Vegetative reproduction favours earlier flowering. For example, *Magnolia campbellii* plants raised by grafting onto selected forms will flower within 10 to 15 years. *Cytisus scoparius* cuttings flower within a few months of rooting, while seedlings may take from 3 to 4 years. The general tendency of young stock toward growth rather than flower in the early years is to the propagator's advantage, but it also affects the gardener and tree grower when the tree is planted and is growing in its final position. There must, however, always be some growth, and a tree which fails to maintain the growing points usually dies, often after flowering and seeding profusely.

Early and premature flowering may seriously affect the symmetry of a young tree. A Sycamore, for example, in a poor position may flower prematurely even from the terminal buds. Thus forking occurs on the leading growths and the process is continued each year with the result that the crown too is produced prematurely thus affecting the ultimate dimensions and shape of the final tree. From this it will be seen that the flowering stage plays an important part in crown formation.

These are factors which must be considered both when propagating material is selected and throughout the period of training. It is important to produce growth in the nursery. Without this, pruning and training are impossible.

CHAPTER TWO

The Pruning of Trees and Conifers

Classification: tree or shrub – Types of tree – Conditions for tree production – Initial training – Training to produce specific types – Natural branch formation – Notching – Nicking – The semi-mature tree nursery – Semi-mature trees taken from woodland – Young nursery stock – Large transplants – The development of a new and stronger head – Semi-mature trees – Recovery from a poor start – Continuity of training – 'Lifting' – Crown thinning – Crown reduction – Epicormic shoots – Sucker growths – Lopping – Young trees up to 20 years old – Semi-mature trees 20 to 60 years old – Mature trees over 60 years old – Hedgerow trees growing close together

TREE TYPES AND TREE PRODUCTION

Classification: Tree or Shrub

The main difference between a tree and a shrub is that the former has a strong branch system which is built upon a trunk. This in turn strengthens to keep pace with the extending framework which develops as the tree grows. The shrub on the other hand forms a head of branches near ground level. The result is that with the former considerable height is often built up as, for example, with our larger trees which may extend up to a hundred feet or more. There is, however, considerable variation in the mode of growth among shrubs. A number adopt a suckerous habit, producing a crop of growths annually from ground level as the plant spreads. In some cases these growths extend and build up from year to year, as with the Blackthorn (*Prunus spinosa*), while with others the growths or canes die down after flowering in their second year, e.g. the Blackberry (*Rubus fruticosus*). The suckerous habit, however, is not confined to shrubs, for some trees such as the Aspen (*Populus tremula*), the False Acacia (*Robinia pseudoacacia*) and the Tree of Heaven (*Ailanthus altissima*), will also spread by this means.

It is recognised that with many species the early training does affect the ultimate form and size. The retention and vigour of the leading growth will often be the deciding factor. By training, *Colutea arborescens* may be grown into a small standard tree, though normally it is a shrub. For general purposes, however, with comparatively few exceptions, woody plants may be broadly divided into trees and shrubs.

The problems of forming a stem which will develop into a trunk do not exist with shrubs, but it is important to train these on sound lines. Details are given in Chapter Three, and also in Six which deals with the individual genera.

Types of Tree

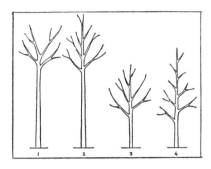

Fig. 5. Some of the types of tree described in the text on pages 16 and 17.
(1) Standard with branching head.
(2) Standard with central lead.
(3) Bush tree.
(4) Feathered tree.

Trees which are being grown in the nursery for final planting should have a sound framework, for when they are mature they will often carry considerable weight and may be exposed to gales and other strains. A tree is well equipped for this provided the framework is mechanically sound, *see* Plates 14, 15 and 16. A British Standard has been produced, No. 3936:1965 Part 1, 'Specification for Nursery Stock', which deals with requirements for trees and shrubs. Broadly, so far as trees are concerned, the following types have been specified (the conversion to the metric system is approximate).

(i) *Bush Tree*. 0·3 to 0·8 m. (1 to 2½ ft.) leg and a balanced head.

(ii) *Standard with Branching Head*. A balanced head on a length of clear stem which should be strong and reasonably straight with a minimum diameter of 19 mm. (¾ inch) at a height of between 0·6 to 0·9 m. (2 to 3 ft.). The length of leg or clear stem varies, but some indication is given as follows:

> *Half Standard*, 1·0 to 1·4 m. (3½ to 4½ ft.)
> *Three-quarter Standard*, 1·5 to 1·7 m. (4¾ to 5½ ft.)
> *Standard*, 1·7 to 1·8 m. (5½ to 6 ft.)
> *Tall Standard*, 1·9 to 2·1 m. (6¼ to 7 ft.).

(iii) *Standard with Central Leader*. A balanced head on a length of clear stem which is strong and reasonably straight with a minimum diameter of 19 mm. (¾ inch) at a height of between 0·6 to 0·9 m. (2 to 3 ft.). One of the main features with this type of tree is that there is a central leader which is well defined, while there is a 1·7 to 1·8 m. (5½ to 6 ft.) length of clear stem. In the case of the *Tall Standard with the Central Leader* this is 1·9 to 2·1 m. (6¼ to 7 ft.).

(iv) *Weeping Standard*. A well-grown, straight stem and the same minimum diameter requirements, with a minimum height of 1·7 m. (5½ ft.) from ground level to the lowest branch.

(v) *Feathered Tree*. A good prominent leader running straight up through the young tree, well furnished with lateral growths along the complete length, except for the very bottom.

In addition there is an increasing demand for the *Large or Heavy Nursery Tree* to fill the need for transplants which give immediate effect and as a means of overcoming the serious problem of vandalism which the smaller nursery trees are prone to suffer in some areas. They are similar to a Standard with a Central Leader, but larger, being 4·6 to 6·0 m. (15 to 20 ft.).

It will be noticed that, disregarding the Bush and Weeping forms of tree, there are two main types, the Standard with the Branching Head and the Standard and Feathered Tree both with a central leader. This distinction is important, for the Standard with the Branching Head is regarded as suitable only for smaller trees such as *Malus* and *Prunus*. Where larger trees are concerned the single central leader gives a stronger tree which is more likely to be mechanically sound, for, as the large tree reaches maturity, the huge weight of the branching system is evenly spread over a large number of small branches. These also tend to come away from the central stem more or less at right angles and are therefore strongly attached, *see* Plate 16.

Sometimes, through damage to the main shoot, two or more rival leaders develop. Should there be just two, this is referred to as a 'forked leader'. Beech trees, in particular, often split up into several rival leaders. These should be reduced to one at an early stage, for this condition should never be allowed to develop. Rival leaders develop into very large main and ascending branches, *see* Fig. 10. Thus the weight is carried by two or more main branches which are comparable to tree trunks in size. Such a tree may well be furnished with the branches symmetrically placed, but they will only be on one side of each of the forked leads. Thus, as the branches extend, the leaders are pulled apart leaving the centre open. In addition, there will be a narrow crotch or angle between the central leads which is a weak form of junction. This is a serious condition when it is remembered that a large tree may be exposed to heavy gales. A major part of the tree may be lost by one clean split which may also cause a tear down the main trunk. Even a small crack in the crotch from the inner core to the outer bark will cause weakness which will become worse as air and water cause rot and decay, *see* Plate 2.

It will be noticed that the Feathered tree may be formed into a Standard with a Central Leader merely by clearing the stem of branches up to the required height, *see* Plates 15, 19, 20 and 23. The one important advantage with this type of tree is that it is easier to stake, not being as top heavy as the Standard with the Central Leader.

In no way should this section be regarded as a substitute for the British Standards publication. It is not complete in any way and the types have only been quoted to illustrate the progress towards standardisation.

Conditions for Tree Production

Trees of the desired specifications can only be produced under good conditions. It is hardly within the scope of this book to describe these in detail, but a brief account will show how they have a direct effect upon growth and the form of young trees even in the early years.

Shelter. Growth will not be good in an exposed position. Not only is there a danger of the leading shoots and main branches being broken in a very exposed site, but they may not even develop properly or evenly. The prevailing winds in this country are Westerly and South Westerly and shelter from the North and East is also desirable with the more tender subjects. This does not of course mean that the nursery site needs to be completely sheltered from all wind, for growth under such conditions might be too lush and the trees loosely formed, and this would be undesirable.

Frosts. Severe frosts may affect the young growth of some evergreens and the unripened tips of deciduous subjects, in severe cases killing them completely. Certain genera and species are tender when young and, until they have developed substantial wood, are thus more likely to be affected than any others. It is, however, worth noting that even the young developing growths of the Common Oak (*Quercus robur*), can be badly damaged by late spring frosts. It may be necessary to prune off frosted portions at a later stage when developing buds lower down indicate the nature and extent of the damage and when the most promising buds or young growths can be selected, *see* Plate 49.

A reasonably fertile and well-drained soil. A soil with these characteristics produces a balanced growth, which is neither too strong nor too weak and, in the case of deciduous subjects, one which ripens fully in the autumn and is thus less prone to winter damage. There is another factor in this connection. Such soils are easy to work by comparison with the heavier types and thus regular transplanting may be carried out under better conditions, while the root system itself is more likely to be lifted and transferred without breaking up.

From a consideration of these factors it will be realised that the whole process of tree production must be treated as one and pruning and training are not just isolated operations in the nursery.

TRAINING IN THE NURSERY

Now that the forms of tree have been established and the main requirements for good growth have been considered, the methods of training required to produce the various types of tree may be described.

Initial Training

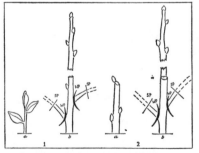

Fig. 6. Stages in training:
(1) Training from a seedling and from a softwood cutting. (a) At a stage when extensive growth can be expected. (b) After one season's growth, an extension of the terminal shoot has taken place. If it is desired to form a clean leg, the lateral growths may be removed, first stopping back at SP during the season of growth and pruning back hard to the main stem at WP during the dormant season.
(2) Training from a hardwood cutting. The procedure is the same, except that the topmost bud becomes and acts as a terminal (a).
The side growths, originating from the buds in (a) are treated as shown at (b) in just the same way as with the seedlings or softwood cutting.

From a seedling. Development under good conditions is perfectly natural and straightforward and very little pruning is necessary during the early stages.

With most subjects the terminal bud or growth extends from year to year, growths being stronger as the tree builds up in size, but if the leading growth is considered to be weak it may be shortened, perhaps by two-thirds or more, during the winter to a strong bud which will take the lead under training during the following season. The lateral growths also increase in size and vigour, their production and development keeping pace with the leading shoot, so that often the young tree is broadly pyramidal. If desired the vigour may be directed into the leading growth by stopping the laterals to 5 or 6 leaves half-way through the growing season, see Fig. 6 (1, a and b). If the specimen is very weak, however, the loss of leaf surface which results from this might be harmful. It should be noted that the strongest growths are often those which are produced when the young tree is 4 to 5 years old. The first few near ground level are usually small and do not develop extensively, see Plate 15. This explains why even the feathered tree has a short leg, for these are removed during training in two stages, as described for a cutting.

From a cutting. A number of trees, most Poplars for example, can be propagated from hardwood cuttings. In the preparation of the cutting, the uppermost portion of the stem is often removed and the lower part is retained for propagating purposes. Thus the terminal bud is removed. However, the uppermost bud on the cutting normally assumes the lead as growth is produced and will grow the most strongly. The remaining buds usually grow out, in some cases rivalling the main one in vigour, but these should be stopped back to 100 to 150 mm. (4 to 6 in.) after approximately 230 to 300 mm. (9 to 12 in.) have been formed. This has the effect of channelling the vigour into the leader shoot which should not be stopped. The stub ends of the laterals are not removed until the autumn or early winter as they have a strengthening effect upon the portion of the stem to which they are attached, and this is an advantage, see Fig. 6 (2, a and b).

From a root cutting. A few plants, for example *Ailanthus altissima* may be propagated in this way. Often a number of adventitious shoots arise from the one cutting, but if a well shaped tree is to be formed only one is needed for the main trunk and central leader. The most suitable one is therefore selected and the remainder are taken out.

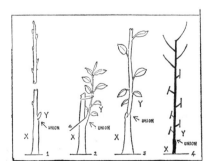

Fig. 7. Pruning and training from budding.
(1) The stock x budded at y.
(2) Growth being put on during the following season. The stock has been headed back, the stub end being used for support. The final cut, an operation referred to as 'snagging', is made toward the end of the season at (a). *See* Fig. 52.
(3) The subject after snagging has been completed.
(4) The growth at a later stage being trained to form a clean leg with a head. The growths on the stem below the selected branches are shortened, and are cut back flush to the stem during the winter.

From budding, *see* Fig. 7. As the bud grows out the stock is headed back, but often this is carried out in at least two stages, the first cut being 100 to 130 mm. (4 to 5 in.) above the union. By this method the snag may be used with a tie for support to the young growth. Finally the stem is cut back cleanly above the scion which has by this time grown perhaps for one season and has become woody, *see* Fig. 52. When tree subjects are budded the growth may be clear of laterals and extend for one or two metres. Such a clean stem, developed in the one season from the bud on the scion, is referred to as a *maiden*. If the maiden growth itself has branched into laterals which have been produced also during the first season, it is referred to as a *feathered maiden*. Any growths produced by the stock are rubbed out or taken off at an early stage.

From grafting. The effect which is produced is very similar. The topmost bud on the scion develops into the maiden growth, *see* Fig. 8 (1, 2 and 3) at X's, while the lower ones also grow out and would, if they were left, form rival leaders, thus producing a low bush rather than a tree. When these reach a length of approximately 230 mm. (9 in.) they should be stopped back 80 to 100 mm. (3 to 4 in.) at Y's, *see* Fig. 8 (1, 2 and 3). In this way vigour is directed into the leading growth. These stub ends are cut back cleanly to the main stem during the winter, *see* Fig. 8 (4), at Y's. Any growths from the stock are taken off at an early stage as with budding, *see* Fig. 8 (2) at Z's.

    The clean young growth produced in this way is also referred to as a *maiden*. If possible, maiden growths should be staked as a safeguard against wind damage, *see* Plate 17.

    In all cases, if the growth is not considered to be sufficiently strong, the maiden shoot may be headed back to a lower bud. The effect of pruning growths of deciduous subjects hard during the dormant season is to reduce the number of buds, and the fewer growths thus produced are relatively stronger, provided the specimen is healthy. To respond properly, however, the root system and the tree as a whole must be encouraged, and care should be taken, for not all subjects will respond to cutting back. Many evergreens and conifers, for example, will not.

    It is likely that in future years the use of special dwarfing rootstocks may increase among ornamental trees and shrubs. This development should take

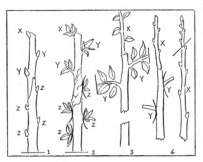

Fig. 8. Treatment during the first season after grafting.

(1) The graft as soon as it has been made and before waxing. Note topmost bud on scion at X, two other buds on scion at Y, four buds on stock at Z.

(2) A few weeks later when the graft has taken. The growths at Z on the stock are rubbed off.

(3) Again a few weeks later. The two growths at Y have been shortened.

(4) At the end of the season. The two growths at Y are removed close to the stem. The tip of the maiden growth is reduced to a promising bud if necessary.

place with an increased knowledge of the existence of virus diseases. The responsibilities of the nurseryman may eventually include the propagation and distribution of a wide range of ornamental plants which conform to a guaranteed stock system.

Training to Produce Specific Types

The training and pruning system which is followed depends entirely upon the type of tree to be produced.

Training of a Feathered Tree. This is one of the most natural types and a strong and definite leader should be well furnished with lateral growths. A natural growth, provided the central leader retains its dominance, ensures the desired effect. Occasionally some thinning of the laterals may be desirable, *see* Plates 15 and 19.

Training of a Standard with Central Leader. The main difference between this type and the feathered tree is that the laterals are removed close to the main leader, up to a predetermined point to form a length of clear stem. The process of removal is carried out in two stages. As they form during the growing season they are stopped back to approximately 130 mm. (5 in.) when about 300 mm. (12 in.) long. They are not cut off close, because if left they have a strengthening effect upon the main stem. They are cut back cleanly during the dormant season.

The head which is formed may develop naturally without any pruning, but this depends entirely upon the extent and habit of growth and this varies considerably with the species. Crossing and crowded branches should be taken out. Even hard pruning back may be necessary to encourage stronger growth, either on the laterals or the leader. Sometimes this is necessary before the head is formed, but if the leader is pruned, care must be taken to train a replacement as the new growth breaks out.

It should be noted that a standard with a central leader may be formed from the feathered tree by cutting back the laterals up to the required height. This may be carried out gradually each autumn as the head is forming, *see* Plates 20 and 23.

Training of Bush Trees. The feathered tree is a natural form taken up by the larger trees. The bush form is for the smaller tree species and hybrids but also it is a natural form. The main stem is cleared of growths to a length of 0·3 to 0·8 m. (1 to 2½ ft.) by the method already described, of stopping the laterals back to 100 to 130 mm. (4 to 5 in.) in the summer and cutting the remaining basal portions back flush with the main stem during the dormant season which follows. The difference is that no central lead is formed. Instead, with such smaller growing trees as *Malus* 'John Downie' (the example quoted in the B.S.I. publication 3936 Part 1. 65), the leading shoot quickly breaks up to form a head. Apart from the removal of crossing branches and any thinning which is necessary, little is required by way of training. In the early stages a bushy habit may be encouraged by hard pruning.

Training of Standard with Branching Head.   The first essential is to run the leading growth up straight and clean until a sufficient height has been reached. Laterals which appear on this length of stem are stopped during the summer in the manner already described, the basal portions being cut off flush in the dormant season. As explained earlier, they are dealt with in this manner in order to strengthen the stem, *see* Fig. 7 (4).

The single growth is then pruned back so that the laterals may form the head. It should be noted that the length of the leg is measured from the lowest branch to ground level. Allowance must be made for this when the position of the final cut is decided upon. The 60 mm. or so above the height allowed for the clean length of stem is the portion which produces the branch system. It should be noted that the cut removes the lead, but during growth in the following season, the topmost shoot usually takes over. Should a completely open cup-shaped centre be required, this growth is removed with a portion of the older stem, otherwise a new leader will quickly form. Even after planting, this type of tree frequently throws up rival leaders and often they are allowed to develop without such a small tree suffering in any way. It is possible that the branching head will be less in demand in the future for a central leader is becoming more popular, even for smaller trees.

The production and training of large or heavy nursery trees.   The normal practice is to move trees from the nursery once the head has been formed, planting them in the permanent sites where they are to mature. However, where a high rate of vandalism is expected the larger transplant has become popular. This more mature stock with a stouter branch system is difficult to destroy and is thus a considerable advantage.

There is no vast difference in the training of this type of tree, for the need for a central lead is just as important. That this should be sturdy and substantial with a good, well-spaced supporting framework, is essential. Growth, during the extra years which are spent in the nursery should not be too vigorous, the laterals being healthy but short. The aim is to produce a tree which has every chance of growing out strongly once it has been planted in the permanent site.

Sufficient transplanting to ensure that the root system is of a reasonably compact and fibrous nature is one of the most important operations in its production and it is a help in this respect if there is a high proportion of organic material in the soil. In this way growth is regulated without excessive pruning, but sufficient is required to maintain a good form and to keep a clear stem up to a defined height. The total height may be from 4·5 to 6·0 m. (15 to 20 ft.). In some cases a more compact head is ensured by pruning back the main branches during the winter. Even in the nursery some form of staking may be necessary, *see* Plate 17.

Training for group plantings.   There is an impression that the beautifully symmetrical tree or shrub is the only one which should be grown. This is not correct, and one has only to take natural woodlands and groups of trees as examples. For landscape layouts and plantings in our parks, roadsides and gardens, group plantings are often desirable. Even so, it is generally true that the best results are from plantings which have been made from well-trained stock in the first instance. Trees in groups and woodlands must have a sound structure if the woodland is likely to be frequented by the public. It is noticeable that in 'natural' woodlands the trees are of various sizes, species and ages, and an attempt should be made to adopt this policy in plantings of this nature, *see* Plates 21 and 23.

Training trees with character. There is sometimes a place for a twisted and gnarled tree, for example on the edge of a small coppice. Few would deny that such trees have character, but the raising and training of such stock must be on sound lines, and the trees must not be allowed to grow too large for a framework which is not structurally sound. There is only a limited demand for such trees and the vast majority of plantings should be made with well managed and selected trees and shrubs. Often too, trees develop their attractive character long after planting. Suitable trees to grow on for this purpose may be selected at lifting time from nursery stock.

Natural Branch Formation

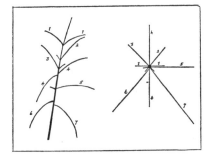

Fig. 9. A diagrammatic illustration (side view and plan) of the natural branch formation which exists among many tree and shrub species. The lowest and oldest branch is No. 7, No. 6 being at right angles. No. 5 is at a completely different angle, and the opposite bud has only made a short growth. The two branches at No. 4 have been formed from opposite buds and have developed to fill in important compass points. So with No. 3 and No. 2, while the two growths at No. 1 are opposite to each other, one being over No. 5. It will be noticed, however, that there is a considerable distance amounting to several metres between the two.
These diagrams were made from a young specimen of Acer. This mode of growth was already decided at the bud stage. The branches did not assume these positions during growth.

The impression may have been given that the formation of a branch system in a young tree is to a certain extent accidental. This is not so. The buds on a stem or twig are dominated by the terminal bud. This bud reduces the vigour of the remainder; in fact, those near the base often do not develop but remain dormant. They may remain in this condition for many years, perhaps throughout the life of the tree. However, should a break or a pruning cut be made in the upper portion, these lower buds may develop and grow out. It should be noted that dormant buds often keep pace with the developing stem over the years, ready to break out should the need arise.

Other instances of natural control exist and examples may be found in the Acers, *see* Fig. 9. The diagram is of the growth and formation of an actual young specimen of Acer. The leaf formation is opposite and decussate and one would expect the branches to be in tiers and opposite to each other, but in fact they are spaced out, often singly, along the length of the leader. The explanation lies in the fact that some growths are suppressed. Thus, for example, shoots 2 and 5 are strong but the opposite growth to each is short and has been suppressed. This is a natural habit and it does ensure that the main branches are evenly spaced along the length of main stem.

Twig shedding is another form of natural pruning, though often lack of light is the primary cause. Dead twigs on a rapidly expanding branch or trunk are quickly cut off by the thickening bark and callus, and thus they are unlikely to become a serious source of infection, *see* Plates 22 and 24.

Notching and Nicking

These are established practices used in fruit-tree training. More particularly, they are used in the formation of the 'Delayed Open-Centre Tree'. In a well-formed tree of this type the branches are spaced evenly on a short central leader, which may be 0·6 to 1·2 m. (2 to 4 ft.) long. Nothing can be left to chance over such a short length of stem, and selected buds are encouraged to break and develop by 'notching'. This is carried out during the dormant season, when a notch is cut about 10 to 15 mm. above the bud, completely removing a wedge-shaped piece. This has the effect of stopping the flow of growth-inhibiting substances which are produced by the buds higher on the stem and as a result the selected bud breaks out into growth.

'Nicking' is carried out below selected buds in order to reduce their vigour. Again, this has been applied mostly to the production of fruit trees as a means of securing a more horizontal branching where the growths from the main stem tend to be erect. The ascending branch is cut back at one or two, or even three buds above the one which it is intended should grow out strongly to form the horizontal branch. Preferably, the bud selected for this should be a lower one. The remaining buds above this are prevented from growing out strongly by cutting a small 'nick' just below each. The small amount of growth put on by a treated bud is sufficient to discourage an upward extension on the selected growth, thus forcing it into a more horizontal position.

THE PRUNING AND TRAINING OF SEMI-MATURE TRANSPLANTS

The Semi-Mature Tree Nursery

There has been considerable debate upon the advisability of using the semi-mature tree for transplanting, owing to the high percentage of failures which there has been in the past. There is, however, a growing awareness that adequate preparation has an important part to play in any ultimate success. Mainly, this concerns the production of a compact root system, a condition which is brought about by root pruning. Plantations are set up which are sometimes referred to as 'tree banks'. Good nursery stock is planted out and a few years later the trees are thinned and treated as large nursery transplants. Later still, the semi-mature trees are taken for planting into their permanent quarters.

This procedure is to be recommended, for both the shoot and root systems can be given adequate preparation. It is not proposed here to give full details of the various methods of preparing and transplanting semi-mature trees. But, whichever method is used, the main roots must be cut, preferably two seasons before the final move takes place, in order to encourage a compact, easily moved system. Undoubtedly this is better when carried out at intervals of 2 to 5 years while the trees are in the nursery, which is possible with row planting and by using machinery. Greater use is likely to be made in the years to come of plastic sheeting and containers, perhaps with a form of ridge-planting, as a means of facilitating the final lifting.

The leading growth is just as important as the root system and it must be vigorous and healthy with the main branches well spaced. A compact branch system can, if necessary, be maintained by winter pruning while a clear trunk to 2·4 m. (8 ft.) helps the final move.

Semi-Mature Trees taken from Woodland

The removal of trees from woodlands where they have been growing for many years is fraught with difficulties. Often, growth is strong and rank, indicative of a root system which will be difficult to move, as it will be large and extensive with the fibrous roots spread over a wide area. Preparation by root pruning is important, but the shoot system should also be reduced and at the same time improved in shape. It is an advantage to develop a clear leg to a height of 2·4 m. (8 ft.) at least so that lower branches do not impede the use of machinery. Careful selection is important, for trees which are malformed, perhaps with forked leads, are not suitable.

Wounds on a shoot or root system which are over half an inch in diameter should be dressed with a sealant.

CARE OF TREES AFTER PLANTING

Good nursery stock, adequately prepared is essential in the first place. But if strong, healthy growth is to be achieved in the years following planting the root system must be active and well fed. If the transplanting is into poor, dry soil there will be very little growth to train, and hard pruning to encourage it may be disastrous.

Young Nursery Stock

It is most important to establish a newly planted tree as soon as possible, and it may be necessary to feed and water to ensure a speedy establishment and the good growth which is required. So far as pruning and training is concerned, one of the most important points is to retain and encourage the lead (unless it is an open-centred bush tree), see Fig. 10. Adequate staking is also important until the tree grows away and is established, see Plates 19 and 20.

The desirability of pruning hard at the time of planting is often debated. This question may never be settled, but provided that all care is taken in the operation and it is done at the right time, establishment is more certain and there is not the same need for pruning. Where lack of roots is suspected, hard pruning of the main shoots, back to more dormant buds, is often a great help. The demands on the root system are more gradual, as growth commences from the less advanced buds.

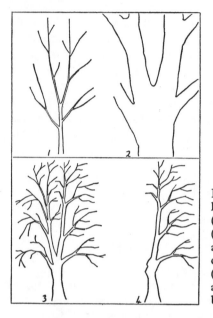

Fig. 10. The development of a tree with forked leader and the possible consequences.
(1) A young tree in the early years after planting.
(2 and 3) The same specimen many years later at maturity, with a close-up view of the main crotch and an outline plan of the whole tree.
(4) The calamity which is likely to occur to such a tree. This may happen during high winds or bad weather and the tree is ruined.

When growth is under way, increased vigour often results in the production of suckerous and epicormic growths from the trunk and branch system. Any which break out should, if possible, be rubbed out as they develop; otherwise they should be cut out in the autumn, *see* Plate 86.

There may also be a need for thinning the branch system if this is at all crowded. Care must be taken to make the cuts cleanly to good branches, and without leaving snags.

Large Transplants

The same advice applies with these, and great care should be taken over the retention and development of the leader. Growth, to begin with, is often a little slower owing to the fibrous and restricted nature of the root system. As the tree develops, some thinning of the branch system may be desirable, for under nursery conditions the crown may be close and crowded. There should be no hurry to do this, for as growth develops freely, it will become more obvious where any cuts should be made.

Sometimes, through years of restriction in the nursery, growth is so slow that it does not break out readily even after two or three years of careful attention in the new site. This may be due to the bark and surface tissues of the stem being hardened, thus preventing expansion. There is a technique of deliberately slitting the bark of a young tree which is in this condition. A simple cut is made with the point of a sharp knife deep enough to penetrate the surface tissues to the wood. The cut should be longitudinal and it may run the complete length of the trunk. This may be carried out after the first flush of growth is over in the spring, when callusing will be complete by the autumn. Stronger conducting tissues will be formed beneath this, and a better and more typical growth is speedily produced.

The Development of a New and Stronger Head

The period of rapid growth following establishment is often very noticeable, especially with the faster growing subjects such as the Silver Birch (*Betula pendula*). A completely new head is often formed, and this is to the good, provided that it has developed from the original lead. If desired, the lower branches of the old head may be gradually removed, choosing the late summer period for this, and spreading it over three or four years if necessary.

It should be noted that this cutting off of the lower branches is required in the case of a feathered tree as the main head forms if a length of clear stem is desired, *see* Plate 23.

Semi-Mature Trees

A good tree will have a sound branch system and a prominent leader. When growths develop freely a few years after planting, a further selection and training may be desirable.

On the other hand, growth after planting may be slow, or there may even be some die-back. Cutting back may be desirable in order to restore the balance of shoot and root growth. This must be done carefully, choosing positions just above good growing points or back to main branches, avoiding snags which may die back to cause infection later.

It is often desirable to carry out this pruning in two stages:

(1) during the summer, when the dead and weak portions are easily recognised. Any major cuts to be made back into the living wood should also be carried out at this time, for excessive bleeding, a risk with large spring cuts, would be disastrous to a tree fighting for its life.

(2) corrective pruning in later years as strong developing growth becomes established. This is carried out on the older growths which have, by reason of the move and check, become stunted.

Recovery from a Poor Start

The ability to grow away and make a good tree from a poor start varies, *see* Plate 28. Some trees, such as *Abies*, seldom recover from a poor or broken lead. Again, young strong shoots do not break readily from weak wood and the hope of recovery may lie with the development of buds lower down, often near the base. Vigour, and the capability of growing and developing from dormant or adventitious buds are important if there is to be a recovery from a condition in which much of the former framework is poor or dead. Sometimes, freshly planted trees may die right down to ground level, breaking up strongly from there. Where more than one regenerating growth arises in this way and a single stemmed tree is desired, the selection of the strongest and best positioned one may be made at the end of the first season, when a general clean-up and pruning may be made, *see* Fig. 11 (2a and 2b).

The Sycamore (*Acer pseudoplatanus*), is an example of a tree which will grow a strong lead and develop into a shapely specimen even after a poor start has

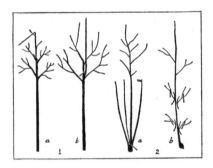

Fig. 11. Ways of overcoming a poor start.
(1a) A young tree with a broken lead, showing the position of a cut which could be made to a suitable bud or growth from which a new lead is likely to develop.
(1b) The position of the final cut is shown after the tree has responded by forming a new lead.
(2a) In this case the stem and branch system has either died or is very weak. However, suckerous growths are springing from the base. If it is desired to select just one of these the position of the pruning cut is shown.
(2b) The summer and winter pruning cuts carried out on the new stem, if a standard with a clean leg is desired. The laterals which have grown out below the level of the intended head are often so strong, that they branch in the first season, in which case the summer pruning should not be too severe, otherwise a considerable amount of secondary growth may appear.

been made. Secondary and annular thickening which follows the development of a new lead from a dormant bud or lateral gradually evens out any kinks in the stem of the young sapling and after a number of years there may be little evidence of the poor start. The damaged or broken leader should be cut back to a suitable growth or bud as soon as it is noticed, but the final cut may need to be adjusted later as a new leader develops, in order that healing and the formation of a callus may take place with the development of the new stem, *see* Fig. 11 (1a and 1b). Even at a later stage, good pruning may help a tree to overcome the effects of the loss of the original leader, *see* Plate 28. It is pointed out that a broken lead as well as a snag may become a source of infection.

To sum up, the need for the early correction of any fault is important for the following reasons:
(i) the balance of the tree may be lost and a gap will occur which will often take several years to correct itself;
(ii) there is a reduction of the conductive tissues in the region of a wound until healing is under way. This will be more serious with the larger wound caused by delay, for this will take longer to heal;
(iii) the increased light which falls on the stem following the removal of a large limb may promote the production of epicormic growths in this portion of the branch system;
(iv) the loss of a large limb is a severe check to a young tree's root system. A portion of it may be killed and this will increase the risk of infection.

THE PRUNING AND MAINTENANCE OF MATURE TREES

Introduction

This section deals with the training of the tree as it reaches maturity and thus includes the removal of large limbs, crown lifting and thinning, the treatment of lopped trees and work among the roots.

The term 'tree surgery' is often used collectively to cover these and other tasks connected with work on mature trees. In this context it is rather a loose term and is therefore a bad one and yet it conveys a sense of knowledge and skill. Both these qualities are needed, for often the work is undertaken at great heights and involves the removal of a considerable weight of wood. In the hands of an incompetent climber the risk of a serious accident is great, while a tree may be ruined by the faulty removal of a limb, perhaps causing considerable damage as it crashes to the ground.

The successful tree pruner must have a full appreciation of the growth and habit of the species or variety on which he is working, and a complete knowledge of the best way of achieving his object. He must be able to make the best of the material available, having in mind the safety of the tree after he has left it and the need for a natural effect when the work is completed. Thus something more is needed than just technical skill.

Many corporations and other public bodies, in addition to private establishments and commercial concerns, carry the tree surgeon's craft to a very high standard. Yet there are far too many 'jobbing people' who go from door to door during the winter, offering to lop trees in order to 'let in the light', or to prune, on the pretence that this is a task which should be carried out periodically. They work to gain profit from whatever they do at the time and also from the sale of logs for firewood afterwards. The trees which they work on are more often than not left in a mutilated state and beyond repair, an eyesore and eventually a liability. Those who engage in tree work should have a full knowledge of the recommendations set out on this subject by the British Standards Institution and be able to work to these standards. (B.S.I. 3998:1966. Recommendations for Tree Work.)

The leading man in a tree gang is the climber. He is supported by one or more as necessary, who work from the ground helping him to secure the ropes and ladders, holding the safety line attached to his harness when necessary, clearing the fallen branches and generally assisting him in his work. It is important that they work together as a team and that they all understand and are fully conversant with the nature of the work. A climber can only work effectively and safely when he is well supported from the ground. Never should climbing and ladder work be undertaken by one man on his own.

In addition to ability, the climber must have pride in his work, for many flaws and cavities can only be seen when viewed from above, *see* Plates 25, 26, 34 and 35. Even the standard of the cuts which are made high in the tree cannot always be judged from the ground. A supervisor should make sure that he has a climber and team who can be relied upon to carry out all types of tree work efficiently, safely and conscientiously.

As mentioned in the Preface, no attempt has been made in this book to deal

D

with the subject of Tree Surgery in detail and the object of this short introduction is to stress the need for employing a specialised team on tasks of this
nature which involve work at heights, often with weighty limbs.

Continuity of Training

It may seem sufficient to say that training never ceases until a tree has reached
maturity, *see* Plates 27 and 28. This is true, but there is much more to the subject
than just this. A watch must also be kept upon general condition, for without
good healthy growth there cannot be effective pruning and training. It is, therefore, necessary to take account of all the factors which affect growth, and it is
to help the reader to grasp this that the table at the end of this chapter showing
the stages in the life of a tree has been produced.

'Lifting' or the Removal of the Lower Branch Systems

Fig. 12. 'Lifting' a roadside tree to allow the free
passage of tall vehicles or loads. The branch
systems in 'broken' outline should be removed.
Although the lower branch which is over the bus
is to remain, a careful watch would need to be
kept on this, particularly during wet weather,
and if necessary this will need to be adjusted by
further pruning.

The need to allow sufficient head-room for vehicles and machinery that may
use certain service roads is dealt with in Chapter Four. The removal of the
lower branches is also essential on roadside trees to allow head-room for the
traffic, which may include double-decker buses, furniture vans, loaded lorries,
etc. In addition to a definite clearance being necessary, allowance should be
made for the sway of the branches caused by wind and gales and the local
turbulence which results from the speedy passage of large vehicles beneath the
trees.

This operation may also be justified when the lower branches are close to a
building and are thus liable to cut light off from certain windows. Again, there
may be plants nearby whose well-being is important enough to warrant the
removal of the lower branch system. By careful planning, however, and the
selection of suitable subjects, it is often possible to overcome this latter problem without such drastic treatment. The cultivation of such shrubs as Rhododendrons, many of which require a light shade, is most successful when there
is an overhead canopy, provided that it is not too heavy. But so much depends
upon the planner. With branches cut-off at one level, the whole becomes unnatural, with a scattering of bare trunks in sharp contrast to a more natural
planting, where branches are left, and encouraged in places to trail down to
the ground, perhaps onto open patches and areas of grass, *see* Plate 23.

The best time for this work is during the late summer, for the branches are weighed down with foliage at this time, and this gives a better picture of the extent of the problem. Callus formation will also start before the winter sets in, when the rate of healing will be much slower. There is also little danger of bleeding at this period.

The removal of the branches flush with the main trunk is straightforward. It must be neatly finished, not only for the good of the tree which is important enough but, if by the roadside, it is a means of educating the public to appreciate good tree work, *see* Plate 32. The crown and the tree as a whole must be left well balanced, both in appearance and weight. In other words, a branch moved on one side means that some balancing may be needed on the other, *see* Fig. 12.

Such work on a large scale should, like any other tree operation, be carried out under strict supervision and with a good, well-trained and disciplined team, but with roadside work and with the safety of the public in mind, there is a need for special precautions, *see* Plate 31. Often it is helpful to have some form of gauge made as a guide to the height and width of any vehicle which is likely to pass by.

It should be noted that the term 'lifting' is generally thought of as applying only to mature trees, but this operation may also be undertaken on younger specimens as part of their training. It may, for example, be desired to train a young feathered tree into a specimen with a clear stem or trunk. In this case, as the young tree becomes established in its permanent quarters the lower branches are removed, ideally spreading this over several seasons as the tree develops, *see* Plates 20 and 23.

Crown Thinning

This is an operation which should not be taken lightly, for it will affect the future shape and life of the tree. Obviously, that which is removed cannot be restored to its former growing position, but the full significance of this may not be realised until a piece has been taken off by mistake. It is of little use experimenting without any thought and far too many undertake thinning because it is something which they think should be done to trees, especially young ones, 'to assist in the formation of a shapely crown'. Thinning is not a means of beating time and of improving upon natural growth which includes branch shed. It is, however, a different matter if branches are removed which have started to decline in health and which are obviously dying. Crossing branches, especially on a young tree, may be corrected by the removal of one or both of the offending pieces, but it should be remembered that a full branch system has a strengthening effect upon the framework as a whole, while a strong and vigorous root action is also encouraged.

The reasons for crown thinning may be outlined as follows:

(a) The operation allows light to penetrate the crown. This could be an advantage where there is heavy shading, for example near a building, to allow sunlight to reach windows, or over plants which are considered valuable and which should have more light.

(b) Wind resistance is reduced and this may be important to a tree which has a weak branch system.

(c) Weight is reduced and this may also help such a weak system. It should be remembered that the fall of heavy limbs may not only be dangerous to life, but often other branches on the trunk itself may be split or injured. This may ruin one entire side of a branch system, *see* Plate 60.

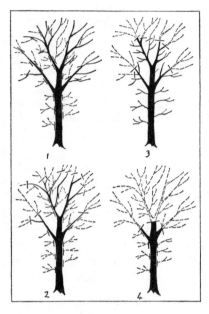

Fig. 13. Good and bad methods of dealing with a mature tree which is unsafe and is in need of attention. It should be borne in mind that only the main branches have been shown. The broken lines indicate branches which are to be cut out.

(1) This is correct. Those branches which are to remain have been left at full length with very little if any shortening.

(2) The branch systems which are to remain have been shortened. This may lead to cavities in the region of these cuts at a later stage and such shortening should not be carried out.

(3) This form of lopping is definitely wrong.

(4) Lopped to this extent it would make a suitable support for a climber, but the strong shoots resulting from the cuts would need to be cut out occasionally.

(d) It may be necessary as a means of restoring balance. It must be emphasised, however, that experience is needed to decide whether or not thinning is really necessary and, if it is, how extensive it should be.

Once it is decided upon, the procedure should be carried out in the following order:

(i) Remove any dead limbs and also those which show definite signs of dying through lack of light. It is to be expected that many of these will be found on the inside of the tree.

(ii) Remove badly shaped limbs, those with a narrow crotch angle and also any other dangerous limbs. Crossing and rubbing branches should be attended to.

(iii) The remainder of the branch system should be thinned to the required amount, *see* Fig. 13.

It should be noted that the work to be carried out in stages (i) and (ii) is really obvious, but while it is being undertaken the operator will naturally become more acquainted with the nature of the branch system and a decision upon the remainder of the work will thus be easier. As experience is gained it is possible to complete all the stages in one area before removing the ladder and equipment. Often it is better to start thinning in the top of the crown and then to work down, but the actual method of working will vary with the type of tree. The cuts should be made flush to the stem or branch and the wounds carefully painted, taking care not to weaken the remaining framework, *see* Fig. 14.

A decision upon the best time of year at which to undertake the operation is sometimes difficult, for it is generally easier to gain an impression of shading, leaf formation and shoot density when the foliage is full and mature, but on the other hand, with deciduous subjects, the work will often be easier when it is carried out in the dormant season. Timing will therefore be a matter of judgement and convenience. The late winter or spring should be avoided with subjects which bleed, for example birch, maple, hornbeam and many of the Leguminous species.

Crown thinning, which may result in the removal of one third or more of the branch system, is generally confined to deciduous trees. It is seldom necessary or desirable to treat hardy evergreens or conifers in this manner.

Crown Reduction

Fig. 14. Part of a branch system under consideration for thinning. The broken lines indicate two branches which would be removed under a moderate thinning, the cuts being made at (a). Whole lengths are removed, making the cut as close to the parent branch as possible. Under a severe thinning policy, three additional branches are suggested for removal by making cuts indicated by (b).

Thinning in the normal way does not result in a reduction of the overall size of the crown. With crown reduction, however, the branches are shortened, the cuts being carefully positioned just above a substantial limb growing in the right direction, *see* Fig. 2. It is carried out over the entire main branch system if need be with the result that the tops of leading branches are taken away and selected laterals form the outline to the crown. It is important to maintain a balanced appearance and condition.

Where the cut-back is extensive, this is obviously a drastic treatment, but it is justified where the branch system is considered to be inadequate for the full height and weight to be carried, or where the tree as a whole is failing in health and has, as a result, become 'stag-headed'. Good husbandry should always form the basis of programmes connected with the management of trees, but a more definite feeding and watering programme is necessary as a means of overcoming the condition of poor health.

Epicormic Shoots

These are strong shoots which spring directly from the main branches or the trunk. A number may spring from adventitious buds but they often originate from dormant buds which keep pace with secondary thickening. Normally they remain dormant unless activated by an extra supply of food as a result of an injury higher in the branch system. Thus the removal of a limb, even though the cut is made close to the main stem, may result in a flush of epicormic shoots round the wound. As these are cut back, more appear and there seems to be no effective and permanent cure. All that can be done is to cut them back year after year during the dormant season. If left, they extend and take vigour from the crown itself and may cause this to die back, particularly in a dry season. An annual flush of these growths may also appear on the trunk, even down to the base and they should likewise be pruned back as hard as possible, *see* Plates 29, 30 and 33.

Sucker Growths

These spring from below ground level, either from or in the region of the root system, *see* Fig. 45 and Plate 29. They should be taken off cleanly as close as possible to the point of origin on the stem. It may be necessary to scrape the soil away to reach the bases of the sucker shoots. The exposed piece should be wiped free of soil with a cloth, so that the secateurs or knife do not come into contact with grit which may spoil the cutting edge.

Lopping

Lopping is the practice of cutting back the main branches of a tree, often severely, either to leave it in a safe condition or in sympathy with a belief that it is something which should be carried out on trees periodically. There is certainly no case at all for the latter and too many of our present-day problems with trees are the direct result of this practice, which generally is a bad one. Not only does a tree which is treated in this way lose its natural shape, at least for many years, but also it is such a short term policy. A later paragraph explains how a tree which has been lopped can eventually become dangerous, and the practice can only be justified in very rare circumstances. As an example of such a case, a tree which was already in a dangerous condition might be kept, after lopping, to form an effective screen and help to baffle the noise of traffic at a study centre. Every effort, however, must be made to overcome the problem in other ways which will be more satisfactory, provided they leave the tree in a safe condition. For example, the branch system may be thinned to reduce the density and weight of the crown. An alternative method is to carefully reduce the size of the crown, while still retaining its natural outline. On the other hand, bracing may be the answer, thus leaving the framework in a safe condition. Sometimes it is possible to fence in a dangerous tree, but the barriers used must be effective against the public, including children.

If lopping is undertaken, a planting scheme should be put in hand at the same time, so that the lopped trees can be removed as soon as possible when the young ones are becoming established and are gaining height. With a small area, where space is not sufficient for the establishment of a young tree near an old one, the short term policy of lopping would not be justifiable, for eventually it would become necessary to take the tree out and valuable time would be lost in growing and training a young and perhaps more suitable one.

Factors to consider when deciding upon the future of a lopped tree.
(i) *Age, vigour and general health.* Provided there has been a vigorous response in growth, the stubs will be partly hidden. It may also be possible to thin these

and improve the otherwise unsightly appearance, which is especially apparent during the winter. A tree which is very vigorous may, however, even after lopping develop heavy wood which quickly becomes dangerous. It is important that any growth which has taken place after lopping, shall be safe and securely attached to the branch or trunk from which it originates. It should be remembered that the growths which are produced after lopping originate from buds which are maintained and developed by the tree in the tissues just beneath the bark. They often grow very rapidly, and for many years at least are only held and supported by the surface layers of the branches from which they originated.

The general health of the tree should also be considered, taking into account the rate of growth and the condition of the foliage. It can be taken for granted that lopping has caused some setback in health, for the serious reduction of top growth affects the root system. This may, however, be only temporary.

(ii) *Condition of the wood.* This must also be taken into consideration, for rot may set in with a large limb once it has been cut, despite a wound dressing as a covering, for this is often pushed aside by vigorous sap flow. Deterioration may already be in progress at the time of making the cut, and this will be speeded up afterwards. Soon a cavity will develop on the top of the branch or trunk, breaking up the cut surface. In time, the trunk will become completely hollow, leaving just a shell to support the branch system which may have grown to considerable heights. Thus the tree will become very dangerous, *see* Plates 34 and 35.

(iii) *Size of branches which are cut back.* Small branches which throw regenerating shoots after they have been lopped usually increase in girth with this development. Thus the scar may eventually heal over completely, making a direct continuity of wood between the old and new stems. In such cases there is no weakness and the actual lopping line may disappear completely. It should, however, be noted that callusing across the top of a branch is rather slow and even a small wound may take several years to heal, *see* Plate 37.

Most of the cuts, however, which are made on lopped trees are large ones. Complete healing is therefore very unlikely indeed and any attempt to restore shape and balance must necessarily be short term. It is even possible that the process of thinning the young growths which is often connected with restoration work on lopped trees will hasten the time when the same drastic process has to be repeated, for the selected growths will develop faster and their length and weight will render them dangerous. Subsequent loppings to make the tree safe must often be more severe in order to take the cuts below the areas of rot. It may also be necessary to cut back severely in order to correct an unsightly appearance, *see* Plate 36.

There is another point to consider. One of the main principles in good training and formation is that narrow angles between main branches should be avoided. Yet this often results after lopping, for two or more upright growths may originate from one point and the angle between them is most likely to be a small one. This, with the additional hazard of exposed and rotting heartwood in the narrow crotch, causes a serious weakness at the junction.

(iv) It is also worthwhile to give some thought to the reason for the lopping.

As stated earlier, most lopping has in the past been carried out needlessly, or perhaps to let in extra light to a building and it should not be taken for granted that the specimen was unsafe, even though it was perhaps thought to be.

Method of inspection of a lopped tree.   After the above factors have been considered, the following procedure should be adopted.

(i) Inspect the old cut surfaces, paying particular attention to the condition of the wood; also to any dressing which may have been applied.

(ii) Inspect the junction of the new growth and the old wood with the aim of deciding upon the strength of the union. It should also be decided whether any thinning of these growths is desirable, remembering that while a more natural habit is obtained in this way, even more vigour will be thrown into the remaining shoots. More wounds will be made and any weaknesses will thus be increased.

(iii) Inspect the remainder of the trunk, looking in particular for any cavities and make borings if necessary to discover the condition of the heart-wood.

(iv) In addition to looking at the topmost branches which originate from near the cuts, the remainder should also be inspected. Lopping often results in the production of a large number of epicormic growths over the whole of the framework and it must be decided whether they can be thinned and trained to form future branches or be cleaned off as surplus.

Action after inspection of a lopped tree.   When inspection has been completed, one of the following courses of action must then be decided on.

(i) *When the tree is unsafe.*
    Lop again, back close to the old cuts, but only if all the wood which will remain is completely sound;
or lop more severely, and as far back as is necessary to reach the sound wood (this is merely repeating the earlier mistake);
or head the stump back to a height of 3·0 to 4·5 m. (10 to 15 ft.) and use this as a support for a climber, *see* Fig. 13;
or remove the wretched specimen altogether and replace with a suitable young tree.

(ii) *When the tree is safe, with the wood at the original cut undamaged.*
    Leave the bushy head intact;
or thin out the overcrowded branches in an effort to balance the crown and thus produce a more natural growth.

    In the latter case, the larger branches may be reduced in length in order to lessen wind resistance, making the cut just above a suitable point so that the development from this point may be according to the good principles laid down in other sections of this book, *see* 'Crown Reduction', page 33.

    In all cases, arrangements should be made for the future inspection of the tree at regular intervals.

Lopped street trees and their treatment.   Another form of lopping is often practised on the street trees in many of our towns and cities. It consists of cutting back at intervals, often every other year, to a definite level, usually one or two metres above the main branching. This results in the formation of a mass of shoots springing from a swollen head at the end of each branch on the level of pruning. This method of restricting the size of a large tree such as the London Plane, which should never have been planted in the first place, is a bad one and cannot be recommended. Once this stunted and distorted framework has been formed, however, it is difficult to break it down and form something more presentable. One method of attempting this is to thin the mass of branches thoroughly, making the cuts just above suitable growths so that no snags are left. Some of the branches are shortened, others cut out completely. It is necessary to shorten branches which remain, otherwise, as they extend and grow rapidly, they may be blown over or weakened before they have ripened and hardened. It must be remembered that an attempt is being made to form a balanced and natural head. Young stock in the nursery would not be left to develop long and over-vigorous shoots which were soft and out of character. They would be shortened during the winter. This is the danger when the lopped head is under conversion to a normal habit, for the vigour is thrown into the reduced number of branches which remain. Remember that the head is exposed and that a street is often subject to localised and severe blasts as the wind whistles round buildings. This process of conversion may take several years of pruning and training.

Other terminology. Various other terms are applied to the practice of lopping, for example *topping* or *beheading*. *De-horning* is a practice which is carried out with fruit trees, particularly apples, when they have become too tall and out of reach for harvesting. The term *pollarding* is also used, but it is usually applied to the practice of cutting back to a definite head, perhaps to provide poles or firewood, or deliberately to give a mop-head effect.

HEDGEROW TREES IN DEVELOPMENT SITES

When the pruning and training of hedgerow trees in a developed area is considered it must be realised that the environment as a whole has probably been changed. This may mean drastic changes in the soil, which will affect the root systems. Extra drainage means less moisture in the soil and the water-table as a whole may be considerably lower. The conditions are often adverse to the well-being of the roots, which no longer have a comfortable existence, often being enclosed and covered by unkindly masses of tarmac and concrete. The changes can include an alteration in the soil level which stifles the feeding roots, or the laying of nearby mains and cables may, unless care is taken, involve the cutting of the main arteries of the system.

On the credit side, however, the hedgerow tree in the developed area, properly cared for and maintained, often has a more settled and even happier existence than before, for there are no grazing cattle sheltering beneath to compact the soil, to rub off the bark or to eat the lower branches, while there is little chance of damage from hormone sprays or close cultivations.

It is important, however, if this happy state is to be realised, that the knowledge and experience of the arboriculturist is enlisted at a very early stage, preferably before the site for development has been planned. He should certainly be consulted before the work starts, so that he will know exactly what has happened in the vicinity which is likely to affect the trees and their growth when they are finally in his care. Even the removal of a nearby hedge, if this is to be carried out, needs to be done carefully and under strict and knowledgeable supervision, as otherwise the roots of a tree to be preserved may suffer unnecessary damage.

In contrast to such an early and timely consultation, the arboriculturist who is brought in at a late stage to advise upon a tree or planting is placed at a great disadvantage. He may have to advise upon the fate of a tree which has been saved at considerable expense and is a vital part of the planned effect, but which has been ruined by ignorance and a complete disregard of the laws of nature.

The reader may well question the relationship of this to pruning, but the answer is that every new condition will finally affect growth and this in turn affects the arboriculturist and his pruning. This pruning should be carried out, not as a routine task which needs to be done, such as the final surfacing of a road, but as a means of correcting or improving conditions where necessary and possible. The pruning of a tree depends upon age and maturity and much of the advice which has been given in the previous section is applicable. However, there are certain factors which need special consideration.

Young Trees up to 20 Years Old

It is obviously necessary to train a lead, and encouragement and selection are usually necessary in the first instance. This may not be possible until good new growth is evident and is strong enough and feeding, mulching and irrigation may be needed to encourage this. Some form of staking is necessary if the selected tree is very young and is likely, for instance, to miss the support of a hedge. When growth is very long and straggly, perhaps as a result of development through a tall, sheltering hedge, some cutting back may be advisable. This can only be carried out when there is a fair certainty that the tree will break out to enable a lead to be selected. As much care and skill is necessary with the selection and training of young trees from the hedgerow as with nursery stock. Trimming to form the desired length of clear trunk may also be required, remembering that it is better to cut at this stage than later when the wounds would be larger and the fault more difficult to correct.

There should be no hesitation in deciding to destroy poor and unsuitable specimens, especially if there is some injury or malformation which will be a continual and increasingly serious weakness as the tree grows older. Always bear in mind that fast growth is put on by good nursery stock after establishment and that replacement may be the better policy.

Semi-Mature Trees 20 to 60 Years Old

At this stage there will be some indication of the ultimate form and size of the tree. It may be too late to select a lead if the branching has split to form a head, but the first opportunity should be taken if this is possible and can be carried out without damage. Trimming to clear the trunk is often required, but there may also be such wounds as bark grazes etc. to clean up. Trees are frequently used as a means of supporting fences with nails or staples driven into the trunk. The policy must be to remove them if they can be pulled out without further damage, but otherwise it is better to cut them short leaving the remainder to be buried. If wires encircle the trunk these should be cut. Epicormic growths on the trunk and branches should be cleaned up.

Mature Trees over 60 Years Old

It is necessary first to look over such trees for dead wood. Branches die back inside the tree as it develops and these need to be removed. Considerable work is involved if the die-back extends over the branch system as a whole, and it is possible that a tree in this condition is dying rapidly and is not worth retaining. Expert opinion should, if necessary, be consulted at this stage. In addition to pruning back, the aim must be to improve the condition of the tree as a whole by feeding, aeration etc. Dead snags, the cleaning up of epicormic shoots on the trunk, and the treatment of scars and cavities will naturally be dealt with at the same time.

With these older trees the soil is often compacted by cattle round the base with the main roots bare and damaged by constant wear and erosion. This is a condition which needs correction. Another effect due to cattle may concern the lower part of the branch system, for they will greedily eat the growing shoots. This leads to a stunted and congested shoot system at a definite level, referred to as the 'grazing line'. Growth is often reluctant to break out freely, even when this is possible after grazing has ceased, and the only solution is to thin as a means of relieving this congestion. The work may have to be spread over several years, choosing the dormant season.

Hedgerow Trees Growing Close Together

Mature or semi-mature hedgerow trees growing close together call for special care. In many cases these are Elms which have originated from suckers and are thus placed closely but at irregular intervals. It is wrong to expect too much of each one of these trees individually, for a shapely specimen cannot be produced under these conditions. However, the clumps of windswept Elms growing alongside the sunken lanes in the exposed parts of the North Devonshire coast have a character which is all their own and thinning would spoil them. In a line of trees running in the direction of the prevailing wind each benefits from the shelter of its neighbour and is thus slightly taller, see Fig. 21 (b). Each one relies upon its neighbours for protection and the removal of one may affect the others to such an extent that if a gap is formed the remainder on the lee side may be blown out or severely damaged. Rather, as with other clumps of trees, the outline and form of the group as a whole should be studied, and if the removal of one or more of these live trees becomes necessary, it must be carried out very carefully in order to avoid damage to those which remain. In order to minimise root disturbance it is often advisable to cut off at ground level, leaving the stump. It may also be wise to reduce the height and spread of those in the immediate vicinity of the gap so that there is less chance of them blowing over.

Often, after opening out, thickets of epicormic growths appear on the main branches and even on the trunks as a result of more light. These may be thinned, taking out the weakest and leaving just a few of the strongest to train in to fill up the gaps and to balance the tree.

Regular inspection should be carried out at least annually following the take-over and treatment.

TABLE OF TREE CARE AND MAINTENANCE

	NURSERY TREE	DEVELOPING TREE
Central lead or balanced head types	Train according to type. Maintain good growth and a fibrous root system.	Maintain principles of early training and correct faults as soon as possible.
Narrow crotches through rival leads	The best stage at which a tendency for these to form can be corrected. Pruning should be carried out with care. Protect even small wounds.	As the tree becomes established, vigour increases and the rival leads which tend to develop as a result of this often form a narrow angle with the main stem. Take care to avoid damage with ladder.
Branch Pruning	Correct any harmful tendencies by careful pruning.	Watch for small snags and dead branches which may continue unhealed and are thus a danger. Gain the ultimate length of clear trunk desirable.
Wound healing	Provided that the cuts are made carefully, pared and dressed, healing is usually rapid.	Wounds must be properly treated, for although callus formation is vigorous the areas over which healing must take place will be larger and it will take longer.
Cavities	These are not likely at this stage, but snags are a potential danger and may lead to trouble later.	With rapid growth they are less likely. Watch, however, for possible sources, and dangers which may develop later.
Support	Staking and tying is often necessary to avoid damage and assist in the formation of a strong, straight leg with a balanced branch system.	At this stage strong anchorage and a stout stem and branch system makes staking unnecessary provided that growth has been balanced and ripened.
Cultivation	Ground kept clean to encourage good growth.	Planting circle kept free of weeds to allow feeding and watering is necessary until establishment is secured. On a large scale herbicides may be used. Grass down later after establishment.
Pest and Disease Control	A young nursery tree is likely to be swallowed up or permanently spoilt in cases of severe attack. In these formative years effective control is vital.	In the early stages control is still vital but later, as the tree reaches semi-maturity control becomes more difficult and expensive. Unless the attack is serious, control measures may be unnecessary.

MATURE TREE	DECLINING TREE
If a central leader has been formed it should have opened out at the top as part of the crown. Maintain a balanced head.	Check and correct weaknesses in the main branching system.
It is too late to correct this fault in a major branch, although the removal of an offending limb may still be possible. The wound will be a large one. Bracing and/or thinning may be necessary.	An extended area of degenerated and weakened wood can be expected, and this would make the specimen with this weakness dangerous. Bracing often advisable. Thinning may also be required.
Dead branches may appear from time to time as the crown extends and thickens, causing shading to a number of the branches. Corrective shaping may be necessary to meet the needs of a changing environment.	Some careful heading back may be necessary if dead branches appear. Dying back is likely from the extremities downwards.
It must be recognised that a large cut or wound made at this stage may never heal completely.	Large cuts or wounds will not heal completely and even callusing, if active, may be very weak. It is important to inspect old wounds carefully and renew dressings if necessary.
A cavity which forms at this stage often remains for the life of the tree, although development may be arrested and the harmful effects reduced.	Cavity development or extension is likely at this stage, for the heartwood may naturally deteriorate beyond control.
When a mature tree needs staking, or a support of any kind, it is normally considered to be an unsatisfactory state of affairs. A tree should be at its strongest at this stage.	Propping of the main lower branches may be necessary, especially with very old specimens. Bracing is also a means of support which may be necessary. Safety is always the first consideration.
Maintain healthy growth by regular mulches and good husbandry.	Correct any poor conditions, e.g., impoverishment or lack of aeration.
As youthful vigour is left behind and more heartwood is formed, the danger is from the wood-penetrating saprophytic or parasitic fungi.	Control may be needed as a means of maintaining vigour. Weakness and pest or disease attack may hasten the end at this stage. The danger from wood-penetrating fungi increases. A decision must eventually be made as to whether the specimen is worth keeping.

CHAPTER THREE

The Pruning of Shrubs and Climbers

Reasons for pruning – Habits of flowering – Extent and regularity of pruning – The natural effect – Variation of habit – Hard pruning – The need for constant vigilance and records – True climbers – Non-climbing shrubs planted against a wall – Free standing supports – Wall supports – Self clinging climbers

GENERAL PRINCIPLES

Shrub pruning may be necessary for a variety of reasons and the method and timing vary considerably with the species or variety and with the age and condition of the subject. Regular pruning is only necessary with comparatively few shrubs, while for many it is not necessary or desirable at all.

Reasons for Pruning

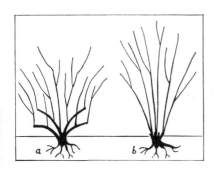

Fig. 15. The wrong and right methods of pruning a shrub which is to be encouraged to produce a quantity of new wood each year from near to the base – e.g. *Forsythia*.
(a) This shrub has not been cut sufficiently hard. Too much of the old wood, which has arched over as it has become heavy with flower and fruit, has been left. The result is an ugly bush and weakened growth.
(b) The correct pruning of this type of shrub. There is no really old wood above ground level.

The main reasons for pruning are given below, but it should be remembered that they are often inter-related. When a shrub is pruned there may be one or more objectives in mind. The main ones are as follows:
(i) to cut out dead or diseased wood and sometimes to free the subject of pest- or disease-ridden material.
(ii) to correct or improve shape; for example, a branch may be considered to spoil the general outline, *see* Plates 38 and 39. It may also be necessary to prevent a shrub from overgrowing a weaker neighbour or a path, etc., *see* Plates 43 and 44, Figs. 17 and 18. A crossing branch may shut out light and air from the centre of the bush, or may be bearing down on others to spoil the general shape. It must always be borne in mind that certain shrubs such as *Poncirus trifoliata* have a tangled growth, and it would spoil them to train them too severely. This cannot be over-emphasised. A further example is provided by many of the Ericas and Callunas. They need an annual pruning, for otherwise they become tall and out of character in the garden where they grow under

E

comparatively sheltered conditions compared to those which prevail in their natural habitat. Also the soil tends to be rich by comparison with that of moorland or heath and this again leads to rank, unnatural growth.

(iii) to maintain or improve flower display. For this to be fully effective, correct timing is very important, for the growth and flowering habits of shrubs in particular must be taken into account when deciding when to prune. This will be found to vary with position and locality and with such general conditions as soil type, rainfall, exposure to wind and sunshine, etc.

Habits of Flowering

Shrubs may be grouped according to their flowering habits.

Group 1. *Those which flower on the current season's wood or growths.*

Generally, these subjects flower in the middle or towards the end of the growing season, the earlier part being spent in growth from buds which have rested during the winter on the previous year's shoots or on older wood, see Figs. 48 and 50. It will be noted that by drastic pruning, the number of buds or growths which can develop will be reduced and as a result extra vigour will be thrown into the remainder. An example of this is *Buddleia davidii*, for if this subject is left unpruned, the result is a large number of smaller flower trusses, whereas, if pruned hard, the reduced number of growths which develop produce much larger trusses. The pruning is in this sense a form of thinning.

The timing for this hard pruning is important, for if it is left too late, growth will have developed only to be wasted when subsequently cut off. With subjects which are treated in this way and which are not fully hardy it is important to wait until the severe weather ends, when the overwintering buds begin to break out in the spring from the living wood. In this way the top growth is left for protection during the winter, and it can easily be decided just where to make the cuts in the spring. If it is necessary to cut evergreen shrubs during the winter period the collections should be light and as scattered as possible, see Plate 48.

Group 2. *Those which flower from the previous year's wood.*

Many of the hardy deciduous shrubs are in this group. They can be divided into two main classes based upon their period of flowering:

(i) Those which blossom really early, often before leaf or growth is produced, the flower buds opening directly upon the older wood, e.g. *Forsythia spp.*, see Plate 40.

(ii) Those which blossom later, producing short laterals during the spring and flowering from these in the early summer, e.g. *Philadelphus spp.*

Many shrubs in these two classes benefit from annual pruning, when wood may be cut out immediately after flowering, allowing the maximum period for the young growths to develop in the extra light and air, but the extent of this varies with the subject and the season. With Forsythias for example, or similar subjects which respond vigorously, some form of annual pruning after flowering is beneficial, while no pruning at all is needed with *Daphne mezereum*.

This cutting out of the older wood with subjects like Forsythia can be looked on as a means of retaining vigour, *see* Plates 38 and 39. Another example is the *Cytisus* hybrids, which may be cut back as the flowers fade and by this method spared the effort of producing heavy crops of seeds. Instead, this energy is put into developing growth, *see* Fig. 29. There are many other examples to be found in Part II of this book.

Group 3. *Those which produce flowering spurs on the older wood.*

These spurs normally develop from year to year and are thus found even on the really old wood of the main branches. This habit is found, for example, among Rosaceous trees and shrubs, *Malus*, *Pyrus* and *Prunus spp.* to quote only three. Flowering may not be confined to the spur systems, for it sometimes occurs on the previous year's wood as well, e.g. *Chaenomeles spp.* Normally, a free-growing shrub of this group needs little if any pruning. Instead, shoot production in the early years followed by spur formation results in the achievement of a balance between growth and fruiting. In confined spaces, where some form of training is necessary, stopping rather than pruning may give better results. Stopping during the growing season provides a check to growth and in this way encourages spur formation and flowering.

Extent and Regularity of Pruning

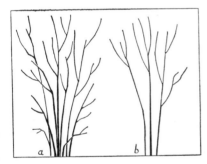

Fig. 16. A well-furnished shrub which is pruned hard fairly regularly, compared to one which has been over-pruned – e.g. *Forsythia*.
(a) A well-maintained shrub with lower twiggy growths which provide a furnishing down to ground level. No really old wood remains.
(b) An example of over-pruning. Only the youngest growths have been left and there is no lower furnishing. Such over-pruning, carried out year after year, would eventually weaken the shrub.

This depends upon the subject, it's vigour and general condition. Furthermore, pruning is not necessarily required as an annual operation and the only guide which can be given is to consider the extent of flowering and growth before a decision is made. Why for example prune a young Forsythia which is growing and flowering well? The same specimen may on the other hand need some pruning a year or so later when the proportion of old wood may be too high. In a sense, the pruner endeavours to regulate and adjust the balance between growth and flowering, but a poor or very good growing season can upset this.

It has already been mentioned that no pruning is necessary on *Daphne mezereum* and many other shrubs are in this category. It is difficult for the beginner to have a clear picture and to decide which subjects will benefit from pruning and which will not. It can, however, be stated that the response to pruning for invigoration and better flowering should be growth. Before a cut is made the pruner must be sure that the specimen will respond to such treatment by producing suitable growths, unless of course some form of thinning is being carried out, when it is important to leave a good spacing of the right type of wood. Experience and reference to Part II will help the reader to decide.

The main framework requires special consideration, for it must only be cut out if it can be readily renewed, unless of course it is diseased or dead. Many shrubs such as *Hamamelis mollis* have a permanent framework and this cannot easily be replaced, *see* Fig. 18. The stool habit, with its free production of young growths at or below ground level, obviously lends itself to quite severe pruning, when some of the older wood may be cut down completely to the base. Failure to cut this type of shrub sufficiently hard when the occasion demands will often spoil its appearance, as a considerable build-up of old wood results which will in time become ugly and support only weak growth, *see* Fig. 15.

Although there are exceptions, as a general rule the slower growing shrubs do not need much pruning. They are not likely to encroach but in addition they often retain their main framework, e.g. *Magnolia stellata*.

The Natural Effect

It is important to retain a natural appearance when pruning for an informal effect. This is emphasised again and again in Part II of this book which deals with the individual requirements of the genera and species. Some shrubs, again to mention *Daphne mezereum*, as an example have a close, almost dome-shaped outline which is their natural habit and is not the result of pruning. Indeed, as stated earlier, pruning is undesirable with this subject. The majority of shrubs, however, have a more open habit, often with arching branches, and when they are pruned this can only be kept by cutting growths out individually. This will often mean making the cut well back into the bush where it is hidden by the growths which remain and which are left at full length. In addition, for a fully furnished and natural effect, the branching should be left to develop down to ground level. This is also emphasised frequently in Part II. It is often helpful to leave the lower twig growth in order to gain this fully furnished effect. The lower branching near ground level also helps to check weed growth and keep the soil moist through shading, *see* Plates 41 and 42. The complete removal of these small growths creates a vase-shaped outline which is undesirable, *see* Fig. 16.

Special care is necessary when pruning prostrate or dwarf compact shrubs to an edge. An unnatural surface will be built up very quickly by merely cutting all growths indiscriminately to this line. Some should be cut off, back into the shrub, well away from the edge. In this way an irregular effect is obtained, possibly with small patches of bare soil here and there along the edge, *see* Fig. 17. With a border planting of Ericas, a wall effect may be avoided by lifting some of the younger and top-most growths and by cutting the older and dead ones away from beneath, taking them back close to the centre of the plant.

The same care to avoid a straight and hedge-like appearance should also be observed when pruning a larger shrub as a means of restricting growth, for instance, across a path. Such attempts are not successful with subjects which do not readily throw out new shoots and regenerate. In fact, some adjustment to the layout in these cases may be advisable if the specimen is to remain and develop properly, *see* Fig. 18. It would be wrong, for example, to cut back a

Hamamelis in this way, but a Yew or Box, *see* Plate 46, would respond very well indeed. To achieve an irregular and informal surface, the cutting back should be done at various levels on the framework of the bush instead of to one hard

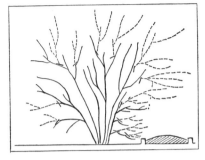

Fig. 17. When it is necessary to restrict the size of a subject which responds well to pruning, the task is a relatively simple one. The subject of the diagram is overgrowing a path (shown in section) and the suggested pruning cuts with the pieces to be removed are shown in broken line. By this method an informal and natural surface effect is maintained.

and definite outline, *see* Plates 43 and 44. It should be carried out in three stages as follows.

(i) The large cuts are made on the older wood, often at points right in near the centre of the bush. They should be made very carefully and an impression of the effect which the removal will have upon the appearance of the bush as a whole should be gained before the cut is finally made. It is of little use being sorry afterwards. Often, only two or three such cuts are necessary, the object being to shorten the longest growths into the bush where they will break out again. They should be taken from the parts of the bush which are most crowded and where their loss will not be noticed.

(ii) The medium cuts are made, often on wood which is perhaps in the region of 5 to 10 years old. They should be made after the larger cuts, exercising the same care to avoid drastic cutting and to position each cut with accuracy. The overall effect should be taken into account as the operation continues, removing pieces over the entire surface one by one, carefully and cautiously.

(iii) The final stage involves the removal of a number of the tip growths which may be no more than 150 to 300 mm. (6 to 12 in.) long.

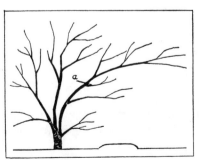

Fig. 18. This specimen, overgrowing a path (shown in section) might well be a bush of the Witch Hazel (*Hamamelis mollis*), one of the shrubs which retains a permanent framework of branches and which does not respond well to regular pruning. Under these conditions, the only real alternative to pruning would be to replan the surrounding area so that the path is re-routed or removed completely.

The drawing was taken from an actual specimen growing in such a situation, with a background of trees on the side opposite to the path, and this has led to an unbalanced habit, with the specimen drawn towards the light across the lawn. Some would prefer to balance the bush by making a cut at (a), but in this setting, this mode of growth is quite in keeping. The background of trees and bushes would also need to be held in check.

All this obviously controls growth, but the process may need to be a gradual one spread over a number of years. The fact that more light and air is let into the bush, results in the development of growths from the older wood, and by repeating the process on other branches in the following year or two if necessary, the shrub can be reduced still further.

The best period for this type of pruning depends upon the subject, but generally the spring is the best for evergreens. Deciduous subjects may be dealt with at any time during the dormant season, but the few weeks from late summer to the fall is also a very good time for the effect on the existing foliage may then be seen.

When engaged on work of this nature it is often necessary to scramble and work inside the bushes, and it is advisable, therefore, to wear old clothing. It is a dirty job, particularly with large evergreens which are growing in the vicinity of industrial cities, and hosing down with a forcible jet a day or so before the work is to be undertaken will wash away most of the dust and dead material which has accumulated.

Variation of Habit

This has to some extent been touched upon in the previous section, but consideration must be given to those forms of growth found among shrubs which do not conform to the normal bushy habit. The prostrate habit of, for example, *Cotoneaster dammeri* as compared to the upright rigid growth of *C. simonsii*, must be taken into account. The former will seldom require pruning, except perhaps to halt the advance of the mat of creeping growths. There are many other examples of contrasting habits, even among closely related plants. For example, two *Viburnum* species provide another illustration where common sense and a full use of the powers of observation are absolutely necessary, if the varying habits are to be taken fully into account. *V. plicatum* has an upright stem which bears horizontal branches, whereas in close and crowded conditions, *V. opulus* is often a thin grower with long shoots which may develop through neighbouring shrubs if they are taller thereby gaining support in their search for extra light. Under these conditions it would be wrong to cut these long growths back in order to gain a bushy habit. Constant pruning would deprive the subject of sufficient light to the detriment of the shrub.

Hard Pruning

It will be apparent from the principles which have already been outlined that there is an advantage to be gained in cutting some shrubs hard back annually, but the position may be made clearer by the following summary.

(i) Half-hardy subjects cut back annually. As indicated earlier, these are not cut back in the spring until after the danger of severe frosts has passed and as new growths break out from the older wood. Much of the young growth may be killed during the winter, e.g. *Fuchsia*. *See* Plate 45.

(ii) Those subjects which respond to annual pruning with an improvement of flowers, foliage or stems, e.g. *Cornus alba atrosanguinea* (Stem effect). With the majority this is carried out in the early spring, *see* Fig. 28.

(iii) Those subjects which respond to hard pruning by the production of adventitious buds or the development of dormant buds from the older wood. Such treatment is often followed by an improvement in shape which may be a good reason for doing this.

It will have been noticed earlier in this chapter that pruning is mentioned as a means of correcting shape. The nature and severity of the pruning will depend upon the necessity, and the ability of the subject to react favourably. Subjects which do respond readily and are completely out of shape may be cut right back, almost down to ground level as an alternative to the gradual shortening described earlier in this section. Many evergreens such as Yew and Box, for example, will do this, *see* Plate 46. The period for this drastic cut-back varies, but with most deciduous subjects which respond the work may be carried out during the dormant season although if there is a danger of bleeding it should be completed before Christmas. Evergreens, on the other hand, should not be cut back during the winter. The work is best done in the late spring after the danger of severe frosts is past, otherwise the young growths may be damaged and the root systems checked when there is no foliage to feed them, *see* Plate 49. Conifers in particular suffer from winter pruning. Hard pruning often seriously checks the root system, and any form of feeding, mulching and if need be irrigation, is helpful. The fresh rooting which develops with the new shoot system is encouraged by this treatment. There is the point too that hard pruning, carried out annually, drains the soil of nutrients and that it is necessary to make good this loss.

Heavy cutting back on occasion, when there is a favourable response, helps to correct any poor pruning which has been carried out in the past, perhaps through the use of unskilled labour.

The new growth which follows pruning may not be sufficient even to hide the large, ugly cuts which have been left behind on the old wood or stumps. In such cases it may be advisable to propagate from any growths which break out, and start again. Such growths breaking from the old wood often root quite readily.

The need for Constant Vigilance and Records

With a specimen in a poor condition, perhaps continually showing dead twig and branch growth, some improvement in the culture is required, that is, of course, if the plant is to be retained and not destroyed. The danger is that one piece after another may be cut off by the conscientious worker in his efforts to keep the place tidy, without the plants condition coming to the notice of the person in charge. This is only likely in a very large department, but there is much to be said in favour of a recording system which will prevent this happening.

It is also very important for the pruner or gardener to report any serious and widespread die-back which may occur over the collection, not just to cut it off and say nothing, otherwise a serious trouble may be present unidentified, e.g. Fire-blight.

Due care must be taken with labels which are attached to a shrub for they can easily be cut off and destroyed with the prunings.

Care is also needed with tools, for if they are left lying about they are quite easily picked up with the prunings and perhaps lost. Brightly-coloured tools are an advantage as they can be readily spotted if accidentally dropped, e.g. the bright red handles of the Felco 3 secateurs.

THE PRUNING AND TRAINING OF WALL SHRUBS

Many shrubs are grown against or within the shelter of walls. Not only do they provide a pleasant and interesting contrast and relief to the structure, but the warmer and more sheltered conditions, particularly with a south- or west-facing wall, provide a means of increasing the range of subjects which can be grown in the garden as a whole, *see* Plate 47. There is a great variety of form and habit among plants which are normally grown in this situation and this must be taken into account when deciding upon their management and pruning. It is emphasised that large and vigorous growers are not successful when restricted in height and size, e.g. *Celastrus articulata* is better planted where it has ample scope for development.

The following examples show how pruning can be related to the variable habits of growth and flowering found among these plants, and it is only by having regard to these that the best results can be obtained. The account is by no means complete, and the reader is advised to consult Part II of this book for more details of any particular species.

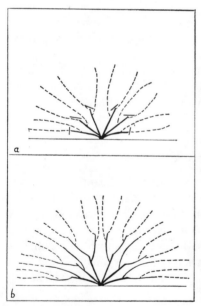

Fig. 19. Two diagrammatic illustrations of fan training in the early stages.

(a) A young specimen which has been trained from an early stage in the nursery, is planted in position against the wall. The side growths are tied out on canes which are attached securely to the horizontal wires. All the growths must radiate from the centre like the spokes of a wheel; indeed, throughout the life of the specimen this principle should be followed. The actual centre must not be filled by a growth, another rule to adopt throughout the life of the bush. The growths are pruned back by approximately one third to an equal length. The subsequent growths, which may be tied in during their development, are shown in broken lines.

(b) The process is repeated as growth develops, but the use of canes may be dispensed with after the original branches are secured by the growths above them.

True Climbers

Subjects which cling hard against the wall or support.

Hedera helix, Ivy. The adventitious roots freely produced by the stems which are tightly pressed against the wall hold the plant up securely. The mature growths, which branch freely, are produced at a later stage. There are two methods of treating this subject;

(i) The whole surface may be clipped over once or twice, e.g. before and during the growing season. This keeps the wall surface furnished without allowing the mature branching to develop, see Fig. 35.

(ii) No pruning in order to allow the mature branches to develop, perhaps partially cutting them back at a later stage if they are considered too large.

Hydrangea petiolaris. From the creeping mat of growths, lightly held by adventitious roots against the surface, mature branches short and spur-like are produced. These are the flowering shoots and they are therefore retained, perhaps being pruned back a little at a later stage if they become too long, Fig. 37.

Subjects which are trained hard against a wall.

This is often effected by tying them to a support system. They are in fact natural climbers and may be used to develop over an old tree or pergola system. By a suitable arrangement of wires or stakes, many of these subjects may be encouraged to cover the available wall space. They can be grouped for pruning purposes into four main categories.

(i) Those which are *pruned back to a permanent framework and spur system*. An example is the Wisteria, which has a spur system of flowering. A few permanent branches are trained fanwise against the wall as a supporting framework. As the space is covered and throughout the life of the plant, the extension growths which develop and are not required for framework purposes, are pruned back by stopping to 150 mm. (6 in.) during the growing season, cutting these back in the winter to the lowest one or two buds. They are not cut back hard during the summer, as the secondary growths which are often produced would not ripen properly. Any which do develop from the lighter summer pruning will naturally be cut off by this shortening back during the winter. In this way, growths which are not needed for extension are taken off and the energies of the plant directed into the production of flower buds. Such pruning also confines the plant, for the long growths would prove to be a nuisance to free passage, for example, by a path. In addition, shoot pruning during the summer provides a check to vegetative growth and thus promotes flowering, see Plate 54 and Fig. 51.

(ii) Those which are *pruned annually after flowering by taking out the old wood*. This is done to encourage the production of young wood which flowers the following year, e.g. *Lonicera* × *americana* K. Koch responds in this way. This policy may result in much of the older wood being cut out each year, although it is usually necessary to leave the oldest stem wood. Also it is difficult to carry out this replacement pruning cleanly with many climbers, for the growths naturally twine round each other and it must be done carefully, without injury to those which are to remain. The subjects treated in this way usually flower along the length of the previous year's wood, see Fig. 38.

(iii) Those which are *pruned back hard each year, often to near ground level*. Clematis in the Jackmanii and Viticella Groups are examples. They grow rapidly and flower on these growths during the same season. The pruning, carried out in the spring as the new growth buds swell, takes away the old growth, much of which has been killed during the winter, and thus prevents a hopeless tangle between new and dead wood.

(iv) *Shrubs which have a scandent habit, gaining height by this means.* Many of these subjects, if grown on a wall in a restricted space, become thick and untidy if left completely unpruned. *Forsythia suspensa* provides a good example. It is by nature a scandent shrub, producing large growths which clamber, but such extensive growths must be checked when grown on a restricted space such as a wall. This subject produces young growths from the old wood very freely and these can be used for the replacement of parts of the main framework as this becomes necessary. In the same way, a proportion of the trailing growths which furnish the surface of a mature bush, can be pruned away each year on a replacement system. Normally, as this subject flowers from the previous year's wood, pruning is carried out immediately after flowering, *see* Fig. 31

With *Forsythia suspensa*, this may with advantage be carried out annually, but with many others, only a light and less frequent pruning is necessary. This pruning is often most effective when whole lengths are taken out, rather than short pieces (which is merely a form of formal clipping). When an annual pruning is required much of the framework is only semi-permanent.

NON-CLIMBING SHRUBS WHICH ARE PLANTED AGAINST A WALL

The following classification is based upon habit of growth and training.

Those with a permanent framework trained fanwise hard against the wall. Subjects which produce a crop of growths freely after pruning, may be cut back annually to near the main framework, the period being adjusted with the flowering. For example, *Vitex agnus-castus* flowers on the current season's growths at the end of the season. Thus, these are pruned off in the early spring, being left for protection during the winter, *see* Fig. 50. On the other hand, *Prunus triloba* 'Multiplex' flowers in the spring on the previous year's wood. It is therefore cut back after the flowers fade and the new growths which develop bloom in the following year.

Chaenomeles speciosa Nakai and the various hybrids flower on a spur system as well as from the previous year's wood. They are typical of those subjects which respond to hard pruning close to the main framework, and this is often most effective when it takes the form of summer pruning, which promotes spur formation. In its simplest form, the summer growths are pruned back to approximately one-third of their length as the basal portion commences to harden. These are later taken back to two or three buds during the winter. A more intensive form of pruning consists of a periodic stopping, taking the young growths back to 50 to 80 mm. (2 to 3 in.), or even less as they develop, repeating this with any sub-laterals which arise a few weeks later. It is often necessary to start with this system of pruning as early as May, but the leading growths for the main branches are left to grow freely while there is wall space to cover. This frequent stopping during the growing season, results in a reduction of leaf surface. This inhibits free and rank growth in both the shoot and root systems and thus encourages spur and flower formation. In addition to *Chaenomeles speciosa*, a number of other shrubs in the Family *Rosaceae* such as the Cotoneasters and Pyracanthas respond to this treatment. It is really a type of 'Lorette' Pruning, which consists of frequently stopping back the growing shoots during the summer months, as sometimes used with apples when grown on a cordon system.

It is emphasised that under this system the effect of the close growth and flowering from the main branches is a formal one. The original main branches should be carefully laid out to produce a near perfect design, whatever is decided upon. Usually the lay-out is fan-shaped. Pruning and training is therefore necessary so that as the original branches grow and become more widely spaced, suitable laterals, usually two on each, must be retained to fill the gaps. Therefore, before any stopping is carried out, the required growths should be selected and secured to canes or wires laid in the right directions, *see* Fig. 19.

Weaker-stemmed shrubs which need support when grown against a wall. Generally, these are the more tender shrubs which need a wall for shelter. The provision of a support, while not absolutely necessary, enables such shrubs to reach a greater height than otherwise possible and thus achieve the desired coverage. Many of the Escallonias, such as *E.* × *langleyensis*, provide examples. Pruning is often necessary in order to keep the shrub within bounds, and this may be carried out after flowering, when lengths of the older wood should be cut back to younger growths nearer the centre of the bush. Also, in this way the shrub is saved from expending energy needlessly on a crop of fruits, *see* Fig. 30.

Strong-growing, self-supporting shrubs grown in the vicinity of a wall. Again it is usually the tender shrubs which are planted in such a position, for shelter. Often, branches are held back nearer to the wall, but no actual support is necessary. *Garrya elliptica* provides an example, for it can stand entirely without any support. Lengths of the older wood are taken out if any pruning is required in order to restrict size, *see* Fig. 32.

SHRUBS GROWING WITH OTHER PLANTS

Shrubs are sometimes grown among plants of a bulbous or herbaceous nature. In the wild or woodland garden, for example, it is common to find Primulas, *Meconopsis* and Lilies thriving with woodland-type shrubs including Rhododendrons. It is important to plant with a good spacing in the first place, otherwise the smaller subjects may be overgrown. Many of the woodland shrubs such as the Large-leaved Rhododendrons, *R. falconeri* for example, are loose-growing and are not commonly pruned nor do they take kindly to it.

Shrubs in sunny positions among herbaceous and bulbous plants are often used for background or framework purposes in order to provide sufficient height for smaller herbaceous plants which do not require staking. They must be sun-lovers, suitable for an open position and must have a reasonably compact growth. The latter is by no means the least important, for by making a suitable selection pruning is reduced to a minimum. With a large growing subject in the wrong position, for example, in a small narrow border, the pruning may need to be severe. Not only is extra work involved, but also it is difficult to mask the cuts and avoid a mutilated or hedge-like and formal appearance which would be completely out of place. To be fully effective, the selection should provide shelter, background and height, with the minimum of restrictive pruning. It is a great advantage if they provide a display, either of flowers, berries or foliage. As an example, the larger Cotoneasters such as *C* × *watereri* would have few flowers and be difficult to control in a small herbaceous border, *C. conspicuus* being more suitable in every respect. It is also important that the herbaceous plants should not be allowed to swamp the shrubs, for if these suffer the effect will be very tattered during the winter when the herbaceous tops have been cut down.

Any pruning which is necessary must be done carefully in order to keep a neat and attractive surface, at the same time retaining the natural habit. This is particularly important when the border is in display during the summer months.

Shrubs suitable for the mixed herbaceous border may be placed in one of the following groups.

(i) *Shrubs which respond to early spring pruning.* These are very easy to maintain, for when the pruning is due the herbaceous plants are either just above or below ground level and thus do not impede the work. When the selection is made, height must be taken into account, for some are taller than others by reason of the amount of annual growth which they make; for example, *Hypericum inodorum* 'Elstead Variety' grows taller than *Caryopteris* × *clandonensis* even when they are both cut to ground level. *Spiraea douglasii* is much taller than either, for not only is the annual growth more extensive but extra height is gained as some of the previous year's wood is left after each annual pruning.

In addition to those which have been mentioned, there are many other suitable subjects which may be pruned in the spring. These include Callunas and many of the Ericas. They may be planted near the front of the herbaceous border and, although their inclusion is a departure from normal practice, it is not wrong, being purely a matter of taste.

(ii) *Shrubs which respond to summer pruning after flowering.* Obviously, pruning at this time restricts growth, but only to a limited extent. Many of the medium or large growers are in this group. However, this type of pruning often results in the removal of arching growths which interfere with the development of the herbaceous plants and in this way it is an advantage, for the younger growths which are left are more upright.

(iii) *Shrubs which form a close matt surface and which respond to pruning.* There are many shrubs which qualify, but again natural height and size must be considered, so that the need for pruning is reduced to a minimum. Such a compact grower as *Berberis verruculosa* needs very little attention in this respect. When pruning is needed, it may be timed so that any pruning cuts are speedily covered by developing young growths. Many of the suitable subjects in this group are the smaller-leaved evergreens.

(iv) *Dwarf Conifers.* Many of the dwarf conifers can be used in this mixed planting, but it is important to ensure that these slow-growing subjects are sufficiently isolated so that they receive full all-round light, as otherwise their surface will be spoilt, becoming bare and unsightly. It may therefore be necessary to check the herbaceous subjects or perhaps to plant more suitable ones.

COLOUR BORDERS OR SPECIAL FEATURES

There can be no definite set of rules, for the pruning policy will vary according to the soil and growing conditions and of course with the species of tree or shrub being used. The purpose of the pruning, particularly if carried out annually, is to produce the best foliage effect, and the main object of this section is to give some general guidance on the pruning policy for a colour shrub effect, be the feature a large one or only a small corner in a shrub border. For full details of the pruning of individual species or varieties the reader is referred to Part II.

Before pruning is considered, the planting distances need special consideration. As a general rule, the larger subjects should be in the background and be planted at such a distance that pruning is reduced to a minimum. A wide feature is needed for the larger subjects. Not only does the use of large growers in a small feature mean extra work, but frequent pruning throws them out of character. *Acer negundo* varieties often lose their variegation on the growths which arise after pruning. Therefore, such large growing subjects as these should be planted at least 8·0 to 9·0 m. (25 to 30 ft.) away from others which are likely to be permanent and fillers may be used for immediate effect. Also, an adequate spacing allows the blocks of colour to develop a bold and well defined outline.

Pruning

The pruning falls into two categories:

(i) *Occasional pruning, carried out to correct size and formation.* Normally, this is done during June and July when the full effect of the growth and foliage can be seen and the adjustments made accordingly. The watch upon growth and effect should, however, be a constant one, so that it may be appreciated much earlier than mid-summer that some attention is necessary. Often too, some thinning may be necessary as a particular colour or specimen becomes too dominant. If possible, this should be carried out at the same time, when the effect can be fully appreciated.

This type of summer pruning may only involve the removal of a few growths. For example, assume a Yew and a Variegated Holly are growing at 6·0 m. (20 ft.) apart. The Holly is 1·8 m. (6 ft.) from the front of the border and the Yew is farther back. The Yew is naturally the stronger grower and the long arching growths tend to smother the Holly and the whole effect becomes untidy. The offending growths need to be pruned in the mid-summer period taking them back in such a manner that an informal and natural surface is left, There may be an underplanting of *Mahonia aquifolium* beneath and between the two subjects. This will need to be cut back, often annually, otherwise the natural development of the lower branches of the Holly and the Yew will be quickly spoilt. In time, of course, these will smother the underplanting, presenting a surface on the edge of the border down to ground level. Very skilled pruning will be needed when the edge is reached, in order to avoid a hedge-like effect, especially with the Yew.

Plate 41 shows a somewhat similar situation.

(ii) *Annual Pruning* (*a*) *Early Spring*. On many subjects this is carried out before the new growth commences, e.g. *Cotinus coggygria* and *Cornus alba* 'Spaethii'. Often the pruning is severe, taking the previous year's wood back to a common line near the older wood, *see* Fig. 28. (*b*) *After flowering in the Early Summer*. A few subjects are dealt with at this period, for example *Weigela florida* 'Variegata' and *Philadelphus coronarius* 'Aureus'. The old flowering wood is then cut out, leaving the new growths which have the strongest and best foliage.

Culture

It is emphasised that the best possible growing conditions should be given to trees and shrubs grown for foliage effect. They must not suffer from lack of moisture, organic material or nutrients, otherwise growth will be poor.

SUPPORTS FOR CLIMBERS AND SHRUBS IN RELATION TO THEIR PRUNING

It is not proposed to go into details on the structure of the various supports which can be used. However, the type of structure has an important bearing upon the pruning and it is not just a case of choosing the support and the climber and relying upon nature to do the rest.

The subject has to some extent been mentioned in the previous section, but it is hoped that by describing the type of support in relation to the pruning, understanding will be more complete.

Essentially, the structure should provide a means of support which is well adapted for climbing. This is important for the true climbers which gain support by twining stems or by tendrils, but not for most of the scandent or clambering subjects such as Rambler Roses and the weaker-stemmed shrubs e.g. *Forsythia suspensa*, for most of these need only be tied in position.

Some climbers are more adaptable than others; for example, many of the Clematis are weak stemmed and rely upon leaf-tendrils for support. The straight metal pole with no laterals and a smooth hard surface is not suitable for these unless some help is given. Once the top of a support is reached, there is usually no difficulty, for the growths bend over this, thus securing a hold which is increased as branches are produced to form a bushy head. Support for the main vines or stems is, however, desirable even when the head is well supported, as if they are loose and hang freely they are liable to be broken and the climber ruined.

Judged from the planning and lay-out point of view, the type of structure and species of climber should be in keeping with the surroundings. Whatever structure is used, it is important for the support and ties to be strong, and well able to withstand the strains of gales under the full weight of summer foliage and growths.

Free-standing Supports

Living trees and shrubs. This type of support is often a very successful one and as the combination of climber and support plant is a natural one, it is used to full effect in informal plantings. Shrubs, or even the smaller trees, are not suitable for the larger climbers, as they may be speedily swamped and broken down by the heavy growths. The right selection is therefore important. The trailing growths of *Tropaeolum speciosum* are not of sufficient weight to damage medium-sized shrubs, whereas the stronger and more rampant grower, *Polygonum baldschuanicum*, will quickly smother all but the larger trees.

Pruning is not normally carried out on a climber growing under natural conditions, although at times it would undoubtedly be of benefit; for example, some of the older wood, could with advantage be removed from the Honeysuckle after flowering, provided of course that this could be done without damage to the younger shoots or the main vine. Again, it would be often advantageous to cut out dead wood, but this must be done very carefully, otherwise a vital piece may be removed which is acting as a support, even though it has long since ceased to function as living tissue. The scope for pruning a climber in such a position is very limited and must, therefore, usually be confined to the pendulous and free branches. It may also be necessary to prune away growths which have extended the climber beyond reasonable bounds and, if this is necessary, it should be carried out carefully in order to provide a good finish and not leave a ragged appearance.

It is often difficult to establish a climber to grow successfully upon a vigorous and extending subject, such as a medium-sized or mature tree in a full state of health. Much depends upon the soil and its moisture-retaining capacity, for a deficiency of the latter may prove to be a limiting factor. It is possible to control the support plant, but the advisability of doing this should be carefully weighed

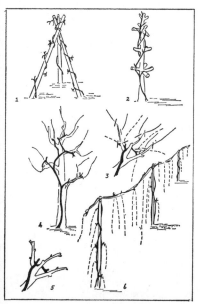

Fig. 20. Support for climber.
(1) The tripod system of support. Obviously a rigid method.
(2) The larch pole with the stub ends of the laterals left on for additional support.
(3) Part of a medium-sized living tree which is used as a support for a climber, in this case a *Wisteria* over a *Laburnum*. The position of the pruning cuts on both subjects are indicated. Both subjects are pruned, but the growths of the *Wisteria* which are to be removed are shown in a broken line as a means of distinguishing them.
(4) The over-all effect after pruning.
(5) A close-up of the branch shown in (3). Note that both subjects will respond to this type of spur pruning.
(6) A vine trained to a pergola system. The broken lines indicate the growths which are pruned back to the main vine each December.

up before any cuts are made. Few would agree that the deliberate spoliation of a shapely tree in order to encourage a climber is a sound or justifiable policy. An old apple tree is ideal, for the canopy of foliage is not too thick, and sufficient light is let into the centre of the tree to enable the climber to become established.

A tree which is declining in health can be cut back to act as a support; indeed, this is one of the policies which can be recommended for dangerous trees, provided that the setting is a suitable one. Trees used for this purpose must be left in a safe condition and should be inspected from time to time afterwards, *see* Plates 50 and 51, and Fig. 20(4).

A tree may be deliberately planted and grown for the purpose of supporting a climber. The tree is pruned, perhaps on an annual or biennial basis, in order to reduce vigour, thus giving the climber a fair chance. An interesting combination is *Laburnum* as the supporting tree for *Wisteria*, but in this case the latter is more likely to require a regular cut back as it is such a large grower, *see* Fig. 20 (3, 4 and 5). By contrast, the stronger trees such as *Acer platanoides* 'Schwedleri' may need annual attention.

Poles.   These are successful for the stronger-stemmed and scandent climbers such as many of the *Rubus spp.* and Roses, *see* Fig. 41 (1 and 3), where the support gained by tying the subject to the pole is sufficient. Climbers, may also be grown on such a support, *see* Fig. 38 (1 and 2), although control with such a limited scope for climbing is difficult with the larger growers such as *Celastrus*.

Subjects which climb by means of leaf tendrils may find it difficult or impossible to find sufficient support on a straight and unbranched pole. This is especially true of the metal poles or piping which are often used. In this case, and also with wooden poles, a sleeve of wire netting, loosely wrapped to cover the entire length, will overcome the difficulty. It is important to preserve the lower end of a pole for as long as possible, whether it be of wood or metal. A preservative should be used for the former, while the base of the metal pole, set in concrete which is carried just above the surface, will ensure a longer life.

Tripod of Poles.   This support, *see* Fig. 20 (1) and Plate 53, has much to commend it from the point of view of stability, and if the poles are secured together 300 mm. (12 in.) or so from the top end, it provides additional support when the climber forms a head. Usually one plant is placed at the foot of each leg of the tripod. As the head develops, pruning may be difficult, but it can be carried out with some subjects such as *Akebia quinata* by lifting the head and cutting out the weaker wood beneath.

Conifer poles with side branches.   With the side branches cut back to approximately 0·3 m. (1 ft.), these supports can be used for a variety of climbers. Those with tendrils or sensitive petioles in particular are well suited for the stub ends of the branches, being radially placed and in tiers, are well positioned for their attachment. This type of support is much favoured, for example, for Clematis; *see* Fig. 20 (2).

Hazel or Birch Brushwood.   This does not last in condition for very long – usually for a period of only a few months. However, it sometimes proves useful when placed against the main support in order to help a climber on to this. It may also be used for such climbers as *Eccremocarpus scaber*, which are often killed down to ground level each year.

Old tree stumps or roots.   These form a suitable support for subjects which are to be allowed to grow naturally, perhaps in the more informal parts of the garden. Neat pruning to give a formal effect would be out of place and must be avoided, especially along the edges where the subject meets the grass or the path. Many climbers in this position spread extensively and it may become necessary to cut away weed growths or saplings if they appear from beneath the canopy of these spreading growths. It may also help if a few growths are pegged down or tied in position, especially during the early years. This serves to emphasise the point that even in a wild setting, some work is occasionally of benefit if the best results are to be obtained.

Pergola and Arch Systems.   These take various forms but the subject chosen should be a strong grower so that it is able to cover the horizontal bar systems adequately, *see* Fig. 20 (6). Thus, the stronger Honeysuckles, the Vines and many of the Ramblers or Climbing Roses may be used. Such structures are found in the more formal settings and thus the climber which can be pruned hard annually either to the main vines or on a replacement system, is likely to be easier to manage, and the effect will be a tidier one.

Wall Supports

Horizontal Strained Wire System.   This is one of the most satisfactory methods of giving support to those subjects which need it, *see* Plate 55. The main essentials are that the wires should be good and stout, and held securely 50 or 80 mm. (2 or 3 in.) from the wall. They should be stretched tight by means of strainers at the ends. The wires, set at about 230 mm. (9 in.) apart, are threaded through 'vine eyes' which are driven in between the brick courses. From the gardener's point of view, one of the drawbacks to this system is that in the early years after planting, when the subject is being trained to cover the available space, there is a tendency for the growths of such subjects as Honeysuckles, which clasp their support by twining round them, to travel horizontally along the wires. This may be overcome by tying in bamboo canes, and using these as a support and encouragement for the growths to develop in the right directions. Alternatively, wires may be stretched vertically between the horizontal strands, *see* Plate 56.

Trellis systems.   These are quite popular and give good support for a wide variety of climbers. It is preferable that they should be well made and preserved, but it is also important that they are secured about 80 mm. (3 in.) from the wall to allow for the development of the vines or stems which have grown behind the trellis. Otherwise, as these swell and enlarge, the trellis may be wrenched from the wall or broken, *see* Plate 52.

F

Wire fencing. The stronger forms may be used, but obviously there is a danger that these will be pulled out of place by the heavier climbers such as *Wisteria*, as their size and weight increases. The chain-link fencing is much stronger than pig netting and is therefore more suitable. The plastic-covered material is long lasting.

Wall nails. These may be used on brick and mortar walls, provided of course that they are driven in between the bricks. Their use should, however, be limited, perhaps to a few main branches. They are not suitable for the shrub or climber which needs a large number of ties.

Self-clinging Climbers

Included in this class are such subjects as Common Ivy, *Hedera helix*, and *Hydrangea petiolaris*, which adhere to the surface by means of adventitious roots produced in quantity beneath the creeping stems as they develop, Fig. 36. *Parthenocissus quinquefolia* is representative of a number of other species in this genus which produce tendrils which flatten upon contact with a solid object. Thus discs or pads are formed which cling very tightly to the surface, giving support to the whole climber.

These self-clinging climbers may cause damage to buildings by way of loose tiles, blocked gutters and deteriorating wall surfaces. It is advisable to keep the growths of all climbers away from the eaves of a building so that there is no chance of the roof or drainage system being damaged or rendered ineffective. Even such climbers as *Clematis armandii* have been known to grow so vigorously that on reaching the eaves and the roof the tiles have been in danger of being loosened.

Self-clinging vines are detrimental to walls which have a rough coating. A tiled wall is unsuitable for most climbers.

CHAPTER FOUR

Pruning in Special Circumstances

Balance – Planting distances – Trees and shrubs under normal conditions – Mechanics of a well-formed tree – Pruning hard to increase stability – Pruning to balance the head – Maintaining a balanced branch system – Maintaining balance in a clump or group of trees – Branch thinning – Pruning and maintenance in exposed positions – Material for decoration or shows – Propagation material – The use of machinery – Conservation of organic material – Irrigation – Planned accessibility – Weed control

THE PLANNED EFFECT

The success of a planting finally depends upon the skill and judgement of the horticulturist or arboriculturist. Not only have the selected trees and shrubs to be planted properly, but they must be established and trained and finally pruned correctly if need be, to achieve the planned effect. It is emphasised, however, that good culture and pruning cannot overcome the effects of a bad selection. All the various factors including hardiness, soil preference, habit and ultimate size should be taken into account before a selection is made.

It is important that the landscape architect or planner should provide a permanent record of the final desired effect for reference as the plan is established and put into being. Clumps of trees and shrubs may quite easily spread extensively and well beyond the boundaries which were first intended for them and, as a result, open spaces may be restricted or views completely spoilt. Even the removal of a few low branches to facilitate maintenance may change the character entirely, perhaps spoiling individual trees and the effect as a whole, *see* Plate 58.

Here are a number of policies which need to be laid down and properly recorded so that those who carry out the plan shall know exactly what is expected of them.

(i) The intended limits in size of trees or shrubs either singly or in clumps.

(ii) The extent, width or dimensions of any views and open spaces which should be retained.

(iii) The extent and depth of shade which is required, for example in paved squares or forecourts.

(iv) The extent to which a natural low branching is desired, bearing in mind that the natural and desirable habit of most trees is to produce branchlets which sweep down to or hang near ground level when mature.

(v) The size and outline of trees planted to hide or to frame buildings.

(vi) The extent of branching which is to overhang water. This should be based upon a proportion of the total surface area of water, but the areas in which shading is desirable should also be indicated. It is not healthy to have an entire water surface shaded, *see* Plate 57.

(vii) The extent of the grass stretches which are to be kept open, in particular the sweeps down to the water's edge. In this connection it should be borne in mind that willows and alders, for example, grow and spread very rapidly and the whole edge can be quickly overgrown and hidden.

These are a few of the points which need to be considered in the formulation of a long term policy. Some flexibility may be necessary on certain points such as the time and extent of any thinning. Where this applies it may be laid down when the policy is formulated and agreed upon. Of course, it must be recognised that it is possible to improve upon the intended plan, perhaps by pruning and thinning.

ISOLATED SPECIMENS AND GROUPS

Some trees and shrubs growing under natural conditions maintain a perfect symmetry, but there are many factors which often combine to make this impossible for the majority. Competition is often a cause of unsymmetrical growth, for it is impossible to maintain a perfect all-round form if the plant is subjected to one-sided light; indeed it would be wrong to expect it and unnatural to achieve it. Trees on the edge of a clump of shrubs in a mature border will often, when viewed as individuals appear poorly shaped. Such a planting must be viewed as a whole, for it is only by this means that a perfectly natural and balanced effect is appreciated.

This must not be taken as an excuse for a crowded planting. Our gardens are made up of a heterogeneous collection, resulting from a desire to grow as many species as possible. Such large mixtures do not occur in nature where the trees and shrubs may be crowded but fewer species are represented in a given area. Bushes or trees in groups of one species often grow well together and a close planting is not such a serious matter. Each individual in these cases is able to fight for light, moisture and nutrients on equal terms with its neighbours. This is not so in a close mixed planting where the weaker species often need protection from the stronger by pruning invasive growths in addition to giving any extra attention which the weaker ones may need.

Balance

When it is intended to grow trees or shrubs as specimens they should be given equal light on all sides, thus obtaining the good symmetrical growth which is essential. Two interesting points are connected with this. Firstly, even the shaded side of an isolated specimen often grows and flowers at the same rate and manner as the remainder of the tree. An equal exposure to light and air often seems to be the critical factor rather than the influence of direct sunlight. Secondly, a tree – or shrub for that matter – balances growth as a means of maintaining stability. This stability and balance is obtained either by an equal distribution of the production of branches over and on all sides of the crown if possible, or by increasing the strengthening tissues in the root system, in order to counteract any unilateral development or strain. Examples of balancing have been observed where a large tree with a perfectly shaped crown remains standing even during gales with many of the main roots in an advanced state of decay. A tree in this condition is dangerous even to fell, for unless care is taken the balancing nature of the crown may be lost, the tree suddenly crashing to the ground. In the same way, once the balancing weight has been removed with the crown, even a light pull on the winch may bring the trunk down very quickly.

Examples of strong anchorage on one side of the root system are quite common when the distribution of the weight in the crown is unequal, or in cases of a very strong prevailing wind. The strengthened rooting, with the thickened and extensive development of buttress roots and trunk on the sides where it is likely to be the most effective, can be very apparent.

Some of these points are also dealt with under 'Minimising wind damage' on page 62, which goes to prove that many of the factors connected with growth and practice are closely related and cannot be considered separately.

Planting Distances

The success of specimens will depend a great deal upon the planting distances, but the ideal spacing varies both with the habit and rate of growth of the species concerned and with the soil and conditions generally. Close plantings are often made deliberately for the production of a quick effect, or as a means of encouragement to the desired specimen in the early years. In the latter case, such a close planting acts as a nurse crop, giving shelter and forcing the development of a good stem and lead. It is important that removal of the unwanted plants be timed so that the specimen does not suffer in any way. When fillers or nurse plants are used, the planting plan should indicate which individual trees or shrubs are to be finally retained either as specimens or in groups. The person in charge can then arrange for those not required to be removed at the right time before they outgrow and spoil the remainder.

The specimen tree need not be completely isolated; in fact, one or more smaller shrubs may be planted in the vicinity to form a group. The choice of subjects for a group of this nature should be very carefully made, as it is most likely to succeed when the associated subjects contrast completely with the dominant tree. Sometimes they need to be planted many years later than the main specimens as they are often shorter lived. As an example of a combined planting for effect, *Cedrus atlantica* may be grown in association with *Parrotia persica*. The latter may need to be planted 50 to 80 years later than the Cedar, but once established, one or two branches of the *Parrotia* may even develop beneath the shade of the larger and evergreen subject.

What connection has this with pruning? Such an effect is not produced by accident and the pruner must keep a close watch to ensure that growth by the larger specimen does not harm the smaller in any way. At the same time, however, he must not spoil the overall grace and beauty of the Cedar. But even the pruner cannot be expected to do his work properly if the planting distances in the first place were poor and insufficient.

MINIMISING WIND DAMAGE

Wind is the one element which is likely to give the arboriculturist the most concern. It is, however, important to differentiate between plantings in inland areas at the lower elevations and those in coastal situations or on high ground. In the former positions the devastating effects of a strong gale-force wind are seldom taken into account when the selection and plantings are made. This is not intended as a criticism, for our gardens and arboreta would be considerably poorer without the enterprising and adventurous spirit, which has prompted past generations to plant up exotic and ornamental species. The point to remember is that should high winds of gale force penetrate such plantings, the results can indeed be devastating, and the aim must be to maintain shelters on the edge against the prevailing winds. If the impression is given that only exotic trees suffer from gale damage, this is wrong, for mature stands of native trees may also suffer severely. It is noticeable that the heaviest damage often occurs during the summer when trees are in full leaf, perhaps laden with flowers or fruits, see Plate 59. A heavy gale with driving rain can be disastrous at such a time.

Trees and shrubs which are growing in an exposed position will, of course, suffer from exceptional hurricane-force winds which are usually at their strongest in such areas, but at least some comfort may be derived from the fact that growth is inured to such conditions, while a suitable selection has been probably made in the first instance. There is also a natural selection which takes place over the years as a result of these conditions, the unsuitable subjects being blown about so much that they either do not grow, or are killed completely. Many of the exposed positions in this country are in coastal areas where the full effects of salt spray must also be taken into account, and this proves to be another limiting factor.

Trees and Shrubs under Normal Conditions

Admittedly it is difficult to define exactly what is meant by the term 'normal conditions.' Broadly, those sites which are not unduly exposed come within this category. However, each site varies considerably in this respect, and indeed this is true of one part of a site when compared with another. Again, a site may be sheltered from the prevailing winds and yet be badly exposed to those blowing from the opposite direction. Sometimes winds blow at gale force from unusual directions and do considerable damage.

Mechanics of a well-formed Tree

The healthy tree with a good central lead is mechanically sound and is therefore better able to withstand the buffeting and swaying caused by a full-force gale. If there is damage on such a well-formed specimen, the loss of a branch or two may not seriously affect the tree as a whole. Also a well-grown nursery tree with a number of strong and well-spaced branches is better able to develop into a wind resistant form and habit than a poorly shaped one. At this stage it must be emphasised that the small feathered tree is better suited for such a development than a larger standard.

Pruning Hard to Increase Stability

A trained tree cannot be pruned hard back to near ground level for stability, but subjects which generate freely after such hard treatment may be dealt with in this way. Such a shrub may thus be stabilised and this is often better than correcting the position by staking or by the use of guys. On occasions, it may be advisable to encourage stability and improve the shape of a leaning shrub by the careful removal of weight on one side. It must be remembered, however, that shrubs which retain a permanent framework and do not throw out freely after being cut back should not be pruned in this manner.

Pruning to Balance the Head

Quite often limbs grow out well beyond the general outline for the tree. While it would be undesirable to train and prune to a symmetrical outline it would be equally wrong to allow one or more branches to grow so extensively that the tree was out of balance and perhaps dangerous. A large limb jutting out beyond the general line may be caught by an unfavourable wind and be broken off at a point which spoils the appearance of the tree. In addition, the large, lower limbs of the Horse-chestnut, for example, often produce strong upright branches, forming a large surface exposed to the wind, and with the increased weight a break is likely under stress. It is of course desirable to correct such tendencies at an early stage rather than to leave it until the removal of a large limb is involved, as this inevitably means a shock to the tree and a wound which may never heal completely.

Maintaining a Balanced Branch System

The influence of balance in a well-shaped tree, particularly with one which is symmetrical, should not be underrated. A large, shapely specimen, often with the lower branches pendulous and reaching the ground, has a low centre of gravity which adds to stability. This is why a balancing for weight in addition to appearance is necessary after the removal of a limb.

Maintaining Balance in a Clump or Group of Trees

A balanced and unbroken outline is desirable with a clump or group of trees as a whole. It is for this reason that there should be a reluctance to remove any one which will leave a gap in the outer 'skin' of foliage and branches. This would let the wind into specimens which as separate individuals may lack balance to such an extent that they would not be capable of standing up even in a moderate wind. A community of trees with a given area has grown up under a certain set of conditions, with the growth and shape conforming to the general pattern of the forces which normally prevail. The removal of one or more of the trees or a building, or, alternatively, the erection of any form of structure, particularly a large and solid one, may seriously alter these conditions.

The importance of this may be more easily appreciated by considering the effect on the waterweed of the current in a rapidly flowing stream. Under normal conditions, the clumps of weed are compact and moulded to definite shapes. But the removal of a large stone will so alter the flow that its effect on the weed can be detected over a considerable area.

It is also common knowledge that the water rushes with increased speed between large stones or in narrow places and this has a direct analogy in the effect on airflow of the large blocks of flats or offices which are often erected near plantings of trees and shrubs. As with the stream, the increased speed is in the narrower reaches but the effects are felt both above and below these points, and the strong eddies and turbulence stretch over a wide area.

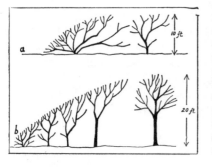

Fig. 21. Showing the effect of a shelter belt under exposed conditions.
(a) The effect of a single line of sheltering shrubs. The specimen shrub growing in the lee of this screen can be expected to reach the height of this shelter and to be of reasonable shape. However, this will depend upon several factors including the nature of both the screen and sheltered plants.
(b) A screen planting in depth. This is very necessary if height is to be built up under exposed conditions.
It is not claimed that shapely specimens can always be grown behind such screens. The position is not always clear cut, as there are so many local factors to consider. For example, sloping ground may make it impossible to build up any height with the screen plants.

Branch Thinning. Trees or groups of trees which are suddenly isolated and left in an exposed position as the result of an alteration or development, may not be strong enough to have a form and habit which is capable of withstanding high gales. There may, in these circumstances, be justification for carefully thinning the branch systems to allow a freer passage for strong winds through the crowns. Again, trees which are suspected of being weak, perhaps through over-growth or old age may, after careful consideration, be dealt with in this way. The reader is referred to the section dealing with this operation, but it is emphasised that the crown must be left in a balanced condition. There is evidence that once the wind is let into the crown, the branches on the lee side may be subject to extra strains and stresses.

Pruning and Maintenance in exposed positions. A careful selection is important when the planting up of an exposed site is considered. A windbreak of com-moner subjects which tolerate and grow under such conditions is usually a necessity and, if one is not already growing, it should be one of the first con-siderations. Coastal areas are subject to high winds which, blowing directly off the sea, are laden with salt spray driven in in the form of a drenching mist. Trees or shrubs in order to withstand such rigorous conditions must either have a tough, resistant foliage or be capable of rapid regeneration as one set of growths is cut away prematurely, even during the height of the growing season, by adverse conditions.

It may be advisable first to construct a fence and to plant up hedging material behind this. For this purpose such shrubs as *Prunus cerasifera*, the Myrobalan Plum are ideal. *Euonymus japonica* is an example of an evergreen which will thrive well in exposed positions on the south coast. The object of this is to build up height gradually. The windward side of such a screen will need very little, if any, pruning; in fact the wind will do this and it is advisable to leave the close, stunted growths which form under these conditions completely alone. Even dead branches and twig growth give some shelter and should be left, for the training of any plant in such a position is almost impossible. With the subjects which are in the lee of this it is a different matter. Training and shaping is possible but only until they grow past the shelter of the hedge, when growths will become windswept and stunted, see Fig. 21. If extra height is required, taller, wind-resistant subjects such as *Acer pseudo-platanus* and *Ulmus montana* may be planted behind the first planting. These should be planted out when small so that they may be staked securely and establish quickly. Gradually in this way height may be built up sufficiently for well-trained trees to be grown in the lee.

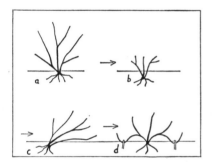

Fig. 22. Methods of planting on a very windswept site, e.g. privet for use as a shelter. This is a subject which throws up strongly from the base and thus with encouragement will produce a thicket of cane-like, almost suckerous growths.
(a) The shrub planted under normal conditions. Alternative methods in exposed positions are shown in b, c and d.
(b) A deeper planting with hard pruning.
(c) Planted at a low angle away from the wind.
(d) A normal planting with the outer and lower branches being held in position by pegs, thus adding to the stability and encouraging rooting.

The leggy shrub which requires a stake is not suitable for planting in this situation for the top growth will have a levering action and even the slightest rocking will delay or even prevent establishment. The low, bushy plant which has been formed by stopping or pruning is more suitable, for it can be planted to rest close to ground level where the surface area will be small and where there will be little resistance to the wind until further growth is put on after rooting and establishment. This treatment is only successful with those shrubs which generate readily, see Fig. 22 (b).

Shrubs may be set out with a slightly deeper planting as an aid to extra rigidity and firmness and with many subjects extra rooting will be promoted from the buried positions. Great care must be taken to ensure that the subject treated in this way is able to respond naturally and freely to the new conditions. Often, it is possible to plant so that the shrub leans away from the prevailing wind. Another alternative is to layer the longer growths securely and thus give extra stability. Again, this is only possible with subjects which are likely to respond readily, see Fig. 22 (c).

LIGHTNING DAMAGE

The extent of the damage to a tree struck by lightning may vary enormously. In extreme cases trees may be completely ruined, with the crown broken up, the trunk spoilt or even the whole tree blown completely asunder. When repair is out of the question removal is the only course to take, but if only a few branches are affected, it is possible to retain a tree, provided that it is left in a safe condition. Often, however, the loss of a crown or a proportion of the main branch system proves to be such a check that there is a gradual decline in condition and eventually the tree may die prematurely.

With the harder-wooded trees such as the Oak, a continuous groove may be taken out running the complete length of the trunk. Quite often this is not deep with only a narrow strip of the bark and a V-shaped portion of the wood affected. Such a wound should be cleaned up, the surface being left smooth and free of splinters. A dressing is also helpful. The edges of the bark should be cut back cleanly.

COUNTERACTING THE EFFECTS OF SHADE

The effects of shade are well known on sun loving subjects, for with the longer internodes which result, the growths are weak and far from typical, there being little or no flowering. Often too, a tree or shrub in a position where light strikes on one side only is drawn out of shape toward the sun and away from the shaded quarter, *see* Fig. 18.

Shrubs which are poorly shaped as a result of too much shade can be improved by hard pruning, but only if they are capable of breaking into growth from hard wood after they have been cut down. The growth which follows will also be quickly drawn up unless the condition causing the shade is corrected. If overhanging trees be the cause, the effects may be reduced, perhaps cut out completely, by carefully taking back the offending branches, *see* Fig. 26. It may, however, be more desirable to leave the tree intact, even to the extent of destroying the shrub in order to allow a lower furnishing of the tree, with grass sown beneath it. This is one of the many instances where planning is related to maintenance. When first laying out, the close planting of shrubs near young trees may be desirable if a fully furnished effect is required quickly, though it is intended to remove them at a later stage when the trees have developed.

A number of trees grow well in shade in their earlier years as seedlings. The Common Ash (*Fraxinus excelsior*), is one example. When young, on the forest floors it is in a shady position, and is thus encouraged to grow up toward the light. Later, as this is reached and the crown is formed, the tree is light-demanding and this is essential for healthy growth and flowering. Growth will only be upright if the shading is equal on all sides. The leader is then forced up as it is in the nursery by fairly close planting.

It is emphasised here and elsewhere that it is not intended to recommend, nor is it desirable, that every tree or shrub should be shapely and well balanced. The drawn specimen which is poor in shape and condition because it cannot reach the light is in no way desirable as a single specimen, but a completely furnished effect is often produced by a combined planting made up of subjects which, if isolated and taken away from these surroundings, would be very poor indeed. A typical natural woodland is made up of good and bad specimens.

REPAIRING SNOW DAMAGE

Evergreens are more affected by heavy falls of snow than deciduous subjects. Those with long, comparatively slender branches such as the Bay Laurel, (*Laurus nobilis*), may be weighed down considerably, thus presenting a very sorry picture. Conifers may also suffer badly, especially those with a flat branch system forming a tiered effect such as *Cedrus libani*. The horizontal branches have a fine network of growths and the snowflakes are held and accumulate to such an extent that the strain under a heavy fall is very great indeed, *see* Plate 60. It must, however, be remembered that branch systems are supple and that they bend under the weight perhaps to shed part of the fall before it sets hard in the freezing weather which often follows snow. When a heavy fall is accompanied by gales and high winds the damage may be severe, for limbs under a heavy load of snow may be bent to capacity, without a margin of 'spring' being left for the sway which is essential if they are to survive without breaking.

The arboriculturist is, of course, powerless to act during a heavy fall, especially if this occurs at night. It is possible to dislodge snow with a long bamboo cane or pole, provided this is attempted before it becomes frozen in the low temperatures which often follow. The timing of this operation is important, for under ideal conditions even the slightest disturbance is sufficient to dislodge a considerable weight. Naturally the operation can only be carried out on the lower branch systems of trees, but such shrubs as Rhododendrons with their very heavy foliage will be greatly benefited and perhaps saved from severe damage.

Branch shortening may be considered, but it should only be resorted to when severe damage has occurred and is likely again. Where the framework is permanent and cannot be replaced by regenerated growths, great care should be taken to avoid spoiling the shape or habit of the tree or shrub concerned. Specimens of the Bay Laurel, may have their long, whippy branches, not actually broken, but bent beyond recovery. This shrub regenerates freely from the base and it may in this condition be cut down hard. This treatment will also be successful with other subjects which behave similarly. Care must be taken to avoid damage to neighbouring shrubs, as the wood is very brittle during cold weather. The final cuts to repair damage may be left until more suitable conditions prevail, but emergency attention is necessary if a broken or damaged branch is resting on a lower one.

CUTTING FOR DISPLAY AND PROPAGATING MATERIAL

By exercising due care it is possible to avoid unnecessary damage to the parent plant when a collection is made for these and other purposes. Often this entails the removal of a large amount of growth at an unsuitable period, e.g. the collection of Holly at the Christmas period. It is therefore necessary to deal with the varied and often conflicting requirements in detail.

Material for Decoration or Shows

The need for great care has been emphasised and therefore it is important to allow sufficient time so that the cuts may be accurately positioned and treated afterwards if necessary. It must also be emphasised that in many cases it is a pity to have to remove anything, but there are exceptions. Forsythias, for example, are pruned, if necessary, after flowering and therefore there may even be some advantage in an earlier pruning, for the young wood may have an even better chance to develop freely and to ripen fully. Shrubs such as *Hamamelis*, on the other hand, which have a permanent framework that is not readily renewed, should not be cut for this purpose. The removal of one small piece does no harm, particularly if it is a side branch, but the loss of larger whole branches would be serious.

The collection of show material without harm to the tree or shrub is more difficult, for there is an understandable temptation to put in the finest sprays or blooms which are usually on the best growths. The advisability of taking such wood from the specimen in question should be carefully considered, and it is really a matter for the owner to decide. With sufficient care, the dangers of permanent damage will be reduced, and this may mean ladder and secateurs work rather than the use of standard pruners from the ground.

The temptation to cut too much should also be avoided. It is easy to be so keen on providing enough that eventually there is a large surplus. It is also better to distribute the collecting over the entire specimen rather than to cut in one place only, which may leave it ragged and unbalanced. If a growth is essential to the good of the specimen it should not be taken.

Christmas decorating material often poses a particular problem, for it means cutting such evergreens as Hollies, Yews and other subjects at the wrong time of year completely. It is worth noting such a requirement several months in advance and, if it is possible, delaying any cutting back which may be needed until the material can be used. This, however, is only advisable with a light cutback, *see* Plate 48. The severe pruning of evergreens should not be carried out until May.

Propagation Material

Material for propagation is gathered as scions or cuttings. Usually, small pieces are involved and there will be a natural tendency to avoid strong leading shoots as these will not be suitable for propagation purposes. Apart from this, however, care is needed to avoid both snags and tears as the material is removed, *see* Plates 61 and 62. In many cases where semi-ripe cuttings are removed they are taken directly and singly from the bushes. With these it is possible to cut the material cleanly and close to the stem taking the very thin slice of the older wood which will facilitate rooting. The pieces should not be torn off if the parent branch is to remain on the shrub. It is a mistake to remove all the growths from one branch; rather, a suitable selection should be made over the entire bush.

With a limited number of subjects which are mainly coniferous, such as *Araucaria*, the leading growth may be pruned back to provide a number of upright growths for use as cuttings, owing to the inability of the laterals to grow into shapely specimens after rooting. This would only be carried out on surplus stock or on specimens which are considered to be unsuitable for growing on, as the loss of the leading growth usually spoils the shape, perhaps permanently.

In the case of specialised propagation departments or with larger establishments, the practice of growing special stock to provide cutting or scion material is a good one. Such stock plants should be selected as being true to type and free from virus and other diseases. The Myrobalan Plum, for example, grown in a hedge and hard pruned each year during the winter, will provide good material for rooting as hardwood cuttings. A tree or shrub grown purely as an ornamental specimen should not be used extensively for providing propagating material.

PRUNING IN RELATION TO MAINTENANCE OPERATIONS

The Use of Machinery

The growing use of machinery must be taken into account and it is becoming more than ever necessary to co-ordinate tree and shrub pruning with the needs of administration and maintenance. Many of the routine tasks such as leaf collection, fertiliser and top dressing applications, grass cutting and other operations have been extensively mechanised and the tendency is to use larger machinery and equipment which require more headroom. The temptation to cut off the lower limbs to allow free and effective use of such machinery is very real, and it may in certain situations be justified, but usually the more natural effect of low branches and twig growth reaching the ground is preferable.

Service roads to key points should have sufficient head room for large vehicles, and it often pays to clearly mark these routes in order to avoid mistakes and damage in other parts. Mowers and leaf-collectors are, however, now in production which need a reduced amount of headroom and these are ideal for use in tree plantings where a natural effect is considered desirable. On big establishments the use of the larger machinery is justified but its use should be confined to the wide open areas, using suitable machinery for the confined spaces and under low branches. Justification for the need for care may be taken from the illustrations, Plates 63 and 64, for extensive damage can be caused by gang mowers working close to a branch system. The little extra care which is necessary in order to conserve the lower branches is well worthwhile when the increased beauty which results from this is taken into account, see Plate 66. In some situations naturalised bulbs may be desirable among the lower branches thus reducing the need for regular mowing, see Plates 23 and 65.

The Conservation of Organic Material

Low branches also reduce the wind force at ground level and thus the stabilisation of the annual leaf-fall is encouraged with obviously beneficial results, see Figs. 23, 24 and 25, Plates 67 and 68. Litter, all too commonplace, can also be held or grounded in the same way so that it can be collected more easily. There is a gread need, therefore, for the landscape architect, the horticulturist and the arboriculturist to work together when the creation and maintenance of a planting is considered. Shrubs have a part to play in this field but planting distances must be carefully considered. Sun-loving shrubs should not be over-shadowed by the trees, remembering that it is only to a limited extent that such ill effects can be overcome by pruning, *see* Fig. 26. If planted very close it may even be necessary to cut half the trees away to prevent overshadowing. Shrubs which are used in this way should be encouraged to furnish right down to the soil surface. Care is therefore necessary to avoid removing this growth during pruning.

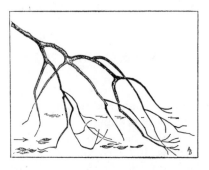

Fig. 23. The effect of low branching is that it retains leaf fall. The finer branch systems of some subjects such as *Crataegus* have an almost 'spring-like action' which tends to hold them to the surface.

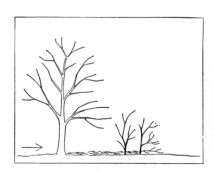

Fig. 24. A carefully planned and maintained planting of smaller trees and bushes on part of the perimeter of a group of large-growing species provide a means of retaining a portion of the leaf fall. Careful pruning may be necessary in order to maintain such a planting.

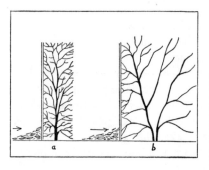

Fig. 25. A method of retaining leaves or litter by a hedge, with a wire netting fence against the formal edge. It is possible to allow an informal growth on one side as shown in (b), but the planting should be a greater distance from the fence to encourage a more balanced growth.

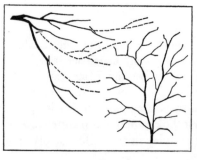

Fig. 26. A background of trees or large shrubs may be essential to neighbouring subjects, either for effect or shelter (or both). The encroaching branch systems may spoil the selected subjects unless they are pruned and kept in check occasionally. This needs to be carried out very carefully, otherwise a hedge-like effect will result. The broken lines indicate the branches to be removed.

Irrigation

Automatic irrigation is now used to an increasing extent with a permanent network of sprinklers and irrigators. When deciding upon their location, the sizes and forms of any existing shrubs should be taken into account in order to ensure a wide and even distribution of water. Severe pruning is often a bad way out of difficulties resulting from a bad placement, but the careful removal of one or two branches may be sufficient to ensure a better distribution, and provided that care is taken to retain a natural habit, this is often advisable. With trees, it may be possible to remove the lower branches which impede the course of the irrigator without destroying their beauty, but careful consideration is necessary before doing this.

Planned Accessibility

It is a great help toward good pruning and maintenance if the pathways and main rides are kept regularly mown and are thus free from long grass. Where branches are left to sweep the ground a regularly mown area round the trees gives good clearance to coarser cutting machines if there is any long grass left to cut. Other essential work, such as regular inspections or repair work after gales, is made easier and is carried out more efficiently. Young trees may also suffer in long and rough grass, and accessibility by means of mown paths is always worthwhile enabling the trees to be pruned and trained in a more satisfying manner. Most workers respond to work being carried out properly by such an improvement in standards.

Weed Control

Weeding is one of the major tasks in a collection of trees and shrubs, especially during the early years after planting. Training in some form is often required, but this cannot be carried out properly without good healthy growth. Rank weed growth may prove to be such a check that the young tree is ruined, the lower branches often suffering the most. Very large groups of such thorny subjects as *Berberis* are difficult to keep weed free and for this reason single or restricted plantings are often to be preferred. The control of seedling trees and bramble is often difficult with large and close plantings. Most *Berberis* regenerate freely if cut down to ground level and this can be used as an effective control. It should be carried out in the spring.

WILDLIFE CONSERVATION

Tree lovers are also nature lovers. They like to think of trees and woodlands as providing a home for the many kinds of birds and associated forms of life which are part of our heritage. The sounds of bird life contribute towards a full appreciation of trees and woodlands; for example, the call of the Green Woodpecker is part of the atmosphere and background for a scene which would seem empty without it. However, it must be faced that good arboricultural practices, extended over large areas, would bring about a vast reduction in the numbers of some species; in fact, this is actually happening as man takes over ever larger stretches of the countryside.

It is easily possible to be too tidy in the informal garden, perhaps edging and mowing to standards which are more in keeping with neat and formal layouts. A parallel may be drawn with trees which are growing in nature reserves. The natural nesting place for the Little Owl is in a cavity, often quite high up, *see* Plate 69. The Woodpecker feeds on grubs which are found in the wood of branches and stem systems, and often such trees are declining in health. Thus the requirements of nature seem to clash completely with the standards required of good arboriculture. This is true to some extent in areas which are open or accessible to the public, for example, where the trees are in public parks and woods, or by the roadside. Cavities, rotten branches or dead trees are dangerous, and the safety of the public in these situations must be given the first consideration. There is a great need for more reserves which have centralised areas, properly enclosed by secure child-proof fencing, in order that dangerous trees can be left to provide natural homes and feeding grounds for the birds and animals. The provision of nest boxes is of course helpful to those species which normally nest in cavities.

In these protected areas the role of the arboriculturist changes, and safety may no longer be the first consideration, provided that the fencing is secure. Cavities and decaying wood may be left, excepting of course where there is an end product on a commercial basis, in which case it will not be a true nature reserve.

Even in such protected areas nature must never be left to run completely wild, e.g. alien trees such as the Sycamore may soon predominate and perhaps spoil a natural woodland. This would be wrong and some control is necessary in such circumstances. Regular inspection is therefore necessary. Again, Bramble, one of our best native ground cover plants, providing an ideal shelter and home for many birds (*see* Plate 72), can become too extensive. Hazel coppice, also valuable as shelter, becomes leggy and loses the lower branches unless it is cut down once every 5 to 7 years. A rotational system of cutting in blocks is advisable in order to avoid the whole area being cut in any one year.

These ideas may seem to some to be taking the matter beyond all reason, but it must be remembered that many of our rarer species will only thrive in a balanced community. With urban spread and in the age of the motor car, man must keep man from selected areas if these species are to survive.

1. A graft which has not healed completely and has been attacked by Woolly Aphis. The callus tissues are young and tender and thus encourage the pest.

2. Part of a split crotch on a Cherry. The rooting from the callusing tissue is interesting. Often it occurs in the cavities of many trees, e.g. Beech.

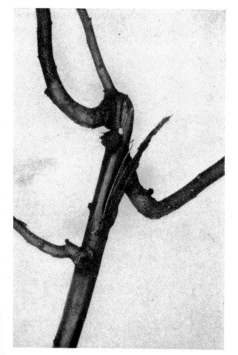

3. A healing wound on a lower branch system, but the torn bark is complicating and slowing down this process.

4. Lime with a badly angled main branch. The cement filling, always bad at height, is now loose with movement.

5. The results of the lack of training and poor pruning, rival leads are forming a narrow crotch and a developing snag with torn bark.

6. *Pinus nigra* var. *cebennensis* with a wide but strong branch junction at the base – not 'text-book' trained but a sound tree, full of character.

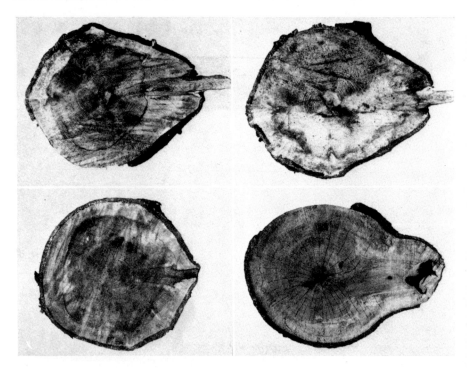

7. Cavity formation in three stages. (7a) Discoloration and infection extending into the heartwood. (7b) Later – healing prevented by the snag. (7c) Lastly – a cavity forming. (7d) Young specimen overgrowing a snag.

8. A large but good pruning cut. Callusing is more active at the sides than on the vertical axis.

9. Healing after a bark injury. The heartwood is intact, but a further dressing is needed to combat the woodworm already present.

10. Section through a large Beech trunk where the breakdown of the centre is complete. The small opening and callusing hide the true position.

11. Stump showing the restrictive nature of a strong girdling root.

12. Careful digging will preserve much of a root system. Sacking or straw to reduce drying out would be a wise precaution.

13. Alterations, involving constructional work in close proximity to trees need care, understanding and hard-work, as was the case when this kerbing was laid. The planner, the engineer and the arboriculturist should meet over problems of this nature.

14. A perfectly shaped specimen of *Carya tomentosa*. A straight central trunk and well-spaced branches with the lower ones sweeping gracefully to ground level.

15. A feathered tree of *Populus lasiocarpa* two years after planting. The weaker branches at the base are cut off as the tree develops.

16. The massive strength of a large tree of Lucombe Oak. Note the grafting line (on one of the parents, *Q. cerris*) and the strong right-angled branching.

17. A swelling caused by a tight tie. Certain patent ties allow for expansion, but a regular inspection of stakes and ties is necessary.

18. A young *Magnolia* growth tied down to act as a replacement for a broken and poorly shaped branch.

19. A young feathered specimen of *Alnus glutinosa* 'Aurea'. The stake and the lower growths are ready for removal.

20. Gradual removal of the lower feather growths on a Spanish Chestnut to give a clear stem. A watch must be kept for rival leads.

21. An informal group of small trees such as Birch and Mountain Ash, which would be spoilt by spacing and training.

22. The leaf-fall which has collected in the lowest branches of *Crataegus prunifolia*. This will rot down to be returned to the soil, while the problem of keeping the area clear of fallen leaves is also considerably reduced.

23. A good straight lead on a Birch which was planted as a feathered tree. Gradually upon establishment and growth the lowest branches have been cut away. Soon the cultivated circle will be filled in and sown down to grass.

24. A branch of *Ulmus villosa* showing scars formed during the natural process of twig shedding.

25. Cavity which was completely hidden by Ivy. This has been partly removed while a cut is being made for cleaning and draining purposes.

26. The forking head of a badly trained Elm. The right-hand half of the crown is in very poor condition with snags and a torn trunk. Repair work and bracing are needed.

27. A *Sorbus* throwing up strong sucker growths from the stock. They should be removed cleanly as close to the stem or roots as possible.

28. A young tree recovering from the loss of a lead but in need of training in order to regain a good shape.

29. Burrs and suckers at the base of the Common Lime. These superfluous growths should be cut back hard each winter.

30. The removal of epicormic growths from a Poplar. The cuts are made as close in to the trunk as possible.

31. A fine Beech which has taken kindly to a new life in an urban setting. The 'lifting' necessary because of its situation has been carried out properly, leaving the head well balanced.

32. Overcoming the effects of lopping. Careful thinning and a slow build up of a stout branch system by hard pruning in the early years appears to give the best results.

33. Epicormic growths to cut back and an old wound to attend to. This is developing into a cavity for the dressing has deteriorated.

34. Head of a Horse-chestnut which has grown substantial branches from the region of the lopping cuts. One cavity can be seen.

35. A close-up of the cavity referred to in Plate 34.

36. A difficult position. The best policy would be to cut back to the growths just above the forks and thus to train a new head.

37. Callusing on a cut which is made directly across an upright branch does not occur extensively until the surrounding growths thicken.

38. Bush of *Forsythia* before pruning. The two or three straggly branches spoil the shape of the bush.

39. The same bush after pruning. The straggly branches have been removed with thinning on the shoots springing from ground level.

40. *Forsythia* bush being pruned as the flowers fade, when the new growths are prominent. Care should be taken to leave any labels securely attached.

41. A complete furnishing but the large specimen of *Cotoneaster frigidus* in the background must be kept in check to avoid overshadowing, otherwise the top of the Holly in particular would be spoilt.

42. Pruning on this *Cotoneaster horizontalis* at the level of the window ledge must be carried out carefully in order to preserve an informal effect, cutting out lengths of branch rather than clipping to a definite line.

43. Yew growing over the edge of a path and in need of pruning to correct this.

44. The same specimen after pruning. The cuts have been made at different levels within the bush in order to avoid a straight formal edge.

45. *Fuchsia magellanica* pruned almost to ground level in the spring. Note the fine specimen of *Pyrus salicifolia* 'Pendula' trailing down to ground level. Larger shrubs than the *Fuchsia* would spoil this effect.

46. A sprouting stump of Box showing the rate of growth in one season following a drastic cutting back in the spring. This was done because the specimen was overgrowing the path and was rather unsightly.

47. An old plant of *Myrtus communis* trained on the south wall of an old cottage in North Devon. The surface is clipped over annually.

48. *Cotoneaster glaucophyllus serotinus* being pruned to supply Christmas decoration material. The selections are made with care and the well being of the bush in mind.

49. The terminal growth of a young Holly damaged by frost. A serious set-back for nursery stock but fortunately the axillary growths are undamaged.

50. *Euonymus fortunei minima* 'Kewensis' grown on a dead trunk. The mature branching has formed from the small matted growths which have reached the top.

51. A close-up of the mass of intertwining growths on the specimen in Plate 50. The habit is similar to that of Ivy.

52. The space of an inch or so between trellis slats and the wall allows intertwining of the climber on both sides.

53. Ornamental Vine trained on a tripod system. Low branching is encouraged for furnishing at the base. It has just been spur pruned.

54. *Wisteria floribunda* 'Macrobotrys' trained as a bush. Free flowering is encouraged by summer and winter pruning.

55. A wire system in use for a wall. Bamboo canes are used to take the growths to the lowest wires.

56. To assist with training, vertical wires have been tied across the horizontal strands. Bamboo canes have also been used to support the lowest branches.

57. *Pterocarya* X *rehderiana* with a graceful sweep of the branches over the waters surface. The extensive rooting which is apparent on the bank and down to the edge is a protection against erosion.

58. A low branch of a large Cedar. Great care is necessary when carrying out such operations as mowing, in order to preserve this feature, for the lowest growths are less than a metre above the surface.

59. The tear on a fine old Beech which had formed rival leads at an early age. Note the weakness of the attachment. A difficult wound to clean.

60. Heavy snow caused the upper limb of this Cedar to tear off bringing down three other limbs. A difficult repair operation.

61. Care must be exercised in the selection and removal of propagation material to avoid spoiling the parent plant.

62. Shortening a growth for despatch which was cut longer to avoid leaving a snag. The cuttings are detached at their destination just before insertion.

63. A mower unit close in to low branching, showing how damage can occur. Mowers with protected cutters are suitable for this work.

64. A close-up of mower damage. Apart from such unsightly tears, a hedge effect is built up which is unnatural.

65. Low branching and naturalised bulbs. It is only necessary to cut once or twice after the bulb foliage has died down.

66. The rotary mower is a good machine for cutting beneath low branches without causing damage.

67. Good furnishing at the base. Part of the leaf-fall is thus held down and acts as a mulch when rotting sets in.

68. A poor furnishing. Few fallen leaves are collected, weeds may be encouraged, while movement of the branches on the surface cause soil erosion.

69. The Little Owl at its nest in a cavity. This bird is most active in the dark, catching both moths and small animals.

70. X *Cupressocyparis leylandii* as a hedge plant in November. Clipping was carried out with shears three months before.

71. X *Cupressocyparis leylandii* specimens during a high wind. The trees lean gracefully yet retain their form, a central lead running through the tree.

72. The Dunnock nesting in Bramble, an ideal ground-cover plant for natural woodland areas as it provides shelter for bird life.

73. A Holly hedge which had been cut back hard from 3·0 to 1·4 m. (10 to 4½ ft.) seven months beforehand. The width had also been reduced.

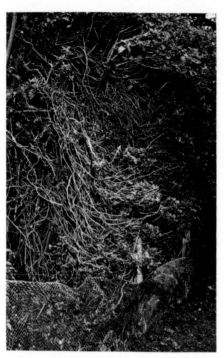

74. A large Holly hedge which has broken down. First the sides should be cut back hard, lastly the top.

75. A vigorously growing specimen of *Pinus ponderosa* at 14 years from seed. Note the strong leading growth and supporting laterals.

76. The base of an old specimen of *Acer campestre* with plenty of character. The concrete filling is many years old.

77. Well-trained fastigiate Yews. The positions of the green plastic-coated wires which are stretched round the circumference are just visible.

78. A fine specimen of *Cedrus atlantica* at Kew. The straight central trunk and branching is typical of this species.

79. Care is necessary when removing faded blossoms from a flowering head but the appearance of a bush is greatly improved thereby.

80. The base of a Hybrid Tea Rose Bush. Note the pruning cuts, clean and close, with the young wood and buds at the base.

81. Corrective training would still be possible on this fastigiate Yew but a central stake would be necessary before tying-in was attempted.

82. Strong vigorous Roses may be trained by bending the growths over. The effect after pruning and tying down new growths in March.

83. Hybrid Tea Rose bushes after pruning. The well-positioned cuts can be seen just above an outward pointing branch of bud.

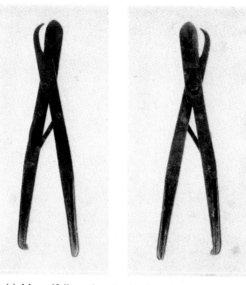
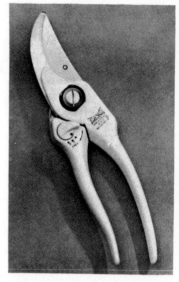

84(a) A beautifully made pair of early 19th century secateurs.

(b) A modern pair of secateurs, precision built with shaped handles and blades.

85. Long-handled secateurs or loppers in use. An ideal tool for larger wood and crowded branches.

86. Thorny and crowded suckers in need of removal. A use for the long-handled secateurs.

CHAPTER FIVE

Pest and Disease Control

Black spot of roses – Bacterial canker – Bacterial canker of poplars – Brown rot – Canker of apple and pear – Die-back of poplar – Coral spot – Die-back of roses – Elm disease – Fire blight – Fomes disease – Apple mildew – Rhododendron bud blast – Silver leaf – Witches' brooms – Aphis – Ash bud moth – Goat moth – Leopard moth – Pine shoot moth

Pruning may be regarded as one of the weapons of defence in the fight to prevent the spread of a number of pests and diseases, but the effectiveness of this means will obviously be influenced by many factors. This account should only be taken as a guide, and no attempt has been made to include a detailed account of each pest or disease and its control. It is limited to a number which may be controlled by pruning, and this section has been included with the intention of showing how some troubles at least can be checked or even controlled by this means.

Hygiene plays an important part in pest and disease control and dead branches should be cleared from the trees and ground and, if possible, destroyed by burning. Normally this clearance should not take place in the type of conservation area referred to in the previous section. With the bacterial diseases and some others it is important to disinfect any tools which are used, after each cut is made through diseased wood.

DISEASES	TREATMENT
Black Spot of Roses (*Diplocarpon rosae*)	The prunings should be gathered up and burnt.
Bacterial Canker (*Pseudomonas mors-prunorum* and related organisms) This may occur on a variety of Ornamental Prunus. The most serious infection is through wounds, including leaf scars in the autumn.	Winter pruning is advisable since over-wintering cankers infect the leaves to produce shot holes in some spp., and the leaves carry the infection through to the summer, the bacterium passing from the leaves into fresh wounds in the autumn.
Bacterial Canker of Poplars (Primary parasite not certain)	Dead wood should be cut out and cankered branches should be removed although it may be difficult to do this without spoiling the tree. Some species and varieties are more susceptible than others and if a tree is badly affected it should be taken down and replaced.

Brown Rot and Allied Diseases of Plums, Apples, etc. (*Sclerotina laxa* and *S. fructigena*)

A variety of ornamental Cherries, Plums, Peaches and Apricots may be attacked. It is usually associated with the fruits, but the infection may pass on to the spurs and supporting wood.

Cut out dead branches, twigs or spurs during the summer months when they may be evident among the foliage. Never leave until the following spring when the infection will pass on to the new buds.

Canker of Apple and Pear (*Nectria galligens*)

Ornamental Malus and Pyrus and other Broad-leaved trees are attacked.

All small branches and shoots which are infected should be removed during the winter. Cankers on branches which cannot be removed should be cleaned-up to expose healthy wood over the entire surface. Paint this with an approved preparation. A watch should be kept for new developing cankers during June, July and August. Cut these out and cover with a fungicidal paint. The protection of cut surfaces is a form of control. These controls will only be possible on small trees. Old and badly diseased trees should be destroyed.

Die-back of Poplar (*Dothechiza populea*)

Affected patches are often found round wounds.

Nursery stock should be pruned during the summer when healing is rapid.

Coral Spot (*Nectria cinnabarina*)

The dead and dying wood of a wide range of trees and shrubs are affected, but the fungus may become parasitic, especially on specimens which are in poor health with unripened wood and after a very long wet period, particularly Plums and Acers.

Cut out and burn infected wood as soon as the pustules are noticed to healthy wood. Also cut off dead wood whether infected or not.

Die-back of Roses and other woody subjects (*Botrytis cinerea*)

Spores may enter through pruning cuts particularly where snags are left. The blackened, diseased areas spread down the stem.

It is important to make good pruning cuts and to avoid leaving snags. Prune back dying shoots when observed to the first healthy node.

Elm Disease (*Ceratocystis ulmi*)

This fungus is spread by the Elm Bark Beetle and others.

Dead and dying branches should be removed and burnt. Badly affected trees may need to be cut down.

Fire Blight (*Erwinia amylovora*)
Many Rosaceous trees and shrubs are liable to attack. Infection is most likely during and immediately after flowering.

The diseased portion should be cut well back beyond the visible zone of infection. No wood with a foxy brown stain should be left. Destroy badly infected specimens. A daily inspection during and immediately after the flowering period is essential. The disinfection of tools after each cut is particularly important with this disease.

Fomes Disease (*Fomes pomaceus*)
This fungus is a slow-growing wound parasite, but it may eventually affect a large part of the tree.

Dead and dying branches should be cut back to healthy wood.

Apple Mildew (*Podosphaera spp.*)
These are found on a number of Rosaceous trees. Infected growths are covered with a white powdery Mildew.

Diseased growths should be cut off, carefully collected and burnt as soon as they are noticed, particularly primary infections in the spring.

Rhododendron Bud Blast (*Pycnostysanus araleae*)

Infected buds which become apparent during the winter should be removed by hand and burnt.

Silver Leaf (*Stereum purpureum*)
This attacks a wide range including Plums, Apples, Peaches, Morello Cherries, Laurels and Poplars.

Cut back any branches which are affected and are dying, well beyond the brown stain which may be seen in the wood. It is useless just to cut off silvered parts. The fungus is not usually present in them, but below. Pruning should be done where possible shortly before mid-July. Protect wounds immediately.

Witches' Brooms (*Taphrina spp.* on broad-leaved trees, *Melampsorella* on Silver Fir)
A fungus which invades the branch systems causing malformed growths. Mites, insects or 'bud-sports' may also cause this type of growth.

All branches or brooms should be cut out cleanly and to the standards of good pruning.

PESTS

TREATMENT

Aphis
The heaviest concentrations of this vast tribe of sap-feeders often occur near the tips and growing points of the current season's shoots.

With trees and shrubs which are summer pruned, this provides a partial control. The prunings should be collected and destroyed.

Ash-bud Moth (*Prays curtisellus*)
The terminal buds may be destroyed.

Infected shoots should be cut out. Reduce rival leads resulting from the loss of terminal buds to one.

Goat Moth (*Cossus cossus*)

The larvae tunnel into the main trunk and branches.

Cut down badly attacked trees. Dying branches may be cut beyond the tunnel. It is sometimes possible to kill the larvae with a piece of wire pushed down to the full length of the holes.

Leopard Moth (*Zeuzera pyrina*)

As for Goat Moth.

Pine Shoot Moth (*Evetria buolina*)

Pines, and in particular the Scots Pine, are attacked. Often, the leading shoots are affected, the tunnelling larvae causing distortion and perhaps their death.

Provided that the tree is vigorous and there is a replacement growth suitably placed to form a lead, affected shoots may be cut out.

CHAPTER SIX

The Specific Pruning Needs of the Genera

INTRODUCTION

In the following list I have described the pruning of nearly 450 genera of trees, shrubs and conifers. The emphasis is on hardy subjects, but many species classed as half-hardy or tender in this country have been included.

It was not possible in a book of this size and scope to include every species, still less all the garden cultivars and hybrids. The habits of growth and flowering have, however, been described for many species and in the larger genera the species have been grouped, where possible, according to these habits and to their pruning needs. If, therefore, the reader finds that a particular species or cultivar is not mentioned he can, in the vast majority of cases, apply the treatment recommended for a species with similar growth and flowering.

Botanical classifications and nomenclature are subject to constant change and I have taken as my main guide the *Manual of Cultivated Trees and Shrubs* by Alfred Rehder (Second Edition, 1947), Macmillan, N.Y. After each botanical name I have quoted my authority for that name, usually in abbreviated form, so that there shall be no doubt as to which species or variety is being referred to. As a result, however, of these frequent changes many plants have two or more botanical names in current use, and in Appendix I I give a list of the more likely synonyms to be met with. If the reader can find no mention in the text of any particular plant he should check whether the name he is using is one of these.

The botanical names of the genera and species have been used throughout, but I have included, in Appendix II, a list of common English names with their botanical equivalents. These English names also appear in the General Index.

ALPHABETICAL LIST OF GENERA

AND

THEIR SPECIFIC PRUNING NEEDS

Abelia

These shrubs love a sunny, rather sheltered position where they will flower well, producing fresh growths freely from the base. Thus, sufficient growth is produced to allow some of the older wood to be cut out completely and by this means the development of the younger shoots is encouraged.

A. chinensis R.Br. is usually grown as a bush in sheltered borders in the South and West, but, even so, some die-back can be expected after a severe winter.

The final pruning should therefore be left until the spring when the exact extent of the winter's damage can be ascertained. If it is desired, one or two of the very oldest branches may be cut out in the late autumn but there seems to be little point in this as they do form extra protection for the plant as a whole. With *A. serrata* Sieb. & Zucc., another deciduous species, treatment may be similar, but often there is more dead and twiggy growth to be cut out. *A. triflora* R.Br. produces a thick mass of erect growths but this is a natural habit and there should be no attempt to thin these out extensively, cutting out just the dead and oldest shoots. *A. schumannii* (Graebn.) Rehd. is definitely tender and may die right back in a severe winter. Should the wood survive for several years, the oldest growths may be cut out in the spring, but small furnishing shoots should be left at the base and the natural arching habit of the growths must be retained to preserve the typical habit of this species. *A. umbellata* (Graebn. & Buchw.) Rehd. is a large spreading bush and it may be necessary to prune the longer branches back to more upright growths in order to retain a specimen within a given space. The larger wood has an ornamental bark effect and size and girth is worth developing for this. *A. spathulata* Sieb. & Zucc., an upright grower, requires little beyond the thinning of the oldest wood in the spring.

The evergreen species and hybrids are typified to some extent by *A.* × *grandiflora* (André) Rehd. This usually needs wall protection when the growths are tied up to the supporting wires. The development of free growth may be encouraged by leaving the laterals unpruned, but new growths which are strong and fast growing must be tied in as they develop, otherwise once they have arched over, the laterals which are produced will be upright. Then, when the growth is finally tied up, these vital shoots which are to produce next season's flowers will be turned in to the wall and thus spoilt. The strong growths are well worth saving and they can be used to replace the oldest branches which may be cut out after flowering. As a rule this subject flowers on laterals from the previous year's wood but the season is extended by the production of blossoms on the earliest of the young growths. *A. floribunda* Dcne. has a similar habit and the same general principles apply.

Abeliophyllum

The only species is *A. distichum* Nakai, which is hardy. This shrub should be encouraged to grow vigorously for it flowers early in the year on growths made during the previous season and the stronger these are the better will be the flower display. Good culture and feeding are therefore important.

Worn and twiggy wood should be cut back after flowering to strong growths in the centre of the bush. The general shape and natural effect should be taken into account.

This subject is often grown against a south wall for the protection of the early flowers. In this position strong shoots develop which are 2·4 to 3·0 m. (8 to 10 ft.) in height. The best policy is to tie in the framework and then to allow the laterals to develop, cutting back a proportion of these each year in order to maintain vigorous growth. This should be carried out after flowering, but in addition some tidying up may be done during the growing season. The very pendulous lower branches often root freely on touching the ground and quickly develop into young plants. These must be removed at an early stage as otherwise they will compete with the parent and a bare patch will be left at the base.

Abies

It is essential that these should have a strong lead at planting time, a characteristic which develops at an early stage in the nursery provided that the stock is kept healthy. The task, after planting into the final quarters, is to encourage establishment as quickly as possible, in order that the rate of growth and development of the lead is maintained without check. An essential feature of these trees is the long, straight trunk which is formed from this lead. Under ideal conditions the lower branch systems are often retained and this greatly adds to their beauty. When the lower branches are lost, sometimes even to half the height, their beauty is to a large extent spoilt. It should be remembered that they are difficult to grow well on dry soils and many species thrive best on a moist soil, with shelter and a fairly high rainfall. Generally, any branches which are seriously dying back should be taken off at the trunk. No other pruning is normally necessary.

Abutilon

The hardiest species is *A. vitifolium* Presl but it is only possible to grow this shrub or small tree in the open without protection in the milder parts of the country. It is usually grown with wall protection, but even so, it is likely to be severely damaged or killed during very hard weather.

As wall culture is more common this will be described. The plants should go into their final position directly from pots, planting in the spring when the growth is about 0·3 m. (1 ft. high). The leading shoot should be retained and it is therefore advisable to stake this with a strong bamboo cane, making further ties as it extends. The lead is continued for almost the complete height of the plant. No support is needed other than ties on to the main stem to prevent the plant from blowing out or coming away from the wall during gales. It is fully capable of supporting its own weight, for it is a single-stemmed bush, not a climber. Should the leading growth be broken when the plant is young it will often form quite a broad-based bush with rival leads. Thus if it goes unattended without the selection of one of these, there is often considerably more lateral development away from the wall. As it is, the laterals from a mature plant will often grow out from 1·2 to 2·4 m. (4 to 8 ft.).

Little pruning is needed other than the cutting off of the old flower heads, but this is very necessary in order to avoid wasted energy in the production of a heavy crop of seed. This, together with a watering if this is necessary, will often prolong the life of this shrub for many years, for it is often short lived, dying suddenly usually just after flowering.

Grown in the open there is no difference in culture. A sunny position is needed.

A. megapotamicum St. Hil. & Naud. This is an attractive shrub to grow in a warm, sheltered corner against a wall. A small plant set out in the spring soon establishes itself, and the growths are tied fanwise against bamboo canes which are themselves secured to the wires. Each year, provided the plant survives the winter, further growths are produced from the base and over the shrub. These should be tied in to gain the utmost protection from the wall, cutting out some of the older wood each March or April when the extent of the winter's damage can be seen and taken into account. There should be no cutting out of old wood in the autumn as this is more likely to survive the winter.

Acacia

These are not hardy and they will only succeed in the mildest parts of the British Isles where they are often best when grown as wall shrubs. They may be planted 0·3 m. (1 ft.) or so away from the base. Staking may be necessary. Sometimes in a favourable position they will assume almost tree-like proportions even away from a wall. Most Acacias will respond to pruning if they become too large for their position, provided that this is carried out in the late spring. At this period living wood is apparent and frosted and dead growths can be removed.

Acanthopanax

These do not require regular pruning, for although they are often untidy in growth this is a natural habit. They should be looked over for dead wood during the summer months for it is often difficult to distinguish this from living material during the dormant stage when free of foliage. Generally, the branch system originates at or just beneath ground level.

A. lasiogyne Harms is one of the larger growers. The lower portions of the mature branches should be kept free of small growths, for the spines which are found on the strong upright shoots develop and become quite broad and thick with age. The extremities of the branches have a pendulous habit and this gives the shrub a well-furnished appearance enabling the foliage, flowers and fruits to be displayed to good effect.

Part of the interest of these shrubs is in their manner of branching and this should not be interfered with by pruning.

Acer

Acers vary considerably in their form, habit and size and in their soil requirements and uses in the garden. This complex genus is divided botanically into groups or sections and this is a convenient form in which to account for the pruning. Only those sections which are commonly grown are dealt with here. It may, however, be stated that with good, healthy and free growth very little pruning is necessary or desirable beyond that which is required for training purposes and for the retention of a lead with the larger growers.

The liability to bleed, especially if cut in the spring, is a weakness which is common to most, less with *A. campestre* L. It is important, therefore, to carry out any pruning which is necessary in the late summer or early autumn.

Sect. I. Platanoidea

A. platanoides L. has a close head with heavy branching and often with a free production of dwarf shoots along the length of the framework. These should not be removed nor should the branches be thinned for this is the natural habit of growth. In addition to the well established varieties, a number of selected clones have appeared, particularly in America, which have a more compact form making them suitable as street trees. These are often termed 'tailored trees'. Examples are 'Armstrong Red Maple' and 'Columnar Norway.'

A. platanoides L. 'Schwedleri', the Purple Norway Maple, is sometimes grown as a support for climbers, e.g. *Clematis tangutica* Korsh., the growths being pruned back hard to a main framework each winter or, if preferred, at longer intervals. The Acer provides support and also acts as a foliage contrast, Fig. 20.

Most of the remaining species in this group are also of tree size and thus a 1·8 to 2·4 m. (6 to 8 ft.) standard is normally planted. *A. cappadocicum* Gleditsch var. *sinicum* Rehd. in particular should be encouraged to spread and sweep down with low branches, as the foliage, flowers and fruits are most attractive.

Sect. II. Campestria

This group is typified by *A. campestre* L., the Common Maple. It may be grown as a 1·8 m. (6 ft.) standard and be trained well in the early years to retain a lead and have well-spaced branches. The natural growth however, is to produce a very close branching and this should be left to develop and no attempt be made at thinning. Occasionally, a strong growth is produced which extends up through the centre of the tree. Should such a growth originate in a mature tree close to the central axis it may be left, for usually it is a sign of renewed vigour. An upright growth on the extremities of the branch system will eventually throw the tree out of balance, in addition to the danger of the extra weight breaking the branches. It should, therefore, be carefully reduced, keeping a watch for any subsequent growths which may break out.

An attractive trunk and branch system may be formed by planting two or three young trees of this species together, allowing them to grow with their heads interlocked as one, *see* Plate 76.

This subject forms a very good hedge plant where, to gain full benefit of the attractive foliage, it may be clipped during the winter. It is also ideal for training over a framework to form an arbour. The annual shoots from this framework should be pruned back hard each winter.

A. monspessulanum L. is similar to *A. campestre* in form but *A. orientale* L. is usually much slower in growth and needs encouragement, with a good deep soil.

A. opalus Mill. Although this is a strong grower there is often considerable difficulty in retaining a lead as the vigour is thrown into the lower branching. A system of stopping may check this at an early stage but the habit, although variable, is to open out to form a head very quickly with a dense crown. Should the branches be clothed with dwarf shoots these are best left. *A. hyrcanum* Fisch. & Mey., very similar in appearance, is a slower and smaller grower but tends to retain its lead more readily.

Sect. III Saccharina

A. saccharum Marsh., the Sugar Maple. This should not be confused with *A. saccharinum* L., the Silver Maple, which in this country is a much larger tree. *A. saccharum* often produces a short branching head in this country and tends to be compact.

Sect. IV Spicatum

A. pseudoplatanus L., the Sycamore. This species, although not a true native, is found throughout the British Isles even in the most exposed areas. The main reason for its success in the exposed positions is that it is a strong, quick grower and is capable of a speedy reaction to damage to growth by development from the remaining axillary or dormant buds. In the nursery it is a strong grower and responds well to training; thus, with care, perfect standards with a good central lead can quite easily be produced.

This species seeds profusely and is distributed far and wide in a most efficient manner; in fact, the resultant seedlings will grow so rapidly that the general effect of an ornamental or amenity planting is quickly ruined. The saplings growing on the edge of a clump of trees where there is more light will in a matter of a few years increase the size of the wooded area thus changing its whole character and in many cases spoiling the lower furnishings of the mature trees. In addition, therefore, to carrying out the required maintenance on mature trees, it is important to eradicate surplus Sycamore seedlings at an early stage.

There are a number of varieties which differ from the type in growth. For example, *A. p.* 'Brilliantissimum' Bean is slow growing and compact, and it is difficult to maintain a central lead. *A. macrophyllum* Pursh develops into a large tree with fairly upright main branches. The outer and lower branches develop a semi-pendulous habit as the tree matures. This form should be encouraged as it brings the yellow racemes down to eye level where their beauty and scent can be appreciated.

Sect. V Palmata

A. palmatum Thunb. Considerable variation exists among the many varieties and forms of this species. The type plant ultimately forms a large bush or small tree, but it is slow growing and takes many years to reach full size. The typical habit which should be encouraged is one in which the branches, originating from low down, almost at ground level, grow up at a sharp angle supporting a twig and leaf pattern of great beauty, many of the lower and outer branches sweeping down almost to ground level where they can be seen to best effect. Often, the only pruning necessary is on neighbouring trees in order to encourage the free branching and unrestricted development of this species, *see* Fig. 26. This advice may also be applied to the many varieties and the most common mistake is to crowd specimens, thus spoiling growth. These plants require shelter from cold winds, while they are prone to damage from late frosts. *A. japonicum* Thunb. and other species in this section have similar habits and the general advice above applies to these also.

Sect. IX Macrantha

This important group is made up of species with a smooth bark which is striped white. *A. davidii* Franch. as an example has a typical habit of growth. The branches originating at the termination of a short trunk sub-divide to a very limited extent but instead produce many dwarf shoots along their lengths creating a graceful 'fox-tail' effect. A lead should be retained for as long as possible allowing branching on a leg of 0·9 m. (3 ft.). The early training consists of the removal of crossing branches which originate at the base of the head. At a later stage any small branches which tend to hide the bark effect should also be removed. For the best effect, the long branches must not be restricted through lack of light or pruning. In most respects the remainder of the species in this group are similar in habit. Among these are *A. crataegifolium* Sieb. & Zucc., *A. pensylvanicum* L., *A. grosseri* Pax var. *hersii* (Rehd.) Rehd. and *A. rufinerve* Sieb. & Zucc.

Sect. XII Rubra

Two large-growing species are in this group, *A. rubrum* L. and *A. saccharinum* L., the Silver Maple. The latter is a most distinctive tree and as it is a large grower it should have a 1·8 to 2·4 m. (6 to 8 ft.) leg with a strong lead. As the tree develops, the length of the leg may be increased even to 3·0 to 4·6 m. (10 or 15 ft.) in order to display the shaggy bark to best effect. The lower branches become pendulous at a later stage but this habit is seen at its best with *A. s. f. laciniatum* (Carr.) Rehd. which has deeply cut foliage.

Sect. XIII Trifoliata

A. griseum (Franch.) Pax, the Paper Bark Maple. In addition to the general effect, the great beauty of this tree is in the bark. This may be seen at its best when there is a definite short trunk 0·9 to 1·2 m. (3 to 4 ft.) with a well-shaped head. The lead should be kept for as long as possible until the head is formed. The branches, if allowed to grow freely without crowding or lack of light, produce an almost tiered effect. The outer branch tips sweep down to ground level, but with care the mower can work beneath them as they are not stiff.

    A. nikoense Maxim. is normally trained on a 0·6 m. (2 ft.) leg and the head quickly splits up into several ascending branches.

Sect. XIV. Negundo

A. negundo L. This and the variegated forms are fast growing but the type plant is the largest and will form a sizeable tree. However, once the clear stem is formed and the crown is developing, the vigour in the lead is reduced and finally fades completely as more and more growth and weight is put into the branches. In time these become heavy and spread out to open the crown, causing epicormic shoots to break out as a result of the extra light. Also, strong upright shoots are often produced in the region of any cuts which have been made on horizontal branches. This extra weight should be reduced and it is often advisable to brace really old specimens as the wood is brittle.

The form 'Variegatum' is often planted in a colour border to add to the general effect. It will, however, quickly outgrow the slower ones such as *A. palmatum* and should not be planted too close. A distance of 6·0 m. (20 ft.) is suggested. This variegated form must be allowed to grow freely without pruning for most of the buds which break out near a cut will produce green foliage and the general effect of the tree will be spoilt.

Acradenia

A. frankliniae Kipp. This evergreen shrub of dense growth is tender and needs a sheltered position in the warmer parts of the country. No pruning is required apart from the removal of dead growths but it must have sufficient space to develop. It may grow up to 3·0 m. (10 ft.) high and be 1 or 2 metres in spread.

Actinidia

These vigorous climbers require an extensive support if they are to be allowed to grow freely, for they produce long growths which twine round each other if there is no other means of attachment. Thus, in a confined space, unless they are pruned, they form an untidy and hopeless thicket.

Grown on a wall, the best method is to train the growths to cover the space which is allocated. Afterwards, growths which extend beyond these bounds are stopped back to 150 mm. (6 in.) when about 0·6 m. (2 ft.) in length. Thus it is necessary to look over the shrubs several times during the growing season. These shortened growths are then cut back hard to one or two buds during the winter. Some species, such as *A. chinensis* Planch., produce shorter growths or spurs on their older wood and this system of pruning encourages their development. Young growths springing from low down and in the centre form ideal replacements for the older and worn growths. They should be tied in as they develop. This replacement pruning should be carried out during the winter.

Another method is to use a tall pole or a tripod of poles for a support, *see* Plate 53 and Fig. 20 (1). The growths are left to arch down once the height for the shrub has been reached, but again stopping is necessary to prevent a chaotic tangle. Some of the older branches may be cut out each year during the winter, tying in the younger ones as replacements.

When the larger growers are used to climb over trees the added weight often becomes a problem. However, it is often possible to reduce this by breaking off the dead growths of the climber. This may be carried out during the summer. Pruning should be carried out with care as living wood can easily be severed.

Adenocarpus

These are deciduous or evergreen shrubs or small trees and are half-hardy. *A. foliosus* DC. is an evergreen which needs the protection of a sunny wall. It should be planted approximately one foot from the base and if trained to a single stem it may reach a height of 1·8 m. (6 ft.) before the head opens out. The horizontal branches are in tiers. Staking may be necessary when the plant is young. Pruning back is necessary where single growths are overlapping the edge or interfering with neighbouring plants. They may be cut back after flowering to leave a furnished effect. *A. decorticans* Boiss. is a deciduous shrub and also needs shelter. Pruning is much the same, making careful cuts to remove offending growths after flowering, in such a way that the cuts are hidden.

Aesculus

The most common species is *A. hippocastanum* L., the Horse-chestnut. At maturity it often forms a very large tree with heavy branching. In addition, the mature branchlets have a heavy downward sweep, some even becoming long and pendulous. To allow for this habit and to produce a good, safe, long-living tree, nursery stock should consist of standards with a good central lead. It is important to retain this lead for as long as possible so that the weight may be evenly spread over a number of well-positioned branches.

Large trees sometimes show a tendency to produce upright branches and to grow vigorously from these, even though they may originate from near the extremity of a lower limb. Such growths are best cut back, at an early stage if possible, for not only is the outline of the tree thrown out of balance, but also the extra weight which builds up on the branch may cause it to break off leaving a tear on the trunk. It is difficult at times to account for this, but extra light on one side of the tree or a succession of wet summers and good growing years are frequent causes.

Sometimes the main branches exhibit longitudinal cracks on the bark and these should be examined carefully from time to time. Should they not extend beyond the bark they have probably been caused by the rapidly swelling stem and there is no danger, for they heal rapidly, leaving just the scar for the remainder of the life of the tree. Deeper cracks or splitting caused by gale or storm damage occur frequently on trees in exposed sites and these need attention. Often when a wound is made, a large number of growths are produced in the following spring from the cambium on the outer edge of the cut. This is one of the reasons why unnecessary cutting should be avoided, for these growths, even after selection by thinning, are seldom strong enough to replace any branches which have been lost. Their attachment to the tree is weak as they have originated from surface tissues and are never directly connected to the heartwood of the parent branch or trunk. It is sometimes possible to thin to one or two growths on the lower edge of a wound and to leave these to hide the full view of this from the ground, thus improving the general effect. The other danger, in common with most trees, is that of the heart-wood rotting before healing takes place, but although the rate of healing is often rapid the heartwood of this species quickly deteriorates.

A considerable variation in growth and form occurs among seedlings, and there are a number of varieties which display this to an even greater extent. *A. h.* 'Memmingeri' often has dense branching with dwarf or epicormic growths over the entire system. These should not be removed, as even more will develop in their place which will involve further cutting. It is important to recognise these habits and to prune and train accordingly.

A. turbinata Bl. and *A. h.* var. *pyramidalis* (Henry) Schn. both tend to produce their branches from one point, the head opening out as soon as branching occurs. It is difficult to form a lead with these.

A. × *carnea* Hayne produces a dense canopy and with free, unrestricted growth and full light the branching will develop closely down to ground level. This is the best form in which to grow this tree and there should be an open foreground to allow this. There seems to be a tendency for this hybrid to form cavities and it is therefore important to retain the lead and to avoid narrow forking, at the same time keeping a close watch on old specimens in particular for any trouble which may be developing.

Another characteristic of this particular hybrid is the formation of large burrs which occur on the trunk and main branches. These appear as cankerous, corky eruptions, but healing and callusing may keep pace with their increase in size as the trunk or branch itself enlarges. In such cases, apart from the unsightliness, there is little to worry about. There should be no attempt to cut or gouge out this mass of corky tissue for it will often go back deeply to the centre of the limb or trunk and there will be no hard surface on the face of the wound with very little healing taking place from the edges. Should rot have set in, however, without any visible callusing, it may be taken as a sign that the tree itself is beginning to decline in health. The decayed and unhealthy tissue should be cleaned out, if possible back to healthy wood, the surface being treated afterwards as for a cavity. At the same time an attempt should be made to improve the health of the tree. Seldom is there sufficient girth on a limb to allow this cavity work to be carried out on a rotted burr and it is often better to consider complete removal of the affected branch.

With *A.* × *carnea* 'Plantierensis' the lower branches not only reach the ground but they will actually grow along it for a short distance afterwards. This produces a very good effect and great care must be taken with the mower when it is used in the vicinity of these growths. It is better to use the rotary type beneath the branches with an assistant to lift these as the cutting proceeds, *see* Plate 66.

A. californica Nutt. is not a large grower, branching low and wide with the outer branches becoming almost pendulous. A 0·9 m. (3 ft.) leg is sufficient. Growth is better in a sheltered position. Any wounds must be watched continuously, for the soft heartwood rots very readily before callusing is complete. The tree normally produces plenty of shoot growth from the region of any cuts.

A. indica (Camb.) Hook. produces a very shapely tree with clean growth, the main essentials being to start with a good standard tree and to retain the lead afterwards. The same is true of *A. octandra* Marsh., although the habit of growth is completely different.

A careful study of the ultimate size of each species must be made before a site is selected, for some, e.g. *A. pavia* L., make only small trees. However, it is important to retain a short lead through the crown, for the branches on a poorly-shaped tree are prone to damage from summer gales. The smaller growers suffer very quickly if denied light by invasive overhanging limbs, the affected portions dying back perhaps to spoil the shape of the tree.

A. parviflora Walt. has quite a suckerous habit and thus expands into a clump which, although only 2·4 to 3·0 m. (8 to 10 ft.) in height, may be quite extensive.

There is no pruning, apart from limiting the spread if it becomes necessary. This should be carried out with great care in order to preserve unpruned, flowering growth on the outer edge with furnishing down to ground level.

Ailanthus

A genus of large, strong-growing trees of which only one is commonly grown in the open, *A. altissima* (Mill.) Swingle. In its early years is it very fast growing but competition after planting is desirable for this helps to draw the lead up. Often, the branches develop horizontally, but turn to grow vertically for a considerable height, even to the level of the leading growth. This is a habit of growth which is difficult to check and old specimens with heavy branching may need bracing or a prop beneath a large horizontal branch. The tree heals very well but new growths appear near old cuts and these must be removed. Rival sucker growths formed on the root system should also be taken out. *A. vilmoriniana* Dode is similar in growth but the branches are more upright. Both species are fast growing when young.

In former days *A. altissima* was frequently grown for the tropical foliage effect which it produces if cut down to near ground level each year. By planting in a group or bed at 0·6 to 0·9 m. (2 to 3 ft.) apart, and by feeding and watering if necessary, strong growths 1 or 2 metres in height are sent up annually.

Akebia

These climb by means of slender, twining stems which are freely produced from a few short, stout branches at the base. They may be used for covering old stumps where little training is needed. The whole will eventually become an untidy mass of dead and living stems, but this matters little in the wilder, more natural parts of the garden. Posts and pergolas are also used for training, but some tying is often necessary, otherwise the whole climber may easily slip down and form a mass of growths at the base of the support. It is also an advantage to allow the growths to grow over the top of the arch or stake, as extra support is gained in this way. A few short stub-ends of branches may also be left on the stakes in order that growths may coil round these and thus help to hold the mass of twining branches in position, *see* Fig. 20(2). A tripod system of poles is also useful, *see* Fig. 20(1) Plate 53. It is possible to reduce the weight and general untidiness by carefully removing dead wood, doing this in the winter or early spring.

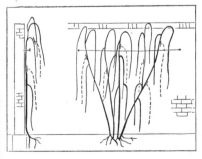

Fig. 27. An *Akebia sp.* trained to a wall. The pendulous growths are trained behind the horizontal wires for support (see p. 57). The dead and weak growths which would be cut out are shown in broken line. With a large established plant a greater proportion would need to be cut out each year.

When grown against a wall the stems should be trained behind one to three strands of horizontal wire. These wires should be stretched at approximately two inches from the wall face. The upper strand may be at 0·3 to 0·46 m. (1 to 1½ ft.) below the height of the wall as the growths are capable of a limited amount of self support, *see* Fig. 27. In addition, they arch over and the long pendulous growths are attractive. Often, a few of the growths twine together but this does not matter a great deal. Pruning consists of cutting out the weaker and dead growths during the winter. Sometimes also there are dead tips which need to be cut back, especially after a severe winter.

Alangium

A. platinifolium (Sieb. & Zucc.) Harms. A half-hardy shrub with an interesting stem formation and leaf pattern. Even when grown in a sheltered position the young growths are often killed back into the older wood. However, the plant will break out from living tissue and even from the base at soil level, thus making good its appearance and the only pruning necessary is the removal of dead wood in the spring.

Albizzia

A. julibrissin (Willd.) Durazz, this is the hardiest species but even in the warmer parts wall protection is usually necessary. However, owing to the fast rate of growth and the fact that it is capable of developing into a tree 9·0 to 12·0 m. (30 to 40 ft.) high when grown under good conditions, a high wall and some pruning will be necessary. It needs no support beyond a strong stake.

The pruning to restrict this subject should be carried out in the spring, taking the previous year's growth back if necessary to 5 or 6 buds. It is wise to encourage as much furnishing on the lower part of the plant as possible for the main stem quickly becomes bare as growth is concentrated more and more at the top of the plant.

Alnus

The strongest species are good growers, naturally producing a definite lead and thus developing straight trunks with well-spaced, small branches. They tend to be pyramidal in outline and, as they develop, the trunk may be cleaned to a height of 1·5 to 1·8 m. (5 to 6 ft.) when the lower branches may be left to sweep down to the ground as they extend. The following species and hybrids are in this group: *A.* × *aschersoniana* Callier, *A. cordata* Desf., *A. glutinosa* (L.) Gaertn., *A. matsumurae* Callier, *A. rubra* Bong., and *A. hirsuta* (Spach) Rupr. Also *A. nitida* (Spach) Endl. and *A. subcordata* C. A. Mey retain their leads well.

A. japonica (Thunb.) Steud. has a definite tendency to branch from ground level and may become a large shrub. This is even more marked with *A. maritima* (Marsh.) Nutt. and *A. viridis* DC. which are definitely shrubby, and no attempt should be made to form a lead. The latter species may not be more than 0·9 m. (3 ft.) in height.

A. incana (L.) Moench may develop into a shrub or small tree. It shows a tendency to form rival leads, especially in exposed positions and is therefore not the best alder for height. The golden form, *A. i.* f. *aurea* Dipp. also shows this tendency while *A. glutinosa* 'Aurea' has a better colour and gives height quite readily, *see* Plate 19.

The following also show interesting variations in growth. *A. firma* Sieb. & Zucc. retains a lead well with long, graceful branches but the shade cast is very light. *A. glutinosa* 'Imperialis' is a thin grower with delicate branching and should have a sheltered position. *A. maximowiczii* Callier is a small tree but the lead slows down as heavy thickening goes into the lower branches. *A. tenuifolia* Nutt. is a dense grower and it is difficult to retain the lead beyond 2·4 m. (8 ft.). *A.* × *spaethii* Callier is often difficult to grow to any height and occasionally, after a very severe winter, considerable dead wood is produced.

To produce an informal effect by the waterside, an even spacing should be avoided and a number may even be planted in pairs or in threes allowing them to grow together to form clumps.

Amelanchier

It is most important for the nurseryman and the arboriculturist to be aware of the two distinct forms of growth which are found in this genus – *suckerous* and *non-suckerous*.

Suckerous or stoloniferous species. Generally these form a thicket of stems and branches which vary in height according to the species. The following species are examples: *A. humilis* Wieg., *A. oblongifolia* Roem., *A. stolonifera* Wieg.

Non-suckerous or non-stoloniferous species. These may be single or multiple stemmed and to some extent this is dependent upon the initial nursery training. A 1·8 m. (6 ft.) length of clear stem may be formed, although some delightful old trees have a much shorter length of clear trunk. With a shorter, feathered young tree it is possible to start with a lower branching at 0·9 m. (3 ft.), and to maintain the lead for 1 or 2 metres. Although the branching under this system may not be regularly spaced, some quite attractive forms are developed and it is a pleasant breakaway from the stereotyped standard. The species only develop into small trees or large shrubs and once a head is formed the leader breaks up very quickly. It should, however, be borne in mind that most of the small tree species readily throw strong shoots from the lower stem system as they become established in their permanent quarters. These must be rubbed out as they appear if it is desired to retain a clear stem; alternatively, the required number may be trained to alter the shape of the tree, provided there is sufficient space and light for the additional branches in the head system. Normally, this can only be carried out when the head is in the early stages of development. *A. asiatica* (Sieb. & Zucc.) Endl. and *A. canadensis* (L.) Med. will form larger trees than many of the other species in this group. *A. sanguinea* (Pursh) DC. is shrubby and forms one or several stems. The same is true of *A. alnifolia* Nutt., *A. florida* Lindl. and *A. amabilis* Wieg. The latter, if trained

H

to a single stem, with a definite branching which commences at 1·2 m. (4 ft.), forms an attractive head with a mass of pendulous branches.

X Amelasorbus

X A. jackii Rehd. This bigeneric hybrid is a strong-growing shrub and requires very little pruning beyond the removal of dead wood. It is seen at its best with an open foreground and with furnishing down to ground level.

Amorpha

These are deciduous shrubs or sub-shrubs, either retaining a permanent branch system or dying down to a woody stock near soil level. *A. canescens* Nutt. usually dies back each winter to a woody stock. Thus all the previous year's wood should be cut back, dead or alive, in the spring, just before the new growths break out and these will flower the same year. *A. fruticosa* L. forms branches which remain and thicken year by year. Again, flowers are produced on the current season's growth. Left to develop freely, the branches spread and become ungainly. Occasionally, therefore, some pruning is necessary, either to shorten these back to a suitable growth or to cut them out entirely. The shrub freely produces young growths which will act as replacements. Never should pruning be carried at one level year after year, otherwise mop-heads of growth will be produced which are unsightly. For foliage effect, this species may be cut right down to near ground level in the spring but the growths will not flower. The remaining species are similar in general habit to *A. fruticosa*.

Ampelopsis

The Ampelopsis and Vitis climb by means of coiling tendrils and are therefore distinct from Parthenocissus, which produces flattened discs which adhere strongly to their support. The strongest species, for example *A. brevipedunculata* (Maxim.) Trautv., are suitable for growing over trees, in addition to such structures as sheds, walls or fences. They are often better in the wilder parts of the garden where they can ramble at will. Training and pruning under these conditions is difficult, unnecessary and undesirable, unless growth goes beyond the intended bounds. When they are trained to single poles and left to develop freely, growth becomes tangled and unmanageable in such a restricted space. A method of control is to prune back annually to two or three permanent rods, which are tied to the support. Under this system, spurs build up which are twisted and knotty and have great character. The young growths are taken back to the lowest bud each December after leaf fall, when there is least likelihood of bleeding. When trained along horizontal pergola systems the young growths, which are long and slender, hang down to form a curtain. Annual pruning back to the permanent rod is carried out in just the same manner, *see* Fig. 20 (6).

   A. arborea (L.) Koehne is better suited to wall culture. Supporting wires are needed and annual pruning may take the young growths back to a permanent rod system.

Anthyllis

The most commonly grown species is *A. hermanniae* L., which has a compact habit in the earlier stages of development. As maturity or old age is reached, bushes often become heavy, with a loose habit which is caused by the crowded condition of the growths on the ends of the branches. A limited amount of careful cutting back after flowering will correct this, but this may need to be spread out over 2 to 3 years before this is corrected. The shrub benefits from the protection of a sunny wall or corner in the rock garden. *A. barba-jovis* L. is a subject for wall culture, the main branches being tied and trained as the shrub develops. No pruning is normally required in the nursery.

Aphananthe

A. aspera (Bl.) Planch. This rare tree forms a rounded head with pendulous branchlets. It should be given a sheltered position but it must have full sun as it is important for the wood to ripen properly. It is a difficult tree to grow well in this country, as any wood which is only partially ripened is often killed back during the winter. It should be trained with a clear trunk of 1·8 m. (6 ft.).

Aralia

These are plants for a light, well-drained soil, for, while growth may be stronger in a moist, rich medium, the wood which is produced is inclined to be pithy and unripened and in this condition may not winter well especially in cold districts. On a stiff clay, growth may be very poor indeed and it is usually impossible to develop these shrubs beyond the bush size.

A. elata (Miq.) Seem. is usually the largest woody grower and under ideal conditions extends its branch system to become a very large shrub. It requires plenty of space and should be allowed to branch freely. Pruning which involves cutting back large branches can easily spoil the curiously crooked and twisted framework which is quite attractive in the winter. In a position where the shrub is against a dark background, the growths often sprawl out towards the light and as the branches grow older, longer and heavier, some of the lower ones may need neatly propping. The inflorescence terminates the current season's growth, but the short, woody shoot tip which supports this remains attached, extension for the following season being taken over by the topmost bud beneath this. Thus, in time, a number of old, dead shoot tips remain attached to the branches. These should not be mistaken for die-back which is usually extensive with specimens on a wet heavy soil after a severe winter. This species is often suckerous but unless an enlargement of the clump is needed, the suckers should be removed. The variegated forms should not be allowed to sucker as they are propagated by grafting onto stocks of the ordinary type. Any suckers which are produced are, therefore, stronger and will soon outgrow the required form.

A. spinosa L. is similar to *A. elata* in many respects but it does not grow as large and will not branch as freely, consisting more of upright stems and branches but suckering extensively. *A. chinensis* L. is also similar, but is a smaller grower.

Araucaria

A. araucana (Molina) K. Koch, this is a tree which must be grown as an isolated specimen if it is to be seen at its best. With a clear surround, for example on a lawn, the branch systems can reach down to ground level with a graceful and natural sweep. The tree should retain the lead until the ultimate height has been reached. However, should the central growth be killed or removed for some reason, a number of adventitious buds may be produced on the central stem and near the original growing point. Often they arise at the point of origin of the highest, and of course youngest, tier of branches. When these have developed sufficiently the strongest may be selected to extend the central trunk and lead. The branches retain their character as such and will not assume the role and character of leading shoots, even if the adventitious buds fail to appear or a lateral is actually rooted as a cutting, *see* page 13.

This tree will appear very ragged if dead branches and wood are apparent and any work carried out to remove these is very rewarding despite the difficulties and unpleasantness of the task. The die-back of a branch is usually progressive and it is advisable to remove the whole of it, back to the main trunk, in the first place.

Arbutus

Normally, this group of evergreen shrubs requires little pruning. It is important in the nursery stage to give them shelter but to allow them to grow freely. Normally they are grown in plunged pots to avoid a check in growth at planting time and staking will be necessary at an early stage. After planting they should be left to grow freely and no attempt must be made to form a trunk. As the leading shoots extend, the smaller branches inside the bush are deprived of light and die. They should be cleaned out as growth extends, for the bark is attractive. Most species form spreading trees when mature, the lower branches assuming a low angle of growth as they are weighed down by extensive development. This is a fortunate habit, for with a clear foreground of grass running up to the perimeter of the tree, a close and rewarding inspection may be made of the flowers and fruits during the autumn and winter. One feature which is common to all *Arbutus* is that they regenerate freely if cut back quite hard, provided that the root system and the plant as a whole are in good condition. It may be necessary to be drastic in this manner following storm damage, or after a very severe and long spell of cold weather when the foliage and small twig growth may have been killed. In the latter case no pruning should be carried out until new growth breaks out.

The above introductory notes serve for *A. andrachne* L., *A.* × *andrachnoides* Lk. and *A. unedo* L. with its other form *rubra* (Ait.) Rehd. A larger-growing species, *A. menziesii* Pursh, should if possible be trained with a definite trunk. Shelter will be needed for this in the more exposed gardens and this may be obtained by planting in a very small clearing, which has a surround of fairly large Rhododendrons. Both genera have similar soil requirements and the young *Arbutus* is encouraged to grow for the light with a good clean stem. The site may be carefully and gradually opened out at a later stage.

Arctostaphylos

Quite a common prostrate plant, particularly in alpine collections, is *A. uva-ursi* Spreng. It forms a mass of growth and foliage and is thus ideal as a ground cover plant. If the plant grows to the edge of the border and needs cutting back to restrict the spread, an informal and pleasing effect is obtained by continually cutting out growths individually with the secateurs. The shears, used to clip along the edge, will result in a hard line which will not be in keeping with an informal effect. Occasionally it may be necessary to dig the rooted pieces out along the edge to check spread.

A. manzanita Parry is a rare species which usually grows to a height of 1·2 to 2·4 m. (4 to 8 ft.). It needs a sunny position with some shelter. It requires no pruning and should be allowed to grow freely, when it will usually form a short leg and branch rather stiffly from this. Good growth should be encouraged, for if this subject becomes unhealthy it often dies off very quickly.

Aristolochia

A few woody species may be grown in the open. They are vigorous climbers, twining in an anti-clockwise direction round supports such as arches, branched stakes and other supports. *A. durior* Hill and *A. tomentosa* Sims are among the most reliable species. Pruning consists of cutting out any dead growths as the buds commence to break in the spring, but it is not possible to retain a tidy habit.

Aristotelia

A. macqui L'Hérit. This evergreen shrub normally needs wall protection, but it may be grown in the open in milder areas. The main branches are strong and upright, the laterals spreading. The shrub is grown as a bush and is thus planted a 0·3 m. (1 ft.) or so from the base of the wall. Pruning to restrict size, if necessary, is carried out in the spring and again in the late summer if further shortening is required. The cuts are made into the bush to keep an informal surface. Sometimes long, strong shoots are produced in the crown of the shrub and these may become top-heavy with growth after a year or so. This tendency, which is more likely to occur as a result of the shrub being cut back by frost, should be corrected at an early stage.

Aronia

The three species of deciduous shrubs have a stool-like habit and when healthy a good supply of strong young wood is thrown up from the base. This allows for good replacement branches as the older ones need to be cut out. These shrubs have a spreading and arching habit and this is part of their natural beauty. Pruning, if it is necessary, should be carried out after the autumn foliage and fruiting displays are over. This is often in January and the cuts should be made as close to the base as possible, provided that there are the required number of replacement shoots.

Artemisia

This is a genus of herbs, subshrubs and shrubs. Their foliage is the most attractive feature and for this reason it is preferable to keep the growth strong and healthy by fairly hard pruning to prevent them from becoming old and woody.

A. abrotanum L. is the most common. Without pruning, this subject becomes very straggly and unsightly with bare stems which become prominent as the branches are weighed down. It should be cut back quite hard in the spring just as growth commences, to prevent this happening. Sometimes mice will eat away the surface bark on the stems at ground level and a watch should be kept for this, especially during the winter.

A. arborescens L. should be cut back hard to the older wood at the base of the shrub in the spring. It appreciates the shelter of a sunny wall. The remainder of the woody subjects of this genus respond to hard cutting back in the same way, although many may be killed back by hard weather during the winter, especially in exposed conditions.

Arundinaria – *See* Bamboos.

Asteranthera

A. ovata (Cav.) Hanst. is a small climber but it may, under ideal conditions, reach a height of 1 or 2 metres when grown against a wall. When it is growing freely it produces comparatively long growths which give the shrub height. It is necessary to tie these in position, although the shrub will clamber into neighbouring plants on its own account. Sometimes the long thin shoots will run along the surface of the soil as a form of ground cover. If required these may be tied up against the wall to thicken and improve the effect as a whole.

This subject will withstand cutting and it is beneficial to cut out the weaker wood. This should be carried out in the spring.

Atraphaxis

This small genus of deciduous shrubs have, even in a sunny position, a rather untidy and sprawling habit which, however, may be improved by cutting out some of the older wood in the spring. This may mean taking back quite large shoot systems as with *A. muschketowii* Krassn. or small ends as with *A. frutescens* (L.) K. Koch.

Atriplex

A. halimus L. is very good near the coast, although it can also be grown inland. The branching is stiff to begin with, but as the bushes reach maturity they open out and become loose. However, annual pruning in the spring, as the new growth commences, corrects this tendency. In addition, the growth tips damaged by frost may be cut back to living wood at this period, but a formal outline should be avoided. This subject also forms an excellent hedge plant near the coast when trimming should take place in the spring as the new growths appear.

The treatment for *A. canescens* James is similar.

Aucuba

The species most commonly grown is *A. japonica* Thunb. It is a strongly growing shrub and will thrive in poor, dry positions, often in quite dense shade beneath trees. Sometimes after very dry periods there is some die-back which needs to be attended to for appearance's sake. As this subject is often grown to provide a background to a border or to fill an awkward gap, it is desirable to have it as large and free-growing as possible and thus it is very seldom that it needs any pruning. The minor branches keep extending year by year and even mature bushes throw up strong cane-like growths each year which reach almost the height of the plant before they branch out. An annual mulch of leaves and a discontinuation of the annual forking through the odd corners every spring to 'tidy them up' is more effective in getting good growth than the pruning knife. Any pruning to shape should be carried out so as to leave an informal effect, cutting out whole growths near to ground level rather than snipping off small branches.

There are many varieties but they all have the same habit of growth. The narrower-leaved forms, such as 'Salicifolia' form a bush which is lighter in foliage effect than the broad-leaved types such as 'Hillieri'.

This is not a good subject for formal hedging for, if it is clipped, portions of the large leaves are left on the plants, and the whole effect is very unsightly. Also, it is difficult to keep the base of the hedge well furnished unless a sufficient width is allowed, leaving the lower branches at almost full length.

Azara

The various species are similar in many respects in that they are bushy and will form a strong framework of branches. Also that they will respond to careful pruning if this is needed to restrict them, while maintaining a surface which is pleasantly evergreen.

A. microphylla Hook. f. may be grown in the open in the milder localities, but it should have shelter. It will then form a large shrub or small tree 6·0 to 9·0 m. (20 to 30 ft.) in height. Usually it is left to branch naturally from the base. It may also be grown on a south-facing wall, when the main branches should be trained fan-wise, six to eight being selected. From these the laterals are used as furnishing and, if it is necessary to restrict it in any way, the pruning of a few growths every May taken well back into the framework will still leave the plant adequately furnished. Another method of growing this subject in the shelter of a wall is to plant it a foot or so from the base and allow it to grow naturally as a bush. *A. lanceolata* Hook. f. produces slender branches from the base of the bush but it is tender and needs protection. The other species may also be grown as self-supporting bushes with a wall for protection, *A. petiolaris* (D. Don) Johnston being one of the largest often developing into a very dense bush or small tree.

Baccharis

Two species are commonly grown, *B. halimifolia* L., deciduous and *B. patagonica* Hook. & Arn., evergreen. Grown in the open in a sunny and windswept position these subjects need very little pruning as the bushes keep compact and rounded. In the shade, growth is weakly and effective staking difficult. Rarely do they flower in a shady position. Both species respond to hard pruning in February in deciduous species, but the evergreens are left until later.

Bamboos

These require very little pruning; in fact, over-thinning or cutting out all the dead wood can be a mistake. This is because the old and dead canes are rigid, and thus act as a support to the new and living ones which are more supple. Some support of this nature is necessary especially during periods of heavy rain or snow.

Pruning will not prevent Bamboos from flowering.

Bambusa – *See* Bamboos.

Berberidopsis

B. corallina Hook. f. This climbs by means of twining stems and is normally a subject for a cool, shady wall. It should be trained up vertical wires, or bamboo canes tied to the horizontal wiring system and will usually climb up these quite readily, but an occasional tie may also be necessary.

It is seldom necessary to prune this subject, especially on the main branch systems. On occasion, the minor branches benefit from thinning if it is felt that they are too thickly placed. In this case the older and weaker ones should be removed but this must be carried out very carefully in the Spring.

Berberis

Many of the species and varieties have a growth and a habit which is quite distinct and any pruning which is carried out should be aimed at retaining this. Great care should be taken in the selection of species and position so that there is no need to restrict growth and size by pruning.

The more vigorous species are really large growers; for example *B. chitria* Buchholz ex. Lindl. may reach a height of 3·7 to 4·6 m. (12 to 15 ft.). In addition, they have an arching and wide-spreading growth and should be left to do this naturally. Where there is sufficient space, groups may be made up of several bushes in proximity to form a complete tangle. A thorough weeding of such clumps may be impossible and eventually sizeable saplings of such trees as Ash appear and must be eradicated. One method of overcoming this problem is to cut the whole clump down drastically to within 300 mm. (12 in.) of ground level during the winter. This will allow the site to be thoroughly cleaned over a period of three or four years before the plants grow together again.

With an arching species it is sometimes difficult to keep the lower growths. The pruning of deciduous bushes, if it becomes necessary, should be carried out during the growing season when any dead branches will be evident and the living ones can be retained. It is important to retain these with the large growers as otherwise bare stems will be exposed which may not readily furnish up again. Any cuts which are made should be back to a suitable growth, the tendency being to cut out lengths of branches, rather than small pieces. The branches are often close together and it is not always possible to cut cleanly without snags. *B. manipurana* Ahrendt among others is very heavily branched and if there are smaller plants beneath the spread they are likely to be smothered, particularly after heavy rains or snowfalls. The most difficult species to restrict without spoiling are the dense and very compact growers such as *B. candidula* Schneid. Any cutting back must be carefully carried out in order to retain the natural surface.

B. dictyophylla Franch. is attractive, especially during the autumn and winter, when the young stems, covered with white 'bloom' are very prominent and there are often brilliantly coloured leaves on the older branch systems. The production of strong young wood may be encouraged by pruning out some of the older wood as occasion demands, accompanying this with mulching and feeding. *B. virescens* Hook. f. & Thoms. also has young stems which are attractive, these being light brown in colour. Their production may also be encouraged by careful and selective pruning with general feeding and mulching.

B. × *stenophylla* Lindl. is often used as a flowering and informal hedge plant. The arching growths are cut back after flowering to suitable developing shoots and by this method the general outline and proportions of the feature are retained. The quickest and easiest way is to clip over the surface, but a better method is to prune each growth individually with the secateurs, choosing a suitable point just beyond a replacement shoot. Feeding and mulching and, if necessary, watering should be carried out after the operation is completed. *B.* × *stenophylla*, like a number of other *Berberis*, develops creeping stolons, a characteristic which in the case of this hybrid is inherited from one of the parents, *B. darwinii* Hook.

Berchemia

These are twining shrubs, but the strongest growths which extend for 1 or 2 metres in one season are often scandent and arch over onto nearby shrubs and even small trees. One of the strongest growers is *B. racemosa* Sieb. & Zucc. and this free habit is more in keeping with the wild garden. *B. flavescens* Brongn., which appears to have a more definite twining habit, will throw strong scandent growths which twine later, or even produces laterals which have this habit.

When grown in a natural setting little pruning is required, although it may be necessary to restrict size by cutting back any long arching branches which exceed the bounds. This may be carried out during the winter.

Under a more restricted system of culture, for example against a wall, the ordinary horizontal wiring system will support the growths in the early stages. As the bush matures the many growths may be held in position by extra horizontal wires tied over the branches and original strands. Thus the branches are held between two wires. Lateral growths are left to branch freely from the main stems. Pruning consists of cutting out the weaker branches and even some of the main stems if these are crowded, as otherwise the shrub soon becomes a mass of congested growths.

Betula

Birches require very little pruning but it is desirable to maintain a central lead among the tree-producing species. It is important therefore to recognise that there are small bush forms such as *B. nana* L., the Dwarf Birch. While this species may only be 0·6 to 1·2 m. (2 to 4 ft.) in height, *B. occidentalis* Hook. is still a shrub at 4·6 to 6·0 m. (15 to 20 ft.) high. The tree species will mostly develop height whether or not they develop rival leads, but one species, *B. nigra* L. will sometimes divide at ground level to develop into a large bush with a rounded head. Should a single lead be retained it may develop into a large tree.

It is important when Birches are to be taken from the nursery that they should be young and well shaped with a good lead and that they are planted up in well-prepared positions. Strong and rapid growth should be maintained by careful treatment thus reducing the shock to a minimum. It is often noticeable that the strong lateral growths which ultimately form the main branch system are produced when the young tree is growing fast in its final position at 1·5 to 1·8 m. (5 to 6 ft.) in height. There should be no attempt to train a clear stem in the nursery, but the small lower branches may be trimmed up gradually when the trees are growing rapidly in their final positions. This should be carried out in August and the whole operation spread over 2 to 3 years, leaving a clear trunk of 1·2 to 2·1 m. (4 to 7 ft.), *see* Plate 23. This allows the coloured bark to be seen to best effect but some of the lower branches can be left on a few outside trees of a group planting as this produces a more natural furnishing.

Sometimes when a lead breaks the strongest growths develop, not immediately below the broken portion but lower down in the branch system. In such cases the new lead should be selected from these stronger growths. Such pruning must be carried out in the late summer or autumn, never in the spring when wounds bleed very badly.

Birches develop better in full all-round light. In a position which is shaded on one side by a large tree the main stem will be weak, and later as growth extends the top may arch over, especially when it is heavily laden with fruit.

Bignonia

B. capreolata L. is the species which is normally grown against a wall in warmer parts of the country. It is a climber and will in nature reach heights of 12·0 to 15·0 m. (40 to 50 feet), using even large trees as a support. On a wall, although the tendrils which it produces are an aid to climbing, the growths or main stems must be spaced out and tied to supporting wires. In the spring the laterals which are produced from these should be pruned quite hard, by at least a third or more. The weaker growths should be cut out entirely during the summer, as new shoots are produced. In this way, the air and all the available sunlight is let into the wood to encourage flowering the following year. The aim is to maintain the vigour of the shrub by encouraging young and strong wood, at the same time cutting out the weaker shoots which shade them and prevent good ripening.

Billardiera

B. longiflora Labill. is not really hardy and needs a sheltered position in a mild locality. It climbs by means of slender twining stems and thus a vertical wiring system is needed. If wall culture is attempted the vertical strands can be secured to the horizontal wires, *see* Plate 56. With a pergola system wires may also be necessary.

Little pruning is required, but dead stems may be cut out in the spring. Weak growths may also be treated in the same way, but great care is necessary to avoid damage to the remaining growths.

Broussonetia

B. papyrifera (L.) Vent. This forms a small spreading tree, the main branching often starting low, often near ground level. This is the natural habit and it should be allowed for in the nursery. It is fast growing when young, but is liable to late frost damage at this stage. Any suspected cavities should be dealt with promptly, as the wood is liable to decay quickly when it is exposed.

Bruckenthalia

B. spiculifolia (Salisb.) Reichenb. This is a dwarf heath-like plant which requires similar conditions to that group of plants. Often after a few years it becomes bare in the centre through the growths bending over and exposing the main stems which are devoid of foliage. The development of this stage may be delayed for a few years by removing the old heads in July after flowering, at the same time shortening the straggly growths, but never cutting back into the older wood. Eventually old plants need to be replaced. In the nursery, compact and bushy plants may be encouraged by snipping back the young growths two or three times during the growing season with a pair of scissors.

Brunnichia

B. cirrhosa Banks is the only hardy species in this genus but it may be killed down to ground level in a severe winter. It produces slender stems and climbs by means of tendrils. A stake is necessary, but the stub ends of the branches should be left on this as further support, *see* Fig. 20 (2). Pruning consists of cutting out any dead wood from time to time.

Buddleia

The growth and flowering habits of the plants in this genus may be classified into three types:

(a) those which flower terminally on the current season's wood,
(b) those which flower from the previous season's wood,
(c) those growing out in the spring to flower from large terminal buds or growths which develop on strong wood made in the previous year.

Those which flower terminally on the current season's wood.

With these, the habit of growth and flowering is such that the late spring and early summer are devoted to the formation of shoots which are often 1 or 2 metres in length. These are eventually terminated by the inflorescence, which opens and sets seed all in the same season, as that in which the growth is made. *B. davidii* Franch. and the various cultivars of this species all have this habit. Left unpruned, they develop into large spreading bushes full of dead wood and small branches which blossom very poorly. Hard pruned annually in the spring, taking each shoot back to the lowest growths, the vigour is channelled into fewer shoots which as a result are strong with correspondingly large panicles of blossom. The pruning may either be carried down to ground level or to a main framework of a few branches about 0·9 to 1·2 m. (3 or 4 ft.) in height according to vigour. The need for a larger framework is indicated when the growths are excessively vigorous, especially at the top of the bush, and in order to achieve it, selected, well-positioned growths should only be pruned to half their length for the first two or three years after planting.

The plant which has this framework is large and needs a suitable setting and position, while that which is hard pruned to ground level is more suitable for the front of the border. However, for the first few years the hard-pruned plant may be so vigorous that the growths may have to be stopped when 0·6 to 0·9 m. (2 or 3 ft.) in height to encourage a shorter and bushier habit. This species comes into growth early in the spring, but as pruning encourages more active growth it should be delayed until there is no danger of really cold weather returning. It should, however, be carried out before the open growths extend otherwise some vigour will be lost.

Among the other species which also flower on the current season's wood are :– *B. crispa* Benth., best grown on a small framework; *B. forrestii* Diels, and *B. nivea* Duthie.

Those which flower from the previous season's wood.

B. alternifolia Maxim., a popular garden plant, is in this group. It produces long arching growths which become pendulous under the weight of flowers and growth. On a healthy specimen, new growth, if freely produced and left un-attended, causes the older growths to die through lack of light as the others are formed above them. To prevent this happening and to maintain the balance in favour of young growth, the old, flowered shoots are cut out as soon as the blossoms drop, back to promising growths which are developing at this time. In the early years much of the older wood is supporting extension and must be left, but as the shrub reaches a mature size the pruning can be more severe. At all times dead wood should be cut out.

This plant is sometimes grown as a standard on a 0·9 to 1·2 m. (3 to 4 ft.) leg. It is trained in the nursery by staking a selected strong growth once the plant has become established and removing all superfluous shoots which develop beneath the head as it is formed by hard pruning at the required height.

Those which grow out in the spring to flower from large terminal buds or growths which develop on strong wood made in the previous year.

B. globosa Hope may be taken as an example of this group. The pruning is based on a policy which retains the larger terminal buds which remain leafy throughout the winter. During late February or March the weaker and dead wood is cut back to suitable points leaving the flowering wood. If the shrub becomes too large, however, it may be cut back quite hard but flower will be lost for one season at least depending upon the severity of the pruning. *B. colvilei* Hook. f. & Thoms. is also in this group although, unlike *B. globosa*, it is completely deciduous. The large terminal buds must be retained and, as the annual growth is quite extensive, this shrub will reach heights of 6·0 m. (20 ft.) or more. Except in the milder regions a high wall is needed as the plant is not fully hardy. Pruning consists of cutting out the weaker shoots in the spring.

Buddleias are sometimes grown as wall shrubs and for this purpose the tenderer species may be selected. *B. colvilei* has already been mentioned. It is an upright grower which is almost self supporting and ties are not required to support weight but only to keep it into the wall. *B. fallowiana* Balf. f. & W. W. Sm. is a tender species and is not considered hardy throughout the country. It flowers on the current season's wood and these growths are pruned back to the lowest pair of buds early the following spring to a main framework which is trained fanwise to the wall. An ample supply of growths is produced from the base and these should be thinned at an early stage. They may be used for the renewal of some of the old and worn out branches if this is required.

All Buddleias are sun lovers. The soil should be well drained but they are strong growers and require feeding and mulching. This is especially true of those which are pruned hard each year. They all respond well by growing from really old wood if the shrub is cut back hard.

Bumelia

B. lycioides (L.) Pers is grown as a small tree from 3·0 to 3·7 m. (10 to 12 ft.) high. It should be trained with a single lead and as the lower branches are removed a 1·2 m. (4 ft.) leg can be formed. The growths and branches are distorted in an interesting way. This species, which is the hardiest of this genus, may lose wood during the winter and the specimen should be looked over for this as the buds break in the spring.

Bupleurum

B. fruticosum L. is not really hardy but it may be grown in favoured spots or in the shelter of walls in the southern part of the country. As the shrub reaches maturity at a height of 1·5 m. (5 ft.) or more it often becomes untidy with thick, twiggy wood which weighs the branches down and eventually they may trail on the ground. When the shrub has reached this condition it may be cut hard back to within a few inches of soil level in April or May when it will regenerate strongly forming a good shapely bush by the autumn. The curious flower display will, however, be lost for one season.

This shrub is very good in exposed positions by the sea and it may be used for hedging purposes. If grown for this purpose it should be clipped annually in the late spring.

Buxus (Box)

When grown informally as a bush very little pruning is necessary unless it is required to keep bushes down to a definite size. Size may be controlled by carefully cutting back the longer growths as they extend beyond the desired limits. These should be taken out individually making the cut with a pair of secateurs, loppers or saw at a suitable point well inside the bush. Thus, an informal matt surface remains. This type of pruning may be carried out at any time during the summer months after May as for Yew, *see* Plates 43 and 44.

Very old and large specimens which have completely outgrown their position may be cut back really hard to within 150 to 300 mm. (6 to 12 in.) of ground level. Often when this is carried out the lower branches will be found to have layered and thus the area of the stool is a large one. It is often better in the long run if these are taken out, restricting the remains of the shrub to the very centre. Provided that the shrub is healthy there will be a rapid reponse, but feeding and mulching will help this. The best time for this drastic cutting back is during May when the resultant growths will have a long period before them for development and ripening before the winter sets in, *see* Plate 46.

Overgrown and straggly specimens which have grown in shade may be dealt with in the same way, but it may be desirable to thin neighbouring trees to encourage better growth. However, there should be a wide consideration of the whole planting before this is done for the surrounding specimens may be more valuable.

B. sempervirens L., the Common Box, is a variable shrub and has given rise to many named varieties some of which are very old indeed. As examples which illustrate this variation '*Handsworthensis*' is a strong-growing erect form while '*Prostrata*' develops into a large, spreading bush with a horizontal branch system. It is important to recognise any particular habit before pruning is undertaken. It is difficult and sometimes impossible to correct and adjust the habit of growth of some varieties by pruning, hence the desirability of selecting the one most suited to the situation in the first instance.

B. balearica Lam. will develop into a small tree 6·0 to 9·0 m. (20 to 30 ft.) in height, especially if a leader is selected and retained in the early years during and after the period of nursery treatment. None of the remaining species require any special training or pruning.

Some of the stronger-growing forms have been used for many centuries for formal hedging and topiary work. Clipping should be undertaken during July and August. With constant clipping it is important to keep the bushes in good condition by feeding when necessary as otherwise bare patches occur.

Caesalpinia

C. japonica Sieb. & Zucc. may be grown against a sunny wall in the warmer localities. The foliage effect and the tracery of branches are quite pleasing but it does not often flower. In the nursery it should be encouraged to branch from the base, if necessary by stopping. It is difficult to train this species hard against a wall and it is better grown as a bush, being planted one foot from the base. Reaching a height of approximately 1·5 m. (5 ft.), the branches have a horizontal habit. Where restrictive pruning is necessary, and it often is, for this shrub is most formidably armed with recurved prickles even on the leaf stalks, it should be carried out in the spring, taking last season's growths back hard to the basal 50 or 80 mm. (2 or 3 in.). Staking or tying may be necessary to keep the shrub in to the wall.

Calceolaria

C. integrifolia Murr. is commonly grown in the shelter of a wall as it is definitely tender. It may be grown in the open in the milder south-western counties. When healthy the growth is very bushy. Protection should be given during very severe weather by using bracken or sacking, but even so there is often damage during the winter and severe cutting back may be necessary in the spring. However, the wood, if living, will break out freely and the shrub will soon recover.

Callicarpa

These shrubs have a bushy habit and throw shoots from the base very freely. When young they have an erect and almost crowded growth, but often at maturity the branching is spreading and even horizontal. This is partly due to the weight of the extending growths and the heavy crops of fruits they often carry. Any branches which have grown out of shape, old and woody, may be cut back in the spring just as growth commences. It is better left until this period as the younger growths may be damaged in a severe winter. The above advice applies particularly to *C. americana* L., *C. japonica* Thunb., *C. japonica* var. *angustata* Rehd. and *C. bodinieri* Levl. var. *giraldii* (Rehd.) Rehd. although allowance must be made for the fact that the latter is taller growing.

    C. mollis Sieb. & Zucc. is tender and needs wall protection. *C. dichotoma* (Lour.) K. Koch is compact and every effort should be made to retain a well-balanced but informal effect as the foliage is quite attractive. It will also need a sheltered and warm position.

Callistemon

These must have the protection of a sunny wall and even in this position they are best suited to the milder localities. Training hard up to the wall is difficult and they are better when planted 0·3 m. or so away from the base. By stopping at an early stage a bushy plant is encouraged. Finally, as the plant grows it may need staking. Pruning is not desirable as the characteristic spikes of flower are produced along the upper lengths of the stronger growths. *C. citrinus* (Curt.) Stapf 'Splendens', *C. linearis* DC., *C. subulatus* Cheel and *C. salignus* (Sm.) DC. may be grown in this manner.

    C. sieberi DC. forms a compact bush of upright growths branching from ground level. It also should be given wall protection and be planted at approximately one foot from the base. The spread is at least 1·2 m. (4 ft.) and owing to the type of growth only a limited amount of pruning is possible. It is therefore important to allow sufficient space for development.

Calluna

C. vulgaris (L.) Hull. Although there are many different forms and varieties of this popular shrub they all look neatest and at their best when they are thick and well furnished with young growths of good length which completely hide the bare woody stem system as it builds up over the years. Often after a number of years, if they are left unattended, growth becomes poor and the plants present a thin and worn appearance. They may even die off in patches to become woody and straggly with the result that bare soil is exposed and weeds spring up to choke the remaining growth. Long before this stage is reached the old plants should be replaced with younger stock.

However, by annual pruning of the young growths in the spring the branch system is kept more compact and the plants will have a longer useful life. The need for this arises from the fact that growing conditions are artificial for these plants in the average garden for the soil is rich and the area sheltered, and thus in the initial years growth is stronger. On the moorlands where this plant is frequently found the almost constant winds, the sun and the poorer soil encourage a more compact growth. It should, however, be remembered that a proportion of old and woody plants do occur even in their natural habitat.

The pruning should be carried out annually just as the new growths appear in late March or April. This consists of cutting back at least half of the previous year's growth. The new growths which are along the length of the old flowered shoots are thus cut off and a more compact framework results as the lower tips are encouraged into activity and take the lead. The cut should not be made into the old wood for often this does not break freely and generally about one half of the previous year's growth is removed. Pruning should not be attempted if the growth is very short and poor. Replacement is then a better proposition. A variety of tools should be used in order to avoid a completely uniform or domed effect. This is most likely to occur when the shears alone are used and so the pruning knife and secateurs must also be considered if a varied and more natural effect is required. Care must be taken, however, when using a knife on plants which are very old and woody, for at this stage they are brittle and are likely to break easily. Electric hedge-trimmers may also be used although the tendency to prune too hard with these should be guarded against.

Young nursery stock should be tipped soon after being planted out from the cutting frames in order to keep growth short and stocky. Left unpruned, the few shoots on each plant will be long and straggly. It is important throughout to take the character and habit of growth of the variety into account when a pruning policy is decided upon. Thus, such dwarf forms as 'Foxii Nana', 'Mullion' and 'Hypnoides' need not be pruned in the normal way, although the latter occasionally throws strong reverted growths which should be cut out as soon as they appear. 'Ruth Sparkes' has bright yellow foliage but green reversions frequently appear and these must also be cut out. 'Elegantissima' is an upright grower with long flowering shoots and care is necessary in selecting the point at which the pruning cut is made to ensure that sufficient young growth is left.

Finally, seedling forms frequently occur among established plants and these should be searched out at flowering time because they normally revert to the colour of the type species.

Calycanthus

These have a stool-like habit of growth, freely producing young shoots from the base. Thus quite a dense canopy is produced, the lower branches even spreading on the surface of the soil, producing good ground cover and keeping weed growth to a minimum. These should be encouraged.

The habit of growth is such that old branches which are cut out are quickly replaced and this pruning is carried out, if necessary, in the spring. *C. fertilis* Walt. is the neatest grower while *C. occidentalis* Hook. & Arn. spreads out extensively with horizontal branches and thus has a more open habit.

The flowers are produced terminally on the young wood during the summer.

Camellia

These popular evergreen shrubs require very little pruning. It is, however, advisable to prune the young growths in the spring before the new buds break, if a young plant shows a tendency to be leggy. A thick bushy habit is desirable. *C. japonica* L. is grown in many varieties which vary considerably in habit and form and the typical habit of each variety should be taken into account if it is found necessary to prune any growths which appear to spoil the general shape of the bushes. In an exposed position it may be necessary to remove any growths which appear to be too tall or heavy or affect the stability of the shrub in any way. Normally, staking should not be required but it may be used for the correction of a poor shape. For general effect branching should be allowed to develop right down to the base of the plant.

Some young plants flower so freely that it may be advisable to disbud them before the flowers open in the spring in order to encourage growth. On the other hand, old plants which have become weak may be cut back quite hard, removing as much as one third of the shoot system. This should be carried out just as growth is about to begin in March or April, making the cuts at the most suitable point. Mulching and feeding help to ensure a good response. The resultant shoots may be thinned if necessary.

The young growths in the spring are sometimes damaged by frost. If so, these should be left until it can be seen just where the new breaks are going to be produced. The removal of faded flowers by careful pruning will give the bushes a tidier appearance.

Often Camellias are grown in sheltered areas against a background of screening trees and shrubs and it may be necessary to prune these carefully from time to time in order to retain a shapely bush, *see* Fig. 26.

C. cuspidata Veitch has a graceful habit with an upright twiggy growth. *C. sasanqua* Thunb. has a comparatively loose habit. It may be grown as a bush

I

but it also responds to wall culture. The branches are tied fanwise to the wire support system and laterals are encouraged to grow out from these. Overgrown shoots are shortened by a system of selective pruning after flowering. Occasionally, an old worn branch may be cut out completely to be replaced by the promising new growths which are freely produced.

Campsis

This is a genus of strong climbing shrubs. *C. radicans* (L.) Seem. produces aerial roots which are of some assistance, even in the garden when it is grown under natural conditions over old tree trunks etc. Usually, however, both *C. radicans* and *C. grandiflora* (Thunb.) K. Schum are grown against a sunny wall for protection and support. Under these conditions ties are made to the wiring system. Often, growths develop against the wall beneath the wires and this provides support. When a site is selected it should be remembered that these species, their varieties and hybrids are vigorous and are only at their best when able to develop to considerable heights, for example 6·0 to 12·0 m. (20 to 40 ft.).

With a young plant, the early training consists of covering the available wall space with the main branches. When the pruning of a mature plant is considered it should be remembered that they flower from mid to late summer on the current season's wood. The young growths produced during the previous season are cut back in the early spring close to the main stems leaving only one or two of the lowest buds. Each spring and summer the growths produced may flower in the late summer. However, in the following spring they are cut back hard, unless required for replacement. If needed for this purpose they should be shortened by approximately one third, back to the stouter wood.

Caragana

These are rather sparsely branched shrubs although *C. arborescens* Lam. can be trained to form a small tree. They require very little pruning. Raised from seed, like so many other shrubs, they gradually build up a strong branch system. In the first instance the growths are short and very twiggy, but stronger ones develop from the base of the plant over two or three years as it becomes established. The natural growth of many of the species is almost suckerous but centralised at the base of the shrub. This natural development is emphasised, for shrubs which are raised from cuttings do not pass through the successive stages of this progressive build up. Instead, one or two strong growths are often thrown up which, unchecked, will produce a very leggy plant which may not have the necessary stability without staking. A bushy plant should be encouraged by stopping in the nursery after one season's growth. This not only encourages the production of laterals but will also promote suckering from the base of the plant. When pruned back in this way good breaks are more likely on the young wood. Caraganas build up a spur system on the older wood and the buds in this region do not break as freely.

In training the tree form of *C. arborescens*, a leading shoot is selected and all suckerous and lower branches are removed. Standards of the other species can also be raised but by grafting on to 0·9 m. (3 ft.) stems of the above species.

Grafted plants often sucker badly and a constant watch should be kept for these during the growing season.

Dead wood should be removed in the spring for the new growths will then show this up very plainly.

Carmichaelia

One or two species are grown in the open in the warmer localities but normally they need the shelter of a sunny wall and should be planted 300 mm. (12 in.) or so away from the base. Staking will probably be necessary, while any of the growths which have been frosted during the winter should be patiently cut back as soon as the shrub is active in the spring.

Carpenteria

C. californica Torr. When it is healthy and vigorous this forms a well-furnished shrub with many growths originating from the base while the older branches are attractive with flaky bark. However, the older wood thins out at the top over the years through exhaustion from flowering and as a result of damage during the winter. These may be periodically cut out at the base, to be replaced by the young growths which spring from this region. The natural habit of the more vigorous branches is an upright one but lower furnishing branches should be left to improve the shrub's appearance. One interesting characteristic is that whatever the angle of the branch the growing parts usually assume an upright position.

This shrub requires the shelter of a south or south-west wall but it should be planted well away from it and allowed to grow as a bush. It is difficult to train hard up against the wiring system.

Carpinus

C. betulus L., the native hornbeam, is one of the most handsome trees in this genus. It is advisable to train a young tree as a 1·8 to 2·4 m. (6 to 8 ft.) standard with a clear stem, for the bark effect on a mature tree is very attractive. This also allows plenty of headroom for standing beneath the tree to study the fine tracery of branches during the winter and the leaf canopy and shade effects in the spring, summer and autumn. Apart from the retention of the lead through the crown in the early stages very little pruning is necessary. As the wood in the centre of the crown dies it should be thinned out, but it is not necessary or wise to attempt a premature thinning of a dense crown of living wood.

A beautiful effect is gained by allowing a mature tree to produce outer branches which grow right down to near ground level. The fruits hanging down like small lanterns remain on for several weeks after the leaves have fallen and thus increases the effect.

This species is also an effective one to plant by the waterside. Sometimes, as the branches extending over the water become heavier, they may be weighed down beneath the surface for part of their length. Provided that the growing tips of the branches are not submerged this does not seem to harm them in any way.

Often this species bleeds rather badly in the early spring both from old wounds and rotted snags and although this seems to do no permanent harm it does emphasise the need to effect a complete healing as speedily as possible after making a cut.

C. b. 'Fastigiata' has a close-branching habit forming a pyramidal head.

The Common Hornbeam is a good hedge plant. It should be planted 0·3 to 0·5 m. (1 to 1½ ft.) apart, and if it is to be a tall hedge over 1·2 m. (4 ft.), it should be allowed to go unpruned for two or three years after planting in order that strong growths may be produced which will carry the height better. If the hedge is to be over 1·8 m. (6 ft.) in height a much wider spacing is required.

C. caroliniana Walt. forms a fine network of twiggy growth. It is a small and slow-growing tree and should be given sufficient light and air on one side at least to allow the branches to come down to eye level. *C. japonica* Bl. should be treated in the same way for it is a small tree but has a very delicate and beautiful leaf effect. *C. orientalis* Mill. is a tree or large shrub which needs very careful training in the nursery if it is to reach any size. It has a close branch system which is often coated with dwarf shoots. These should never be cut off, as with this species they do no harm and add greatly to the character of the tree.

Carya

This is a very distinctive genus as all the species are fast growing and will normally form good straight leads ultimately developing into fine, shapely trees. It is important that they grow away without check even from the seedling stage. They should be sown in pots after a stratification period and be planted out into their permanent positions from them. As the lead and upper branching extends, a clear trunk of at least 1·8 to 2·4 m. (6 to 8 ft.) should be formed, choosing July to August as the pruning period. Usually, with a straight trunk and lead the lateral branching is not extensive. The lower and outer branches should be left to grow down to eye level and with a dark background to the autumn colouring the effect is very pleasing, *see* Plate 14.

C. pecan (Marsh.) Engl. & Graebn. does not thrive well in this country, mainly because there is insufficient sun to ripen the wood properly. It is thus prone to attacks by Coral Spot (*Nectria cinnabarina*), and other destructive organisms.

Caryopteris

The species grown in the open are semi-woody and may be cut back to near ground level during the winter. Even during a normal winter much of the top growth is lost as a large portion dies back after flowering.

C. × clandonensis Simmonds is the most widely grown. The growths which spring from the short, woody branches at the base produce a terminal inflorescence in the late summer and autumn. These growths are pruned back hard to near their base in the spring just as the buds are breaking. The pruning is left until this period in order that the cuts may be made into the living wood without leaving any dead. By pruning back hard to within approximately 25 mm. (1 in.) of the older wood height is only slowly built up but the number of growths is reduced and thus the heads of flowers are larger. Also, by pruning hard the wood is kept close to the soil and is thus more protected.

C. *incana* (Houtt.) Miq., C. *mastacanthus* Schauer. and C. *mongolica* Bge. are very similar in their pruning requirements but they are taller and need not be cut back so hard; in fact it is only necessary to cut back the dead tips of the shoots as the buds break in the spring.

Cassia

C. *marylandica* L. is the only species which is normally grown outside in this country. It must be given wall protection and should be planted about 300 mm. (12 in.) from the base. It is treated as an herbaceous plant, being cut down in the autumn to within 25 mm. (1 in.) of the base. As a protection for the winter the crowns and the surrounding soil should be covered with bracken lightly held in position with string and pegs.

C. *corymbosa* Lam. may be grown as a wall shrub in the mildest parts of the British Isles. One method is to train the framework of branches to the wall supports. When the buds are active in the spring the growths made during the previous year are pruned back close to the framework. These in turn flower in the late summer.

Cassinia

This genus consists of evergreen shrubs which are heath-like, and all the four species which may be grown outside will withstand hard pruning, an operation which is necessary to correct an untidy habit. This cutting back hard into the old wood, perhaps only 300 mm. (12 in.) or so from soil level, should be carried out in the spring. Thus, the basal portion of the branch system may be retained. C. *fulvida* Hook. is the hardiest and can sometimes be grown in the open border in the South. For the remainder, some form of wall protection is advisable, where, with staking, a height of 1·8 m. (6 ft.) or more is sometimes reached. Generally, however, if staking is necessary it is because the shrub has become untidy or weak-stemmed, and some form of pruning is therefore desirable to correct this. In the nursery young plants should be stopped to encourage a bushy habit.

Cassiope

There is no need to prune these apart from the removal of any dead pieces which make the plants unsightly. The upright growing species such as C. *tetragona* (L.) D. Don may blow over and their shape be spoilt unless they are closely planted, staked or sheltered.

Castanea

C. *sativa* Mill., Sweet Chestnut, is the most widely known species in this genus. It will form a heavy branching system but, provided the tree is in good health, it is strong and safe. However, when a specimen dies back, especially in the crown, it should be held suspect and be carefully inspected. Declining health with heavy branching can be dangerous as they are liable to drop limbs suddenly through the wood becoming very dry. Often, by a careful reduction of the branch system the life of such a tree may be extended for many years.

Establishment after the final transplanting often takes two or three years but growth is then very rapid with the tree forming a good straight lead quite readily. A 1·8 m. (6 ft.) clear length of stem may be formed in the nursery or when the tree is growing away in its final position, *see* Plate 20. The bark effect is an attractive feature of this tree. Suckerous growths are freely produced even from the base and trunk of mature specimens and these should be removed annually. This ability to sucker freely is made use of when it is grown under a coppice system for large stools are formed which are very long lived.

In addition to the numerous fruiting varieties there are several variegated and dissected forms. The former in particular revert very readily and an inspection should be made during the summer to cut out any offending growths. No attempt should be made to control reversion in a large tree which has lost a considerable portion of its variegation.

Of the remaining species, although a tree form can be trained with *C. dentata* (Marsh.) Borkh., they do not seem to be as adaptable to our climate as *C. sativa*. *C. henryi* (Skan) Rehd. & Wils. forms a stunted tree with rather graceful growth while *C. mollissima* Blume is often a very slender grower and may split up into two or three stems at a very early stage. *C. seguinii* Dode and *C. pumila* (L.) Mill. should be left to grow as large bushy shrubs or trees. The former is ideal on the edge of a clump of trees and its foliage retains a green colour for longer than many other trees.

Castanopsis

C. chrysophylla (Hook.) DC. is the only hardy species. It is a low branching shrub or small tree which forms a very dense growth. It should be allowed to grow unpruned and thus to form a complete canopy down to ground level.

Sometimes a random branch dies back leaving a gap when it is cut out. However, regeneration often takes place strongly, especially with mulching. This will occur even though the top is almost entirely killed by severe weather.

Young plants should be left to branch naturally in the nursery.

Catalpa

The most commonly grown species is *C. bignonioides* Walt. When mature it forms a spreading head with a strong branch system. In the nursery stage it should be trained with a lead up to 1·8 to 2·4 m. (6 to 8 ft.) so that when the head is formed there is a good length of clean trunk. Once branching is established it is difficult to maintain a lead and the crown quickly forms and opens out. The lower branches sweep down to ground level on a mature tree but there appear to be two forms. With one, the branches actually touch the ground and develop close to the surface from this point, while the other form has branches which sweep down at the same angle until within 0·3 to 0·6 m. (1 to 2 ft.) of the surface when the ends turn upwards again. The effect is more natural where the branches reach the ground but grass cutting is difficult and damage easily occurs. They should be carefully lifted, with assistance, when mowing is attempted beneath them.

Large old trees which are considered unsafe can have their branches shortened and bracing or propping may also be necessary. Even old trees will regenerate very freely from cuts and a branch which has been shortened to reduce weight may be even heavier after a few years as a result of the new growth which has been put on. Growths often develop near wounds even though these may be large and on the main trunk.

C. speciosa Warder is a pyramidal tree and naturally develops a lead through the tree although this may need to be trained during the transplanting period and immediately afterwards for these disturbances often have a retarding effect. When training, if a young tree has opened its head too early, the rival leads may be stopped to encourage growth in the selected shoot. This is better than cutting out the offending branches. At planting time there should be a clear stem of 1·8 to 2·4 m. (6 to 8 ft.) for this allows the main branches to develop a natural and almost pendulous habit after growing out a good distance from the trunk. Thus the lowest branches will, from a height of 2·4 m. (8 ft.), almost reach to ground level.

All Catalpas like a sunny, sheltered position with a well-drained soil, these being the conditions which produce ripe, sound wood. In wet and cold districts die-back and cavities frequently occur. The growths on young plants are also susceptible to frost damage in the late spring.

Of the remaining species, some difficulty may be experienced in growing and training *C. fargesii* Bur. and the variety *duclouxii* (Dode) Gilmour. The strong upright growths in particular do not seem to ripen properly unless the situation and soil are perfect.

Ceanothus

There are two distinct types of growth in this genus. Firstly, those which are mainly evergreen, flowering in the spring on growths made during the previous year. Many of these are not hardy and are grown against a wall for protection. Secondly, there are the smaller deciduous species which flower in the late summer or autumn on the current season's growths. These are often grown in open beds.

Evergreen Species and Hybrids – Wall Training

Generally, these are too weak to be grown near a wall without any support whatsoever, for the bushes grow out towards the light and thus become top heavy, to be finally torn down by gales or heavy snowfalls. It is better to plant them hard up against the wall and to tie the branches out fanwise to the main support system. By this method there is ultimately a greater latitude in training than if a single stem were first trained up to the height of the wall, and laterals trained out from it. With the fan system the replacement of old branches by selected young growths is more straightforward. It is necessary, however, to start off with a bushy plant and this habit must, if necessary, be encouraged in the nursery. Many will naturally branch low and extensively but a few such as

'Dignity' often tend to be single stemmed. Thus, until the allotted wall space is covered the leading growths are tied in, *see* Plate 56. The laterals are pruned reasonably hard after flowering, but never into the older wood which is devoid of foliage. It is desirable to carry out this pruning carefully so that an informal effect is retained with the cuts hidden. In the early stages a large quantity of young growths often appear near the base of the shrub and these need to be thinned out before they develop into main branches. Growths which are needed for replacement must be kept tied in, for if allowed to grow away from the wall at an angle, the laterals from them will become upright. Once such a unilateral development has taken place it is difficult to tie in such growths effectively. Much depends on the adoption of a good replacement system over the years, for the best flowering is from the younger wood and continued cutting back, using the old branch system in its entirety, does not give such good results. Examples of evergreen species are: *C. dentatus* Torr. & Gr., 'Dignity', *C. rigidus* Nutt. and *C. thyrsiflorus* Esch. *C. velutinus* Dougl. is a larger grower than many, reaching a considerable height and forming quite a stout trunk. It therefore needs a large wall and, if trained to a single stem, apart from one or two ties to the wall, it needs no support. *C. thyrsiflorus* 'Repens' may be grown against a low wall for the shoots are held up by their springy nature against the surface.

The hybrid between the deciduous and evergreen groups, *C.* × *burkwoodii* Burkw. may be wall-trained but the pruning back is carried out in April and the young growths which are produced flower in the following summer and autumn months.

It must be emphasised that the evergreen species may be grown out in the open, given some shelter and a suitable climate. Hybrids such as 'Edinburgh' are almost hardy. Sun and full all-round light are important for if there is a heavy background screen on one side the shrubs have a drawn and leggy appearance that even staking does not fully overcome. Some pruning helps to control this untidy habit.

Deciduous Species and Hybrids

Such species as *C. americanus* L. and *C. coeruleus* Lag. are deciduous and produce growths during the spring and summer which flower in the autumn. They have, however, been hybridised extensively and such cultivars as 'Gloire de Versailles' and 'Perle Rose' are quite popular. This group, which is grown in the open border, is first pruned lightly to encourage the formation of a rigid framework up to a height of 0·6 to 1·2 m. (2 to 4 ft.). The previous season's growths are then cut back hard to two pairs of buds just as they become active in April. If this intensive pruning is to be successful it is important to maintain good growth by feeding and mulching.

Cedrela

C. sinensis Juss. At maturity this is quite a large tree and is at its best with a long clean trunk. It is important therefore to train a central lead in the nursery and to encourage this by providing good growing conditions. As the tree develops, the lower branches may be removed to provide a clean trunk. The branching is heavy but sparse and often there is a good covering of smaller branches along their length. These should be left.

Cedrus

C. libani A. Rich. is seen at its best in a lawn setting where, with sufficient space, the branch systems can develop and spread out to show the full beauty of this tree.

In habit, the tree when young is pyramidal and it is only at a later stage when maturity is reached that the branches spread out extensively. A central lead should be retained for as long as possible although, at a later stage, often when the tree is 12·0 to 15·0 m. (40 to 50 ft.) high and growing vigorously, rival leads may develop. It is almost impossible to keep a constant check on a tree at this height and some specimens are more liable to develop rival leads in the upper crowns than others. However, it is often these more upright branches which tear out from the main trunk during gales when the tree is mature, especially if they occur at a time when the tree is laden with snow, *see* Plate 60. This may be looked upon as a natural habit which cannot be corrected but which may ultimately prove to be a weakness.

It is important to cut out as much dead wood as possible for the health of the tree, and also to reduce the weight on the branch systems. These dead pieces are most likely to develop on the undersides of the branches as they are weighed down with extending growth. Sometimes the smaller and lower branches may need to be cut out as they become overshadowed or hidden by larger and higher systems. It is better to anticipate this rather than allow the branches to die back before they are removed for the wounds will callus much better with earlier removal. Another tendency which needs correcting if it occurs is that of weaker branches lying on the stronger ones beneath them. The offending limbs should be sawn off neatly, the position of the cut being selected with great care, otherwise the appearance of the tree will be spoilt. Old or even mature cedars seldom produce sufficient new growth to cover up the ugly effects of poor pruning, especially if the cuts are large ones on old wood.

Large wounds, especially if they are on older specimens, may be slow to heal and callus over but the exposed heartwood, if it is sound at the time and is dressed at intervals as required, will remain in good condition, often for the life of the tree. Normally, pruning cuts should be made as close to the parent branch or trunk as possible but often the latter in particular may be deeply furrowed. A furrow may even be positioned immediately beneath a limb which is to be removed. In such cases the position of the cut should be adjusted for there must be adequate supporting tissue round the wound if the callus is to be complete.

We must now consider the tips of spreading branches. Two kinds of growths are produced, the long extension shoot with scattered leaves and the short spur-like shoots with tufts of leaves round each growing point. A specimen in full health produces a balanced proportion of extension growths during each growing season. A lack of these accompanied by thin and poorly coloured needle growth on the dwarf shoot system is a sure sign that all is not well and that feeding and culture generally should receive more attention. From this it may be gathered that the leading growths even on the branch systems are important.

If these are able to spread out and develop with plenty of space and light the branches will grow out horizontally and the lower ones will eventually sweep gracefully to the ground, *see* Plate 58. When these vigorously growing branch systems are pruned, perhaps to prevent a spread over a path or border, there is often a build-up of arching growths which is out of character and spoils the appearance of the tree. One should try if possible to avoid the need to restrict the natural spread by re-planning the nearby features.

In common with many other trees the cedar will often develop extensively in one direction in response to a one-sided light condition. When placed hard up against other trees, if the light is sufficient on one side, it will furnish up completely on this surface. The fault with this type of planting is that the cedar is a long-lived tree and the chances are that the neighbouring trees will eventually need to be taken down, leaving it lopsided and with no chance of acquiring the balance necessary for it to stand as an isolated specimen.

Specimens sometimes lose their needles completely during the winter months. Such a condition should be watched very carefully, for while it is recognised that some trees are more likely to do this than others, it may also be due to impoverishment. Some trees of *C. atlantica* also have this habit.

C. atlantica Manetti. Much of the advice given for *C. libani* also applies to this species. Growth is variable, apart from the fact that in most cases a central lead is naturally and readily formed, *see* Plate 78. In addition to great variation in colour, some forms have a heavily laden appearance with pendulous sub-branches which will even grow along the surface of the ground if encouraged and protected. Other forms exist where the branching is completely horizontal and a few even have a system where the extremities of the branchlets turn up. Such trees of the latter form often have a thin appearance.

C. deodara (Roxb.) G. Don. The pruning and training of this species are similar in many respects. It is not as hardy as the two species already mentioned and appreciates a sheltered position, especially when it is in the earlier stages of development. The leading shoot, especially when the tree is young, has a natural arching or pendulous habit. There should be no attempt to straighten this out by ties to the stake which must be used to establish all trees of any size in their final quarters. *C. libani* var. *brevifolia* Hook. f. is a stunted grower with no particular pruning or training requirements. It is desirable to encourage and retain a central leader for as long as possible.

Celastrus

These are vigorous climbers producing long growths which in one season extend for 1 or 2 m. (3 or 6 ft.). These shoots either twine round or loop over neighbouring branches or supports, with an arching habit. Laterals and compound branch systems build on these.

With such a vigorous habit these are difficult shrubs to contain in a small area. All that can be done is to cut back the long growths which arch out too far in such a manner that the natural habit is retained. Usually this means cutting back a few complete lengths rather than cutting every growth to a given line, when the outline would be too formal and artificial.

Allowed freedom in the wilder parts of the garden, the long arching growths can spread over old stumps at will. These shrubs can also be planted to climb over trees which have been lopped back, perhaps to a height of 6·0 to 9·0 m. (20 to 30 ft.), because they were unsafe, *see* Fig. 13 (4). Old trunks of *Robinia pseudoacacia* L. are ideal for this purpose as the wood is so durable. Such a position is an ideal one for the climber, for after it has gained the top of the support it produces long branches which hang down and fruit freely.

Little pruning is necessary under these conditions apart from cutting out dead wood. This should be carried out during the summer for it is difficult to distinguish living from dead unless the subject is in active growth. Actually, there is little need even for this and it is really a refinement which few can afford to keep up.

Celtis

These must have good growing conditions and they require careful culture even in the nursery stage. A check causes stunted growth and it may take several years for a tree to grow normally once this has occurred. In the meantime the lead may be lost and this may add to difficulties later when free growth is resumed. The tree species are trained as 1·5 to 1·8 m. (5 to 6 ft.) standards, but a number of them often develop into shrubs rather than trees. Among these are *C. glabrata* Planch., *C. pumila* (Muhl.) Pursh and *C. tournefortii* Lam. These may fail to respond to attempts to produce a trunk.

The largest grower is *C. occidentalis* L., whose general habit allows a lead to be retained up to 11 m. (35 ft.). The lower branches tend to be horizontal and often become pendulous and heavy. In addition, upright growths may be produced on the ends of these lower branches, and their development should be watched for as this can quickly be the cause of excessive weight. This is more likely to happen where thinning of neighbouring trees has in the past been undertaken and the trees are exposed to more light and to better growing conditions.

C. australis L., from S. Europe, N. Africa and W. Asia, does not display the same degree of hardiness as many of the deciduous species coming from China, Korea and Japan. The growths of a young tree in particular, being strong and perhaps not fully ripened, are prone to frosting during the winter. To some extent this is also true of a related species, *C. caucasica* Willd. and, although it is reputed to be hardier, wood which is exposed in wounds tends to rot quickly and produce cavities. *C. sinensis* Pers. displays extensive powers of regeneration and produces a crop of vigorous young growths from the region of wounds, which need to be carefully thinned. Sufficient shelter is an essential part of the successful culture of all the species.

Cephalanthus

C. occidentalis L. This deciduous shrub is very bushy with branches which spring from ground level. The terminal flowerheads are produced on the current season's wood. Little pruning is needed other than the cutting out of old branches in the spring, thus encouraging the long lengths of young cane which will produce good flowering growths later in the season. The tips of the shoots which have supported flowering growths die back and these may be cut to living wood as the new growths break out. This shrub is very late in breaking into leaf. Bushy plants should be encouraged in the nursery by pruning.

Cephalotaxus

These are similar in many respects to yews and they will respond to pruning in the same way, for they will form new growths very readily even from the oldest wood. *C. drupacea* Sieb. & Zucc., the 'Cow's Tail Pine' forms a spreading bush and the habit is very desirable as this species develops sub-branches which sweep gracefully to ground level to form lower furnishing. Too frequently they are crowded in densely-shaded places where little can be expected to grow properly. These shrubs appreciate a very light shade but if it is too dense they become weak and leggy, the branches being bent down and untidy. Shrubs in this condition should be cut back, if necessary to within 100 mm. (4 in.) or so of ground level, choosing April to May for this operation. At the same time it may be possible to lighten the overhead shade by careful pruning.

The species mentioned freely produces branches directly from ground level, but *C. fortunei* Hook. tends to produce only two or three erect stems and in time may be 4·6 to 6·0 m. (15 to 20 ft.) high with tiers of branches.

The cultivar *C. drupacea* 'Fastigiata' is quite distinctive, having an erect fastigiate habit, but older specimens often present an untidy appearance as their branches become heavy and pull the bush out of shape. Careful tying-in can improve this habit, although a specimen which is badly out of shape may need to be cut hard back to the base in the spring, when it will break out readily although it is slow growing.

Ceratostigma

C. willmottianum Stapf is the most outstanding shrubby species. Normally, it needs the shelter of a sunny wall where a woody branch system will build up to a height of 300 mm. (12 in.) or more. From this, growths break out in the late spring and after growing through the summer the flowers are produced in terminal clusters in the autumn. A young plant produces growth shoots which have very few if any flowers in their first year. Pruning is carried out in late April as the buds commence to break and consists of cutting back the old flowered growths to the living wood, generally at their base. The extent of die-back depends largely upon the severity of the winter and occasionally even the old wood is killed entirely. Should a plant become very old and woody at the base it should be replaced by a young plant. *C. griffithii* C. B. Clarke is even more tender but the same pruning treatment may be applied.

Cercidiphyllum

C. japonicum Sieb. & Zucc., developing into a tree often 9·0 m. (30 ft.) or more in height, has a natural habit of forming several rival leads from low down, often at ground level. Thus a mature specimen may have three or more trunks but the growths are ascending and a close crown is formed. The lower laterals have a horizontal habit. This tree is best grown in a sheltered position as it appears to dislike strong winds. The young growths are readily frosted in the early spring, while the tree also appears to dislike a very hot and sunny position, especially on a well-drained soil. A woodland environment on a retentive loam suits it best, while a background of trees and a grass foreground provide an ideal setting. A natural growth should be encouraged in and after the nursery stage and no attempt should be made to retain a single lead. *C. j.* var. *sinense* Rehd. & Wils., however, often develops a single trunk. *C. j.* var. *magnificum* Nakai is generally shrubby and is often the most suitable one to grow.

Cercis

These shrubs or small trees thrive on a well-drained soil and many good specimens are in areas in which the underlying subsoil is chalk. This is mentioned because it is very difficult indeed to grow good specimens in areas overlying a badly drained clay. In such areas the wood often dies back badly after wet seasons and is also prone to attacks by the Coral Spot fungus (*Nectria cinnabarina*). Dead or diseased branches should always be attended to immediately. *Cercis* seem to thrive better in the southern part of the country and is a sun lover.

C. *siliquastrum* L., The Judas Tree, is the most common species. The natural habit is to branch low at ground level into two or more stems which grow upwards almost vertically. Often too, additional growths are thrown up from the base or from the lower parts of the branches. Sometimes this low branching habit proves a weakness at maturity, for a break may occur during summer gales affecting a large portion of a tree and it may be wise to provide support by bracing if this is considered a danger. During a very severe winter this species is sometimes killed down to ground level but it may break vigorously from the base in the spring. *C. canadensis* L. and *C. racemosa* Oliv. are more likely to form small trees and can be trained to a single stem. *C. chinensis* Bge. is more shrubby and often requires the protection of a wall. *C. occidentalis* Gray should also be left to branch naturally and become shrubby in the nursery.

They should be transplanted at an early age as they resent disturbance, while the young growths are sometimes prone to frost damage.

Cercocarpus

In many ways these uncommon Rosaceous plants have the mode of growth which is typical of this family. They produce dwarf and spur-like growths on the older wood as distinct from the young extension shoots. No definite pruning policy is needed, although should it become necessary to restrict the shrub in any way, it is usually possible to take the pruning cuts back to promising extension growths thus keeping a good informal effect. This may be carried out during the dormant season.

Chaenomeles

In many respects these shrubs are very similar to the Malus and thus to the ordinary apple in their flowering and fruiting habits. When young they build up and concentrate upon growth and at this stage very little flower is produced. Two or three years later spurs form on the older wood and flowering commences. Growth slows down over the years as a bush becomes larger and vigour is spread over a large number of growing points. At this stage flower buds are also produced on the young shoots at the end of their season's growth.

C. speciosa (Sweet) Nakai, which is the parent of many of the popular varieties, has a spreading habit and forms a tangled bush which may be 3·0 m. (10 ft.) high and as much in width. It is best grown on the edge of a lawn, or in the less formal parts of the garden, where it can be left to develop freely right down to ground level without any pruning whatsoever. It is even permissible to allow crossing branches, indeed, such wild growth is the habit of this shrub.

This shrub is also very popular for growing against a wall where it is valued for its early display. The first object is to cover the wall space by training the strong young growths fan-wise. In this position the shrub must be restricted and the growths coming away from the wall at right angles must be dealt with, as otherwise they will extend even further the following year. Also, if they are left too long they will sway in the wind and it may be difficult to secure the main branch properly.

One method of pruning and training is to stop all growths coming away from the wall during the growing season at five leaves, unless they are required for the extension or replacement of the branch system. The sub-laterals which develop from these are stopped at two leaves, and this is repeated if further growth is put on. The original laterals which were stopped at five leaves may be pruned back to two or three buds in the winter, alternatively the subsequent policy can be to thin out the branch systems with a view to repeating the stopping on the remaining ones the following year. If treated in this way the shrub has a less formal appearance. Later, this thinning process may need to be more severe in order to keep the shrub within bounds.

There are several variations of these methods but basically they are forms of summer pruning. By restricting growth the leaf surface is reduced, which in turn curbs the activities of the root system and the vigour of the shrub as a whole. In its simplest form the treatment consists of cutting back all the young wood to two or three basal buds during the dormant season, but without the additional summer pruning, the shrub may be longer in coming into full flowering. Summer pruning also helps to control Aphis.

C. cathayensis Schneid. is also a good shrub to grow as a wall specimen. It shows a tendency to throw up a few strong shoots rather than to branch extensively. These growths may be spaced out fan-wise. After the early vigour has been controlled by pruning and stopping this species will settle down to regular flowering and cropping. Occasionally the long growths can be replaced by young shoots springing from the base.

C. japonica (Thunb.) Lindl. is a dwarf shrub approximately 0·9 m. (3 ft.) in height which is suitable for growing at the base of a south-facing wall. With the forms of *C.* × *superba* (Frahm) Rehd., which are hybrids between the above two species, vigour must be taken into account when the type of training is decided upon.

With all the species and hybrids, stopping is a form of pest control, for aphis in particular feed among the undeveloped leaves, and are thus inaccessible as far as contact insecticides are concerned.

Chamaecyparis

This genus includes some very fine species and cultivars which if planted and trained properly will give great satisfaction. One of the most important factors upon which ultimate effect is dependent is the position in relation to the general environment and surrounding plantings. Some shelter is preferable, but it is also important to allow sufficient space and light for the development both of the laterals down to ground level and of the leader itself. These trees are at their best when furnished down to ground level and with a clear foreground, so that this effect can be seen to the best advantage. Too close a planting is a major fault and when planted in a group they should be not less than 4·6 to 6·0 m. (15 to 20 ft.) apart.

C. *lawsoniana* (A. Murr.) Parl. is a variable species and there are many varieties. This variation is apparent among seedlings and with some the lower branch systems loop down onto the ground and root freely giving rise to new leaders and a clump-like growth. Generally it is better to train this species to one definite leader in the early years, but later, as the size increases, rival leaders may form, even along the length of the trunk. This appears to be no disadvantage to a mature tree.

The forms and varieties with a naturally spreading foliage tend to be tidier and easier to look after than a number of the fastigiate or columnar cultivars which may become untidy and bare at the base. 'Erecta Viridis' is an example and some tying-in of stray branches is often needed after gales or snow.

C. *nootkatensis* (D. Don) Spach. has very similar growth to the former species but the branchlets have a distinct drooping habit. Mature specimens are often seen which have a cluster of rigid branches at the base and on one side. This is a natural habit, a type of juvenile foliage and branching which is 'left behind' as extensive and mature growth develops. It has nothing to do with stock growth from grafting, a common but mistaken belief.

Similar conditions and training are required for the remaining species and cultivars which reach tree-like proportions. Special mention should be made of C. *pisifera* Endl. 'Squarrosa', for the branch systems are so densely packed with juvenile foliage that they may be weighed down and spoilt by the build-up of dead material within the tree or shrub. Although the task of removing this is a difficult one it lightens the branch system and improves the general appearance.

C. *lawsoniana* is often used for hedging purposes. The young plants should be set out approximately 0·9 m. (3 ft.) apart, each being staked with a cane tied to a horizontal wire. The leads are retained until they reach from 150 to 300 mm. (6 to 12 in.) beyond the decided height. The tops are then cut to a lateral approximately 150 mm. (6 in.) below this height. The upper laterals then grow up to form the top surface. Undoubtedly the best effect is obtained when the secateurs are used in trimming, when complete and individual sections of the branch systems are removed, leaving a matt surface.

Chamaedaphne

C. calyculata (L.) Moench., the only species, forms a clump-like growth with a mass of thin stems originating from ground level. To keep the plant tidy it is occasionally necessary to cut out individual dead branches.

Chimonanthus

C. praecox (L.) Link. This subject is valued for the fragrant flowers which a mature bush produces during the winter months. A young bush in the early stages of branch formation blossoms very sparsely if at all, and it is not until the rate of annual growth slows down that the shorter, flowering wood is formed. Almost invariably these flowering growths are part of a mature branch system. The flower buds are produced in the axils of the leaves on the current, or youngest, wood and are fully formed before the fall. The shorter growths may produce a bud in almost every axil but more often a number of growth buds remain to extend into wood in the next season.

Undoubtedly this subject flowers most freely if a branch system is left to mature without any pruning. Grown as a bush in the border or in the shelter of a wall it may quite easily be left to develop naturally. Plenty of vigorous renewal wood is thrown up from the base and the older branches may be cut out if they become weak. The same applies when it is actually tied to a wire or support system on a wall. Free growth can be allowed within reason provided that there is sufficient space. Some restriction of growth away from the wall is possible by a reduction of the branch system, taking away whole sections consisting of both old and young wood, and by cutting a whole branch out occasionally using a new shoot springing from the base as a replacement.

It may be necessary to exercise an even more rigid control by annually cutting away all wood growing at right angles to the wall. This must be carried out in February in order to allow a full season's growth for the new wood. The cut is made on the previous season's wood hard back to the buds at the base. The success of this system will depend upon the vigour of the shrub but the type of season and the amount of sun must also be considered. In conclusion, as a general rule, the less the pruning the more the flower.

Chionanthus

The two species in this genus must have good soil and plenty of sun both in the nursery and in their permanent positions, otherwise growth will be poor and stunted. *C. virginicus* L. is the larger grower and will form a small standard tree under ideal conditions. If growing freely in the early stages a 0·9 m. (3 ft.) leg may be formed when tree-like proportions develop, though it is often difficult to produce a shapely tree as the branches develop an upright habit. If this occurs it should be taken as a characteristic which is difficult to correct, and provided that the overall development is satisfactory it need cause no concern. The branch extremities should be left to develop naturally and at maturity they will become pendulous. Often this subject will break freely from cuts on old wood.

C. retusus Lindl. is more often shrubby, producing branches which originate at or near soil level.

Choisya

C. ternata Kunth has a very dense and bushy habit and it will break very freely if pruned back hard to the old wood. It may be necessary to do this after damage from very severe winters or if the shrub has become badly overgrown.

It is a shrub which loves shelter and the sun and is frequently grown against a south wall. There should be no attempt to train it hard against the surface, for a free-growing bush flowers better and gives a more natural foliage effect. The flowering period is during April and May, but occasionally flowers are produced later. However, a second display is certain if the flowered growths are pruned back by about 250 to 300 mm. (10 to 12 in.) as soon as the first blossoming is finished.

Cistus

These are hard-wooded shrubs and most of the species do not respond well to cutting back as they will not break freely from stems and branches once mature bark has formed. Thus, after being cut back by frost the whole plant is often killed. There are exceptions, however, for example *C. monspeliensis* L. shows a great potential for regeneration from the old wood and this allows any sprawling branches to be cut back. *C. parviflorus* Lam. also shows this characteristic.

In some instances, winter damage is confined to the tips and cutting back provides a good solution, provided that the cuts are not taken back into the ripened wood. This should be carried out in the spring just as growth commences. In fact, all forms of pruning, even the removal of dead wood, should be left until this period so that the extent of any winter damage can first be ascertained.

In the nursery, compact and bushy plants should be encouraged by stopping during their first and second seasons of growth, doing this in the spring and never going back into the ripened branches. Straggly plants often blow over in the wind, and this leads to root disturbance while the exposed lower branches are more likely to suffer damage during the winter.

Cladothamnus

C. pyrolaeflorus Bong. This often forms a loose bush with clusters of long twiggy growths which develop from the main branch system. By carefully cutting out the longest of these whip-like branches which tend to make the bush untidy, it is possible to contain the size and shape within reasonable proportions if, of course, this is considered necessary. It will throw out strong renewal growths from the proximity of pruning cuts, provided they are made in promising positions on the branch system. Pruning should be carried out after flowering.

Cladrastis

Grown properly, these form delightful trees. Preferably they should be on the edge of a grass area or as a lawn specimen so that the growths can develop right down to eye level. In the nursery and as a young tree after planting the young shoots sometimes suffer from late frosts. They are best when transplanted into

K

their permanent positions at an early stage and this should be done as soon as a good lead has been developed. The one important point is to retain the lead and to keep the tree growing without check. The reason for this, in addition to the pleasant effect of a well-shaped tree, is that the wood is brittle. An early formation of the crown may result in excessive weight being thrown on two or three branches, with the danger of these splitting at the crotch especially during high summer gales when the tree is mature and in full leaf. Bracing may avert this disaster with an old tree which has branched low. Should any corrective pruning be necessary it must be carried out in the late summer owing to the danger of bleeding at other times.

C. *lutea* (Michx.) K. Koch is the largest grower, reaching a height of 12 m. (40 ft.) or more. It shows a tendency, when a large limb is lost, to throw young growths on the stems of the remaining branch system. These should be thinned, and a watch kept as their extension will produce extra weight. C. *sinensis* Hemsl. is often smaller and the head may open out early when about 6 m. (20 ft.) in height. The top branches, when the tree is mature, develop in one plane, giving a flat-topped effect. C. *platycarpa* (Maxim.) Mak. and C. *wilsonii* Takeda have similar requirements.

Clematis

Clematis are mainly climbers, raising themselves by means of their leaf stalks which coil round any support. The type of support will vary according to taste and position but the larger growers which retain a permanent and extensive branch system, e.g. C. *montana* DC., are well suited to the larger spaces on walls, fences, pergolas or even trees. If the support is smooth, it may be augmented by a trellis or wire system, provided that this is strongly secured. It may be necessary to tie-in some of the main growths whichever type of support is used, *see* Fig. 20.

The ultimate size to which a Clematis will grow must be taken into account when deciding on the position and variety. Excessive pruning to restrict size, especially with the larger growers, often spoils their effect and display.

The extent and type of pruning is directly related to the habits of growth and flowering, and clematis may be classified for this purpose in the following groups.

Group I. *Species and hybrids which flower on the previous year's wood.*

These are mainly the larger growers, often flowering in the spring, and include C. *alpina* (L.) Mill., C. *balearica* Rich., C. *chrysocoma* Franch., C. *macropetala* Ledeb. and C. *montana* DC. They require very little, if any, pruning except to cut out the dead wood or perhaps to attempt a reduction of a hopeless tangle. If these varieties are grown in a small or restricted space they may well appear untidy and, if a clean-up is needed, hard cutting-back may be resorted to in the early summer as the flowers fade.

Hybrids in the Florida, Patens and Lanuginosa groups have similar habits of growth and flowering. The main crop of flowers in the Florida group is produced directly from the old wood in the spring, but smaller flowers are often formed on the young growths in the autumn. Little regular pruning is needed but it may be necessary to tie in a number of the growths.

The Patens group should not be pruned unless some tidying-up is needed and this is best done after flowering. Sometimes there is a second flowering in the autumn on the young growths.

The Lanuginosa group flowers on the previous year's wood during June and July followed by a display on the young growths during August and September. Normally, very little or no pruning is necessary but should the plant become a hopeless tangle and affect neighbouring plants some cutting-out may have to be done in February. In extreme cases this pruning may be taken down almost to the base.

The evergreen species *C. armandii* Franch. is also included in Group I. It produces trailing growths which flower profusely and these may be thinned out annually after flowering, making the cuts back to suitable young shoots which should be apparent at this stage.

Group II. *Species and hybrids which grow extensively and flower from the young wood during the summer and autumn.*

These produce long vigorous growths which break from the older and stouter wood, and the flowers are produced on these growths during the same season. They often develop into a heavy, tangled mass which builds up year after year and looks very untidy. In addition, this mass of growth may become top-heavy and hang down to deprive the lower parts of sufficient light and air to support foliage and growth. In a restricted space this cannot be tolerated and the answer is to cut the last year's growths back in the spring to the stouter wood. Where there is plenty of room, perhaps in the wilder parts of the garden, pruning is to a large extent unnecessary.

Species in this group which may be pruned hard, as strong growths break out within 0·3 m. (1 ft.) of ground level, are *C. campaniflora* Brot., *C. fargesii* Franch., *C. texensis* Buckl. and *C. viticella* L.

A number of the species need only be cut back to about 1 m. (3 ft.) but the position of the cut depends on where the stronger growths break out from the old wood. These include *C. flammula* L., *C. florida* Thunb., *C. orientalis* L., *C. paniculata* Gmel., *C. rehderiana* Craib and *C. tangutica* (Maxim.) Korsh.

The following hybrid groups have similar habits of growth and flowering.

Jackmanii group. Their natural habits lead to most of the blossoms being produced on the upper parts of the plant. The best policy is to prune back hard to within 0·3 m. (1 ft.) of ground level and this should be done annually in February before growth commences. As a result, the new shoots start low down on the plant each year and thus it is kept tidier.

Viticella group. With this group also, growth commences from the living wood below those portions which carried the flowers during the previous year. Hard pruning prevents a straggly habit.

Texensis group. These are in many ways similar and also respond to hard pruning.

It must be emphasised that the hard pruning advised for these three groups of hybrids is not essential for flower production. In fact, the flowering season may be extended by missing out the pruning altogether. As with the particular species having these habits of growth and flowering, they may be left unpruned if they are growing in natural situations.

Pruning and Training after Planting

It is important to distinguish between the two types of growth and flowering outlined above, for some pruning and training is needed soon after planting.

Group I. The growths should be tied in on a fan system if against a wall, fence or similar structure; otherwise they may be tied up to the support. The weak ends should be pruned away in the early spring as growth begins. Good early training will help with any corrective pruning required later.

Group II. As growth begins after planting pruning should be hard, taking the top shoots back to the lowest breaks.

Clerodendrum

In this large genus of shrubs and climbers there are three species which are grown in the open. Two which are strong-growing and will reach a height of 3·0 m. (10 ft.) or more are *C. trichotomum* Thunb. and *C. t.* var. *fargesii* (Dode) Rehd. In training, the head of branches is often formed on a short leg. As this head develops to maturity the standard of flowering may be improved by shortening the wood made during the previous year back to the last pair of buds in the early spring. Thus a restricted number of new growths is produced which are terminated by the inflorescences later in the season. The process should be repeated year after year, but it may be necessary to maintain vigour by feeding and mulching.

Injury to the root system by hoeing or digging will promote the production of suckers and this should be avoided. If they do occur they may be used for propagation.

C. bungei Steud. is shrubby, but even in a sheltered corner it is often killed down to ground level each year. The growths should be cut down in the spring, leaving them during the winter for protection.

Clethra

Both *C. alnifolia* L. and *C. tomentosa* Lam. develop a mass of growths which spring from soil level. As clumps become established the thicket spreads by means of suckerous growths. This habit may be more pronounced in *C. tomentosa*. The frequent production of new wood from the base allows the older branches in a clump to be thinned out at ground level and some of the weaker suckers may also be cut out with advantage. This should be carried out during the winter. When a clump extends beyond the intended limits and becomes too thick and weedy the whole mass is best dug up and selected pieces replanted after the soil has been reconditioned.

C. acuminata Michx., *C. barbinervis* Sieb. & Zucc., *C. monostachya* Rehd. & Wils. and other more tender species form larger shrubs or even small trees. They may be allowed to branch from ground level and renewal growths will be thrown up from time to time. This allows a limited pruning during the winter if growth is weak. *C. barbinervis* has attractive flaking bark on the mature branches and with a specimen near to the edge of a border this may be seen to full effect.

Cleyera

C. ochnacea DC. forms a dense shrub with close bushy growths. Most of the growth and foliage is on the extremities of the branch system, leaving the supporting branches and main stem bare. This shrub requires very little pruning. It often develops a single main trunk, and branches from this and does not renew the main branch system.

The subject normally requires wall protection, where it is grown as a bush near to the foot.

Clianthus

C. puniceus Banks & Soland. The only successful method of growing this subject is by training it closely to a sunny wall for protection. Even so, this is only possible in the most favoured districts. After one stopping, if necessary, in the spring in order to encourage a bushy habit long growths are produced which are tied in for the winter. Finally the wall space is filled, when a policy of thinning out the old lengths of wood to make room for the young growths is carried out in the spring just as growth commences. It is advisable to delay this pruning until the spring as the older wood is more likely to survive a severe winter, after which there may, in addition, be a considerable amount of dead growth to be cut away.

Cocculus

C. trilobus (Thunb.) DC. This climbs by means of slender twining stems and is suitable for growing up pillars, pergolas or a tripod of stakes. A mass of twining stems is formed and pruning, even of the dead wood, is difficult and must be carried out very carefully as otherwise there may be a loss of support. Normally, however, little pruning is required apart from the removal of growths which have trespassed onto neighbouring shrubs.

Colletia

C. armata Miers is the hardiest species. One feature of this shrub is that it will respond to cutting back at almost every stage, breaking out with one or two strong laterals beneath each cut. The main branching is sparse, and bushy plants should be encouraged in the nursery by at least one pruning in the spring. After the initial pruning, and provided the permanent position is open and sunny, the shrub should be shapely and no regular cutting back will be needed. Later, however, the old branches may become heavy and bent down with age, and it is then that the offending branches can be shortened to a suitable point with good effect. Occasionally a young growth springs straight from the old wood at the base of the plant, extending for 1 or 2 m. in one season. These should be encouraged as replacements for old branches. In a position which is shaded on one side the shrub often needs a stake as the growths lean heavily toward the light.

C. cruciata (Gillies) Hook. needs the shelter of a wall in a warm, sunny position.

Colquhounia

C. coccinea Wall. This shrub, which sometimes grows up to 2·4 or 3·0 m. (8 or 10 ft.) high, has a loose habit with wood which is like that of the Buddleia in appearance except that the branching is not as rigid. It may be killed back into the old wood during a severe winter, in which case it should be pruned back to living wood as the growths break in the spring. It flowers on the current season's wood.

In the nursery and afterwards a bushy framework should be encouraged by pruning, as this will provide a stouter and more rigid branching.

Colutea

These leguminous shrubs flower freely for a long period during the summer on the current season's wood. One of the chief aims, therefore, is to keep them growing strongly so that a good quantity of young growth is produced each year, on the principle that the more growth the more flower. One pruning policy which is quite popular is to cut away the annual growth each February, making the cut back to a permanent framework, leaving only the two lowest buds of the young wood. If this method is to be carried out, the framework must be encouraged to branch freely from ground level and the shrub left to develop up to a suitable height before hard pruning starts. This height will vary according to vigour; for example, *C. arborescens* L. is much stronger than *C. orientalis* Mill.

A variation of this is to train a single stem up to a height of 0·6 to 1·2 m. (2 to 4 ft.) and to prune back to this each year, gradually forming a head of multiple spurs. Specimens treated in this manner may have a certain attraction, but they lack the natural beauty of a free-growing specimen. Even the hard-pruned bush lacks natural beauty after a number of years and the response may become weak.

A limited amount of pruning may be carried out with a free-growing bush. This consists of cutting out some of the oldest and weakest growths, or even branches, in February. The cuts are made carefully to a suitable growth making certain that the natural shape is retained.

It is necessary to stake these shrubs when they are planted in windswept sites. Hard cutting back after planting also ensures a firmer hold for the shrub when it is planted under these conditions. *C. istria* Mill. requires a sheltered position and should be planted in the vicinity of a wall.

Comptonia

C. peregrina (L.) Coult. var. *asplenifolia* (L.) Fern. This shrub is a sun-lover. Grown in a suitable position, little pruning is required.

Convolvulus

C. cneorum L. This shrub is often planted at the base of a sunny wall. The short growths are freely produced from a woody rootstock which develops just above the ground. Normally, no pruning is necessary but occasionally old growths become long and woody, ending up in a heavy mop-head of leafy shoots which give the shrub an untidy appearance. Such growths may be removed down to the base or crown of the plant in the spring.

Coriaria

In this small genus of herbaceous plants and shrubs are three or four species which are sufficiently hardy to be grown in the warmer parts of this country. *C. napalensis* Wall. is perhaps the most distinctive and it will keep its wood in a normal winter. It has a stool-like habit with strong, arching branches which spring up from a woody rootstock at ground level. New growths, in addition to arising directly from the base, are also produced along the lower halves of the arching branches in a similar manner to many of the *Sambucus*. This and the other woody species are so strong-growing that considerable height may be put on in one season. Staking for the first year or so after planting may be necessary especially with a pot-grown specimen where the roots are coiled round and lack anchorage.

The main pruning should be carried out in the spring and consists of tipping back any growths which have been frosted during the winter. In addition, any of the older growths, which are considered to be crowding out better growths, may be removed, taking the cuts back to a suitable growth. Thus, the balance may be kept in favour of the young wood, which gives the better effect.

C. sinica Maxim. is similar in many respects and needs the same treatment. *C. myrtifolia* L., being less hardy, is killed down to ground level in most winters. *C. japonica* Gray and *C. terminalis* Hemsl. are semi-woody and die down each year to a woody base which is at or just below ground level. The pithy wood is often dead by the late autumn. Pruning consists of cutting these dead growths back in the spring.

Cornus

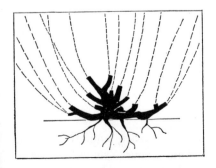

Fig. 28. A stool of *Cornus* which is cut back hard in the spring, just as the new growth is about to begin. It is grown by this method for stem effect.

There are two main types of growth form and habit so far as the arboriculturist and gardener are concerned; the larger growers which will develop a definite trunk under training such as *C. controversa* Hemsl. and the shrubby species such as *C. alba* L., many of which have coloured stems and will respond to annual pruning. It is important for the propagator and nurseryman to recognise these two habits as there are great differences in their training.

The Tree-Forming Species

C. mas L. is in the Sect. Macrocarpium and will form either a very large shrub or a small tree. Much depends upon the nursery training, and unless a lead is selected it will usually branch low down near ground level. The branch system is very spreading and the lowest growths will grow along the surface. Little will thrive beneath the canopy of foliage, as it is very dense. If a lead is selected in the nursery stage a clear stem 0·6, 1·2 or even 1·8 m. (2, 4 or 6 ft.) in length may be formed, this will eventually develop into a trunk which will display an attractive bark. Even with the tree form the lower branches should be encouraged to develop to eye level or lower in order that the attractive flower display can be appreciated in the spring. *C. officinalis* Sieb. & Zucc. is closely related to *C. mas*, but the twig system is somewhat untidy. Neither species normally needs pruning.

C. nuttallii Audub. is in another distinct group, Sect. Benthamidia, trained to a single lead, a trunk will be formed, but if low branching is allowed to develop and it is given a clear foreground, the specimen will be seen to the best effect both when in flower and during the autumn when the foliage is often brightly coloured. Normally, pruning is not required or desirable. *C. florida* L. is more difficult to grow as poor ripening of the wood in the autumn renders it subject to spring frost damage.

C. kousa Hance, in the Sect. Benthamia will readily form a lead, but the lower branches should be left to develop. The horizontal branches give a flattened, tiered effect and these should be encouraged to develop with a clear foreground. No pruning is necessary unless there is dead wood to cut out. The form 'Speciosa' has a distinctly upright, almost fastigiate, habit and no attempt should be made to retain a lead.

The remainder of the tree species to be mentioned are in the Sect. Thelycrania. *C. controversa* Hemsley should be trained to a definite lead which will form a trunk in later years. The lower branches may be trimmed close to the trunk as the head develops, with the lead running through the crown. The horizontal branches are tiered and there should be a clear space round the specimen to allow these to develop to their full extent. *C. macrophylla* Wall. also responds to lead training. *C. alternifolia* L. will form a small tree if a lead is selected, or a bush with a number of upright main branches when left to grow naturally.

The Shrubby Species

Most of these are in the Sect. Thelycrania. As stated earlier, a number of these are pruned annually and are grown mainly for their coloured stems. *C. alba* L.

with its forms and varieties together with *C. stolonifera* 'Flaviramea' are outstanding when grown for this purpose, but a number of other species such as
C. rugosa Lam. and *C. racemosa* Lam. respond in the same way. The method
of culture is to allow the young stock one growing season for establishment
after planting from the nursery. In the following spring, just as growth is about
to commence, the complete top is cut down to within 50 mm. (2 in.) of ground
level. In response to this a crop of young stems is thrown up and these colour
brightly and remain decorative during the late autumn and winter. This cutting
back in the spring is repeated year after year and vigour is maintained by
mulching and feeding, *see* Fig. 28. Under this system of pruning there will be
no flowers or fruit. However, these and many of the other shrubby species are
also effective when grown in bush form when, without regular pruning, flowers
will be produced. When left to grow freely, many are spreading and are thus
suitable for the more natural parts of the garden. An overgrown specimen may
be kept within reasonable limits by pruning away the older growths towards
the centre of the bush, cutting off whole branches rather than small shoots on
the outside. This also encourages a good number of young growths and these
lend extra colour to the bush during the winter.

    C. capitata Wall. is tender and is only suitable for very mild areas. It will
naturally form a dense spreading bush.

Corokia

These are tender shrubs which need wall protection in all but the mildest districts. *C. cotoneaster* Raoul. is best grown as a bush planted 0·3 m. (1 ft.) or so
away from the base of the wall. The stems and growths are curiously twisted
and are difficult to train against a wire system. In the nursery the shrub is
allowed to develop naturally and the branch system is often a permanent one,
apart from minor replacements. The laterals from the main stems develop horizontally and to obtain the full effect sufficient space should be allowed for their
extension. With such sparse foliage as this species produces it is difficult to
gauge health and vigour, and this condition is best judged by the number and
length of the new growths, which are thin, wiry and grey in colour. These show
up quite plainly in the late summer and autumn.

    C. macrocarpa T. Kirk and *C. virgata* Turrill are often even more tender and
need the protection at least of a wall in the average garden. Corokias generally
break freely from the old wood if cut back by the frost or as a part of pruning,
though normally no pruning should be needed except as required for training.

Coronilla

C. emerus L. This shrub has a very pleasing habit, the slender and rather
crowded branchlets springing from a woody framework. Many of these are upright with the tips bent over and almost pendulous. The regular pruning policy
should consist of cutting out any old and worn growths during the winter.
Specimens which have become too large and overgrown may be cut down close
to ground level, when they will break out quite readily. This should be carried
out in the late winter. *C. glauca* L. is tender and should be planted in the shelter

of a wall. It has a dense bushy habit. In the spring as the new growth commences, any dead tips or shoots should be cut back to living wood, at the same time cutting out any very old and worn growths. Otherwise, very little pruning is needed.

Corylopsis

These attractive shrubs or small trees flower on leafless twigs in the spring. Well-shaped specimens are most pleasing to the eye at this period and it is thus important to allow sufficient space for development. If possible the growths should be given freedom to spread out, and when a young plant is finally positioned in a new border, the immediate vicinity should be planted up with Ericas or other dwarf shrubs, so that the horizontal branches can stretch out unimpeded. From this it will be gathered that any pruning required to correct overgrowth in the border, should if possible, be done on neighbouring plants.

In the nursery, the young stock should be allowed to branch freely from ground level. They should also be given a good spacing to allow for natural development.

If it is absolutely necessary, some pruning to restrict size may be carried out, but the greatest care must be taken to retain the natural habit. The best period for this is after flowering. Occasionally it may become necessary to remove old branches but often there are young growths which are suitable as replacements. It is not necessary to thin branches to let in light and air and doing so will quickly spoil the natural habit.

Corylus

Only a few species and hybrids in this genus form trees. The remainder, which form the majority, are shrubs. *C. colurna* L., the Turkish Hazel, forms a tree up to 15 m. (50 ft.) and over. A lead should be selected at an early stage in the nursery and this develops rapidly when the young tree becomes established in its permanent position. Suckers which may appear from time to time should be removed. The shaggy appearance of the bark is quite attractive and for this reason the lower branches should gradually be removed up to a height of 1·8 m. (6 ft.). The main branches are sparse and grow upwards at a slight or distinct angle. The hybrid *C.* × *colurnoides* Schneid. forms a dwarf tree with an interesting branching habit. The dwarf pendulous growths which often clothe the main branches should be left, as they add to the attraction. Other tree forms include *C. chinensis* Franch. and *C.* × *vilmorinii* Rehd. and with these as with any of the tree forms, a lead should be retained and a trunk formed.

The shrubby species have a definite stool habit, forming rootstocks from which suckers, and thus new branches, freely arise. *C. avellana* L., our native Hazel, is a common example. If the suckers are removed at least annually this species and others with this habit of growth will reach heights of 3·0 to 6·0 m. (10 to 20 ft.) with three or more main branches from the base. *C. avellana* is often grown for its display of catkins in the early spring and the best displays are given by mature growths with a strong but compound branch system. Occasionally, it is necessary to cut an old branch right down to ground level, using a young one for replacement. The old wood is best cut out during the winter. This often throws the whole plant out of balance and it may be more effective to cut the bush down to near ground level and to thin and train up a fresh crop of replacement growths. *C. a.* 'Heterophylla' produces interesting, almost laciniated foliage which is at its best on a strong-growing bush furnished right down to ground level. 'Pendula' is grafted on a single stem 1·2 to 1·5 m. (4 to 5 ft.) in height and the most interesting form in which to grow it is by running up a lead for 1 or 2 m. beyond the graft line. The pendulous branches then fall away with graceful effect. *C. maxima* Mill. is stronger-growing than *C. avellana* and the cultivar *C. m.* 'Purpurea' has very dark purple leaves. The pruning policy with this should be to retain the height by keeping mature growths. Vigour may be encouraged by cutting out the weaker wood during the winter.

Cotinus

The most commonly grown species is *C. coggygria* Scop. There are two methods of cultivation.

Grown as a Bush with No Regular Pruning

Under this system the subject will form a large shrub or a small tree with a rounded, bushy head made up of short, twiggy growths. Quite a stout trunk and branch system is built up. Nursery specimens should be encouraged to branch from ground level. The stem system of a mature bush is often covered with clusters of adventitious or epicormic growths, but no attempt should be made to remove these as this is part of the character and natural habit of the bush.

Under this natural system very little pruning is required apart from the removal of dead wood.

Grown for Foliage Effect with Annual Pruning in the Spring

Under this system the shrub builds up a framework which consists of one to three main stems springing from ground level. These may be allowed to divide or branch again until a height of 0·6 to 0·9 m. (2 to 3 ft.) is reached with substantial wood.

Pruning is carried out annually from this point, cutting down the young wood to the two lowest buds in the spring. This careful positioning of the cut is important, for if cut too low the growth from the adventitious buds will be later and thus smaller. This is carried out just before growth commences in the spring. Using this system such coloured forms as 'Flame' or 'Royal Purple' are shown to best effect but flower will not be produced from the young wood. Good growth is maintained by feeding and mulching.

C. americanus Nutt. should be grown naturally as a bush.

Cotoneaster

Most species respond quite strongly even if pruned hard back to the old wood or to the base. Normally, however, there is no need to cut these subjects hard, indeed pruning needs to be carried out very carefully, otherwise the natural form and habit will be spoilt, at least until additional growth has been put on to cover any bad cuts or bare surfaces.

It may be necessary to restrict size, in which case a few long pieces should be removed, cutting back into the shrub so that the wounds and the effects of removal may be hidden by the growths which remain. The selection of the species and position is important so that the need for restrictive pruning is reduced to a minimum, or better still rendered completely unnecessary.

In the nursery a bushy habit should be encouraged, although often this develops naturally without any stopping or pruning.

The gardener must take habit of growth into account. This varies with each species, sometimes even between separate individuals of one species. The following classifications will serve as a guide but it is by no means a complete list.

Graceful Habit

Most of the cotoneasters have a graceful habit but some more so than others.

C. × *watereri* Exell. Indiscriminate pruning easily spoils the fine habit which is at its best when growth is free and unlimited. It is vigorous enough to train to a single stem.

C. *lindleyi* Steud. This species may reach 3·0 to 6·0 m. (10 to 12 ft.) in height with long slender branches. For the best effect they should be left at full length, cutting out complete branches if necessary, not just a partial snipping back.

C. *horizontalis* Dcne. One important characteristic of this and a number of others is the fish-bone effect produced by the main growths with the regular arrangement of branchlets on either side. This characteristic appearance must be retained if any pruning is carried out. A greater height is gained in the border by tying the main growths to a 0·9 to 1·5 m. (3 to 5 ft.) stake.

C. *nitens* Rehd. & Wils. has a graceful habit with a fine tracery of branches and foliage. If pruning is needed this habit must be retained.

Horizontal or Tiered Habit

A number of species which produce heavy and conspicuous corymbs of flower have an almost tiered branching habit. An example is C. *lacteus* W. W. Sm. If pruning is needed, as for example when this is used for an informal hedge, whole lengths should be cut out after the berry display is over. This will ensure that the informal effect is retained; snipping off short lengths will completely spoil this fine habit.

Dwarf and Prostrate Habit

There are many species which come into this group. It is important to arrange a proper spacing but despite this, some pruning to restrict spread may be necessary. Rather than a speedy clipping with shears resulting in a straight and rigid line, an informal effect should be maintained by carefully cutting out individual growths, taking them back into the shrub where the cuts may be hidden by the growths which remain. An example is C. *dammeri* Schneid., a completely prostrate species. *C. congestus* Baker also has a prostrate habit but, in addition, small incurved branches develop as the mat matures. This gives the whole an attractive appearance and the uneven, mounded effect should be encouraged. It may be necessary to uproot and transplant pieces in order to restrict growth. This is best carried out in the autumn when it is more likely that the rooted pieces can be transplanted successfully.

There are many other instances where habit of growth needs to be taken into account if any corrective pruning is needed, e.g. the stiff, erect habit of *C. simonsii* Baker, the vigour of *C. frigidus* Wall. and the spreading, ragged branching of *C. melanocarpus* Lodd. *laxiflorus* (Lindl.) Schneid. Some pruning to improve shape may be necessary with the latter.

A number of the species and hybrids are suitable for planting and training in positions other than in the shrub border or open planting. A number of examples are given below.

Wall Planting

C. horizontalis Dcne. when planted against a wall reacts in a most peculiar manner. The branches press against the wall with a spring-like action, *see* plate 42. However, as height is reached some support by means of ties is needed. This can be kept to a minimum and is required on the main branches only.

C. wardii W. W. Sm. This subject, in company with many others, may be grown on a wall using an intensive and hard system of training and pruning. The branches are spread out, being trained on a fan system as described in Chapter 3 and illustrated in Fig. 19 and the training, once the branch system is established, may be carried out by finger and thumb. As the growths develop they can be pinched out when soft and unripened without the use of knife or secateurs, taking them back to the lowest leaves. In this way flower production is encouraged while this display and fruits are more prominent, as they are not hidden by growth development away from the wall. Specimens treated in this way have a somewhat formal appearance, but they are ideal for positions where there is little scope for development away from the wall or similar surface.

C. glaucophyllus Franch. *serotinus* (Hutch.) Stapf. In common with many other species this can be grown as furnishing close to a wall or similar structure. One or two of the main branches may be tied back to correct any tendency for these to grow away from the wall and arch towards the light. In order to retain the berry display for as long as possible, pruning if necessary, should be carried out in the early spring just as the new growth commences. This, however, is only needed if the shrub outgrows its position or if there is any dead or diseased wood. The longer and older pieces should be taken out in order to retain the natural habit, making the cuts back toward the centre of the specimen, *see* Plate 48.

Informal Hedging

A number of species and hybrids are well suited for this purpose. One of the first to be used was *C. simonsii*. This is a rigid, upright grower and is a natural choice. Some pruning may be required to keep the hedge shapely and within bounds and this is achieved by cutting out whole lengths which have developed beyond the limits. With the informal hedge this selective pruning is the only method of restricting size for clipping over the entire surface will reduce it to a formal feature. It should be after the berry display is over, although on a limited scale old pieces may be cut out during the growing season with, however, the loss of growth and flowers.

+ Crataegomespilus

+ *C. dardarii* Simon-Louis (*Crataegus monogyna* + *Mespilus germanica*). This graft hybrid is usually grown as a 1·8 to 2·4 m. (6 to 8 ft.) standard. Mature trees often develop a mass of twiggy growths in the head, but they should not be thinned as there may be a danger of upsetting the balance between the two tissues.

Should a growth break out which consists entirely of one or the other parent, a careful watch must be kept to see that it does not grow at the expense of the remainder of the specimen, otherwise the nature and shape of the tree may be lost.

The interesting characteristics of the foliage, flowers and fruits can only be appreciated from a close range, and for this reason it is better to allow the branches to develop down to eye level and below.

The cultivar 'Jules d'Asnieres' ('Asnieresii'), also a graft hybrid, has a natural pendulous habit which should be encouraged.

Crataegus

The majority are small deciduous trees, often with a twisted and matted branch system. In nurseries they are usually raised with a clear stem of 1·8 to 2·4 m. (6 to 8 ft.) with a branching head and no central leader. The feathered tree is also quite popular and it is often to be preferred, for it has a central leader which can extend as the crown is forming. If desired, a clear stem can be obtained by cutting off the lower branches in stages as the crown develops. Nursery-trained trees with a clear stem and a central lead are obtainable and these are to be preferred for planting by public highways etc.

A central lead is particularly important with the larger growers, as with an old specimen the branching is very heavy, for the trunk which is often slender. An open-headed tree with branches arising from one point may become weak in later years. In fact, trunks sometimes split down almost to ground level. Should this happen, the trunk and head may be bolted and braced together, for the wood is very hard and the specimen may go on living for many years.

Once a tree has been planted out and has become established, growth is often rapid and the leader may naturally break up to form the head. This happens with some species earlier than others, e.g. *C. ellwangeriana* Sarg. has a very flat head but is also spreading. No attempt to retain the leader beyond its natural 'break-up' point will overcome this habit. This is why it is important to have a good knowledge of the natural habit during and after the training period.

In later years as a specimen reaches the mature or semi-mature stage the head may be so matted that it appears to be in need of thinning. It should be remembered that this is the natural habit and to thin would be a mistake. Also thinning might encourage the development of epicormic growths, giving the specimen an unnatural appearance. Over-thinning may actually weaken a tree, both mechanically and in general health.

Many of the species and hybrids will produce outer and lower branch systems which are so pendulous that they will reach ground level. *C. prunifolia* (Lam.) Pers. provides one example and it is a habit which can be left to develop when the tree is on a lawn with an open foreground. Such branches also act as a trap for fallen leaves which blow across open spaces during the winter and spring, *see* Plate 22.

Again it is emphasised that habit of growth must be taken into account throughout, both in the nursery and in the permanent position. *C. monogyna* Jacq. 'Inermis Compacta' has a compact growth with stiff branches. This branching may be left to develop just above ground level.

Thorn trees in exposed positions are often leaning and may appear to be unsafe. Such trees should be carefully inspected but it does appear to be a natural habit and they may be perfectly sound and safe.

× Crataemespilus

× *C. grandiflora* (Sm) E. G. Camus (*Crataegus oxyacantha* × *Mespilus germanica*). This is a sexual hybrid, an important point, for the tissues are uniform and therefore differs in this respect from the graft-hybrid, + *Crataegomespilus*.

This tree is commonly grown on a 1·8 to 2·4 m. (6 to 8 ft.) clear stem with an open centre and therefore it is planted as a standard with a branching head. Often, it forms a wide but rather shallow head with many of the lower branches almost horizontal but the twig systems on these become pendulous as the tree reaches maturity. They should be encouraged to develop down to ground level for this adds to the attraction of the tree. Pruning consists of cutting out the dead wood which develops from time to time beneath the branch systems. It is seen at its best with a clear foreground.

Crinodendron

C. patagua Mol. This shrub or small tree requires a sheltered position and is often grown in the lee of a south facing wall. In this position it is best when trained as a free-growing specimen without any actual support from the wall. Little pruning is necessary beyond cutting out the dead growths. *C. hookerianum* Gay is even more demanding and requires a partially shaded position in addition to shelter. A healthy specimen requires little pruning beyond cutting back in the spring the dead wood which may develop during the winter.

Cryptomeria

C. japonica (L.f.) D. Don forms a definite lead and, with a straight trunk running up through the centre of the tree, the outline is pyramidal. The lower branches should be encouraged by allowing space for light and development.

The spread of this tree is very fine, particularly in a lawn setting, but seldom do the branches actually reach ground level. Many forms have smaller growths along the length of their main branches and these should be left as it is a natural habit.

C. j. 'Elegans' is a juvenile form which produces a feathery branching system but the main stem, although supple, is weak and a large specimen, perhaps 4·6 to 6·0 m. (15 to 20 ft.) high, is often bent down to ground level by the effects of heavy rain or snow. Staking will help to correct such a position but as more growth is put on, the branch systems become very untidy indeed. The alternative to staking is to deliberately cut the main trunk back to within a few feet of the ground, at the same time pruning back the remaining branch systems, even into the older wood. This subject has been proved to be very good as a formal hedge plant and it reacts well to trimming once a year in August.

The type species prefers a sheltered position, but this is true to a greater extent of many of the forms, particularly such delicate ones as *C. j.* 'Pendula'.

Cudrania

C. tricuspidata (Carr.) Lav. This forms a dense thorny shrub or small tree. It is often easier to accommodate if it is trained to a definite clear stem 1·8 to 2·4 m. (6 to 8 ft.) in height. Dead wood should be pruned out during the summer, when it can easily be distinguished from living material.

Cunninghamia

C. lanceolata (Lamb.) Hook. appears to be the hardiest species, although it is only really suitable for sheltered positions in the warmer parts of the country. Some of the best trees are based on a straight trunk which runs up through the centre and crown, the branching being horizontal from this. On a well-clothed specimen with an open foreground the lower branch systems may come down to eye level.

Multi-stemmed trees are formed when the original lead is lost perhaps through frost or some other injury, either in the nursery, or when they are established and growing freely. Such specimens are not altogether unsightly, but the stems may weaken and bend over as they become top-heavy with growth and this will obviously spoil the appearance. However, these stems may be cut out as replacement growths are sent up from the base. Old and ragged specimens, which are multi-stemmed and therefore no more than large bushes, may be regenerated by hard pruning in May, accompanying this with feeding and, if necessary, watering.

× Cupressocyparis

× *C. leylandii* (Dallim. & Jacks.) Dallim. This is made up of a number of clones which vary a little in habit yet essentially are very similar in their mode of growth to the typical forms of Cupressus and Chamaecyparis. A central lead is developed at an early stage, even from cuttings taken from laterals provided that they are sufficiently vigorous. From this lead a central trunk is built up giving the tree a columnar habit with little spread, see Plate 71. The laterals, which are thickly placed often have an ascending habit but there is some variation among the clones.

As specimens they are ideal, but one or two of the clones which are easier to root than others have become popular hedge plants, see Plate 70. The young plants are set out at 0·9 m. (3 ft.) apart along the site for the hedge, each being tied to a bamboo cane which in turn is secured to a wire strained along the length of the row. The central leads are retained until they have reached 150 to 300 mm. (6 to 12 in.) beyond the intended height for the hedge. The tops are then taken off just above a lateral about 150 mm. (6 in.) below this height. The laterals are left to grow up to the intended height. The best period for this topping operation is during July, indeed, subsequent clippings should also be made at this period. This subject does seem to be very impatient of cutting during the early summer months when growth is very rapid but of course the late autumn, winter and early spring months should be avoided.

Cupressus

The habit of most Cupressus is to develop a definite lead from a very early stage. As this thickens and matures it becomes the central trunk, and the framework upon which the mature tree is built. This mode of growth is readily adopted even by plants raised by cuttings from side growths, but it is advisable to stake the leader carefully in order to encourage a shapely development and as a safeguard against wind-rock or direct damage.

Most species are able to form other leads if the original one is injured and they will do this most readily from the uppermost laterals. However, with strong and vigorous specimens of *C. macrocarpa* Gord., for example, new leads may eventually form from growths originating from much older wood if for some reason an extensive reduction has been made. It is usually desirable to reduce rival leads to one. When a lead has been developed from a misshapen specimen it is often difficult or impossible to hide the effects of earlier troubles.

A number of Cupressus species are not as hardy as those of the closely related Chamaecyparis and in a cold or exposed nursery the young growths are subject to frost damage. However, even when the growth is good the anchorage of the root system may be far from satisfactory. *C. sempervirens* L., for example, may be weighed down beyond repair or even uprooted in extremes of weather such as those experienced during severe gales or heavy snowfalls. A species is only really hardy when the shoot and root systems are healthy and able to function properly.

C. macrocarpa has been used extensively as a formal hedge plant, but although fast growing it is not a good subject for this purpose as it will not respond to severe clipping, whole plants sometimes dying out completely. The bigeneric hybrid, × *Cupressocyparis leylandii* produces the same effect and is a far better plant for this purpose. *C. macrocarpa* is good for screening in the milder coastlines, where it may be allowed to grow freely.

Some conifers of this nature will withstand a very hard pruning if it is carried out during the late spring and summer months, but it is a very severe check

L

which is often a 'killer' if it is done at any other time of the year. The reason for this is that the root system suffers extensive damage through the reduction of the food supply manufactured by the foliage and twig growth. *C. macrocarpa* is perhaps more impatient of this check to the shoot and root systems during the winter months than many, and a very high percentage of the trees treated in this way will often die.

It should be pointed out that a severe cutting back of a mature conifer screen is not advocated at any time of the year. It is really lopping, a drastic and undesirable practice.

Cydonia

C. oblonga Mill. is the true Quince and it can be grown to form a large shrub or a small tree for much depends upon the initial training. It is often suckerous, and will quickly branch low at ground level to form a thick mat and stool-like growth with several upright main branches. The extent of suckering depends partly upon the method of propagation originally adopted. Thus the 'stooling' or 'mound-layering' method which has been extensively used in the past frequently results in the free production of growths at or near ground level, unless these are checked and a central lead built up to form a standard. The standard tree is the best form in which to grow this species and its forms and varieties. Grown as a 1·8 m. (6 ft.) standard, the main branches should be developed with an open centre. As the framework of branches is formed, pruning may be necessary to cut out crossing or badly placed growths but as the head develops no further pruning should be necessary. At a later stage the lower branches should be left to develop down almost to ground level. A large intact crown looks particularly fine in fruit and autumn colour.

Cytisus

The various species and hybrids in this group exhibit quite a wide range of growth, form and habit. This must be taken into account when deciding whether or not to prune.

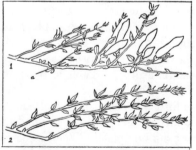

Fig. 29. The pruning of a *Cytisus* after flowering. (1) The growth has finished flowering and the fruits are forming. (a) is the point at which the pruning cut is to be made. It is just above the young growth which may be found below the flowering portion.
(2) Such a growth a few weeks later after pruning.

C. scoparius (L.) Lk. and the other popular hybrids should be pruned annually immediately after flowering in order to conserve vigour and to direct this into growth instead of the production of a useless crop of seed. These shrubs flower along the length of the previous year's wood and strongly growing plants often produce growths which branch freely during one season and flower the following year. Pruning involves cutting off approximately two-thirds of the previous year's shoots and results in the removal of most of the developing pods. The work is carried out with a sharp knife, cutting the growths as they are collected in a bunch by the free hand. New growths will spring from below the cuts, but care should be taken to avoid cutting too low into the old and hard wood as many Cytisus do not break freely if they are so treated, *see* Fig. 29.

Not only does this annual pruning conserve vigour by reducing the strain on the plants at a difficult time of year but it also prevents the bushes from quickly becoming leggy and keeps the plants shapely for a longer period. This is a definite advantage, for straggly bushes often lean over, or may be broken down after a very heavy fall of snow. It is a good practice to carefully brush or shake off snow after it has fallen and before it becomes frozen and perhaps added to by further falls. Summer pruning also reduces the incidence of black fly which often colonise from the developing pods. At this point it should be emphasised that a bushy habit is to be preferred with the young plant and is obtained by hard pruning in the nursery before the season's growth.

Among the cultivars which benefit from annual pruning are 'Lady Moore', 'Lord Lambourne', 'Andreanus', 'Firefly' and 'Sulphureus'. There are of course many others.

The decumbent species and hybrids are seldom pruned, the reason being that it is more difficult, while the growth itself is usually more compact. A limited amount of pruning can be carried out by cutting out individual fruiting stems after flowering.

C. monspessulanus L. becomes straggly and overgrown, but annual pruning is not needed for when a plant becomes unsightly it is better to replace it. Seedlings are often found in the vicinity of a bush and these will transplant readily. It is not fully hardy.

C. nigricans L. flowers on the current season's growths in July and August. It should therefore be pruned back to developing shoots at the base in the spring, and the summer pruning, which is carried out after flowering, restricted to merely cutting off the flowered portion of the stems to prevent fruiting.

C. battandierei Maire is a tall and strong-growing woody subject which may be grown in the shelter of a sunny wall although it is often successful in the open. In the former position it is self-supporting and no training or tying-in is needed. Normally, it throws out plenty of strong growths from the base and these often grow 1 or 2 m. in one season. Thus the very old wood may be cut back and also any growths which stray and lean out too far.

Daboecia

D. scoparius (L.) K. Koch, this species often develops into a straggly bush if it is left unpruned for a number of years. This may be overcome to a large extent by pruning back the old flowering heads to the cluster of growths found lower down on the stem. The best period for this is in the spring just as active growth is about to commence.

Danae

D. racemosa (L.) Moench. This shrub throws up 0·6 to 0·9 m. (2 to 3 ft.) high canes from a spreading rootstock during the summer months. The oldest growths often become ragged with progressive die-back from the tips of the fine branches. These may be cut out at ground level in the spring as new growth is commencing.

Daphne

Normally these do not require pruning and their response if it is carried out is so varied that the advice is, do not try it. *D. mezereum* L. may be quoted as an example. When it is growing in the open in a suitable soil, growth is close and the bush well furnished. Bushes in the shade or among other, perhaps taller shrubs often develop long bare branches and are straggly. The secret is therefore to select the site carefully in order to obtain typical growth. There are, of course, shade lovers such as *D. laureola* L. and *D. pontica* L. but they are fewer in number.

   D. blagayana Frey. and *D. cneorum* L. are dwarf and spreading, and after a few years long, trailing, bare branches develop. Annual pegging down and top dressing of the previous year's growths after flowering prevents this and the plants are happier for it.

Daphniphyllum

D. macropodum Miq. To gain the full effect, this bushy evergreen should be encouraged to branch freely from the base, when it will furnish down to ground level and form a dense, rounded bush. There is little pruning required if this shrub is in full light and can grow unrestricted. Some dead wood collects in the centre of the bush, for the small amount of light which reaches beyond the dense outer canopy will not support healthy growth. Care must be taken if this is cut out to avoid damaging this canopy.

   A plant growing in the shade becomes thin and spreading, with a loose untidy habit. This species will, however regenerate well from the older wood if it is cut hard back.

   D. humile Maxim. seems to thrive better in shade.

Davidia

There is only one species, *D. involucrata* Baill and the variety *D. i.* var, *vilmoriniana* (Dode) Wanger. Both retain their lead naturally without any difficulty. The ascending branches are thickly spaced on the trunk but they are rather sparsely sub-divided. The outline of a mature tree is wide and spreading, for the lead finally terminates in branching at an approximate height of 9·0 m. (30 ft.) or more. The spreading branches should not be restricted by lack of sufficient light or pruning, otherwise the effect will be spoilt. As a tree gains height and grows freely, the lower branches may be removed back to the stem to form a 1·8 m. (6 ft.) clear trunk if desired, doing this in the later summer. This is a good form in which to grow the tree, as the showy bracts, hanging down, may be seen to full effect. The process of forming a clear stem may start in the nursery, but the head will not be complete for at least a year or so after the final planting.

Often with a young tree in the autumn, the leaves on the ends of the branches in the crown, drop earlier than the remainder, and this gives a false impression that the centre and the shoot tips are dying. Wounds on this tree may heal slowly, but seldom does a cavity form.

Decaisnea

D. fargesii Franch. This is an upright growing shrub which throws a number of young growths from the base, and does not branch extensively. The late spring frosts sometimes kill the young growths as they are breaking and this leaves short lengths of dead wood which may be cut out later in the season when new growths below this point are established. Occasionally, the weaker branch systems may be cut out at ground level provided that there are suitable growths to replace them. No regular pruning is required. In the nursery no pruning back is needed as the sparse bushy growth develops naturally.

Decumaria

D. sinensis Oliv. This evergreen climber clings to supports by means of aerial roots on its young shoots, and it is normally grown against a wall. As the plant extends, the older wood may hang loosely from the wall, in which case a tie will be needed. It is a good plan to allow the growth to top the wall when it will often grow down a foot or so on the other side before turning up again. This will help to give the shrub a wonderful support. Flowering lateral growths are produced from the wall. Any which have extended too far from the wall may be pruned back after flowering but normally very little pruning is required. There may be some dead growths to cut out after a severe winter.

Dendromecon

D. rigidum Bentham should be grown against a warm, sunny wall. In the nursery the plants are grown in pots. They develop a bushy habit and these growths are trained fanwise when the final planting is made. Upon establishment, stronger growths appear from the base. These should be trained out so that the plant gradually builds up strength. The flowering laterals are produced from the strong growths. The pruning consists of cutting out the dead and thin wood in the spring as new growth commences.

Desfontainea

D. spinosa Ruiz. & Pavon. This choice subject requires very little pruning, apart from the removal of dead pieces which occur from time to time. The shrub is so difficult to please and to grow successfully that one is rightly hesitant to prune it, even though it may be necessary to limit its size. The main essential is to keep the plant growing freely.

Desmodium

Of this large genus only a few are hardy enough to be grown outside in this country and even these are normally killed down to ground level each winter. They are best grown in a well-drained, sunny border against a wall and may be covered with a layer of loose bracken or straw round the base. In the spring the old growths are cut down to ground level. These shrubs flower on the current season's growth.

Deutzia

These have a stool habit, forming branches freely just below ground level. Thus a sufficient quantity of new shoots is produced on a healthy bush to allow a number of the older branches to be cut right down to ground level after the blossoms fade. Flowering on short laterals which grow from the previous year's wood, the best displays are on the younger growths. With some species, however, the bark on the older wood is attractive and a portion of this may be left each year, cutting back the oldest to good replacement shoots. *D. scabra* Thunb. is one such species. It is a strong grower and the mature branches, which enable it to reach heights of 3·0 m. (10 ft.) or more, are attractive with a loose, shaggy bark. When pruning these large growers a few small, twiggy growths should be left near the base as furnishing and to lend a more natural effect. Some cutting back is desirable on even the older branch systems that are left, as otherwise the taller growths tend to become wind-blown and straggly. The cuts should always be made to a promising growth.

The strongly spreading species and varieties need plenty of space for their canopy of young foliage is attractive even when flowering is finished. *D. scabra* 'Staphyleoides' may be quoted as an example and pruning to confine this shrub would spoil the effect.

D. gracilis Sieb. & Zucc. is sometimes damaged by late spring frosts and the flower buds and young growths, particularly on the upper and exposed portions of the plant, are killed. *D.* × *lemoinei* Lemoine, which is a hybrid between *D. gracilis* and D. *parviflora* Bge, often suffers in the same way. These dead pieces of stem should be cut back later, in the early summer, taking the cut back to strong living wood.

In the nursery young plants which are lined out should be pruned hard before their first season's growth in this position, in order to encourage a bushy habit.

Dichotomanthes

D. tristaniicarpa Kurz. is very similar in growth to the Cotoneaster and in favoured localities it may be grown as a bush in the open. In this position the pruning consists of cutting out any weak and old wood after flowering in June. At this period the strongly growing pieces will be evident and cuts should be made back to these although sometimes it may mean removing an entire branch. Regular pruning, however, is not necessary or desirable.

This plant should normally be grown on a wall and the framework is first trained out fanwise. Once the area has been covered, all growths coming away from the wall must be pruned back to within 25 mm. of the main stems, unless they are required for replacement, when an older piece has been cut out. This should be carried out in the spring just as growth is about to commence. One stopping at five leaves in the early summer helps to control growth and the shoots may then be taken back hard in the early spring.

In the nursery a bushy habit should be encouraged by stopping or pruning the plants after their first season's growth.

Diervilla

The three species in this genus, all from North America, flower on the current season's growth and should not be confused with the dozen or so *Weigela* species from East Asia which flower on laterals from the previous year's wood, as the pruning needs of the two genera are quite different.

D. lonicera Mill. forms a mass of growths from a spreading and suckerous stool. *D. sessilifolia* Buckl., *D.* × *splendens* (Carr.) Kirchn. and *D. rivularis* Gatt. have a similar stoloniferous habit. They should be pruned hard back to just above ground level in the spring as new growth is about to start at the base. Old and worn clumps should be dug up, divided and replanted in enriched soil.

Diospyros

The species most commonly met with is *D. lotus* L., the Date Plum. It will reach from 9·0 to 12·0 m. (30 to 40 ft.) in height with a similar spread. Trained with a clear stem of 1·5 to 1·8 m. (5 to 6 ft.), the outer growths will become pendulous as the tree matures, thus complete coverage to ground level. This displays the beautiful, dark foliage to full effect while, viewed from beneath, the branches often form an attractive and interesting pattern and provide a good position for a garden seat. The tree should be in full sun although it will branch sparsely on the shaded side if grown on the edge of a large clump of trees.

D. virginiana L. is a larger and more loosely growing tree and with a clear trunk of 1·8 m. (6 ft.) the lead should be retained to at least 6·0 m. (20 ft.), or more if the tree is growing strongly.

D. kaki L. f. should have a sheltered but sunny position, for it is not quite as hardy as the former species and will often lose twiggy growth in a severe winter. These and any growths which have died beneath the heavy foliage canopy may be cut out during the early summer. In former days this species and its forms were given wall protection, being trained and closely pruned for fruit production, but specimens have been left to grow out as this policy was discontinued and have eventually formed small trees, the older wood being perfectly hardy.

Diostea

D. juncea (Schau.) Miers. This unusual shrub requires little pruning. It is a tall, erect grower and becomes bare at the base. It is therefore advisable to choose a site among other fairly close growing deciduous shrubs so that it can grow above them. The surrounding shrubs need to be 2·4 to 3·0 m. (8 to 10 ft.) high.

Dipelta

The growth of all three species is very similar. The main branches from ground level are upright but the secondary growths and the finer laterals arch over as the shoots come into flower. Strong, upright extension growths are often produced from this branch system, but these in turn arch over as flowering begins. This development deprives part of the older branches of light and causes leaf-drop and die-back. Occasional pruning is necessary to remove this dead wood at an early stage to encourage healthy development. In addition, however, strong growths are often produced from the base and this gives an opportunity to remove an old branch to ground level if it is weak and worn.

D. floribunda Maxim. has a very attractive peeling bark on the older stems and if the lower furnishing branches are retained the effect is very good.

Little pruning is necessary on nursery stock, as bushiness is naturally produced by growths springing from ground level and these become stronger as the shrub develops.

Dipteronia

D. sinensis Oliv. This forms a large shrub or small tree. It has quite a characteristic habit of growth, for in the first few years after planting the shrub develops a mass of cane-like shoots from ground level. As establishment takes place, strong growths are produced which develop into the permanent branch system of a really large shrub. The smaller growths at the base are then like suckers and may be removed. Epicormic growths which are freely produced on the older branches should be removed unless required for the framework. There should be no attempt to force the early formation of a branch system by pruning and training in the nursery.

Disanthus

D. cercidifolius Maxim. This choice shrub has a spreading habit, with a slender branch system. Shelter is important, especially in the early stages when the young growths are very subject to frost and wind damage. The sheltering screen may have to be pruned in order that the growth of the selected shrub does not suffer in any way, see Fig. 26. The foreground should be clear to allow branching to be as low as possible.

Discaria

No regular pruning is required with D. serratifolia (Vent.) Benth. which assumes tree-like proportions. The habit is for the young plant to branch low or at ground level and these branches should be allowed to extend year by year. The laterals have a semi-pendulous habit, a mode of growth which is adopted by the whole branch system as it develops. Any upright shoots which are produced on the branches grow strongly but arch over to deprive the lower ones of light. Over the years, as these lower branches die and are cut back to healthy wood, a rather untidy habit of growth develops. Gloves are necessary to clean out dead wood. The shrub gives every indication that it would be happier in a sunnier climate. The sparse branching allows underplanting.

D. toumatou Raoul. is a tender shrub for a south wall. A permanent framework should be trained from three or four main branches which should be secured flat against the wall. From the sparse branching pendant growths are produced, which should be left at full length to trail down. They will often grow out several feet from the wall and after flowering in May the oldest of them may be cut back to the main framework to allow space for younger ones to develop.

Distylium

D. racemosum Sieb. & Zucc. Although a tree in its natural habitat, it is more often of shrub proportions in this country. Many of the stiff branches have a horizontal habit with a dense flattened twig growth, which gives an almost tiered effect. Some of the branches in the crown are interlacing, but there should be no corrective pruning for this. In fact, this shrub is most effective when the branches are left to extend over a clear foreground. Should pruning be necessary to restrict size or development in any direction, the cuts should be carefully positioned inside the bush, so that they are hidden and the natural branching habit retained. This should be carried out in April.

Docynia

This is a genus of small trees or shrubs. Under good conditions a lead may be attempted in the nursery, eventually to form a length of clear stem of 1·2 to 1·8 m. (4 to 6 ft.) but more often a natural branching from near ground level is allowed to develop. The head of branches is usually thick and spreading, and in some respects they are similar to the Pyrus, Chaenomeles or Cotoneaster. Pruning may be undertaken to restrict size or spread, taking the cuts back to suitable growths which are usually not difficult to find. Both *D. delavayi* (Franch.) Schneid. and *D. fufifolia* (Lévl.) Rehd. are similar in general effect.

Dorycnium

These may be regarded as subshrubs, but the stems which are produced die back to the woody rootstock each year. The dead top branches serve as a protection for the young basal shoots during the winter and should be pruned back to these in the spring.

Drimys

D. winteri Forst. This strongly growing evergreen is rather tender and normally it needs at least the shelter of a wall. Its habit is to produce strong upright growths, and the wall or sheltering building should be 3·0 to 4·5 m. (10 to 15 ft.) high to allow sufficient room for development. It should be planted a foot or so away from the structure, as no form of training on the wall surface is required or desirable.

Very little pruning is required, apart from the removal of old twisted branches which interfere with the development of the strong growths from the base of the plant. Branches which have been damaged by the winter should be cut back to suitable growths as they break out in the spring.

Eccremocarpus

E. scaber Ruiz & Pav. This is classed as a semi-woody climber. Under glasshouse conditions and in mild districts it often forms a woody base. In warm situations, even in the colder areas, the plant may survive almost untouched provided that the winters are mild. However, the herbaceous stems which are produced from the woody base may be killed back to an extent, even by moderate frosts.

Pruning is best carried out in the spring, when new growth is produced from the living wood. The dead may then be distinguished quite easily and can be cut out. This may mean taking the old growth back almost to ground level.

Pea-sticks or fine wire netting may be used for support, while a sheltered position near a wall is preferred.

Edgeworthia

E. papyrifera Sieb. & Zucc. This shrub should have wall protection and should be planted about 0·3 m. (1 ft.) away from the base, but it only develops into a rather thin bush, and does not respond to tying and training against the wall. It may, however, need a stake. The inflorescences develop in the leaf axils on the newly formed wood in the autumn, but do not open until the spring.

Growth often thins out on the older wood over the years, but strong shoots are thrown up from the base which can be used as replacements. Apart from this, no pruning is necessary, even in the nursery stage.

Ehretia

There are two fairly hardy trees in this genus, *E. dicksoni* Hance and *E. thyrsiflora* (Sieb. & Zucc.) Nakai. With both species the younger wood is often killed back during a severe winter, but regeneration is usually very free, even from the older branches and should this take place recovery is very rapid. The dead wood should be cut out during the early summer, when it will stand out clearly against the young growth.

Full sunlight is essential for good growth, and in positions of partial shade the tree may lean toward the light through heavy wood being put on that side. No growth is made in the shade and if overgrown by taller trees the affected portions will die back.

In the nursery, stock should be given a sheltered but sunny position as the young wood, particularly that of *E. dicksoni*, is tender and liable to winter damage. This is more likely on sappy and unripened wood and thus a very rich soil should be avoided. In training, a lead should be retained for 1·8 to 2·4 m. (6 to 8 ft.), but there is little advantage in forming a clear trunk and the lower branches may be left.

Elaeagnus

This distinctive genus shows quite a wide range of habit, the best known being *E. pungens* Thunb. The natural habit is to branch low and extensively at ground level to form a spreading bush. The form *E. p.* 'Maculata' is variegated and often displays a tendency to revert back to the type plant by developing a number of shoots with pure green foliage. If allowed to remain, these growths, being faster and stronger growing, quickly take over at the expense of the remainder of the plant. They should be carefully cut out as soon as they appear.

    E. commutata Bernh. is slow-growing and spreads by means of suckers. *E. multiflora* Thunb. branches very thickly and a furnishing right down to ground level is required for full effect but it has a very wide spread. *E. macrophylla* Thunb. develops the low branching habit to such an extent that the growth is often thicker in this region than elsewhere. Often too, the manner of branching is such that even the main stems become horizontal or almost pendulous as they arch over when young and become woody in this position. Thus the shrub may form a framework of arching branches, gradually gaining height in this way. It is difficult to form a shapely shrub in the early stages.

    E. glabra Thunb. will ramble over neighbouring shrubs by means of long slender growths which are freely produced from the crown. These should therefore be cut annually unless they are required for extension. In the early stages it is better to have a 1·8 m. (6 ft.) pole for support but, as the shrub increases in size, it becomes self supporting, forming a mass of branches with a domed or pyramidal outline. The long, rambling extension shoots should be cut off each autumn thus forming a fairly compact growth with a slow build-up in height rather than a loose one.

    E. × *ebbingei* (*glabra* × *pungens*) is fast-growing and has an upright habit. As a shrub, it should be left to grow naturally with plenty of space and without any pruning. However, it is very successful as an informal hedge plant. The feature may be kept within bounds by carefully pruning back individual growths to just above a leaf axil or dwarf shoot system in August. The leading growths should be left unpruned until the desired height has been reached. *E. pungens* varieties may also be used to form attractive informal hedges.

    E. angustifolia L. produces strong, upright growths, and nursery stock should be trained with a single lead to encourage the formation of a strong trunk and branch system.

    A general characteristic of Elaeagnus spp. is that they respond well to hard pruning by shooting vigorously from old wood.

Elsholtzia

E. stauntoni Benth. This is classed as a semi-woody plant. When established it produces a panicle of small, pink flowers toward the end of the season, on growths which have just been formed. These are killed back during the winter to near the woody base, from which growth starts again the following year. It should be noted that the lower portion of this young stem survives the winter and increases the woody structure at the base of the plant. The pruning, which should be carried out annually, consists of cutting back the old, flower shoots to the lowest one or two pairs of buds. This should be carried out in March, when the buds on the living wood are apparent as they commence activity. Gradually over the years the old wood and branch system builds up to a height of 0·6 m. (2 ft.) or more.

Embothrium

E. coccineum Forster forms a shrub or a small tree, dependent upon its well-being, position and locality. It is not fully hardy and is suitable only for the milder parts of the country. The form 'Lanceolatum' is hardier than the type.

The young plant should be left to grow freely without any pruning when it will often throw up branches from the base. A successful method is to plant in clumps of three or four. This is a subject which, if it is growing strongly enough, will of its own accord form a small tree. Normally there should be no attempt to train a single lead.

Emmenopterys

E. henryi Oliv. This forms a moderately sized tree with a good straight trunk and lead, the branching from this having a horizontal habit. Great care must be taken to retain the lead while the plant is developing. A careful watch should be kept on the leading growths in the crown of the plant, where most of the extension wood is put on. Part of the answer is to keep the tree growing well, judging the rate of growth by the leading shoots, for lateral growth is very small and slow by comparison. Nursery specimens should have a lead.

Empetrum

E. nigrum L. This is described as a procumbent shrub, and eventually bare stems develop in the centre of the plant to give an untidy appearance. When this condition is reached it is wise to replace it with a younger plant, but the need for this may be delayed by trimming back annually in the spring.

Enkianthus

All the species are densely branched, the main stems springing from ground level and often centrally positioned, the laterals from these being whorled and often in layers. In the early stages most species are upright but a spreading habit may develop with age.

These shrubs need very little pruning, although overgrown specimens break freely if cut down quite hard. They will 'stand still' if they are not happy in their situation, but this is not a healthy condition and sooner or later serious die-back will occur. Their condition may be judged by the amount of new growth which is produced annually.

In the nursery no pruning is required for the production of a bushy habit which will develop naturally with good growth.

Ercilla

E. volubilis A. Juss. This climber is self-clinging, but it cannot be relied upon to support the extensive growth which it puts on after a few years when it is grown against a wall. In its natural habitat of rocks and trees the young growths by which the shrub adheres are able to loop over angles in the support and thus carry considerable weight. There is, therefore, considerable advantage to be gained from allowing the young wood to grow over the top of the wall and partly down the other side. The main growths should also be tied to the wires. Occasionally, the heavy bunches of growth hang down and become very untidy. This may be corrected by carefully thinning them in the spring after flowering.

Erica

Even the few hardy members of this genus exhibit a wide range of growth and this must be taken into account when the need for pruning is considered. Many of the low-growing species and forms need pruning annually for at least 3 to 5 years in order to maintain a compact habit. This would appear to be unnatural and severe, until full account is taken of the conditions under which these plants grow in their natural habitat. Heaths and moorlands are windswept and the plants are exposed to full sun in a well-drained and often poor soil. The average garden is made up of richer soil and is often comparatively sheltered. Under these conditions the plants tend to grow tall with a loose habit.

When annual pruning is considered necessary it is carried out after flowering, and just as the new growth is about to commence. It is not considered wise to prune in the late autumn or during the winter; in fact with a few species such as *E. vagans* L. it may kill the plants completely, especially if it is followed by severe weather. As a general rule the following guide may be applied to those in need of annual pruning.

Spring flowering. Prune in May to June as the flowers fade. This allows the new growths to mature in time for flower production in the following spring.

Summer and Autumn flowering. Prune in March as soon as the new growth commences. The new shoots develop rapidly and are able to flower a few months later.

Winter flowering. Prune in April as the flowers fade and the new growth begins.

When pruning, it is important to avoid cutting into the old wood, for this does not break freely. Old and worn plants do not regenerate readily and replacement is the better solution, provided that the soil is suitably improved before the new planting is made.

A variety of tools should be used in order to avoid a regular and formal effect. The secateurs, the knife and the hand shears should all be used in the same area. In giving this advice it is recognized that the work will be slowed down by using knife and secateurs. Also care is necessary in using the knife in order to ensure that growths are not broken as a result of exerting a pull rather than a cut. Electric hedge trimmers may be used. It will be found that the shoot systems are cut more readily when the foliage is wet. The prunings should be collected in a sack or canvas laid flat and taken up by the corners for moving. It is a task for a light and nimble person, as excessive trampling should be avoided.

While pruning, any seedling Callunas which have appeared should be pulled up by the roots. The beautiful natural effect which results where Ericas are allowed to mingle and grow in association with neighbouring shrubs should also be considered.

The following list gives details of the more common species and their requirements.

E. arborea L. var. *alpina* Bean. Annual pruning not required. Very old and leggy specimens or ones which have outgrown their position may be cut back hard in the spring, even to the woody stems at ground level, for new growths will be produced very freely. In the same way, specimens which have been badly broken as a result of damage by severe frost or snow may also be cut back and will break into new growth provided the old wood is living.

E. australis L. Annual pruning not required. Readily spoilt and even killed by severe weather.

E. carnea L. Annual pruning may be required. These have a naturally compact habit but a limited amount of pruning is often beneficial in the spring after flowering is over. *E. c.* 'Springwood White' is normally low and even prostrate, but given the opportunity it will grow and intermingle with the growths of taller neighbouring plants such as Callunas or Pernettyas and reach a height of 0·6 to 0·9 m. (2 to 3 ft.). It may even be necessary to check it by careful pruning. Should it be necessary to prune to an edge to keep an extending mat within bounds, this must be carried out very carefully to avoid a straight, clipped effect. An informal line may be kept by cutting away the growths individually at different levels. Another effective method is carefully to lift the side of the clump a few inches, cutting away the under branches. When returned the cuts are hidden.

E. ciliaris L. Annual pruning required. This has an untidy growth. The weak stems develop a prostrate habit and upright flowering growths are produced from these. Pruning in March and April as growth commences helps to keep the plants tidier, especially if it is undertaken annually from the time when they are first established. But one should never cut into the old wood. *E. c.* 'Maweana' has a stronger and more erect habit.

E. cinerea L. Annual pruning required. This has a stiff, upright habit but, left unpruned, it becomes straggly and rather untidy. A closer and more tufted habit is encouraged by pruning in the spring just as growth starts and regular annual pruning from the young stage ensures bushier plants. The dwarf, compact forms do not need pruning.

E. × *darleyensis* Bean, 'Darley Dale' and the other cultivars of this interspecific hybrid. Annual pruning required. This is a vigorous grower, but pruning keeps the plants in better condition. This must be timed carefully, as the subject flowers well into the spring and often into the growing period. The operation should take place at the beginning of the growing season. By cutting back, the new shoots which extend beyond the flowering portions are taken away, and growths break out closer into the bush thus encouraging a compact habit. Should this subject need restricting in size, either because it is growing over a nearby edge, or if a neighbouring plant is in danger of becoming overgrown, the offending shoots should be cut out individually in order to leave a natural effect. Merely clipping round the edge to a hard line leaves a very unsightly finish.

This informal edge pruning should be the aim in the Erica garden. A poor or unsightly edge is particularly noticeable when a neighbouring clump has been cleared for replacement and time spent on the finish is always well worthwhile.

E. lusitanica Rudolph. Annual pruning not necessary. This species is tender and is happiest in the mild parts of the country. It does not respond to hard pruning.

E. mackaiana Bab. Annual pruning required. Although some shortening back may be carried out each spring just as the new growth is about to start, eventually the branches build up and lie on each other to produce an untidy mat. When this happens and growth deteriorates, replacement is necessary.

E. mediterranea L. Some annual pruning required. Some varieties are more compact than others, but often isolated shoots will grow up well above the remainder. These should be cut back after flowering in order to avoid a leggy habit, which may lead to wind damage. If after a severe winter the shrubs are killed back, they will usually regenerate from the base, making up well even during the first season. *E. m.* 'W. T. Rackliff' has a compact dome-shaped habit, but very old plants have a worn and gappy appearance. This form seldom responds well to cutting back and a complete replacement is the only answer. No regular pruning is required.

E. scoparia L. Annual pruning not required. This has a loose upright habit and sometimes suffers from wind damage, especially in exposed areas. It is advisable to prune it hard in the initial years in order to encourage a bushy habit. This should be carried out in the spring.

E. terminalis Salisb. Annual pruning not required. This species has an erect habit and is rather a loose grower. If it is desired to keep it more compact the pruning back of the longer and taller growths may be undertaken in the spring. It may be more necessary to do this with specimens which are shaded.

E. tetralix L. Annual pruning required. Cutting back in the spring before growth starts helps to keep a more compact habit, but with older plants the stems are spreading and the plants become untidy. No attempt should be made to induce the plants to break by cutting into the older wood and replacement with young plants is the best solution. *E. t.* 'Mollis' has a compact upright habit, and a limited shortening of old, flowered growths in the spring is advisable.

E. vagans L. Annual pruning required. This species develops a close, clump-like growth but, left unpruned, it will become overgrown and woody and flowering deteriorates. Pruning should take place just as the new growth is showing signs of starting. It must never go back beyond the lowest point where this is breaking out. Specimens which have become old and worn despite annual pruning should be replaced.

E. × williamsii Druce. A limited annual pruning required. This hybrid has a close habit, but leggy shoots, particularly those which have flowered, need to be shortened back to the general level as the new growth commences. One of its main attractions is the young growths which are yellow, particularly in the spring. This effect is spoilt if a general clipping over of the entire clump is carried out.

A number of species and hybrids have not been included in this list, but, provided the habit of growth is recognised, the principles as outlined above may be applied.

Eriobotrya

E. japonica (Thunb.) Lindl. This strongly growing evergreen shrub often reaches tree-like proportions, but it needs the protection of a wall in most parts of this country. With a large wall space which has considerable height, a lead may be retained to form a main stem and the main branches and stem should be loosely secured to the wall. In a more restricted space, branching from near ground level may be encouraged, while good, strong shoots which are thrown up from the base can be used for replacement purposes.

In the milder parts, this subject may be allowed to grow away from the wall, when the branches will spread out for 1 or 2 metres. In this case the shade beneath it will be very dense and only an evergreen ground-cover plant will survive.

Escallonia

One almost general characteristic is the arching habit which develops as a growth hardens and goes into the second year when it flowers. There are exceptions, however. For example, *E.* × *iveyi* Veitch has a completely upright and rigid growth. But the few variations are easily recognised.

Most species and hybrids produce abundant new growths each season from one-year-old shoots and even from older wood near or at the base. Often, at least one new growth is found on the upright portion of a mature stem, or even on the bend as it arches over.

For the most part they flower in June and July from one-year-old wood. Any pruning which is necessary may be carried out as the blossoms drop, removing these growths and making the cut just above a promising shoot or branch.

Another characteristic is their ability to break into growth from old wood after most of the shrub has been killed by severe winter weather. Badly damaged shrubs should not be cut out until they have been given a chance to break in the late spring or early summer.

The reasons for pruning Escallonias may either be to conserve vigour or to control their growth and shape. It is not necessary to prune every year, and the general condition and habit of the species or variety must be taken into consideration. The shrubs should be looked over at least once a year after flowering, first removing the dead and very weak growths. Often it is better to cut in deeply, taking out a considerable portion of a branch, rather than to snip at separate small growths which will give a hedge-like effect.

The south-facing, sunny wall is a fine position for most Escallonias, but in particular for such tender species as *E. macrantha* Hook. and Arn. In the first years after planting the main growths should be tied in, which will ensure that the full height of the wall is reached. The strongest species and hybrids will grow up to heights of 3·0 m. (10 ft.) or more when supported. From this framework strong branching develops to give a considerable spread from the wall.

This outward spread needs to be kept in check by pruning after flowering, occasionally cutting out an entire branch, for renewal shoots are often freely produced from the base, *see* Fig. 30.

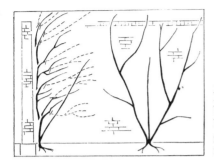

Fig. 30. *Escallonia* trained to a wall. The main branches are tied out to cover the space. The broken lines indicate where the old flowering growths would be cut out after the blossoms fade.

In the warmer parts of the country many of the species and hybrids are successfully grown in the open border. Pruning is often necessary after flowering to conserve vigour and to encourage the young growths, but it may also be necessary to check an invasive habit of the very pendulous forms whose growths, on touching the ground, will root to make separate plants, often to the detriment of their neighbours. The careless application of compost which weighs down and buries parts of the lower branches also has the effect of encouraging such rooting and spread.

The following remarks on individual species will help to give a more complete picture. *E. illinita* Presl is one of the hardiest. It is fairly upright and is unusual in that it flowers terminally on the current season's wood. Any pruning on this and other late-flowering species should be carried out in April, as otherwise, if done immediately after flowering, soft growth will be produced which will not stand the winter. *E.* × *iveyi* Veitch has a very bushy habit and it is difficult to grow hard against a wall. Growth in an outward direction from the wall may be limited by cutting back whole branches.

In a wet, mild summer and autumn some varieties will give a second if reduced display of flowers from short laterals. These are distinct from extension growths. This second flowering, habit may be encouraged by cutting back the old growths after flowering, but not severely. The harder pruning is left until later. Only a few varieties respond in this way, e.g. 'William Watson'. The later pruning is important, as otherwise a close hedge-like surface will result which will look unnatural.

In the mildest parts of the country Escallonias are commonly used for hedging. Under annual clipping, a good surface is formed and the whole genus is able to withstand the salt-laden winds of coastal districts. *E. macrantha* in particular has a dense rigid habit and is ideal for this purpose.

Eucalyptus

E. gunnii Hook. f. is one of the few species which are hardy enough for this country.

Within recent years there has been a revival of interest, which has been partly

M

due to the establishment of improved methods of training and pruning. These are described in detail below.

The plants are raised by seed which is sown in the late summer, and they are kept growing coolly throughout the following winter until planting time in the spring, when all danger of frost is past. By this time they may be in 130 to 150 mm. (5 to 6 in.) pots and they should go straight out into their permanent quarters. There must be no delay in doing this, as otherwise the main roots will be wrapped extensively round the pots, which will spoil the chances of a good anchorage. Trees which start life with a root system which has been cramped and distorted in this way are more likely to be blown down in later years.

The site selected should be sheltered from the north and east winds and additional protection is advisable during their first winter outside, using sacking for screening purposes and a heavy mulch to reduce the chances of the ground freezing in depth. During very severe periods straw, bracken or similar loose and dry organic material should be piled round the basal portion of the stem as a further protection. Effective staking is necessary as the plant grows away.

The second season's growth should be very rapid indeed, and if satisfactory, the plant should be able to stand well on its own without requiring further staking. If not, or if there is any doubt, the young tree should be cut back hard to within 0·5 m. (1½ ft.) of ground level in the spring. This may seem to be rather drastic, but an established plant should respond to this treatment by breaking freely from the base. Often these regenerating growths occur from the swollen base which is normally present on a young tree, which is referred to as the ligno-tuber.

Once these young shoots grow away and are a foot or so in length, the strongest one can be selected and an adjustment made with a final cut on the old stem. This should result in better anchorage, although if it becomes necessary it should be repeated.

Trees which have been badly frosted or killed back during the winter can be expected to react in the same way, unless of course the vital tissues at the base have also suffered. The dead growths may be shortened in the spring, the final cut back being delayed until the regenerating shoots have developed, when some decision as to which are the most promising growths is possible.

There is another method of culture in which the growths are cut down annually or quite frequently to near ground level on a coppice system. This should be carried out in the spring. Tub-grown plants may be treated in this manner, and this will provide attractive young foliage. Bracken and leaves are placed round the tubs during the winter after standing them in a sheltered place.

Eucommia

E. ulmoides Oliv. forms a tree up to 18 m. (60 ft.) in height. It should be raised in the nursery as a 1·8 m. (6 ft.) standard. The reason for this is that the head opens out very quickly once branches are left to develop, and there may be difficulty in retaining a central lead. A good height to the branch system allows the outer and lower branches to develop a fully pendulous habit. Heavy with twig growth and foliage, they are most attractive. This type of growth needs a sheltered position as wind may cause damage.

Eucryphia

These are informal shrubs or small trees which have their own peculiar habit of growth, and they do not take kindly to pruning or training. It is therefore advisable to allow and encourage a natural growth. Often, the lead splits up low down or at ground level, and the main stems are upright. *E.* × *nymansensis* Bausch in particular is a very upright grower with laterals which have a semi-pendulous habit. Often there is some dead wood to cut out beneath these.

Eucryphias are often grown in woodland settings, and care should be taken that low, overhanging branches from neighbouring trees are removed before the general shape and health are affected. In the nursery the young shrubs should be allowed to develop a natural habit, staking if necessary to prevent wind-rock.

Eugenia

E. cheken (Spreng.) Mol. is not fully hardy except in the warmer localities but it can be grown in the shelter of a wall in all but the colder parts of the country. It should be planted about 0·6 m. (2 ft.) away from the base and with its extensive, lateral branching it will occupy a large area. It is upright and close-branching but it will be completely self-supporting. Normally it should be encouraged to branch low by stopping, and it is most effective when furnished right down to ground level. The shrub may be restricted in width by careful pruning, so that the cuts are hidden and an informal surface preserved. The shrub maintains many living growths inside the bush. If severely checked or cut down by frost it will often break freely at ground level from old wood.

Euonymus

Normally, the deciduous species require very little pruning, but it should be borne in mind that there is quite a variety of growth even among these. *E. alata* (Thunb.) Sieb. is a low, close-branching shrub with a spreading habit which must have scope for development if it is to be grown to full effect. *E. bungeana* Maxim. has an erect habit and may develop into a small tree. By way of contrast, *E. latifolia* Scop. has a weaker branching system and the leading growth needs staking, at least when it is young. There are other variations and it is better to see a mature tree or shrub before the choice of species is made. Some of the deciduous species, *E. europaea* L. in particular, act as hosts for Black Fly, (*Aphis fabae*). The developing colonies of insects will often cripple early growths and should be controlled.

E. japonica L. is one of the most common of evergreen species and it will either form a dense shrub or a small loosely growing tree. *E. j.* 'Robusta' has a stiff, upright growth. This subject is often used for hedging purposes, especially near the south and west coasts. It is very good grown as an informal hedge when individual shoots or branches may be cut back, if it is necessary to keep it in shape, in April or May. It does not form an attractive surface when closely clipped although it will withstand this treatment. The coloured forms are attractive; a watch should be kept for reversion which must be cut out as soon as it appears. The forms of *E. j.* 'Microphylla' are attractive when young, but they should be replaced as they become old and woody at the base. *E. fortunei* (Turcz.) Hand.-Mazz. is a creeping evergreen, and in common with the Ivy and some other shrubs it has an adult or flowering stage. In nature, the shrub climbs tree trunks etc. and only when the light is reached, is the mature flowering material produced. *E. f.* f. *carrierei* (Vauvel) Rehd. and *E. f.* var. *vegeta* (Rehd.) Rehd. are mature forms which are bushy and bear fruit. *E. f.* f. *coloratus* (Rehd.) Rehd. forms quite a large spreading shrub which covers a very wide area of 4·6 to 6·0 m. (15 to 20 ft.) wide when it is mature. *E. f.* 'Silver Queen' is most attractive when trained to climb and ramble over the main branches of small trees as *Acer negundo*. *E. f.* f. *gracilis* Rehd. is also a variegated form which climbs. Loose ties may occasionally be necessary for both of these. It is very attractive when planted against a close columnar conifer such as *Juniperus communis hibernica* Gord. The trailing growths are assisted in climbing by threading them through the close branches of the Juniper. The *Euonymus* is not of course allowed to overgrow the Juniper completely.

E. f. *minima* (Simon-Louis) Rehd. is a low, creeping shrub, but it will climb. Even the smaller-leaved form of this, 'Kewensis', will climb for 4·6 to 6·0 m. (15 to 20 ft.) up a tree trunk, to produce a mature branch system with larger leaves, when it reaches the light, *see* Plates 50 and 51.

Many of these forms may also be grown against a wall where they require the minimum of support. The coloured forms of *E. japonica* are also suitable for this situation and in warmer and more sheltered areas a north wall is suitable. Occasionally with the latter, the older growths are cut away in the spring to allow the younger ones to be tied in. Other surplus growth is pruned hard back.

Eupatorium

E. micranthum Less. This shrub is tender and can only be grown in milder districts. It flowers on strong shoots of the current season springing from a woody branch system which is often short and limited in extent. Pruning should be carried out annually in the spring, and consists of cutting back the growths produced during the past season to within 50 to 100 mm. (2 to 4 in.) of their base. This should be carried out before the new growth commences.

Euphorbia

E. wulfenii Hoppe. This may be regarded as a sub-shrub. It forms a mass of erect stems, and this close habit no doubt helps to keep the plant intact and windproof. However, the old growths as they pass out of flower develop small laterals, and this may spoil the general effect. These old flowered stems may be cut down to a really strong growth or to ground level. The plants should be looked over annually, for a drastic pruning in one operation may result in over-thinning and thus wind damage on the remaining growths.

The main attraction of this plant is in the impressive effect which is gained when young and well-furnished stems are massed together. It has great powers of regeneration and quickly recovers from damage which may result in the removal of all the top growth.

Euptelea

This is a genus of small trees or shrubs. The habit of growth and appearance is similar in some respects to that of the Hazel stool. Sucker shoots are thrown up from the base in just the same way, but they are usually not as plentiful and the shrub as a whole is more sparsely branched. In the nursery an attempt may be made to run up a lead with the aim of forming a single trunk and head, but this is not always successful. Little regular pruning is required but the oldest growths may be cut out at ground level or to a suitable growth, if they are weak. Specimens with a single trunk should have their suckers removed as necessary.

Eurya

E. japonica Thunb. This is a stiffly-branched shrub which needs to grow un-pruned and unrestricted in any way; the spread is then considerable, being 1·8 to 3·0 m. (6 to 10 ft.) from the centre of the bush. The branches ascend from ground level at a low angle, while the minor growths are arranged herringbone fashion down the main stems. In the nursery a naturally bushy habit should be encouraged. This shrub will respond to pruning but the characteristic natural habit will be lost unless great care is taken.

Evodia

These trees do not branch extensively. They should be trained with a definite lead in the nursery, which should be extended after planting in the permanent position. If vigour is maintained a clear trunk of 1·2 to 1·8 m. (4 to 6 ft.) can be formed, the lead extending up through the crown to a height of 4·6 to 6·0 m. (15 to 20 ft.). As the trees mature the outer branches are weighed down by extension growths, flowers and fruits, but this habit should be encouraged as it allows the head of blossom which appears in August to be seen to perfection.

    E. hupehensis Dode is one of the commonest species and with its horizontal branches it forms a wide-spreading tree. There is some evidence that *E. henryi* Dode forms a lead and trunk more readily than others.

    Considering the genus as a whole, they need light and it proves difficult to grow a good, shapely tree when it is shaded on one side. For this reason also, encroaching branches from other trees should be kept well clear. They must have good drainage otherwise the wood deteriorates and cavities form.

Exochorda

These shrubs have a fairly upright habit, the branches often being slender and covered with epicormic growths. In addition, numerous suckers may spring from round the base at ground level. These superfluous growths should be cut off annually unless a number are required for the replacement of older branches, in which case selected shoots may be left to extend and develop so that they are suitable for this purpose. The winter period is good for cutting away this crop of annual growths but, in addition, young developing shoots may be quite easily 'rubbed off', or removed with finger and thumb in the spring, just as three or four leaves have formed. Another time for looking over these shrubs is after flowering, when useless old wood may be cut out and surplus young growths removed.

The most erect species is *E. korolkowi* Lav., while *E. racemosa* (Lindl.) Rehd. has a more spreading habit.

Fabiana

F. imbricata Ruiz & Pav. This is normally grown at the foot of a south-facing wall. Apart from the main stems which are upright, the shrub produces a twisted and distorted branch system. It is better in most cases to restrict the shrub to one main stem which will require staking as a head develops with maturity. Should a branch system crack, or break in the wind, the shrub may be cut back into really old wood, as regenerating growths are produced very freely. Any cutting back to shape should be carried out after flowering in July.

Fagus

F. sylvatica L., the Common Beech, is the most common species and is a native, and when well grown is ideal from the arboriculturist's standpoint. Typically, when grown out in the open as an isolated specimen, the upper main branches in the crown are ascending, while the remainder are more horizontal, with the outer and lower ones pendulous. These often sweep down to reach the ground and may eventually root to become a thick, extensive clump round the mother tree. On large estates where there is sufficient space this habit should be developed. The leaf canopy is very dense and quite often the smaller and lower branches die back. These should be removed when this die-back commences, for the healing will then be complete in a young and vigorous specimen, and a length of clear trunk, one of the great beauties of this tree, will develop. Large wounds on an old specimen heal only partially and a considerable area of old wood is left exposed for the remainder of the tree's life, *see* Plate 10. It is therefore more important than ever to renew the protective dressing as often as it is required.

One unfortunate characteristic, particularly with old and mature specimens, is the liability to shed heavy limbs suddenly and without warning. More often this occurs on hot, still mornings in early summer. Invariably, the wood on the exposed surfaces is very dry in appearance. Often, large, ugly tears on the main trunk are made in this way, but they should be cleaned up and smoothed as much as possible, afterwards applying a suitable dressing, *see* Plate 59. An even more thorough inspection should be made of trees which have shed limbs in this way, and if necessary a neat rail should be placed round the perimeter to keep people away from danger. Alternatively, of course, a dangerous tree should be removed.

The good arboriculturist takes soil preferences into consideration when planting young trees and the beech thrives best in well-drained soil. Growth in a young tree is rather slow in the early years, but upon establishment the lead shoots up very rapidly. Much can happen to spoil this lead with the result that rivals quickly develop, for example, the beech is liable to damage from late spring frosts. Rival leads should therefore be cut out at an early stage, for shedding limbs, the one great weakness of this tree, will be more likely to occur where the whole weight of the crown is carried by two or three main branches.

Planted in a group, 12 to 15 m. (40 to 50 ft.) apart, beeches retain their leads more readily than in the open, eventually forming smooth, straight pillars of great beauty.

F. s. 'Purpurea' appears, because of the colour of the foliage, to cast an even denser shade than the type. Generally, it also has very dense branching. Occasionally, reverted growths appear in the centre of the crown, but this is difficult to check and it does not harm the specimen in any way. The forms of *F.s.* 'Purpurea-pendula' are small and compact, forming dense umbrellas of growth. On the other hand, the green weeping beech, *F. s.* 'Pendula', has a distinctive habit, with the tree gradually gaining height and spread, with heavy branches. Many of the older branches are kept alive in the centre of the tree and form branches of dwarf, fastigiate shoots. These should be left, as they add to the character of the tree. *F. s.* 'Laciniata' is a most distinctive tree which is densely but gracefully branched. In order to appreciate this habit to the full the foreground should be open to allow the branching to reach ground level. Some of the forms of this variety are periclinal chimaeras and growths arising from a cut may show considerable variation. *F. s.* 'Fastigiata', the Dawyck Beech, retains a lead naturally with twisted side branches. There should be no attempt to form a length of clear trunk. *F. s.* 'Rotundifolia' is slow-growing and forms a low crown with ascending main branches. This tree will furnish thickly to ground level and will even layer itself at the points of contact. *F. s.* 'Tortuosa' may appear to be untidy to the conscientious arboriculturist, but no attempt should be made to clear the congested growths beyond retaining the lead and clearing the dead wood. *F. s.* 'Zlatia' has an upright, almost fastigiate branching, with a curious bark-splitting habit. The lead should be retained for as long as possible.

The European Beech is often grown as a hedge plant. When kept in a dwarf state it responds to annual trimming in late summer, autumn or winter. In order to allow the young stock time for establishment, no trimming should be carried out for at least two seasons after planting. After trimming, the dead leaves are retained throughout the winter.

The beech seems to be very prone to infection by White Rot, *Ganoderma applanatum*, while the presence of the huge fructifications of *Polyporus giganteus* in the neighbourhood of the root system is indicative of rot on the root system, for this fungus is a saprophyte. A tree in this condition may be unsafe.

Of the remaining species, *F. grandifolia* Ehrh. is quite a strong grower, but the lead should be retained for as long as possible, as it often shows a great tendency to form a crown early in life. *F. orientalis* Lipsky. forms a similar tree and both should be trained with 1·8 m. (6 ft.) clear stem. *F. japonica* Maxim. forms a small slender tree with a very light, twiggy branch system. It should be allowed to branch into several stems at the base, as this is a natural habit.

× Fatshedera

F. lizei (Cochet) Guillaum. is a spreading, low-growing shrub which seems to develop at random, rather than to any pattern. As the shrub grows over the surface, strong shoots are produced which are at first upright, but, as they extend during their second season, are weighed down. The whole process is repeated over and over again in later years as the clump extends.

This untidy habit may to a certain extent be controlled by stopping these upright growths in August. Sub-laterals will be produced, but the shrub as a whole will be closer to the surface. A pair of long-arm or standard pruners may be used for this work, if the clump is extensive and to save walking on the bed.

Fatsia

F. japonica (Thunb.) Dcne. & Planch. is a quite outstanding late autumn-flowering shrub which has a wide spread of some 3·0 m. (10 ft.) as it reaches maturity. The outer branches are weighed down as they extend, although their sub-division into branchlets is very sparse. Most of the branches and the new growths, one or two of which are produced each year, spring from ground level, thus giving the shrub a stool-like habit.

Although it is most impressive when left to grow naturally, it is often necessary to restrict the size by pruning. If this is essential, it is carried out in the spring, when the offending branches may be taken down to ground level. This subject will throw growths from dormant buds, even on the older wood, but provided that there are plenty of replacement shoots, the shrub assumes a more natural shape if they are cut right down.

In the nursery this subject assumes a natural growth without stopping.

Feijoa

F. sellowiana Berg. normally requires the protection of a south-facing wall. It is difficult to train hard against a wall, and it is better when grown as a bush planted about 0·6 m. (2 ft.) from the base. It will then be self-supporting, branching from ground level and forming a rigid, bushy shrub. It will have a spread of several feet from the wall, but it may be restricted by careful and gradual pruning back into the main branch system, on an annual basis after flowering in July.

Ficus

F. carica L., the Fig. This was formerly grown in the larger private gardens for its fruit, and often under these conditions it was subjected to a specialised pruning system.

When grown as an ornamental feature, an upright growth with the main branches should be encouraged, as if there is considerable spread an untidy habit will develop. An overgrown specimen may be cut hard back to ground level; in fact top growth is often killed completely during a severe winter. This subject has great powers of regeneration and will break very freely. It is possible to restrict the size by very careful pruning, taking the cuts into the bush so that they are hidden, and at the same time leaving an informal surface. This may be carried out at any time other than the spring or summer.

Firmiana

F. simplex (L.) W. F. Wight. This develops into a large tree but it can only be grown successfully in the mildest localities. It has attractive foliage, but this is only seen to full effect when allowed to develop freely without being hemmed in by neighbouring trees. It is a fast grower, but the lead should be retained to form a good trunk and strong crown.

Fitzroya

F. cupressoides (Mol.) Johnston. This is usually found as a large shrub rather than a tree with a definite clear trunk. At its best it is conical, well furnished down to the ground with the ends of the branches drooping. The main branching system may consist of a number of upright stems which often spring from near ground level.

Undoubtedly, in a very favourable climate and under good growing conditions, it is possible to build up a small tree form with a definite trunk. Training for this should commence in the nursery when they are but 150 to 300 mm. (6 to 12 in.) high, for there is a tendency even at this stage for the young plants to become bushy and to form several competing leads. The selected growth should be staked, the uppermost tie being on the mature portion of the wood where the stem has ripened. This allows the growing tip to droop naturally.

Fontanesia

F. phillyreoides Labill. and *F. fortunei* Carr. are similar to Privet in habit and appearance. They branch low from ground level. The former has the more delicate and graceful branching habit. Some die-back may occur as a result of severe winters, but apart from cutting this back in the spring very little pruning is needed.

Forestiera

These are similar in appearance to Privet, although they are not as free-growing. They form branches at or just below ground level, and occasionally strong growths are thrown up from the base, which can be retained, either to provide extra furnishing or to replace growths which are weak or overgrown.

Forsythia

The habits of growth and flowering of this genus are that blossoms are freely produced by mature plants in the early spring, directly from growths made during the previous season. Even the strongest of wood on young and vigorous plants often flowers profusely, but occasionally this is devoted entirely to growth. Most species produce a quantity of branches from ground level, and it is their natural habit to grow strongly from this point with growths which, in time, will develop and replace older branches as these become worn and weighed down by a mass of twiggy growths, which have a poor flowering potential.

The object of pruning these shrubs is to encourage this habit by cutting out

the oldest wood immediately after flowering, just as the new growth has com-
menced. This means that annual pruning is not necessary or even desirable.
In a young plant, the future branch system is being formed, and this should be
encouraged to spring from ground level by planting slightly lower than in the

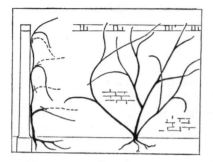

Fig. 31. *Forsythia suspensa* trained to a wall.
Owing to the habit of growth it is rather
difficult to produce a shapely plant. The broken
lines on the left-hand figure indicate the
growths which are to be cut out after flowering.
Entire lengths of the old flowered wood are cut
out at that time. The pendulous habit of the
remaining growths is retained.

nursery. As the plant reaches maturity the balance between old and young wood
should be satisfactory, little or no pruning being required. The growths must be
left full length in order to encourage a natural and free habit.

It is at a later stage, when the plant has been at full size for two or three years,
that a proportion of the older branches may be taken out completely, making the
cut as low as possible on the bush, just above a strong shoot or bud. This should
be carried out immediately after flowering. A furnishing of small branches and
twig-like growths should if possible be left near the base of the shrub, as these
look attractive in flower and in leaf and help to give a natural appearance, *see*
Plates 38, 39 and 40.

It will be recognised that over the years this policy amounts to quite severe
pruning, and that very little wood will be left on the plant which is more than 6
to 10 years old. In order to maintain vigour, therefore, regular mulching and
feeding is necessary.

In cases of neglect, when a specimen is very old, unshapely and weak, it may
be cut back hard to ground level in the winter or early spring. Provided that it
is not too old it will shoot up strongly to produce an entirely new branch system
within two or three years.

Although the relationship between the growth and flowering habits and the
pruning has a general application throughout the whole genus, variations in
size and outline are found among the species and varieties. *F. giraldiana*
Lingelsh. is often a thin grower with a graceful branching habit, a complete
contrast in this respect to *F. × intermedia* Zab. 'Spectabilis', which is stiff
and upright, although, as it matures, many of the outer growths become semi-
pendulous. *F. ovata* Nakai forms a very dense, rounded bush with a compact
habit and is seldom more than 1·2 to 1·5 m. (4 to 5 ft.) in height. Surprisingly,
against a wall the character of the plant changes and longer growths are produced, which if supported add to the height considerably. *F. viridissima* Lindl.
'Bronxensis' is a dwarf and compact grower which seldom needs any pruning.

F. suspensa (Thunb.) Vahl. is a tall grower, reaching 3·0 m. (10 ft.) or more
with long, pendulous laterals and sub-laterals which may reach lengths of
0·6 to 0·9 m. (2 to 3 ft.). In the open this shrub quickly becomes untidy and it is

much better as a wall specimen. The main branches, if trained up and supported, will reach heights of 4·6 to 6·0 m. (15 to 20 ft.) and the long pendent
branchlets may be left to trail down to ground level. Young branches may be
trained up and tied in to replace the older ones as complete lengths are cut out,
and thus overall the plant is kept young and vigorous, *see* Fig. 31. *F. s.* var.
sieboldii Zab. is even more slender and pendent in growth, and may collapse
in the open without support. Forsythias will flower quite well beneath a light
canopy of foliage, provided that there is sufficient moisture for growth. The two
latter subjects are suitable for a north or east wall.

F. suspensa f. *atrocaulis* Rehd., may be grown for its coloured bark, but for
this it is necessary to maintain a good supply of young and vigorous canes by
hard pruning. These are coloured dark purple.

Forsythias are sometimes grown for hedging purposes and *F.* × *intermedia*
'Spectabilis' is the best one to choose for this, as it has an upright, rigid growth.
It will even flower when clipped formally perhaps two or three times during the
growing season, but the best effects are from a more natural growth and outline. For this the standard pruning is adopted immediately after flowering, but
care must be taken to preserve the outline of the hedge.

Fothergilla

These have a stool-like habit, sending up woody and very twiggy growths from
ground level, which have an attractive display of flower spikes in the spring,
with a fine autumn display of coloured foliage before the leaves fall. For this
autumn colour to be shown to full effect, a bush should be well shaped with a
good furnishing of growth down to ground level. The short twiggy shoots at
the base are therefore important and should not be cut off. These shrubs as a
group need very little pruning and often it is necessary to cut neighbouring
growth to prevent overcrowding. Should an old and worn branch need removal,
it should be carefully cut out during the winter, for the growths at the base are
crowded and, unless care is taken, unnecessary injury may occur. Usually there
are a number of young shoots at the base which can be trained for replacement.
F. major (Sims) Lodd. is an upright but slow grower, strongly resembling a
coppiced hazel stool. *F. monticola* Ashe has a well furnished and spreading
habit.

Franklinia

F. altamaha Marsh. requires a sheltered woodland position in a very mild and
favourable locality. It naturally develops an upright habit, and may reach a
height of 3·0 m. (10 ft.) or more. Specimens often display a tendency to branch
from near the base, but there is no need to restrict growth to one stem. No
regular pruning is necessary, apart from cutting back any growths from sheltering shrubs which overgrow it and compete for light. This should be done carefully to conceal the cuts, and to leave an informal effect.

Fraxinus

It is important to retain and preserve the leading growth for as long as possible, for once rival leads occur, a rounded head is quickly produced and this will be difficult to correct. This habit is encouraged by the winter buds being opposite, which means that they develop with equal vigour once the terminal bud is lost through pest damage or a late frost after it has broken into growth. The main branches in a prematurely formed head grow very long and heavy with foliage. These are liable to break during severe summer gales.

Some species, even on generally well-shaped trees, produce long branches with masses of foliage and in exposed positions these may be broken during wet and windy weather. Among the species which are liable to do this are *F. angustifolia* Vahl, *F. oregona* Nutt. in some forms where the laterals are semi-pendulous and *F. rotundifolia* Mill.

F. excelsior L., the Common Ash, is a strong well-branched tree, but when heavy branches are broken or sawn off, large upright growths frequently develop, adding considerable weight to a weakened and often rotted system. Also the general shape of the tree is spoilt. Careful balancing by thinning may be used to correct this. The weeping form of this species, *F. e.* 'Pendula' develops a low, spreading mass of growths, while *F. e.* 'Pendula Wentworthii' will retain an upright lead with pendulous branches. Should an attempt be made to reduce this lead, other upright growths may form on the horizontal branches. *F. e.* 'Myrtifolia' forms an attractive dwarf tree with stunted branching and clusters of small epicormic shoots, which should be left. Occasionally, strong growths with larger leaves are produced, and these should be cut out at an early stage.

Both *F. americana* L. and *F. pennsylvanica* Marsh. retain their leads well, and will form shapely trees with branches sweeping down often to form a thick canopy at ground level. This should be encouraged. One or two of the forms of the latter are very strong in growth, with a dense, almost mop-head of growth. This means that there is plenty of dead wood to cut out from beneath as it dies back through lack of light.

F. ornus L. and the other species which are in this group have a closer, sturdy growth which should on no account be thinned. A clear trunk of 0·9 to 1·2 m. (3 to 4 ft.) is desirable and eventually the branches will reach the ground. *F. spaethiana* Lingelsh. is a small tree with rigid branching, which has little trouble from wind damage.

Generally speaking, the *Fraxinus* species display a considerable degree of hardiness, but some die-back sometimes occurs among species which have been introduced from warmer climates. Not only do these tend to develop into smaller trees, but owing to the frosting of the young growths which sometimes occurs in the spring, it is difficult to form shapely specimens. Examples of the species which may suffer in this way are *F. dipetala* Hook. & Arn., from California, *F. mandshurica* Rupr. from Northeast Asia, and *F. syriaca* Boiss. from West and Central Asia.

F. oxycarpa 'Raywood' has a graceful, upright habit and is worth experimenting with for roadside planting.

Fremontia

F. californica Torr. This subject needs little or no regular pruning. Nursery stock should be grown in pots and trained up to a single lead. This should be staked, a precaution which is also necessary after planting if it is grown as a bush in the shelter of a wall. The alternative method is to train the main stem and branches hard against a wire support system. Wall culture is necessary and the shrub must have full sun.

Fuchsia

This group of attractive shrubs or small trees cannot be considered hardy except in the mildest parts of the country. However, the so-termed 'Hardy Fuchsia' may be grown out-of-doors permanently in the more sheltered parts of the garden especially in the southern part of the country. Normally they are killed down to ground level each year, but the old stem should be left intact until the spring and when the new growths appear the cut may be made down to living wood, *see* Plate 45. As a protection, a loose layer of bracken or a 150 mm. layer of ashes may be placed round the bases of the stems for the winter, this being raked away as growth starts in the spring. Among the hardier forms are the *F. magellanica* Lam. cultivars, the old wood being retained in a normal winter, thus building up a framework.

When the main branches do survive to build up year by year, the laterals are pruned back to the lower buds in the spring, just as they are breaking out. Vigour is taken into account, the weaker growths being cut back harder than the stronger ones. Very old overgrown bushes may be pruned back hard to encourage growths from the base.

The hardy forms are commonly grown as hedge plants in the West Country. This feature is pruned hard back to a formal outline in the spring just as growth is about to commence. The Fuchsias flower on the current season's wood as it extends. Plenty of good growth should therefore be encouraged.

Garrya

G. elliptica Lindl. is almost hardy and in the south and west it may be grown in the open as a bush, provided that a sheltered site is chosen. Normally, however, the protection of a wall gives better results. Although this shrub responds to pruning after flowering, even when cut back quite hard to a branch system which is trained close to the wall surface, the best results are from a free-growing bush which has been trained initially to one or two leads, *see* Fig. 32. It may, however, become necessary to restrict the spread and size of the subject by pruning, and this should be carried out after the catkins fade and before the

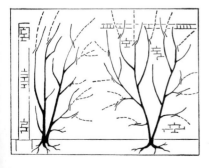

Fig. 32. *Garrya elliptica* when given wall protection may be grown as a free-standing shrub, perhaps with one or two ties on the main branches to keep it in closer to the wall if this becomes necessary. No pruning is necessary unless it is desired to restrict size. The broken lines indicate how this should be carried out after flowering.

new growth commences. The cuts should be taken to a suitable growth well inside the general outline of the foliage and shoot system, so that they are hidden and an informal effect is retained. With an overgrown bush this pruning should be spread over a three to five year period, though an alternative in this latter case is to cut hard back in the spring to the main framework, when it will throw new growths quite freely.

G. × *thuretii* Carr. will form quite a large bush out in the open in the south. Should it be damaged by frost it will throw new, strong growths very readily in the spring. G. *macrophylla* Benth. is normally only suitable for the warmest parts of the country. It may be trained up to a single lead.

Gaultheria

Normally these require very little, if any, pruning. The dead or weak growths would naturally be cut out of the choice species, such as G. *veitchiana* Craib, but this would be difficult and indeed unnecessary with G. *shallon* Pursh, as it generally grows really strongly, and is difficult to curb on a definite line without making it apparent by producing a dense, hedge-like surface. An overall clipping with a pair of shears will produce a close formal line of growth, and it is better to cut or even dig out whole pieces in the spring as the new growth is getting under way. Also, there should be no hesitation in cutting out individual pieces with the secateurs during the summer months if this is required.

A number of Gaultherias produce a dense habit, but G. *procumbens* L. is one of the creeping species and forms a mat which is only 50–100 mm. high. Gaultherias with this type of growth do not need pruning, but mice will sometimes congregate and live in large numbers beneath the close mat during the winter. For food they will nibble away at the bases of the short stems, but the only sign that this has happened, apart from observations made on an occasional inspection, is in the spring when large patches gradually wither and die revealing the extent of the damage. By using a long bamboo cane in a sweeping action to brush over the tops of the growths, any loosened and detached pieces are disturbed and an attack can be detected. In the early stages the mice can of course be dealt with, while the nibbled growths, if taken early enough, can be rooted as cuttings.

× Gaulthettya

× G. *wisleyensis* (Marchant) Rehd. This shrub is very bushy and spreads extensively with arching growths and by means of suckers. On the right soils and in suitable situations it is best when allowed to grow and romp in the wilder parts of the garden. However, by careful pruning in the spring, size may be restricted and it is not difficult to decide on the positioning of the cuts as there are plenty of growths within the bush. Even the low, horizontal growths have upright shoots to which the cuts can be made.

Normally there is little pruning required on a mature bush which has plenty of room for development. The upper branches occasionally develop dead ends and an untidy appearance which needs correction. Also fallen leaves from nearby trees may collect in the branch system in such numbers that they are not even dislodged during gales. The movement of the stiff branch system with a stout stick causes them to fall to the ground where they will act as a mulch and thus be of benefit.

A very old, straggly bush may be pruned hard back in the spring to encourage the production of new wood from the base.

Genista

Genistas are sun-lovers and the most typical growth is obtained in a sunny position. *G. aetnensis* DC. becomes quite a large shrub, or even a small tree up to 6·0 m. (20 ft.) in height. The ultimate height it reaches depends to some extent upon the form and training in the nursery. A low branching, either as a result of a natural break or by stopping, leads to a bushy growth. A lead of a few feet, perhaps by careful staking, produces a standard-like effect. Little or no pruning is required as the shrub matures.

Fig. 33. The basal portion of a growth of *Genista cinerea* which has just finished flowering. The pruning cut may be made at (a). Care must be taken to avoid over-pruning.

G. cinerea (Vill.) DC. and *G. virgata* DC. are similar to each other in habit and appearance. In the nursery and even in the early stages after planting, pruning may be necessary in order to encourage a bushy habit. Once the shrub is growing away, pruning consists of shortening the growths over the whole bush after flowering. They should be taken back to the young growths which develop at the base and along the length of the previous year's wood, *see* Fig. 33. This removes most of the developing seed pods and thus improves growth and vigour. The cuts should not be made beyond the previous year's wood, as the older parts do not break readily. Very old plants which have become unsightly and do not respond to pruning, should be taken out and a fresh start made with young ones.

G. hispanica L. forms low and compact hummocks, but as they become older, dead patches often appear which completely ruin the appearance. This often happens after a severe winter. Any which are in this condition may be taken out for replacement, but another method is to cut away the dead wood, pegging the living portions down as close to the ground as possible. This may be followed by a dressing of leaf mould over the bare stems to encourage rooting. Regeneration and coverage is often speedily obtained in this way. A light clipping immediately after flowering helps to keep a compact and healthy growth.

G. lydia Boiss, has a distinctive habit which could quite easily be spoilt by pruning; in fact, this is true of many of the remaining species such as *G. horrida* DC. and *G. sagittalis* L.

Ginkgo

G. biloba L. The Maidenhair Tree is quite distinctive by reason of its sparse branching and the short spur-like growths on the older portions, in addition to the long shoots which extend from year to year on the extremities of healthy branch systems. There is, however, considerable variation in habit, for some are much more upright with semi-erect branchlets and an absence of heavy branching; they are almost fastigiate in habit and there is a recognised form, *G. b.* 'Fastigiata', which is columnar with semi-erect branches. Others have a more natural form of branching, the main limbs coming away at right-angles, the sub-branches from these being semi-pendulous. In a well-shaped specimen with a strong central lead the main branches are often formed when the tree has reached a considerable height and is many years old.

Essentially, this tree should have a good, well-defined lead running up through the centre. Fortunately, it readily responds to training and naturally forms a good lead in the nursery. The nurseryman only needs to ensure that growth is good and that rival leads, if they do form, are reduced to one. This policy should be continued after the final planting. This is a very long-lived tree, but a weakness caused by the formation of rival leads will inevitably tend to shorten its life as the wood becomes older and the strain greater.

Gleditsia

G. triacanthos L. is the most outstanding tree in this genus. It will retain a good lead and will thus form a long, straight trunk. As the tree develops, this may be cleared of growths to a height of 3·0 to 4·6 m. (10 to 15 ft.). The trunk is also quite interesting, as short but stout spines develop in clusters. These should be left, as they add character to the tree. This species is also grown in several other interesting forms. 'Inermis', is thornless but can be trained and grown in the same manner as the type. This is also true of 'Sunburst', although it is not such a vigorous grower as the type. It is trained with a 1·5 to 1·8 m. (5 to 6 ft.) clear stem in the nursery. 'Elegantissima' Rehd., var. is shrub-like and no definite lead or trunk can be formed. It seldom has thorns and has upright branching. *G. t.* 'Nana' can be trained to a definite lead when young, but the trunk is short and it forms a dense narrow crown.

A good straight lead and a well-formed tree may be trained from the following species: *G. caspica* Desf., *G. delavayi* Franch., *G. japonica* Miq., *G. macracantha* Desf. and *G. sinensis* Lam., although the results are variable according to health and well-being. *G.* × *texana* Sarg. often forms a small flat-topped tree in this country.

Gleditsias should, if necessary, be pruned in the late summer for bleeding is a danger with spring pruning.

Gordonia

G. axillaris Szyszyl. is a tender evergreen tree or shrub which can only be grown in the mildest localities. Often a specimen is restricted to one main stem, but later other upright growths may develop from the base. These should be allowed to grow as they increase the strength and vigour of the bush. Very little regular pruning is needed, but occasionally weak and untidy growths are better cut out to strong and well placed branches. Most of the pruning is needed on sheltering plants if they tend to overgrow and deprive the specimen of light, *see* Fig. 26. This should be carried out carefully in order to retain a natural and informal surface.

Grevillea

This genus is represented in this country by a few shrubs which normally need the protection of a wall if they are to succeed. They are planted close to the foot of the wall for maximum protection, but should not be trained in any way. One essential is to keep growth as compact as possible by allowing full sunlight. If the subject is overgrown or shaded in any way by stronger neighbours, growth will be drawn towards the light and away from the warmth of the wall. In this case it is more likely to be caught by severe weather. Careful pruning may also be carried out in the spring, to cut off straggly growth, thus keeping the bush compact. Also, if growths have been damaged by a severe winter they may be cut back to suitable breaking shoots in the spring.

Grindelia

G. chiloensis Cabrera. It is only in the more favoured places that this survives the winters sufficiently to become a definite shrub, retaining wood to a height of 0·6 to 0·9 m. (2 to 3 ft.). More often the growths are killed to the woody stems at the base. They should be pruned by cutting out the dead growth in the spring, when it can be seen just how far down the bush the winter's damage has extended.

Griselinia

G. littoralis Raoul, this forms a rounded, evergreen bush 2·4 to 3·0 m. (8 to 10 ft.) high, although it will grow higher in sheltered and favourable conditions. In the nursery it will branch naturally from the base. As it develops, laterals are freely produced which in turn become very thick with foliage and additional growth.

This characteristic of breaking freely and strongly, even from short growths, makes it an ideal shrub for use as a windbreak along the milder coastlines. It may also be used as a hedge plant in the milder areas. For this latter purpose, an even bushier habit may be encouraged in the initial years by pruning. This subject grows quickly, and density, with increased rigidity, is encouraged by its habit of throwing up strong shoots through the centre, from the base to the top of the hedge, even during one season.

Although it will respond to 'clipper pruning', it is better with an informal surface, the secateurs being used to cut off individual shoots. This should be carried out in the early summer.

This subject retains a considerable amount of foliage, even in the centre of the bush. The variegated form has a similar growth.

Gymnocladus

G. dioicus K. Koch forms a large, coarsely-branched tree. Even the twig growth is thick and sparse. From the nursery stage a lead should be run up for as long

N

as possible. Eventually, as the head forms, the lower branches can be removed cleanly, thus encouraging a clear trunk of 1·8 to 2·4 m. (6 to 8 ft.). Often the outer branches on a mature tree have a semi-pendulous habit and the attractive foliage is thereby brought down to eye level. In addition to the summer and autumn display of foliage, the effect of the midribs, which remain attached long after the leaflets have fallen, is both pleasing and interesting.

G. *dioicus* 'Variegata' has a distinctive, upright habit, forming a dense head, while, in addition to the variegated foliage, the attached midribs in the winter are quite attractive. Both this and the type species love the sun and a warm sunny spot should be selected where they are isolated from other trees.

To reduce danger of bleeding, any major pruning operation should be carried out in July and never in the late winter or early spring.

Halesia

The most common species is *H. carolina* L., the Snowdrop Tree. It can be trained in the nursery to form a short trunk, but a more natural habit is a free branching from the base. With the latter habit of growth a low, spreading bush is formed and the lower branches assume a horizontal habit. This free spread, with growth down to ground level is delightful, and with a clear foreground, it may be allowed to develop naturally without pruning. If pruning is needed to restrict growth it should be carried out after flowering. It is natural for the branches to be thickly placed and they should not be thinned.

H. monticola (Rehd.) Sarg. has a tree-like habit and may be trained to form a definite lead. Eventually a mature specimen may have a clear stem of 0·9 to 1·2 m. (3 to 4 ft.), but with long trailing branches the growths reach down to ground level. They hang down in an untidy manner, but should not be thinned. *H. diptera* Ell. is trained as a shrub from the nursery stage.

× Halimiocistus

This small group of bigeneric hybrids, in common with *Cistus*, seldom responds well to pruning. Should a straggly and woody growth develop, it is better to re-propagate and then to plant up with young stock. However, dead wood and the old flower heads may be cut off in the spring.

Halimium

This small genus shows considerable variation in habit, but generally the species do not respond well to pruning. This should therefore be confined to the removal of dead growth in the spring. *H. lasianthum* (Lam.) K. Koch and the variety *concolor* Hort. spreads extensively without gaining more than a foot or so in height. It should be planted 0·6 m. (2 ft.) from the edge of a border, so that there is good space for natural development. It is possible to carefully prune the leading growths if it is necessary to restrict size in any way. This should be carried out in the spring as growth is beginning, making the cuts well into the shrub so that they are hidden and an informal effect is retained. *H. alyssoides* (Lam.) K. Koch is also spreading. Often, when either of these two plants are grown near to and develop against larger shrubs, the long prostrate growths will climb through the branches, gaining a height of 0·8 to 0·9 m. (2½ to 3 ft.) and flowering profusely when they reach the light. *H. halimifolium* (L.) Willk. & Lange. will gain height in this way too, but may also be grown against a wall. As a contrast, *H. umbellatum* (L.) Spach forms a fairly compact bush with finer foliage.

Halimodendron

H. halodendron (L.) Voss. This shrub has a spreading habit with spiny branches. It should be allowed to develop naturally, and usually it branches freely at ground level, having this free branching habit as a seedling. Normally no pruning is required.

This plant, however, thrives better when grafted upon seedling stocks of *Caragana arborescens* Lam. as the root system is not well adapted to conditions in this country.

Hamamelis

Normally, the members of this genus require very little pruning. One of the most desirable features, that of winter flowering, is displayed to the best effect by free and natural growth. Some pruning may be required at the training stage in the nursery, especially with *H. japonica* Sieb. & Zucc. var. *arborea* (Ottolander) Gumbleton. Trained to a single lead for 0·9 m. (3 ft.) or more, it will assume the proportions of a small tree, although it should be recognised that the habit of this form is naturally rather ungainly, with the branches assuming a horizontal habit. *H. virginiana* L. is also sufficiently strong-growing to form a small tree; the main branches are ascending and it has an attractive habit. This latter species may also be grown as a bush. Most of the remaining species, cultivars and forms also have quite distinctive habits of growth which must be allowed for in training. It is definitely a mistake to thin branches or to prune with the intention of reducing each to a uniform shape. Should any pruning be necessary in order to reduce size, for example, if a specimen is too close to a path, this should be carried out after flowering and before growth commences. It should be done very carefully with the cuts being made just above promising growths, *see* Fig. 18.

When grown in even slight shade the bushes become very straggly, and the habit and flowering are much better in full sun. Mature specimens have a considerable spread and in a group planting may need to be 5·5 to 6·0 m. (18 to 20 ft.) apart.

The practice of grafting *Hamamelis* on to *H. virginiana* stock is widespread, and a watch must be kept for suckers which may spring from the base. They are best dealt with as they appear, for if they are left until the end of the growing season they are often several feet in length, and may spoil the inner growths of the bush itself. One means of distinguishing the suckers is that the leaves remain attached to these strong shoots long after the bush as a whole is completely defoliated. Shrubs which are on their own roots are usually, of course, free from this trouble, although *H. vernalis* Sarg. often has a natural habit of suckering. Branches which are at eye level are very much appreciated as the flower display can then be admired from close quarters.

Hebe (Veronica)

One of the most important characteristics of this genus as far as pruning is concerned, is the ability to break freely from the old wood when cut back, either by frost or by hand. This is fortunate, for many of the large-leaved species such as *H. speciosa* (R. Cunn.) Cockayne and Allan are tender, and are often cut back severely, almost to ground level, in a hard winter. Should a specimen be badly frosted in this way it is better left with its top, withered and scorched though it may well be, until the spring, for it will afford some protection during the latter part of the winter. Also, when the new growths break out it will be apparent just where the pruning cuts should be made. It is important to cut back to the strongest of these, although it may be apparent when growth is under way a few weeks later that the final cut should be lower, in order to leave a neater bush. There should be no hesitation in doing this, but the earlier in the season it is done the better, for with more light and air there will be a better chance for the growths which remain to ripen.

Form and habit of growth vary considerably, but many species such as *H. anomala* (Armstr.) Ckn. are naturally compact and therefore seldom need pruning to correct a straggly habit. Occasionally however, even such species as *H. brachysiphon* Summerhayes, benefit from hard pruning in the late spring in order to correct an untidy habit, or if the bush has been broken down by snow. *H. dieffenbachii* (Benth.) Ckn. & All. is one of the more untidy growers and restrictive pruning may be necessary, in which case it should be carried out in the late spring. However, as with all plants in an informal setting, it is important to retain the natural habit of growth as far as possible.

It is sometimes necessary to prune back a specimen in the neighbourhood of a path, but this needs to be very carefully done as otherwise an abrupt and ugly edge is produced. Often, it is better to cut the entire shrub hard back and make a fresh start, or even to take it up and plant a more suitable species. A careful watch must be kept on the variegated forms such as *H.* × *franciscana* 'Variegata'. Any growths showing reversion to the pure green type plant should be cut out as soon as they appear.

H. macrantha Ckn. & All. has a poor, straggly habit, but this may be improved by cutting back after flowering.

Many Hebe species and varieties set heavy crops of fruits, and the vast numbers of developing capsules place a considerable strain on these shrubs, particularly during periods of drought. Plants which are suffering in this way will benefit from the removal of the withered heads, and they will look neater during the winter months if this is done, though it is only possible on a small scale. *H. hulkeana* F. von Mueller certainly benefits from their removal, for otherwise it may be short-lived. Sometimes this and many of the other species die back for an unaccountable reason, often progressively, one shoot after another. Little can usually be done to correct this, apart from removing the offending growths, but a bush may be cut about so badly that it is better to propagate from healthy shoot tips and remove the old one completely.

Hedera

H. helix L. The natural habit of this subject is well known, the creeping and climbing growths producing bushy branches when the plant ultimately passes into the mature stage. This sequence of growth allows the developing plant to reach the light before the branches which produce the flowers and fruits are formed.

Fig. 34. The short growths which are produced by Ivy on a wall when it is clipped hard annually.

There is a great need for caution when the health and safety of an Ivy clad tree is considered. Such a tree may be attractive, but it must be safe. There is little danger of strangulation, for the habit of growth is for the main Ivy stems to develop along the length of the trunk and branch system. The extra weight, as the Ivy branches freely, may, however, strain a weak framework causing a loss of one or more of the main limbs. This danger may be overcome by preventing an extension of the growths into the upper branch systems, and once the Ivy has developed beyond the creeping juvenile stage this is not difficult. However, by far the greatest danger is that the matted growths and stems may hide a cavity which will ultimately affect the health and well-being of the tree, making it unsafe. This should give the person responsible great cause for concern, and, if the Ivy is to be retained, the tree must be inspected very carefully – a difficult task!

Ivy is often found on the walls of buildings, etc. where it will, if there is room, reach considerable heights. Actually, it does no harm to such structures until the mature stage is reached. Then the branches, as they become heavier, may strain and loosen the brick or stone as they sway in the wind.

Annual clipping overcomes this trouble, for the subject is kept close to the wall and never in fact has a chance to produce mature growths, *see* Fig. 34. This should be carried out during May and June, for this allows time for the new growths to develop and ripen before the winter sets in. If it is left until later

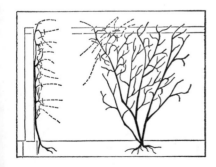

Fig. 35. Ivy against a wall, but only the main branches are shown. The broken lines are the young growths which would be removed by clipping hard back during May and June, after the nesting period for birds.

the young growths may be damaged by the winter frosts. The clipping should be taken as close to the wall surface as possible, despite the fact that for two or three weeks it will look rather bare, *see* Fig. 35. Ivy which is grown over fencing, pillars or similar structures should be treated in the same way, if a topiary-like effect is desired.

'Arborescens' is the tree form of the Common Ivy, obtained by propagating from cuttings of mature growths. Pruning is not required, but some form of staking may be advisable from an early age. This seems to be a difficult subject to nurse back once it has slipped into a poor, unhealthy condition.

The remainder of the species can be treated in much the same way as *H. helix*.

Hedysarum

H. multijugum Maxim. This has a bushy habit, but it is sparsely branched, and after a few years it becomes rather unsightly, with bare, woody stems. The pruning back of long branches to suitable growth in the spring may help to correct this. Long branches may also be pegged down in the spring just as the buds are breaking, and this will produce new, young plants.

Heimia

H. salicifolia (H.B.K.) Link. This light and graceful bush normally needs the protection of a sunny wall, where it should be planted about 0·5 m. (1½ ft.) from the base. It should be allowed to break freely when young, both with main branches and smaller furnishing growths. The flowers are produced along the lengths of the current season's wood in the late summer. Pruning consists of cutting out one or two lengths of the older wood, as this becomes necessary, in the spring just before the new growth commences. If pruning is confined to merely snipping over the head of the bush, a close broom-like effect is produced which completely spoils the graceful habit of the shrub.

Helianthemum

These respond well to pruning after they have finished flowering, which is usually in July. Growths which are straggly and make the plant look untidy may then be cut back, and they will even break freely from the old wood. Often too, older growths which need removing are found beneath the clump. These should be cut off carefully, and it may be necessary to lift the mat of growth to do this.

Helichrysum

These shrubs generally need the shelter of a wall and are suitable for the smaller border. Often, they survive the winter, but in a very ragged condition. However, even without the winter's damage they may become woody with age. They will often respond to hard pruning in the spring as growth is about to commence, but reaction is variable and a very old plant in poor condition may not respond favourably. In the same way, frost-damaged wood will not break out, and this may in part explain some of the failures which have been experienced. Cutting back need not, in all cases, be carried back to the actual wood, thus gaining the advantage that the younger tissue breaks out more readily. *H. scutellifolium* Benth. in particular is often very reluctant to break out after severe damage during the winter.

Hibiscus

H. syriacus L. is recognised as a good late-flowering shrub and is available in several varieties. These vary in habit and form but generally they are upright, often branching low from near ground level. Flowering is on the current season's wood. For good growth they must have a well-drained soil, while a sunny position is necessary for healthy wood which will flower well and stand the winter in sound condition. In particular, this species is prone to infection by various forms of die-back including Coral Spot (*Nectria cinnabarina*).

Pruning consists first of cutting out dead or diseased wood during the spring or summer, but when there is large scale dying back it is often better to replace the plant completely. If it is thought that the die-back is due to an unsuitable site or soil, it is advisable to select a better one for the replacement. Little other pruning is required, although overgrown specimens may be thinned and cut back quite hard, choosing the spring for this operation. Extra light reaching the bush as a result of nearby thinning will have the same effect, for vigorous breaks often appear from very old wood.

In the nursery, a low bush should be encouraged by hard pruning in the spring.

Often, the anchorage or rooting of these plants is not particularly strong and in exposed positions they may rock considerably.

Hippophae

These deciduous trees or shrubs are dioecious, but there is very little difference in the manner and habit of growth between the two sexes. They are spiny, especially when young.

H. rhamnoides L., the Sea Buckthorn, is a native and is often found growing in coastal areas, where it may be partially buried by drifting sands yet continue to survive. It is also grown inland and, under favourable conditions, by reason of a suckerous habit of growth, it will often form large clumps. Under these conditions very little if any pruning is required.

It may also be nursery-trained to form a small tree with a 1·2 to 1·8 m. (4 to 6 ft.) length of clear stem. It is difficult, however, to retain a lead and to form a shapely head; in fact, it would be against the character of this subject to do so. Instead, the branches are curiously twisted, while the head is composed of stiff, semi-pendulous twig growths. It is also difficult to distinguish dead from living wood during the winter and the cutting out of this is better left until the summer.

H. salicifolia D. Don will form a medium-sized tree. It should be nursery-trained to form a clear stem of 1·2 to 1·8 m. (4 to 6 ft.). As the tree matures the bark is attractive, being deeply furrowed. The trunk should be kept clear, but any epicormic growths may be allowed to remain on the branches as they give character to the tree. The branch system is often quaintly twisted and this very habit may lead to weakness in later years, when some form of bracing may become necessary. The stiff outer branches have a semi-pendulous habit.

Hoheria

H. glabrata Sprague & Summerh. and *H. lyalli* Hook.f. are the hardiest. However, they are not completely so and may be killed right down to ground level during a severe winter, though, provided that there is living tissue at the base, strong regeneration and growth can be expected.

Both species have an upright habit, branching from ground level and occasionally vigorous growths are thrown from these low branches or from the base. After cutting out the surplus, the remainder should be left to add to the branch system, or to be used as replacements for the older branches when these are cut out. There should be no hesitation in cutting out a proportion of the older and weaker wood in the spring if this is considered necessary. Both species are subject to Coral Spot, *Nectria cinnabarina* and this is more likely in a damp and shady position.

The evergreen species *H. populnea* A. Cunn. and *H. sexstylosa* Col. are definitely tender and in all but the mildest districts they should be grown as bushes in the shelter of a wall. Both species should be left to branch freely from the base. If necessary they may be carefully pruned to restrict their size, making the cuts at a suitable point inside the bush in order to retain an informal surface. This should be carried out in the spring.

Holboellia

These are evergreen, twining shrubs. They will freely produce a large number of slender stems, and are so vigorous that if a suitable means of support be available they will reach a height of 6·0 to 9·0 m. (20 to 30 ft.).

H. latifolia Wall. is quite a tender species and thus needs a sheltered position such as a sunny wall. The main support should be a horizontal wiring system, some of the growths growing between the strands and the wall. Others may be laid on the wires and tied in position. Vertical wires are also useful, particularly for the young plant as it grows to cover the available space. When the full height is reached, the pendulous growths provide an attractive furnishing. At this stage it has a considerable spread outwards from the wall. Some thinning of the weaker growths may be carried out in the spring and this helps to keep the shrub within suitable proportions. Dead wood may also be cut out at this time or later during the summer, when another thinning of the long growths may be necessary.

H. coriacea Diels. is hardier and may be used to climb small trees or a system of tripod stakes in the border.

A neglected specimen is often full of dead wood in the centre. This may be cleaned out by pulling away the brittle growths by hand.

Holodiscus

The best known and most attractive species is *H. discolor* (Pursh) Maxim. The growth is spreading and arching, and the flowers in the form of heavy panicles are produced on leafy shoots which spring from the previous year's wood. Young canes are produced from the base of the plant each year and thus the older stems may be cut out annually after flowering. This has the effect of maintaining the flowering display year by year and allows the strong growths to arch over freely to produce the best effect. Sufficient older wood must be left on the bush to maintain furnishing and a good framework and the best of the young growths from the base are used to replace this framework as necessary. Usually, just part of the branch system is cut back to suitable young growths, leaving an adequate furnishing. An unusual, but very suitable, setting for this subject is a north-facing wall, where with the minimum of support it will reach a height of 3·7 to 4·5 m. (12 to 15 ft.). *H. dumosus* (Nutt.) Heller is a dense, twiggy grower. The old canes may be thinned at the base after flowering. This will result in a neater plant, and the young canes can develop freely and produce an improved flower display.

Hovenia

H. dulcis Thunb. This forms a large shrub or small tree, although it is more often the former as it is not fully hardy in most parts of this country. As a result, unripened and even woody growth is killed back during the winter. The wood is also very subject to Coral Spot (*Nectria cinnabarina*). Often, therefore, there is a considerable amount of dead wood to cut out in the spring.

In a sheltered and suitable position, a lead with a 0·9 to 1·2 m. (3 to 4 ft.) clear length of stem may be developed.

Hydrangea

One characteristic which is common to this genus, is that the species and varieties grow freely from the base, thus allowing old and worn branches to be removed, even from those which are not normally pruned regularly.

For pruning and management purposes, the genus may be divided into four groups based on their habits of growth and flowering.

Group 1. *Those which flower terminally on the current season's wood*

H. paniculata Sieb. var. *grandiflora* Sieb. may be taken as an example. Growths which extend during the season from the dormant bud stage produce large heads of blossom in the late summer. Left to develop year after year without any pruning, the many growths which result will produce only small heads of flower. The hard pruning which is advised each spring, usually in February before growth commences, is in effect a form of disbudding, for the cut is made just above the lowest pair or two pairs of buds. Thus only two or four buds can grow from each position. An interesting point is that this plant does exercise some control over its flowering, for often only one bud of each pair grows out strongly to flower. Very seldom do four growths develop completely unless the plants are very vigorous. Eventually this treatment, extended over the years, will result in the build up of a short, stout branch system a few inches or more in height.

In an exposed position, lower branching should be encouraged on the plants on the outside of a clump, as these will protect the taller ones which may otherwise be broken. It is emphasised that growth and vigour must be maintained by feeding and mulching as necessary, usually on a planned annual basis.

The other species which respond to annual pruning are *H. arborescens* L. and its varieties, and *H. cinerea* Small.

Group 2. *Those which are low-growing, producing a clump-like growth freely with young growths from the base*

H. macrophylla (Thunb.) DC. f. *hortensia* (Maxim.) Rehd. may be given as an example. It flowers from the strong buds which have wintered, and which were produced terminally on growths which sprang up from the base during the previous season and on growths which flowered then. If the plants are examined after the flowering period, the large, fat buds are those likely to produce an inflorescence the next year, the smaller ones being confined to growth only. It should be noted that a flowering growth may also form flower buds for the following season.

As a result of this habit, which is at first sight rather confusing, the following pruning method can be adopted to assist flowering. It should first of all be understood that, left unpruned, this group will often flower well, especially in a well-drained, sunny position. Pruning carried out on careful lines will, however, improve flowering. The old flower heads should be left on during the winter for protection against very severe weather and in the spring, before growths from the buds have advanced, the weaker and older branches may be cut right down to ground level and the old flower heads cut back to strong buds. The removal of these old heads may mean cutting back 150 to 300 mm. (6 to 12 in.) of stem. The heads of the Lace-cap varieties may be cut off as the flowers fade to prevent wasted vigour in seed production.

In effect, the strong flower buds are retained, crowded growth is avoided, the wood ripens better and this assists flowering. The varieties vary considerably in their flowering capacity.

In addition to the large number of *H. m. hortensia* varieties which may be pruned by this method, *H. serrata* (Thunb.) DC. also responds. Should any of this group be cut back to ground level in the spring, the regenerated growths will be strong, but will not flower until the following year. The cluster of growths may need thinning at an early stage as they develop.

Group 3. *Those which form large shrubs, retaining a more permanent framework*

The following species are among those in this group; *H. bretschneideri* Dipp., *H. heteromalla* Don., *H. quercifolia* Bartr., *H. sargentiana* Rehd., *H. villosa* Rehd., and *H. xanthoneura* Diels. These and the other species which are similar in growth need little pruning. The weaker growths may be thinned or cut out in the spring, or after flowering. A weak or poor bush may be pruned hard and then strong renewal shoots will be thrown up from the base, provided the plant is encouraged by way of mulching and feeding.

Hydrangeas suffer during late spring frosts, and some adjustment by pruning may be necessary when new growths break out.

H. quercifolia Bartr. is rather an untidy grower and staking is helpful in the spring before the new growth is made.

Group 4. *Those species which climb by aerial rootlets*

These rootlets are produced by the young extension shoots to enable them to cling to any support as they develop, *see* Fig. 36. Their hold is often retained for many years as they thicken, and the shoots which flower develop laterally from them. The three species commonly grown in this group are *H. anomala* Don., *H. integerrima* Engler and *H. petiolaris* Sieb. and Zucc., the latter being the most common.

When grown on a wall they will cling naturally without any support, but an even greater stability is gained if the plant is allowed to develop its extensive branching on the top of the wall. This it will do with great freedom.

Fig. 36. A climbing growth of *Hydrangea petiolaris* with the adventitious aerial roots on the undersurface of the stem which allow a secure attachment to a suitable surface.

Normally, pruning consists of carefully cutting back extension growths which are not required, as they are produced during the summer. In time, the flowering branch system has a considerable spread from the wall. These branches may be pruned back closer to the wall by carefully cutting back a proportion of the spurs to a suitable bud. This should be carried out in the spring, but in order that flowering is not affected, the work over the whole surface may be extended over a 3 to 4 year period, *see* Fig. 37. This group may also be planted against trees or other supports.

Another effective method of growing shrubs in this group is to plant them against a boulder or tree stump, so that a low mat of branches and growths are produced. No attention is needed, beyond cutting off any extension growths which are not required.

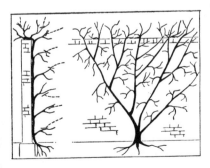

Fig. 37. An established plant of *Hydrangea petiolaris* growing against a wall. It is well furnished with flowering laterals. The diagram on the left shows how these may be shortened if necessary, the pieces to be removed being indicated by broken lines. Notice the strong attachment to the top of the wall.

Hymenanthera

The species in this genus have very distinctive habits of growth which would quite easily be spoilt by regular pruning and therefore should only be pruned if it is necessary to confine them to a limited space. *H. obovata* Kirk is very bushy from the base, most of the branches being rigid and fairly upright. It may be confined to a narrow border by careful pruning, with the cuts being hidden by the thick foliage. *H. dentata* R.Br. ex DC. forms a mass of thick, fairly upright branches. The young, whitish growths are an attractive feature of this shrub, and it should be allowed a width and height of several feet to show this to good effect.

H. crassifolia Hook. f. forms a low mound of congested growths and any form of training would not be practical. It should therefore be in a position where it can develop freely, gradually building up height to 1·5 m. (5 ft.) or more. If it is restricted in width, the main growths, naturally twisted and weak, are without support and may need staking. In many parts of the country these shrubs need the shelter of a south wall and should be planted about 0·3 to 0·6 m. (1 to 2 ft.) from the base.

Hypericum

A considerable variation exists among the shrubs in this genus, for while a number are hardy and retain their wood from year to year, others are semi-woody and are almost herbaceous in nature, most or all of the wood above ground is lost, the growth being made up from ground level each year.

The most common species is *H. calycinum* L. which is seldom more than 0·3 m. (1 ft.) in height. Being stoloniferous it spreads extensively and is a good ground-cover plant. By cutting hard back in the early spring to within an inch or so of ground level, the areas colonised by this plant may be given a general clean up before the new growth commences. This looks quite attractive when it develops a few weeks later. It is, however, a good plan to go round the clumps from time to time during the growing season in order to check the invasive spread of this subject over weaker plants. Large areas may be clipped over for the annual pruning, using the garden shears. A motorised scythe is useful for covering extensive areas.

H. ascyron L. is almost herbaceous and should be cut back each spring. *H. inodorum* Willd. and the form 'Elstead Variety' may also be treated in this way. These two plants may weaken over the years as the soil is exhausted, and the clumps extend, with the area becoming hard and weedy. Regular mulching will delay the need for replacement.

H. androsaemum L. need not be cut back as hard, but it will throw up shoots strongly if occasionally it is reduced to ground level in the early spring in order to clean the area generally.

The distinctly shrubby species, hybrids and varieties include *H. hookerianum* Wight & Arn., *H.* × *moserianum* André and the forms of *H. patulum* Thunb. The extent to which the wood is killed back depends upon the severity of the winter, but in the spring there is no difficulty in recognising the living wood, for the new growth will then be breaking out quite readily. The method of pruning is to cut out the weaker and thinner growths, afterwards shortening the remainder to suitable buds or shoots. Often this will mean only the removal of the seed heads. To some extent the size of the bushes is regulated by this pruning.

'Rowallane Hybrid' is not really hardy and will be killed down to ground level in all but the mildest areas. Normally, therefore, it should be planted against a south and sunny wall, and the dead wood cut down to ground level. It grows up to flower each year in the late summer. Should wood survive the winter it may be left to build up height.

In the nursery, the woody members of this genus should be cut hard back as they break into growth in the second season, in order to encourage a bushy habit.

Idesia

I. polycarpa Maxim. has a distinctive habit. It forms a single, straight trunk and lead, the radiating branches being horizontal and in tiers. The branching is also rather sparse. Provided that it is given a good position with no overhanging branches or competition for light with neighbouring shrubs, it will form a shapely tree and pruning is not necessary. Shading causes die-back on the affected branches.

Even in the nursery, the young trees quickly develop a good lead and a tier system of branching. This should be encouraged by careful handling, spacing and staking.

Ilex

I. aquifolium L., the Holly, a native, is found almost throughout the whole of the British Isles. Both the type and the many garden varieties are commonly used as garden features.

This subject reacts well to close annual clipping and large specimens as well as hedges are sometimes found which have been kept to a formal outline. Unless, however, the surrounds are completely formal, a more natural growth is desirable. The pruning policy may thus be based upon the need to maintain a general outline, cutting back any growths which are obviously extending beyond the intended limits. This pruning should be carried out during July and August, using a knife or pair of secateurs and making each cut well back to a suitable growth. Thus an informal and natural surface is obtained. The aim should be to have a thick coverage right to ground level, for not only does this appear more attractive but bare soil at the base is unkindly, and loose, thin twig growth may brush the soil in the wind, to produce erosion, *see* Plates 67 and 68.

It should, however, be borne in mind that varieties behave differently; some, if left unattended, may even lose their character and grow vigorously into tree forms. Account must be taken of this, and if it is thought undesirable, the tendency should be corrected at a very early stage.

Sometimes, despite efforts to conceal them, cuts appear unsightly, but hollies, if they are healthy, respond to this treatment very vigorously and the pruning points are hidden after a few months. Wound dressings also help to conceal the cuts.

Hollies are tolerant of shade, but the density of growth is often affected and it may be thin. Thus overshadowing and faster growing neighbours may quickly spoil a surface, even to the extent of making it bare and ragged. Corrective pruning on the neighbouring tree or shrub may be thought desirable, rather than that the specimen itself should suffer. It should be remembered that starvation and drought may also cause defoliation, thin growth and die-back.

If cutting out of dead wood is attempted, it should be carried out over a period of 2 to 3 years, otherwise there is danger of living wood being cut too. To carry out this work thoroughly it is often necessary to crawl into and beneath the specimen, which can prove very dirty work.

The nursery training should be based upon the need to form and retain a lead, and this should continue after planting for as long as possible in the life of the tree. A stunted specimen may not at first have a lead, but with good growth, suitable shoots appear and selection is possible at a later stage. Frost damage may also kill leading growths, especially if they are vigorous and sappy, see Plate 49. A further selection of growths may therefore be necessary at a later stage, when new ones have developed.

Finally, it should be remembered that many forms produce naturally pendulous growths from their outer and lower branches as they reach maturity. The extensive lateral spread of large specimens which is sometimes met with, is often caused by seedlings which have germinated and grown beneath the lower branches. Unless the coverage is insufficient they may be removed.

I. aquifolium L. is often used as a formal hedge plant. Clipping should be undertaken in August, but an earlier start may be made if there is much to be done. The holly hedge, if overgrown, will respond to very hard cutting back, provided this is spread over 2 or 3 years. First one side should be cut back, then the other, and finally the top. Great care must be taken when reducing the height of a really old hedge with pendulous growths, see Plates 73 and 74. Cutting back to a definite level may sever these, causing a collapse of several feet. This is the main reason for cutting back the sides first, for there is less weight and length of growth and the position is clearer.

Just as the varieties of *I. aquifolium* vary, so do the other species and full account of their natural habits should be taken when a training and pruning policy is decided upon. *I.* × *altaclarensis* Dallim. naturally forms a strong lead and an impressive pyramidal tree. *I. ciliospinosa* Loes. forms a good lead, but may only reach up to 4·6 m. (15 ft.). *I. dipyrena* Wall. is similar but is much stronger. *I. cornuta* Lindl. forms a dense, rounded bush. *I. pernyi* Franch has a very wide and stiff branching habit. *I. verticillata* (L.) Gray, a deciduous shrub, branches at ground level with rather fine, stiff growth. *I. crenata* Thunb. is variable, some forms being tree-like, others quite dwarf and compact.

Illicium

I. anisatum L. is the best known species. It is slow-growing, but often eventually forms a large shrub or small tree. *I. floridanum* Ellis is a shrub with very thick growth. Little pruning is required, but it may be necessary to restrict growth in certain positions. For example, these subjects should be grown within the shelter of a wall in all but the warmest parts of the country, and the borders to such walls are often quite narrow and shrubs may thus need to be confined. The growths for this type of pruning should be carefully selected, making the cuts at suitable points behind others so that an informal surface is maintained. With *I. floridanum*, whole branches if they are weak and old, may be cut out at ground level. Much depends upon the condition of the shrub, but usually new growths are freely produced from ground level.

Indigofera

A few of the shrubby species are hardy enough to survive our winters in the open, but they may lose most or all of the wood which they make during the late spring and summer months. Usually they are killed right down to ground level, but *I. amblyantha* Craib, for example, will retain a low, woody branch system and perhaps build up height from year to year. The flowers are produced during the late summer and early autumn on the current season's wood. Pruning is carried out in the spring, probably in March, cutting away the previous year's growths down to near ground level. Any which have retained wood above ground may be pruned hard back to this, leaving just the basal portion of the younger wood. If wood is left in this way, it should be checked over later, as the buds become prominent, in order to cut out any that is dead.

Itea

I. ilicifolia Oliv. This subject is grown as a wall shrub in all but the mildest parts of the country where it may be grown as a bush in a sheltered area. Where space is unrestricted both along the length of the wall and in front of it, this shrub will develop up to a height of 3·7 m. (12 ft.) or more and have a considerable spread. In this case very little pruning is required, but a number of ties should be made from the wall on to the main branches to prevent these from being damaged by strong side winds or heavy snow falls. In the colder areas or where space is restricted, some pruning and tying-in is necessary. The best displays of the long catkins are produced on the strong, young growths made during the previous year. Once the framework has been formed against the wall, the policy should be to cut out the older and weaker branches to allow the best of the new growths to be tied in. The young developing growths are often tinted an attractive bronze colour. This type of training is very similar to that advised for *Escallonia*, see Fig. 30. In the nursery the production of a plant with three or four low branches should be encouraged, so that these may be trained out against a wall when planted in their permanent position.

I. virginica L. This will naturally form a bushy plant right down to the base, which allows some of the oldest and weakest wood to be cut out altogether, although this is only occasionally necessary. However, some of the oldest wood on the ends of the branches may with advantage be cut out annually after flowering which is completed in July. The cut should be made back to promising young growths, the majority of which originate from just beneath the flowering shoots. The young growths produce the best foliage and autumn colour.

Jamesia

J. americana Torr. & Gray. This is a rather stiff shrub with erect branches, and grown in the open it produces a close habit. It produces growths freely from the base in the nursery stage, and these may be used as replacements if necessary for any of the older branches which are cut out. However, this subject usually requires very little pruning and the crown should be kept as intact as possible, with the furnishing down to ground level.

Jasminum

In general the hardy species are vigorous growers, and freely develop young growths which are produced as readily from the topmost branch as from near the base. A number are climbers which cling to a support by twining, but others have a loose scrambling or arching growth.

J. nudiflorum Lindl. As a wall specimen, in the early stage this is trained fanwise to bamboo canes which are tied to the horizontal wire supports. Later, as growth increases, the leading shoots may be loosely tied to the wires. The laterals from these hang down and the pruning of these should be hard, directly after flowering in the early spring, taking the growths back to promising shoots at the base which break out at this time. This policy must be rigidly carried out on an annual basis otherwise the subject quickly gets out of hand, with the new growths falling over the old ones and killing them by depriving them of light. This results in a build up of untidy masses of dead wood. At pruning time the ties should be carefully checked. A plant which is untidy and out of hand may be pruned severely and it is also a good plan to cut out a really old branch, using a young one as a replacement.

The pruning is the same when this plant is grown on a fence or pergola, but it may also be tied to a single stake 1·2 to 1·8 m. (4 to 6 ft.) high in the open border. Again, the framework branches should occasionally be replaced.

J. primulinum Hemsl. has similar growth and pruning requirements, but is tender. *J. humile* L. has a stiffer habit than *J. nudiflorum*. It may be grown against a wall, and as it flowers on the previous year's wood, this may be cut out after the petals fall, tying in the new growths as they develop on the framework. It may also be grown in bush form as a border plant. Old and worn growths may be cut out after flowering.

J. officinale L. is a vigorous climber which must have a strong support, especially if left to grow to heights of 6·0 m. (20 ft.) or more. It is difficult to train and to prevent it from becoming a tangled mass; indeed a more natural effect is gained when it is left to grow and develop on its own. This climber flowers from laterals produced from the previous year's wood, but also terminally from growths produced during the summer. If it is thought necessary, some of the oldest wood may be cut out during the summer as it passes out of flower, but great care must be taken to preserve the natural furnishing and foliage effect.

J. beesianum Forrest & Diels is similar, but is not such a strong grower as *J. officinale*. Both are climbers which twine in an anti-clockwise direction for support. *J.* × *stephanense* Lemoine, a hybrid between these two, also has this habit.

Jovellana

J. violacea Don. This is a half-hardy shrub which should normally be grown near the base of a south-facing wall, and then only in the milder parts of the country. Even in such positions growths are usually killed back to ground level during the winter. A protective layer of loose bracken should be placed round the base of the plant before the winter sets in. Pruning is carried out annually in the spring, just as the new growths are breaking from the base. Should there be any old wood which is living it may be retained, but generally the shrub responds better to hard pruning. It also spreads by means of suckers.

Juglans

All the species in this genus have much in common. They are prone to damage from late spring frosts, but particularly so in the nursery stage, when careful pruning back and reselection of the leader is needed if this occurs. In the nursery and in their final positions, a good growing soil is needed in order that strong growth may be produced and that, if the leading shoot is lost, a sufficient number of good leads develop in its place to ensure a suitable selection. It is also important to transplant when young, for they move badly, growth is checked and a poor tree often results. Another important point is that walnuts bleed badly if cut in the spring, and they should, therefore, only be pruned in the late summer.

J. nigra L., the Black Walnut, forms a graceful and shapely tree, retaining the central lead better than many others. This allows the lower branches to be removed as the tree develops, forming 4·6 to 6·0 m. (15 to 20 ft.) of clear trunk. Even from this height the lower branchlets sweep down to ground level to produce a fine effect.

J. regia L., the Common Walnut, often forms rival leads after frost damage. It is important to correct this by selection and stopping at an early stage, as otherwise they quickly become heavy branches and the tree may later become unsafe.

J. californica S. Wats. is a small tree which does not always grow well in this country and the wood is prone to rot from cavities. If these occur they must be speedily attended to. *J. mandshurica* Maxim. is also a poor grower in many parts and much depends upon the early days in the nursery.

With this wide variation in growth rate and final form, it is important that the characteristics of the species or variety are taken into account during the training and shaping period.

Juniperus

There are many varieties of dwarf junipers, but this section is concerned mainly with the tree and large shrub forms. *J. virginiana* L. is perhaps the most common of the tree species. In its best form, it has a central lead and is well furnished with branches, the lower of which may almost reach the ground. Many of the larger growers which will develop into trees, have a similar habit and a central leader is desirable for a good proportion of the height. With both these

o

and the shrubby species and forms it seems important to allow specimens sufficient light and space for healthy development, as otherwise the build up of dead material among the branch systems makes them very unsightly. No regular pruning is normally needed.

Kalmia

These shrubs must have the correct growing conditions and pruning will not in any way compensate for a failure to provide them. It is true that some regeneration often takes place as a result of pruning hard a neglected specimen, but the response will only be maintained if conditions and culture are suitable.

K. angustifolia L., which normally requires very little pruning, may become old and woody, and with the main stems bent over and exposed, the effect is rather unsightly. These may need to be cut right down to the base, leaving only small, thin and perhaps woody growths in this region. The strong growths which are needed will not develop from these, but from completely new shoots which will form at their bases or on the old wood. Often too, several years after establishment, strong growths are thrown well above the ordinary level of foliage. These should be left as they are a sign of extra vigour and well being.

K. latifolia L. forms a rather dense bush with a stout branch system, and no pruning is needed with a healthy specimen. The policy should be to preserve a furnished effect over the bush as a whole. A straggly plant is the result of poor growth and a weak branch system and the general appearance is unhappy. Unsuitable growing conditions are most frequently the cause of this, and if the shrub is in a poor state of health it may not respond well to cutting back. A large specimen which has overgrown its position is difficult to deal with, but careful pruning back over a period of 3 to 5 years will be effective, choosing a few growths at a time and cutting them at a suitable point beneath the canopy of foliage. The only other method is to prune hard to a suitable size, but the rate of regeneration is often slow, even on a healthy bush.

Kalopanax

K. pictus (Thunb.) Nakai. This beautiful tree should be trained up to form a single lead, for not only is the bark more attractive on a large trunk, but the framework is also very much stronger. The main branches have an ascending habit and thus rival leads will form very acute angles with the main stem. The tree as a whole is sparsely branched, with very short spur systems. The latter even form on the main branches and trunk. The trunk should be kept clear of these and of branches up to a height of 1·8 to 2·4 m. (6 to 8 ft.), but the remainder are better if left.

This tree is outstanding for its fine foliage and this is seen to full advantage with an open foreground. Grown in this setting, the lower branches sweep down to eye level, despite a rather stiff habit.

The varieties have a similar habit.

Kerria

K. japonica (L.) DC. forms a close, bushy shrub, throwing up new canes from the base at ground level, which reach the height of the shrub at 1·2 to 1·8 m. (4 to 6 ft.) in one season. They flower in the following year. The shrub also spreads by means of suckerous growths and thus the whole area round it becomes a mass of intertwining stems and foliage. Often, the old, flowering shoots die back to strong, young growths which appear on the stem. This habit of flowering well on the young growths allows some of the old shoots to be cut out, either to a strong, young cane on the stem, or down to ground level, as the blossoms fade.

'Pleniflora' is similar in habit, but the pruning is more extensive, there being a greater need for this as the flowered growths which die back look unsightly. Often the young growths produce a scattered display of flowers in the autumn. 'Picta' is variegated with an attractive spread or tracery of branches. This variety does not sucker readily; in fact, there is a danger of reversion if this happens. Any growths which show reversion should be cut out.

Koelreuteria

K. paniculata Laxm. is the species most commonly grown. At its best it will form a tree 9·0 m. (30 ft.) or more in height, with a definite trunk and a sound branch system. Good nursery stock should have a clear stem of 0·6 to 0·9 m. (2 to 3 ft.) at planting time, with a central lead. After planting out, this lead should be retained, and as the tree develops the lower branches will often die through lack of light, thus allowing a clear trunk to form which may be 1·2 to 1·5 m. (4 to 5 ft.) or even more in height. At a later stage the lower branches will sweep down to within 0·6 to 0·9 m. (2 to 3 ft.) of the ground, if unrestricted by shade or growth. This tree is light-demanding, and growths which are shaded will not flower and may even die. 'Fastigiata', is a rare form with a habit similar to that of the Lombardy Poplar.

Kolkwitzia

K. amabilis Graebn. From the nursery stage, when a bushy habit should be encouraged, this plant sends out strong, arching growths as it becomes established. These should be left to grow freely and unpruned, for the arching habit continues at maturity. From these main branches, whole lengths of old and weak wood should be cut out immediately after flowering in July. Many of these will be found on the underside of the branch system and they should be cut back to a suitable point. The lower, furnishing branches should be left as they are quite attractive and add to a natural effect.

This shrub may reach 1·8 m. (6 ft.) or more feet in height with a considerable spread and yet, with its upright, arching habit, it can be grown fairly close to the edge of the border, for example, 1·2 m. (4 ft.), without interfering with mowing operations.

+Laburnocytisus

+*L. adamii* (Poit.) *Schneid.* This graft hybrid, *Laburnum anagyroides* Med.+ *Cytisus purpureus* Scop. is normally grown as a standard and is similar in habit to *Laburnum*. No pruning is required other than the removal of suckers. Occasionally, however, a specimen will grow out of its chimaera form, eventually becoming a complete specimen of *Laburnum*. This appears to be the result of pure *Laburnum* tissue growing out very strongly and any such tendency should be checked by pruning.

Laburnum

This is a small genus of trees. They are small and quite fast-growing, but often only remain in perfect condition for a short period when compared to longer living trees. Forms and hybrids are often propagated by budding on lined-out stock. Growth from this is so rapid in the first season that a 1·8 m. (6 ft.) leg is quite easily formed. This is quite a popular form, although they are often grown as bushes or feathered trees. Once the head and main framework has been developed they need very little pruning. Any large branches which need to be removed should be attended to in July or August, as bleeding may occur if this is done in the spring. Large wounds do not heal rapidly, especially with a mature specimen, and a careful watch should therefore be kept on these, for deterioration of the heart wood often sets in rapidly once air and moisture gain access.

L. anagyroides Med. responds to spur pruning, the young growths being taken back almost to the older wood, leaving only one to two buds. This should be carried out during the early winter. They are often trained in this way to cover archways and pergolas. In the early years, the positioning of the main growths should be studied carefully. Crossing branches, and those which are badly placed, should be removed at an early stage. Low branching fan-shaped specimens are best suited for this purpose. Wisterias, also winter pruned, are effective when allowed to climb and grow in conjunction with Laburnum which has been trained in this way.

Lapageria

L. rosea Ruiz. and Pav. is a twining shrub which can only be grown outside in very mild districts on a sheltered wall and in partial shade. There should be vertical strands stretched between the horizontal wires. Pruning consists of cutting out the weaker stems in the spring before the new growth commences. Naturally, the best of the growths break from the thicker and healthier stems, and by careful timing, injury to the new growth can be avoided. Should any of the remaining stems become loose on their support during this operation, they should be carefully tied back in position.

Lardizabala

L. biternata Ruiz & Pav. This shrub climbs vigorously by means of long, twining stems. It is only satisfactory against a wall in the warmer parts of the country. Vertical strands should be stretched between the horizontal wires to facilitate climbing in the early stages.

Pruning consists of cutting away old and weak growths and dead wood in the spring. This must be done carefully to avoid disturbance and damage to the remainder of the shrub. Young growths which develop from low down on the stem system should be encouraged. Any which develop beyond the bounds should be cut off, if they cannot be tied in without crowding.

Larix

The Larches are very distinct in habit, and when grown under good conditions a straight trunk is formed through the centre of the tree, the branches radiating from this. A good lead should be encouraged, but it is noticeable that with a vigorously growing tree, a broken leader is replaced by growths from adventitious buds or by the upper branches which develop an upright habit.

Larches are light-demanding, and with close planting the lower branches are lost one by one, as height is gained and the light taken from them. Thinning at such an advanced stage is not the complete answer, for although new growths are produced from the bare trunks, they develop very slowly and may never reach the proportions of the original branches. Thinning, unless carefully carried out, may also lead to considerable gale damage.

Single specimens in sheltered positions may be quite heavily branched, provided there is no shading, but a distinct and straight trunk is essential. *L. decidua* Mill. is fine when grown as a specimen, with its large branches sweeping down almost to ground level. The Japanese Larch, *L. leptolepis* (Sieb. & Zucc.) Gord. is also recommended for this purpose, but the branches often spread more horizontally.

Laurelia

L. sempervirens (Ruiz & Pav.) Tulesne. This must be grown in the shelter of a wall, where it will form a self-supporting tree or large bush. It may be run up on a single lead. It needs considerable head room, but restrictive pruning may be carried out on the width, cutting back into the branches in order to conceal the cuts. Often, the main stem needs one or two ties back to the wall to prevent the specimen from being blown about.

Laurus

These are thickly branched trees or shrubs with a plentiful supply of young growth. *L. nobilis* L. is hardier than *L. canariensis* Webb & Berth., which should definitely be grown in the shelter of a wall. The leads should be left to grow up strongly without pruning, although if it is necessary to restrict the size, this may be carried out in the spring, carefully positioning the cuts inside the bush to hide them. These shrubs regenerate very strongly and will often break into growth even if killed back to near ground level by severe winter weather.

L. nobilis, the Bay Laurel, is often grown in tubs and clipped to a formal design. The shape is maintained by carefully cutting back the new growths several times during the summer, using a pair of secateurs. This species also withstands exposed positions near the south and west coasts.

Lavandula

L. spica Cav. is the most common species, but there is a number of cultivated forms available which vary in height and vigour, a factor which must be taken into account when pruning. Left unattended without any pruning, the shrub eventually becomes weedy with many bare stems. Regular pruning keeps it more compact and decorative. This should be carried out in March or April, just as the new growth has begun, when the branch system may be shortened to a point where only a sufficient number of new shoots is left to develop and furnish the bush. The hand shears may be used for this work. It is unwise to cut back hard into the old wood, as this does not break freely. It is therefore better to keep a plant in condition from an early stage by pruning annually than to allow it to grow unpruned for several years, when it is easier to make a replacement and start again. Young plants are pruned hard, even in the nursery, to encourage a bushy habit. In order to make the shrub appear tidy for the winter the old flower stems may be cut back in the late autumn.

Lavender is often used as formal hedging, but it is pruned according to the same system.

The advice is sometimes given to prune after flowering, but as a general rule the spring is the better time. The young growths are then protected by the mature foliage for the winter, while they grow away without check with the improved weather conditions.

The other species may also be improved by pruning, but a number are tender and need a sheltered and sunny position.

Lavatera

L. olbia L. 'Rosea'. This shrub is not fully hardy and should be grown in a sheltered position. Usually, a woody framework of older branches survives and the new growths break freely from these in the spring. The flowers are produced along the terminal length of the current season's wood and this flowering portion dies back naturally as the fruits ripen. Unpruned, this shrub develops a loose, untidy habit and once the framework is formed, the young growths should be cut back annually in the spring to near their bases, waiting, however, until there is little danger of severe weather.

Ledum

The members of this genus need very little pruning, especially if they are growing healthily. In fact, once it becomes necessary to cut out dead wood, it is often a sign that the shrub is deteriorating. Ledums are often happier when growing in association with other shrubs which have similar requirements and pruning may then be necessary on these neighbouring subjects to prevent encroachment. However, it may be preferable to cut back the occasional long, straggly growth which spoils the appearance of the bush, or even pulls it out of shape. Such cuts should be made in the spring as growth is commencing. Thin bushes may regenerate, if they are cut back and there are sufficient growths left, but conditions generally should also be improved and it is often better to begin again with fresh plants.

Ledums produce young growth during and just after flowering, and their health and vigour is improved by removing the heads as the blossoms fade in order to prevent seed production. Care is needed to avoid damage to the young growths, but with a little practice this can be done by hand. Mulching and watering if necessary may be beneficial at this stage.

Leiophyllum

L. buxifolium (Berg.) Ell. In order to keep this small shrub tidy, the clusters of dead flowers may be cut off as the blossoms fade in the summer. Eventually, when the plant becomes old with a worn, untidy appearance, hard cutting back should be resorted to. This should be carried out in the late spring and new growths will be produced during the summer. At this stage it may, however, be considered better to start again with rooted pieces which may sometimes be found round the plant, or with freshly propagated material.

Leptodermis

L. kumaonensis Parker. This shrub loves to grow in the shelter of a sunny wall in a well drained position. It should be allowed to grow and branch freely when young as most of the growth is put on by the leading shoots. Often, the furnishing at the base of the shrub is poor. While it is young it may be necessary to stake the rather slender growths. It does not always break out well when damaged by frost. Normally, little pruning is required.

Leptospermum

This genus is made up of sun lovers which must also have a mild climate. Wall protection is often necessary, but they should be grown as bushes in this situation and not trained against the surface.

Normally, very little pruning is necessary, and in this country they do not break readily from old wood if they are cut down to it. In order to encourage a bushy habit, pruning should be carried out in late spring, on young growths, before hardening and ripening take place.

Lespedeza

The woody members of this genus are killed down to ground level each winter. They are best grown in a sunny, well drained and sheltered border, with a protective layer of bracken or loose straw placed round the bases for the winter. In the spring the old growths are cut down to ground level. These shrubs flower on the current season's growth.

Leucothoe

Very little pruning is required. Those species such as *L. catesbaei* (Walt.) Grey which have an attractive arching habit should be planted well back from the edge if in a border, in order to show this to full effect. Pruning to restrict the shrubs can easily spoil their appearance.

If it does become necessary, a few of the oldest and weakest growths may be cut out after flowering in May, provided that the bushes are left well furnished with younger growths. The aim should be to make the cut at ground level, thus retaining a natural, branching habit.

Leycesteria

L. formosa Wall. has a stool-like habit of growth, breaking freely from the base with strong, green, hollow-stemmed shoots which reach the full height of the shrub and flower in one season. If it is left to grow completely unpruned it will become thick and congested with many weak growths.

Pruning consists of thinning out the older and weaker shoots in the spring before growth commences, taking these right down to ground level. An alternative plan is to cut all top growth down hard each spring, to within 50 to 80 mm. (2 or 3 in.) of ground level. This treatment, however, must be accompanied by heavy mulching and feeding, with watering if necessary.

In an exposed position, the hollow stems are sometimes broken in strong winds.

Libocedrus

L. decurrens Torr. is the species most commonly grown. It is columnar and should be grown as a single specimen, when, with an adequate amount of light, the foliage will be retained in a good condition down to near ground level, *see* Plate 75. The natural habit, in the early years at least, is to form a single lead, but rivals often appear as the tree gets older and gains height. There is no need to worry about this, as it does allow the tree to gain an increase in width proportional to its height.

Old specimens, particularly those in industrial areas or exposed to the pollution of large cities, often lose a considerable amount of foliage, leaving exposed to view a mass of dead stems and branch systems. This, in addition to spoiling the appearance, is a danger sign and, if left unattended, such specimens deteriorate further until recovery is out of the question. The dead wood should be cut out and a programme of feeding and watering and, if necessary, aeration by spiking, should be adopted in order to encourage recovery and a better appearance.

Ligustrum

This genus is most commonly represented in gardens by *L. ovalifolium* Hassk., the Oval-leaf Privet, as a hedge plant, but there are quite a number of species which will, if allowed to grow freely and pruned correctly, form shapely bushes equally as decorative as many other shrubs. Perhaps it is because it is such a good hedge plant and responds so well to clipping, that it is never thought of as a free-growing bush and it is concluded that the whole genus is therefore worthless for any other purpose. Most of the species regenerate very strongly if hard pruned and many throw young shoots freely from the base.

L. lucidum Ait. is the strongest grower, with erect main branches, and it may even be grown on a 0·6 to 0·9 m. (2 to 3 ft.) leg. The laterals from these main branches are spreading and are gradually weighed down by extending growths.

It is at its best when allowed to branch low on the edge of a lawn. The young shoots, which develop from the main branches as they become horizontal, should be left, as they will help to thicken up the centre.

The remaining species and varieties, if allowed to grow freely, should be pruned when necessary so that the natural habit is retained. The mode of growth varies considerably within the genus; for example, *L. obtusifolium* Sieb. & Zucc. var. *regelianum* (Koehne) Rehd. has a spreading habit, while *L. japonicum* Thunb. 'Rotundifolium' has a compact, stiff habit and also needs shelter. There is even considerable variation in habits of growth among the varieties of such common species as *L. vulgare* L. Three which are stiff upright growers are 'Densiflorum', 'Fastigiatum' and 'Glaucum'. Their habit makes them suitable for close planting to form a screen in exposed coastal districts. The type plant could also be planted more extensively in these and other wind-swept conditions. This plant is found colonising the lee slopes of sand dunes where the winds do all the pruning which is necessary.

L. ovalifolium and the cultivar 'Aureo-Variegatum' are commonly used as hedge plants. After planting for this purpose, the young shrubs should be pruned back to within 300 mm. (12 in.) of ground level and taken back hard for 2 or 3 years afterwards in order to fill out the base before too much height is put on. This hedge needs clipping frequently during the growing season, but if it is overgrown it will respond to hard cutting back on both the top and the sides. The response will be very quick if it is carried out in April.

Lindera

These seldom require pruning, apart from the removal of any dead tips or branches which may have been killed back during the winter. Their powers of regeneration are often very good and they can be expected to break into growth, even from the old wood at the base, after a severe winter has killed all the top growth.

L. praecox (Sieb. & Zucc.) Bl., hardy only in the warmer localities, is bushy from the base and has a stool-like growth with dense upright branches. In the most favoured positions it may be trained, with one to three stems only, to form a small tree.

This species may also be trained against a south-facing wall. At an early stage it is pruned hard back to encourage the development of a number of growths which are then trained out fan-wise. Informal, twiggy growths are left to develop from this framework. They require little pruning, unless they extend too far from the wall, in which case they may be carefully shortened to hide the cuts. A hard pruning of these lateral growths back to the main branches usually results in a free production of young growths round the edges of the wounds which may require thinning. Under this system of culture a cluster of sucker-like growths often springs out annually from the base. It is better to remove these as they appear during the growing season, than to leave them until the end of the season.

L. benzoin (L.) Bl. also forms a rounded bush, while *L. megaphylla* Hemsl. an evergreen, is more upright in growth.

Lippia

L. citriodora H. B. & K. In nature, this species forms a small tree, but it is not perfectly hardy and thus does not reach these proportions in this country. In the mildest parts it may be grown as a bush in the open, but wall protection is usually necessary, and even with this it may be killed outright during a severe winter. A proportion of the young growths are killed each winter, and these should be pruned back to living wood in the spring just as the buds break. Frequently this means going right back to the older wood. The inflorescences, which terminate the current season's growth, are larger and more effective as a result of hard pruning, provided it is accompanied by feeding and mulching.

In addition to growing this subject as a bush at the foot of a wall, the growths may be trained to the surface, when much of the wood will be retained from year to year. The pruning is much the same, the previous year's growths being taken back to the main framework in the spring.

In colder districts a loose bracken protection round the basal branches may be necessary to save the shrub during the winter.

Liquidambar

The hardiest and most widely grown species is *L. styraciflua* L., forming a large and beautiful tree. In the nursery stage it should be encouraged to grow freely with a strong central lead. It should be transplanted at an early stage, but larger trees are said to withstand a move better, if the side branches are drastically pruned just before the move is made in the early winter. A good, mature tree forms a long, straight trunk with a beautiful bark effect. This characteristic may be enhanced by cutting off the lower branches flush with the trunk up to 4·6 to 6·0 m. (15 to 20 ft.) as the overall height increases. Even from this height the lower and outer branches, which are pendulous, will, with encouragement, spread and drop down to eye level, allowing the full beauty of the foliage, especially when tinted in the autumn, to be seen to best effect.

L. orientalis Mill. is a slow-growing tree very similar in general appearance and habit to *Acer campestre* L. When young, this tree is full of twiggy growth, but from this the lead and the main branches form. A sharp watch should be kept to ensure that a central lead is kept for at least 6·0 m. (20 ft.), otherwise the branching becomes very heavy which leads to weakness later in life. At maturity, the pendulous outer branches reach right down to ground level. It is a tree for the edge of a planting.

L. formosana Hance and the variety *L. f.* var. *monticola* Rehd. & Wils. are both liable to be injured by late spring frosts, if they occur just as growth is breaking. This, to a lesser extent, also is likely with the other species. Following such damage, it may be necessary to train another lead by stopping rival branches during growth.

Liriodendron

L. tulipifera L., the Tulip Tree, is commonly found in tree collections. The best form in which to grow this is with a strong central lead. The branches are then well spaced and are able to carry a considerable amount of growth when the tree reaches full size at maturity. The extreme ends of the branches are often semi-pendulous and will reach ground level with encouragement. This will allow the interesting flowers to be inspected at close quarters.

The best form in which to plant this tree is as a feathered specimen, for establishment will be easier than with an older tree. The trunk is cleared of growths up to a height of 2 to 3 m. as the head develops. However, young trees are available as standards and with care they may be successfully established. These should never be without a lead. Specimens which are left to branch low without a central lead, reach a stage when each limb carries considerable weight and weakness may develop in a crotch with disastrous results. Bracing is often necessary with a mature specimen in this condition.

Apart from the training, there is little need for pruning. However, some trees show a tendency to throw strong, upright shoots, even from mature horizontal branches. This should be corrected by pruning, otherwise the head will be thrown completely out of balance. Epicormic growths need not be removed unless they are thick and unsightly. Provided that the tree is healthy with a naturally thick canopy, these are not troublesome.

With the cultivar 'Fastigiatum' which is narrow and upright in habit, branching should be left to develop from ground level.

L. chinense (Hemsl.) Sarg. will also form a good lead, but it appears to have a slender branching system.

Lithocarpus

L. densiflorus Rehd. This is the only species which is normally hardy in this country. In the earlier years it forms a pyramidal tree with a slender branch system. If possible, the lead should be retained, for a strong framework is needed as the foliage is very heavy and the slender stems of rival leads are easily weighed down and broken, especially under snow or during a gale. Even a properly trained specimen should be given a sheltered position. There will often be small pieces of dead wood to cut out, especially after a severe winter.

Lithospermum

L. diffusum Lag. Two cultivars of this species are popular, 'Heavenly Blue' and 'Grace Ward'. Left to grow unattended year after year this species often develops into a large but untidy mat. In addition, exposed parts of a clump die back during the winter. A restricted amount of pruning is beneficial after flowering, taking out the weaker and dead growths and letting light into the clump. An inspection may also be made in the spring. It is possible to lift the mat of growth and cut the dead wood out from beneath.

Lomatia

This is an uncommon genus in our gardens, for the species are not sufficiently hardy for most of the country and can only be grown in the mildest districts of the south and west. Very little pruning is required and the shrubs furnish up well and throw up new shoots from the base. Thus there is a chance of replacing old growths which may need cutting out.

Lonicera

In habits of growth, the members of this genus exhibit a wide variety and yet, as far as the horticulturist and pruning policies are concerned, there are three distinct groups; (a) the shrubs or bushes with branches and growths springing from the base; (b) the climbers which flower on the current season's wood; and (c) the climbers which flower on the previous year's wood.

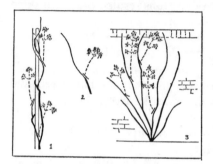

Fig. 38. A simplified diagram showing the pruning of a climbing form of *Lonicera* (Subgenus Periclymenum). This flowers on the previous year's wood.
(1) Trained to a pole.
(2) A close-up showing how the flowering portion, indicated by the broken line, may be pruned as the flowers fade.
(3) The pruning of a wall-trained specimen.

Group (a). *The shrubs or bushes with branches and growths springing from the base.*

These are found in three of the sections of the Subgenus I Chamaecerasus, namely Sect. 1. Isoxylosteum, Sect. 2. Isika and Sect. 3. Coeloxylosteum. Their habit generally is typical of shrubs which regenerate well by sending up young growths after being cut back, both from the base and from the mature branch systems.

Pruning consists of removing old wood when it is weak and perhaps partly dead, taking the cut back to a suitable point just above a promising growth. Branches which arch over will often produce upright growths from their lower portions, and these may be in an ideal position to be used as replacements. Care should be taken to retain the natural habit, otherwise by frequently cutting all arching branches to an upright growth, bare sections of the old wood will be visible, especially during the winter months. It is, however, difficult to restrict the growth of a large-spreading shrub by pruning and at the same time retain the natural effect and habit, and far more attention should be given to selection in the first place, before planting.

A considerable variation in habit is found even among the shrub species. For example, *L. quinquelocularis* Hardw. produces a few branches at the base which later become quite large and, being often twisted and gnarled, are full of character. The same is true of some others, but many more branch freely from ground level and in addition produce a mass of new growths, also from the base. Thus the difference in pruning, for the oldest wood on the latter species may, if necessary, be cut down completely to ground level after flowering. As the species with weaker growths and main stems extend, they sometimes arch over and even spread on the ground during wet weather or as a result of a snowfall.

L. nitida Wils. one of the evergreen, shrubby honeysuckles, is very easily propagated, is fast growing and responds well to frequent clipping on a rigid line, and is therefore suitable as a formal hedge plant. It is, however, liable to be blown over and out of line at the top, especially if the feature is in an exposed position. This fault may be overcome at planting time by the erection of a fence consisting of two or three strands of wire over the actual planting line. The hedge plants grow on either side of this and are thus held firmly in position. After a number of years as a hedge plant, this subject often loses foliage from the older and lower branches and thus becomes bare at the base. Hard pruning, even down to within 150 mm. of ground level, is an effective answer to this and work of this nature should be carried out in the early summer. As stated earlier, this subject is a vigorous and rapid grower, and requires frequent clipping during the summer months.

Group (b). *The climbers which flower on the current season's wood.*

This group is made up of the few species which twine, with their flowers in pairs, they are in the Section Nintooa. The most common species is *L. japonica* Thunb. It is a vigorous grower and will climb and ramble over stumps or small trees. Sometimes it is grown on a pergola or archway, but it is not an easy subject to prune by accepted methods. However, it is possible to keep it within bounds by hard clipping over the entire surface in the spring with a pair of shears. In this way it may be kept within bounds and be grown along a fence, e.g. chestnut paling. Treated in this way, new growths soon break out to flower some weeks later.

Group (c). *The climbers which flower on the previous year's wood.*

Species in the Subgenus II Periclymenum are in this group. The Woodbine or Honeysuckle, *L. periclymenum* L. is an example. They are pruned by cutting out a portion of the vines which have produced the flowers as soon as these fade, *see* Fig. 38 (1 & 2). It should be noted that the flowers are formed on short laterals from a vine which has been made during the previous year. It is this vine or twining stem which is cut out, but great care must be taken to avoid injury to the young, developing ones. These are often intertwined with the older ones. When these climbing subjects are growing in a natural setting, some of the smaller growths may be left to hang down from the supporting branches. In this position the flowering heads are attractive. When these are pruned after flowering, young replacement growths are left hanging down in their place to produce the flower display the following season.

Species for Wall Culture. Generally they are not ideally suited for wall culture. *L. fragrantissima* Lindl. & Paxt., one of the winter-flowering shrubby species, is sometimes wall-trained for the earlier display produced under the more sheltered conditions. It is only really successful if the shrub is attended to especially as far as pruning is concerned. The main branches are tied out to cover the feature and may be replaced later, if necessary, by the promising growths which often spring from the base. The flowering laterals are left to develop from the wall and are pruned back to suitable growths in the spring after flowering. By this system the extension of the lateral branches is restricted and kept reasonably close to the wall. Strong growths, which spring from the base and which are not required for replacement, may be cut out as they develop during the growing season. A wall specimen which is out of control through years of neglect may be pruned back very hard during the winter, either to suitable growths on the main branches or even harder.

The climbing species may also be grown against a wall, but under hot, dry conditions pests are often troublesome. Pruning is on the lines already described, the *L. japonica* types being clipped back hard over the surface in the early spring, and the *L. periclymenum* group pruned after flowering by the removal of the older wood. A vertical system of wires should be attached between the horizontal strands for additional support to the young growth, *see* Fig. 38.

The tender species, *L. sempervirens* L., appreciates wall protection. It belongs to Group (c).

Lupinus

L. arboreus Sims. This rapidly-growing shrub normally branches freely when it is young. Pruning consists of cutting off the old heads of flower, leaving sufficient for seed if desired. This is followed by spring pruning, when the younger growths may be shortened and some of the oldest and weakest wood cut out completely. Despite this treatment the shrub is often short-lived and it is wise to raise young plants for succession.

Lycium

These rather untidy shrubs respond well to hard cutting back and this should be resorted to when the mass of shoots gets completely out of hand. This may be considered part of their treatment every few years. The growth generally is rather spreading, but corrective pruning, carried out annually, delays the need for a more drastic operation. This annual pruning may be carried out during the winter. It consists of cutting away any dead growths, searching for these beneath the branches where they tend to collect, and at the same time reducing heavy horizontal growths back to suitable young and upright shoots near the centre of the bush. Any young growths which are too long may be shortened.

These shrubs are often grown in open spaces near the coast where they do not require pruning. They are also used for hedging purposes, being cut back hard in the spring, although at least one trim may be necessary during the summer if the feature is to be kept close and formal in outline.

Lyonia

L. ligustrina (L.) DC. is the most commonly grown species. It is dense growing, branching freely from ground level, and strong young growths are also sent up from the base if the shrub is doing well. This does give an opportunity for a limited amount of pruning, as the oldest growths may be cut out completely at ground level. The extent to which this is done should depend entirely upon the age and vigour of the shrub. The natural habit is close and the bush should be left well furnished. This advice also holds for the varieties of this species.

Maackia

M. amurensis Rupr. This species is often shrubby but it may develop into a small tree. The lead should be retained on a young nursery plant. Branching is naturally sparse and vigour and health will be the deciding factors in determining the ultimate height a specimen reaches before the head opens completely. The branching has a flattened appearance and there appear to be few trailing branches. *M. chinensis* Takeda has an ascending branch system, and may be trained to a definite tree form. The branching is also sparse but the ends are more twiggy. It may be grown on a 0·6 to 1·2 m. (2 to 4 ft.) leg.

Maddenia

M. hypoleuca Koehne. This is grown as a shrub or small tree and should be encouraged to branch at soil level in the nursery. The main branches are ascending, while the laterals tend to be horizontal in habit. In the initial years of training the centre of the bush should be kept open. Occasionally, strong growths appear from near the base and grow up through the centre of the bush, but unless any of these are needed for replacement purposes they should be cut out, as they may ultimately spoil the shape. Otherwise, no regular pruning is necessary.

Magnolia

Magnolias grow and develop best in a well sheltered position, for the wood is brittle and the branches are liable to be torn off by severe winds. They must be kept growing well in order to produce a good shape. Magnolias usually show great powers of regeneration and may throw strong young growths from really old wood. Advantage may be taken of this by cutting damaged specimens back carefully, if necessary correcting the positions of the final cuts a year or so later, when the most suitable growths may be selected (*see* Plate 18). This power of regeneration is also a great help in overcoming the effects of bad training in a young specimen, especially with bush types such as *M. soulangeana* Soul., which branch low. Large scale pruning, if it becomes necessary, should be carried out in late July, thus avoiding the risk of bleeding, while leaving sufficient time for the healing processes to get under way before the winter sets in. All wound surfaces over 12 mm. (half an inch) in diameter should be protected with a suitable dressing, for the heartwood is soft and rot quickly sets in. Cavities should also be promptly dealt with.

The need to keep Magnolias growing well applies to all plants, trees and shrubs, yet many an old specimen has flowered so extensively that its vigour has been exhausted, particularly when a heavy crop of seed has followed. The result has been little or no growth, followed quickly by death as the energies were completely dried up. The avoidance of such a disaster is sometimes possible by carefully picking off the flowers as they wither and by feeding and, if necessary, watering. As with so many subjects, the main pointer to watch is the amount of growth which is being put on early in the season.

The form of tree or bush should be carefully considered. In the nursery the young plants should be left to grow naturally and to form a lead. Strong rival branches should not be left unattended and the necessary action must be taken early. With the bush forms such as *M. soulangeana*, the vigour of the leader will soon weaken as the branches increase in girth and extent. As specimens of both the bush and tree types reach maturity, the lower branch systems should be encouraged to grow and develop, even down to ground level. The individual flowers are of great beauty and they can be appreciated better if they are within reach.

Many of the vigorous growers throw strong suckers and sometimes epicormic growths, which run up through the centre of the bush. This needs careful judgement for they should be encouraged, perhaps with some thinning, if the older branches are weak or in need of replacement. Otherwise, they should be regularly removed before they become too large, or spoil the character and shape of the bush. Also they may, if left, reduce the vigour of the older branches. Eventually very low and heavy branches may need some support, either by bracing, or by the use of a forked prop.

M. campbellii Hook. f. and the other species and hybrids, including *M. c. sub. sp. mollicomata* W. W. Sm., are strong growers which can be trained very easily to form a central lead. The tendency to form a really strong lead is greater among seedlings, and thus the initial years of training young nursery stock obtained by grafting is important. Young plants of this group take many years to come into flower, but there appears to be some evidence that plants with a lead flower earlier than those which are forced to break and branch low. Seedlings often produce growths from the base when 4 or 5 years old, but if the lead is strong there is little chance of these spoiling the shape. One of the most untidy growers is often *M.* × *thompsoniana* (Loud.) Sarg., for the branches are very widespreading and they rest on each other as they become heavy. It is difficult to correct this habit if it develops.

M. grandiflora L. is ideal for growing in the shelter of a large, south-facing wall. For this purpose it should be trained up for at least two-thirds of its height with a central lead. Often, it is necessary to tie only the main branches to the wall. *M. delavayi* Franch. usually needs wall protection. It produces very strong wood and requires a large wall, where a strong central lead can be encouraged.

× Mahoberberis

× *M. neuberti* (Baumann) Schneid. often develops an untidy habit which may be corrected by pruning back loose, straggly growths to suitable buds. This should be carried out in the spring.

Mahonia

The most commonly grown species of this genus is *M. aquifolium* (Pursh) Nutt. It is a strong-growing subject and will extend and colonise by means of suckers.

It should therefore be planted where there is scope for development, but it can be restricted by pruning and by removing the suckers.

It is very tolerant of bad conditions and can be planted on banks and in shady positions, but often, in such situations, the upright growths are weak and produce little flower. In addition, they may become untidy and full of fallen leaves and dead twigs etc. Such areas and clumps may be cut over in April, taking all the upright growths down to 100 to 200 mm. (a few inches). This may either be carried out at intervals of a few years, or on an annual basis if required.

In the open, a thick mass 1 or 2 m. (3 or 6 ft.) in height is formed and very little pruning is necessary. Some of the varieties and forms such as 'Undulata' have an upright habit, often without suckers, and thus form a bush rather than a clump.

Many of the larger-leaved species and varieties such as *M. japonica* (Thunb.) DC. have a stiff, erect habit and a beauty of form which would be spoilt by pruning. It may become necessary to cut out dead wood, but the need rarely arises. Breaks should be encouraged along the length of the stems and from the base, if they arise. In the same way, branching from ground level should be encouraged in the nursery.

A number of species, such as *M. napaulensis* DC., need a mild climate and all the large-leaved forms appreciate shelter. *M. nevinii* Fedde is not sufficiently hardy to be grown in the open in most districts and usually needs wall protection. It may be grown as a bush in the shelter of a wall or actually tied up to the face fanwise on a supporting wire system. Growths are freely thrown up from the base, and this allows the longer and older branches to be cut out at ground level, replacing them with younger shoots.

Malus

The species comprising this genus are mainly small or medium-sized trees, the larger growers reaching up to 9·0 m. (30 ft.) or more. They are strong and reliable and the main branches on an old specimen, even when holed or full of cavities, are able to withstand considerable strain. This, of course, is no excuse for allowing a tree to get into this condition, or for allowing such a state to continue once it has occurred. The well-balanced tree, maintained in a good condition, will always have much to commend it, and it will be a much better long-term proposition.

The form of tree is important and there is much in favour of the feathered type which has a strong central leader. This may seem at first to be contrary to general practice, for many very good nursery trees are produced which are standards with an open branching head. Yet fruit trees with a central leader are preferred by many, and this does seem to be the more natural mode of growth. The branches will be equally spaced round this leader which eventually opens out to form the topmost system on the crown, thus the weight is more evenly spread along the length of the leader. Also, by using the feathered tree, it is possible to encourage a much lower branching and under certain circumstances this may be desirable, as a tree with a central lead on a 0·8 m. (2½ ft.) clear leg can be very attractive. In other cases, however, a 1·8 to 2·4 m. (6 or 8 ft.) clear length of trunk may be preferred. It may be more difficult to restrict the lateral

P

spread of an open-centred, wide-branching tree, while there is also another important point – often another lead develops and is left to grow through the centre of the tree, making the removal of the first one seem to have been unnecessary.

As the trees mature, epicormic growths may develop on the more horizontal branch systems. These are indeed unsightly, yet they are more likely to be found on specimens which have been thinned out in the centre to let in the light and air. There seems to be little point in doing this; in fact, a twisted and crowded head of branches in a Malus is to be expected and is thus more natural, typical and also more interesting. Once the main framework has been established, a natural head of growth is advocated. Often, this may mean that the outer and lower branches become pendulous. This, for example, is the habit of *M. pumila* Mill. whose trunk and main branches are often very crooked with a matted head, which is characteristic of the species. *M. trilobata* (Poir.) Schneid. is distinct from many others in having an upright growth with a pyramidal habit.

As in many cases Malus are grafted, it is important to remove all suckers, particularly those which spring from below the union, which is usually at ground level.

Mandevilla

M. suaveolens Lindl. This is a slender, twining shrub and is only suitable for a very sunny corner or wall in the mildest parts of the country. On a wall, vertical strands should be stretched between the horizontal wires.

Pruning consists of cutting out the dead wood and weaker growths in the spring as the shrub becomes active. There should be no hesitation in cutting out some of the older wood, provided that no damage is done to the growths which remain, for they are often wound very tightly together. This shrub breaks out readily from the older wood.

Marsdenia

M. erecta (L.) R. Br. This deciduous climber produces long growths which twine in an anti-clockwise direction. It is not hardy and a sunny wall or a sheltered position is necessary. Neither is it particularly ornamental and, owing to the danger of blistering on the skin caused by the milky juice which the plant exudes when it is pruned, it is rarely grown. It is also very poisonous. If it is grown there will be some need for pruning, for the twining shoots will overgrow all but the largest of positions. They should be cut back during the summer and autumn, using the long-arm pruners to keep clear of the cuts. A final check over the plant at closer quarters with the secateurs may be made in the spring, cutting out some of the older wood. This work should be undertaken from the top of the plant downwards, as this reduces the danger of the cut ends coming into contact with the skin. Gloves should be worn.

Medicago

M. arborea L. is not completely hardy and in most gardens it thrives better in the shelter of a wall. Normally, no pruning is required. Some cutting back is necessary after a severe winter, but it may not break out if the damage extends into the old wood.

Melaleuca

These are tender shrubs and need a very mild and favoured locality. *M. squarrosa* Sm. seems to be a little hardier than the remainder and it may be successful in a sheltered sunny corner against a wall. It should be left to grow freely, for it will not conform to rigid training. The younger wood may break into new growth following winter damage, but the old wood is more reluctant to do so when grown in the open in this country. No regular pruning is required.

Meliosma

There are two groups in this genus, one having pinnate and the other simple leaves. Generally, the species in the former group are tree-like, while those in the latter are more shrubby. It is important to recognise these two forms in the nursery, for a definite lead must be formed with the tree species.

Group 1. *Species which should be grown to a single lead.*

M. beaniana Rehd. & Wils. is a very rare species. *M. veitchiorum* Hemsl. is slow-growing, but produces branches which radiate naturally from the central stem with a sparse, almost spur-like habit. Ample all round space should be allowed for development. *M. oldhamii* Miq. has an ascending branch system, but again neighbouring trees or shrubs should, if necessary, be pruned back to allow for development. These are prone to frost damage in the spring as growth commences.

Group 2. *Species which should be left to branch naturally at the base.*

M. parvifolia Le Conte freely produces upright growths from which almost horizontal branches extend. The twig system is often tangled, but there should be no attempt to correct this as it is a natural habit. This species often regenerates well from around cuts. Both *M. cuneifolia* Franch and *M. pendens* Rehd. & Wils. freely produce young growths from ground level, and these can, if necessary, be used for replacing old branches.

Menispermum

M. canadense L. is a vigorous, twining shrub which will quickly cover a wall, trellis or similar structure up to a height of 3·7 m. (12 ft.). Vertical wires may be necessary to assist climbing. Once established, this subject is so vigorous that it can be cut down to nearly ground level each winter, when short woody stems will often build up below the point of pruning.

The alternative method is to cut down periodically, perhaps every two to three years. One other method is to avoid this drastic pruning completely and rely upon the cutting out of dead and weak wood to keep the shrub in condition, but this task, with such a tangle of growth, is a very difficult one.

Menziesia

During the winter these shrubs have the appearance of rather thin-wooded, deciduous azaleas. They are fairly erect in growth, with main branches which originate from below ground level. They are slow-growing, but as the bushes gain strength new growths are thrown up from beneath the soil. Little regular pruning is needed on the rather twiggy branch system, but dead wood and some of the weak growths may be cut out. There is only limited scope for this and it must be carried out carefully. Some pruning may be done after flowering, when the dead blooms may be cut off in order to prevent seeding and thus to encourage the shrub, but it is advisable to look over them again in the spring.

Mespilus

M. germanica L. This is normally grown as a 1·8 to 2·4 m. (6 to 8 ft.) standard. Usually, it has an open head without a central lead. The strong branches spread out laterally in rather an interesting manner and the tree as a whole has great character. The growths should be left to sweep down as low as possible. Often, if horizontal branches are cut short, strong epicormic growths appear which will, if left, thrust up through the crown to spoil the character of the tree completely. Dead wood should be cut out during the late summer. Normally, very little pruning is required.

Metasequoia

M. glyptostroboides Hu & Cheng, so recently discovered, has proved to be quite distinct from many other conifers in its habit of growth. One outstanding feature is the ease with which a new leader is formed, even from the older wood, if the injuries are extensive and provided, of course, that the tree concerned is young and vigorous. The habit appears to be columnar with a definite lead, which is naturally and readily maintained for the whole height of the tree. A furnishing down to ground level should be encouraged, as one of the beauties of this tree is the branch and twig growth, when seen at close quarters, which is effective at all seasons. Some variation in habit and growth can be expected among seedlings.

This subject is effective as a screen, where a planting distance of 3·7 to 4·6 m. (12 to 15 ft.) is recommended if it consists of a single line. If necessary, the laterals may be reduced in spread.

As a hedge plant this subject has not proved entirely successful, yet it makes an interesting feature and is so beautiful at all seasons. One of its faults is that hard pruning results in a considerable amount of top growth, this being very pronounced on forms which have an ascending branch system. A selection of the best forms for hedging is therefore advisable. A height of 1·5 to 1·8 m. (5 to 6 ft.) is suggested for this feature, and clipping should be carried out in July.

Metrosideros

Even *M. lucida* A. Rich, one of the hardiest species, requires a sheltered position in a very mild and favourable district. No pruning is necessary; rather, it is a fight to retain the shoots and foliage intact through the winter. A well-drained and warm soil is essential.

Michelia

These trees or shrubs are more suitable for the milder parts of the country. *M. compressa* Sarg. will, under favourable conditions, develop a lead, and every effort should be made to retain this for at least a metre or so until a head of branches is formed. *M. doltsopa* Buch.-Ham. may form a tree or shrub, depending upon environment, although in a very favourable situation with shelter, it is possible to retain a lead for some time.

M. figo Sprengler forms a very leafy shrub and occasionally the lateral branches have a horizontal habit. Often therefore, it is spreading, the young growths toward the centre of the bush being very upright. It is possible to restrict size by careful pruning, concealing the cuts and leaving an informal surface. In the mildest of localities it needs wall protection, but even so it is better grown as a free-standing shrub rather than hard trained against the surface.

Microglossa

M. albescens (DC.) Clarke is a semi-woody shrub which flowers on the ends of the current season's wood. However, growths which are produced from the previous year's wood are more likely to flower than those which spring up directly from the base. It should therefore be planted near the base of a south-facing wall where there will be more likelihood of the young growth surviving the winter. Pruning consists of cutting out the old growths in the spring to ground level. The strong, young growths which spring up from the base should be retained at full level if living. However, if die-back has occurred, they may be cut back to breaking buds, which are often found at ground level.

The entire removal of top growth often reduces any chance of flowers being produced the same season.

Mimulus

M. glutinosus Wendl. This is a woody subject, but it is tender and is most successful as a wall subject in the south-west. In this position and locality it may be trained to a support system, and pruned fairly hard back to the woody framework each spring. Alternatively, it may be grown as a bush. Often, it survives in less favourable areas if the wood at the base is protected with a mound of coarse sand. Young growths are thrown from the old wood very readily and the shrub will respond to hard pruning in late spring if this is necessary to correct a ragged appearance. When young, the shrub should be stopped once to encourage a bushy habit.

Morus

M. nigra L., the Black Mulberry, is often found in the older gardens, usually as ancient trees and thus of historical value. These old specimens may be heavily branched, this being a characteristic of old or mature trees. The danger that these will break, especially during summer gales when the branch system is heavy with fruit and foliage, is a very real one. Thinning, which should be carried out in the early winter, will help to reduce this danger, but it must be done with great care as otherwise it will spoil the shape and character of the tree. Bracing is often the better plan, for the branching usually gives way in one of the main crotches.

The standard is the ideal form in which to plant this and the other species but the lead should be retained for as long as possible in order to reduce the weight of branching. One of the advantages of a standard is that it is more difficult for children to climb in search of the fruit than a low-branching tree. Even with a standard, however, the lower branches may, with encouragement, grow down close to ground level.

M. alba L. is also heavily branched and the same advice applies. There are a number of varieties but, in general, there is a tendency for this group to throw epicormic growths, often in great quantity, especially from the horizontal branches. These must be pared back annually, otherwise they may spoil the character of the tree and may also cause die-back on the branch tips, especially during a drought. 'Pendula' needs to be trained by tying up the leading shoot until the desired height has been reached.

M. cathayana Hemsl. is quite distinct in growth and is more adaptable to training to a central lead.

Muehlenbeckia

M. complexa (A. Cunn.) Meissn. produces a mass of thin, wiry stems which will intertwine to form a close canopy over the ground. When sufficiently established it will also invade nearby shrubs, covering them thickly with a tangle of thin growths. Should it be necessary to restrict this subject, it will look most effective if care is taken to leave an informal edge. This means cutting away individual growths. A clipped effect, which results from masses of growth being cut off at one level or line, should be avoided. It may be necessary to do this two or three times during the growing season.

In a severe winter it may be cut down to ground level, but it should regenerate.

Mutisia

These climb by means of tendrils which are modifications of the midrib. Unless the district has a mild and favourable climate they should be grown against a sunny wall, at first being encouraged to climb on pea sticks planted nearby, or tied on to the wires. Should growth be healthy and vigorous, they may invade nearby plants, but this will not be excessive or harmful. Pruning consists of cutting out dead or weak growths in the summer, but great care is necessary in doing this or vital connecting growths will be severed.

Myrica

The members of this genus as a whole need very little pruning and usually this only consists of the removal of dead twigs during the summer. *M. gale* L. and

M. cerifera L. need to be grown in a clump with several plants together, as both are to some degree suckerous and therefore invasive. Tall and straggly branches will give a planting an untidy appearance, and such growths may be cut right down to ground level, for there are usually plenty of small suckerous shoots to train as replacements. There is no point in clearing the suckers among established plants as they act as ground cover. *M. californica* Cham. forms a large bush or small tree but does not sucker to any extent. In a severe winter this shrub may be killed back to near ground level, but usually growth will break out from any living tissue which is left in the spring.

Myricaria

This genus is closely related to *Tamarix*. All species flower on the current season's wood, and they respond to hard pruning back to the main framework in the spring. Without hard pruning, even while the frame is being built up, they quickly become straggly and unsightly.

Myrsine

One of the hardiest species in this genus is *M. africana* L., which forms a compact bush 0·6 to 0·9 m. (2 to 3 ft.) in height. It should be given wall protection and planted approximately one foot from the base. However, after severe weather or through old age, the shrub may develop an untidy appearance. Often, this takes the form of long, woody, bare shoots terminated by small bunches of bushy growths. Hard pruning in the spring will correct this.

Myrtus

M. communis L. is the most commonly grown, and it is one of the hardiest of a genus of evergreen shrubs or small trees, all of which are tender. In all but the most favoured districts it needs wall protection, but even in this situation it cannot be grown in the colder parts of the country. Normally it is not trained hard up against the surface of the wall, but is grown as a bush, being planted about 0·5 m. (1½ ft.) from the base. It has a dense habit with branching from ground level. The main branches are somewhat erect and it is completely self-supporting. Normally, no pruning is required, unless it becomes necessary to restrict the shrub, in which case the longer branches may be cut back to a suitable growth inside the bush, so that the wounds are hidden. This should be carried out in the spring. Should it be severely damaged or killed down to ground level by frost, it will often break freely from the old wood right at the base.

This shrub is sometimes grown hard up against the surface of a wall, where it will grow to considerable heights with only the minimum of support. Sometimes one sees the walls of old cottages in the West Country completely covered in this way, *see* Plate 47. The surface is clipped over once during the spring or early summer, and again at a later period if it becomes necessary.

The dwarf forms such as 'Tarentina' are compact and seldom need pruning, even to prevent encroachment.

The advice given for this species may also be applied to others which may be attempted in the milder districts, they seldom need any pruning.

Nandina

N. domestica Thunb. This subject is only really at home in the warmer localities, where it requires a sheltered position. In other areas, even though it may survive, it often has a ragged appearance, especially after a severe winter. With a strong growing specimen, vigorous growths are freely produced from the base and these may be used as replacements for the ragged growths, which can be cut out at ground level in the spring. Even young plants in the nursery will branch freely. The upright stems are unbranched and pruning at any point down this stem is not effective. They should be cut right off at ground level, if pruned at all.

Neillia

These shrubs have a stool-like growth, freely producing young canes from the base. Often, too, suckers are produced one foot or so from the parent, originating as adventitious buds on the roots. Pruning consists of cutting back some of the oldest wood to ground level, at the same time shortening the other mature branches back to suitable growths. Thus the old flowered portions are removed at the same time, letting light and air into the bush. This should be carried out immediately after flowering.

The extent of the pruning will depend upon the amount of young wood being produced; for example, *N. ribesioides* Rehd. does not always have sufficient for all the old wood to be cut away annually. The essential thing is to leave these shrubs well furnished with young growths which spring from the base and from older wood.

Nemopanthus

N. mucronatus (L.) Trel. This shrub is closely related to the deciduous group of Hollies. No pruning is necessary and it should be left to grow naturally from the nursery stage.

Neviusia

N. alabamensis Gray. This shrub develops a stool-like growth, gradually spreading as new canes are produced on the outside of the bush from ground level. These extend to the height of the shrub, 1·2 to 1·8 m. (4 to 6 ft.) in one season. Pruning consists of cutting out the older and thinner wood, either back to suitable growths or right down to ground level after flowering in May. In the nursery, the stool-like habit develops naturally.

Nothofagus

N. obliqua Bl. is a fast grower but care must be taken that a single lead is maintained. Trained in this way, the branches are well spaced round the trunk and the whole habit is attractive, as they sweep down at an angle. Eventually, as the tree gains height, additional lower branches may be removed to expose the trunk for 4·6 to 6·0 m. (15 to 20 ft.), as it has an attractive bark. In exposed positions growth is more stunted. *N. procera* (Poepp. & Endl.) Oerst. can suffer frost and wind damage and is more successful in the West. Staking is important to prevent wind-rock in the early stages.

N. antarctica (Forst.) Oerst. The arboriculturist should make due allowance for the fact that growth is not always free with this species, and that often the main shoot and branches will adopt a twisted habit. *N. dombeyi* Bl. usually forms a small tree in this country with a spread which is often equal to the height. This species, especially if it is growing in an open site, develops rival leads and the whole tree becomes very bushy with many of the lower branches horizontal and just above the ground. There is evidence that a definite lead develops more naturally, if there is competition for light with other trees of a similar age in the early stages after planting out. Grown either way, it forms an attractive tree.

Notospartium

The species are not fully hardy and generally need wall protection. They are particularly tender when young, and should be grown on in the nursery for 2 to 3 years where they can be protected during the winter. When the stems are definitely woody, they may be planted out in a sunny position approximately 0·5 m. (1½ ft.) from the wall. Branches may be allowed to form from ground level, and they maintain an upright habit of growth to begin with, but the growths from them are pendulous. Often, as the bushes grow older, staking is needed, otherwise the heavy branches lean badly. Very old bushes which are unsightly may be cut right down to young growths, which are often found at the base. Normal pruning consists of carefully cutting out any dead wood, or growths which appear to make the bush untidy.

N. carmichaeliae Hook. f. will reach 1·2 m. (4 ft.) or more in height, and *N. glabrescens* Petrie forms a rather larger shrub.

Nyssa

N. sylvatica Marsh. When mature, this species will form quite a large tree, 15·0 m. (50 ft.) or more in height. However, there appears to be some variation in height and, where the crown forms at an earlier stage in development, a more compact tree is produced which has shorter growth. This variation may well be due in part to soil conditions and a good deep loam is most likely to give the strong growth essential to the production of a lead which will run right up through the crown as height increases. As the tree becomes established in its permanent position, the lower branches may be gradually removed, eventually to a height of 1·8 to 3·0 m. (6 to 10 ft.). This allows the remaining branches to develop their typical semi-pendulous habit and display their fine autumn colour at eye level. Also, access beneath the branches allows the autumn foliage to be viewed from the inside against the light and this is very pleasing.

In the nursery, good, strong growth and a lead should be encouraged, for a stunted specimen, when established in its permanent position, may break out with a strong shoot from low down or near to ground level which will run right up through the centre of the head and spoil the shape. However, should this happen and it is thought that this growth has sufficient vigour to develop beyond the existing branch system, it may be left to supply the future framework of the tree.

Olea

O. europaea L. normally requires wall protection, even in the milder parts of the country. Generally six to eight main branches are trained fan-wise, with additional laterals tied in as growth extends over the wall. The growths, or 'breast-wood', which develop from this system must be restricted and thinned by careful pruning, always allowing an adequate and natural furnishing. This furnishing should consist mainly of young growths which are the most attractive parts of this plant. Promising shoots may also be used as replacements for any older branches which show signs of failing.

With age, large, woody stems or branches develop and the shrub may become unsightly. The remedy for this is to cut the whole back close to ground level, in the spring so that a fresh start may be made with the young growths which break out freely. Alternatively, the old shrub may be removed completely, planting up a young one in a fresh position.

This species may also be planted out in a sheltered position in the open, provided that the climate is sufficiently mild and sunny. However, after severe winters there may be considerable die-back and dead wood to contend with. A central lead should be trained for this purpose.

Olearia

This is a genus of evergreen trees, shrubs and subshrubs. There is a great variety of growth, but the majority will only survive in the mildest parts of the country. Many are happiest in coastal areas where the full sun and wind results in a closer habit, which is more typical.

One general characteristic is that they break freely from pruning cuts, a response which can be made use of in various circumstances. Thus, worn and untidy bushes may be pruned very hard in the spring when growth will break out very freely from the old wood. In the same way, severe injury by frost may be followed by hard pruning. However, the operation should be left until new growths appear, which will indicate just how severe the damage has been. Specimens which have grown too large for their positions may also be carefully pruned in the spring, making the cuts inside the bush at suitable points in order that an informal surface is retained. This restrictive pruning is, for example, needed with such large growers as *O. avicenniifolia* Hook. f. when grown in a fairly confined space near a wall. The gradual process of shortening may need to be extended over two or three seasons, unless a more drastic hard pruning is given over the whole shrub in the first instance. Olearias in such a situation are not trained hard against the surface of a wall, but are left to form free-growing bushes, *see* Fig. 32.

O. gunniana Hook. f. may, with advantage, be cut back after flowering by several inches once the bush is two or three years old and has grown to full size. An even harder cutting back is necessary following damage by frost.

It will be seen, therefore, that the same principles apply throughout the genus. Even *O. nummulariifolia* Hook. f. may at times need pruning, for although it has a stiff and rigid growth, the outer branches sometimes have a tendency to spread and spoil neighbouring shrubs.

Ononis

O. fruticosa L. is a hardy, shrubby species which is sometimes found in collections. The actual growth is quite compact, but it does benefit from a light clipping over after flowering, as useless seed production is thus avoided. The pieces should be brushed or picked off. *O. rotundifolia* L. is semi-woody and should be cut down in the dormant season.

Orixa

O. japonica Thunb. This is a very densely foliaged shrub which grows from 1·2 to 2·4 m. (4 to 8 ft.) in height, and sends out spreading growths. These are horizontal at first, but the extended branch ends become pendulous. As they touch the soil they root and form strong shoots, and so the mass of twig growth and foliage moves forward. This shrub shows great promise of becoming a first-class ground cover subject. If necessary, the spread can be checked by careful pruning so that the cuts are hidden and the natural habit is retained. The layers may be uprooted in the dormant season and planted elsewhere.

Osmanthus

A common characteristic of all the species of Osmanthus is that they regenerate very freely from old wood. Thus they may, if overgrown, be cut back quite severely.

O. ilicifolius (Hassk.) Mouillef. is slow-growing. It should be left to branch freely from ground level, the lower branches being almost horizontal. Small growths are produced freely on the old wood, even inside the bush. This shrub may be restricted in size by cutting any long growths back to suitable laterals inside the general branch system, and thus preserving the beautiful effect of an informal surface. This should be carried out in May, but hard cutting back of the whole bush, if hopelessly overgrown, is better done in April.

This subject is quite good as a hedge plant, but trimming should be carried out before the end of July. A formal hedge cannot be expected to flower a great deal. The flowers are produced in the axils of the previous season's wood and are followed a few weeks later by more flowers from the bases of the young growths. As a hedge it is often slow to fill out.

The remainder of the species also respond to pruning if it is necessary to restrict size, using the same method as with *O. ilicifolius*. Where the individual leaves are larger and the growth stiff and upright, even more care is necessary in carrying out this operation.

O. delavayi Franch, although it may be grown in the open border in the South and West, is often planted as a wall shrub. The main branches are trained out fan-wise and the laterals produced from these provide the furnishing as they extend and branch. This subject flowers in the spring from the previous years' wood. Pruning may be carried out immediately after flowering and it consists of cutting out any overgrown branches, which may even be weighed down and spoil lower growths. The pruning cuts should be made to suitable growths and, at a later stage, the long, strong shoots may be tied in with the aim of using them as replacements for the older branches forming the framework against the wall. On no account should the wholesale snipping back of growths take place during the summer months, as this will spoil the next season's flowering.

This subject will, however, conform to close clipping several times during the growing season, and is thus suitable for a formal hedge in the milder South-West.

× Osmarea

× *O. burkwoodii* Burkw. This is a compact and slow-growing shrub, particularly in the first year or so after planting out from the nursery where it has in the course of training been regularly transplanted. When it does become established in its final quarters, strong, upright growths are put on which stand well above the remainder of the close branch system. Following this, growth often tends to slow down.

If it is necessary to restrict the size of this shrub in any way, pruning should be carried out after flowering in early May. The longer branches should be cut back inside the bush, taking care to leave an informal surface.

This subject regenerates well after being cut back, and it forms a very close surface as a hedge plant when it is given an annual clipping which should be carried out in July. A later clipping results in secondary growth being put on in the autumn, and this, being soft, may be damaged by frost.

Osmaronia

O. cerasiformis (Torr. & Gr.) Greene. Although this shrub is unisexual both the male and female forms are similar in habit. The shrub suckers freely and a single specimen soon develops into a clump which also layers freely. With this habit it is suitable for the more natural part of the garden. In this setting an enlarging clump is formed and pruning is difficult to carry out effectively.

In a more limited space, some pruning of the older wood may be carried out after flowering and the cuts may be taken right down to ground level. It may also be necessary to remove offending suckers. With age, as they carry more and more wood, the growths often arch over and spoil neighbouring plants. Pruning these to upright young shoots relieves weight and thus corrects the position.

Osteomeles

O. schwerinae Schneid. is not fully hardy and needs to be grown against a wall in most parts of the country. However, the long branches conform quite readily to training, which should be fan-wise and hard up against the surface. Pruning, once the framework is formed, consists of cutting out the older branches in sufficient quantity to allow the younger ones to take their place, perhaps after further growth and training.

Ostrya

These are medium-sized trees which in a suitable setting can be trained up with a central lead and become very shapely. A 1·8 to 2·4 m. (6 to 8 ft.) length of clear stem is to be preferred.

O. carpinifolia Scop. will perhaps produce the most shapely head, the branching being light and evenly spaced round the central lead. One of the main beauties of this tree is in the finer branching, and the lower limbs should be left to sweep down to eye level, where the beauty of the fruits and later the catkins can be appreciated after the leaves have fallen. This species does not take kindly to competition for light from neighbouring trees and branches will be lost on shaded parts of the specimen. It is not advised that every specimen should be perfect, in fact, it is an interesting tree to plant on the edge of a natural clump where a tree with rival leads which leans toward the light, produces a more natural effect.

O. virginiana (Mill.) K. Koch is similar in habit but the branching tends to be heavier. *O. japonica* Sarg. retains a very good lead and has slender branches. The shaggy bark of this species is very attractive and it should be grown with a good clear stem.

Ostryopsis

O. davidiana Dcne. forms a stool-like habit and occasionally throws strong growths from the base. The new growths which extend from ground level often appear 0·3 m. (1 ft.) or so away from the main clump. If necessary, thin and old wood may be cut out at ground level during the winter, but regular attention, even on an annual basis, is seldom required.

Oxydendrum

O. arboreum (L.) DC. requires little or no pruning, but this is often needed on neighbouring, sheltering trees and shrubs to prevent a specimen from being overgrown and spoilt. This subject needs good treatment in the nursery to promote free growth with a single lead, and this policy should be maintained after it has been planted in its final position. In the early years, staking may be necessary. Branching should be encouraged to ground level to provide an adequate furnishing. The side of a lawn is an ideal setting.

Ozothamnus

This genus is allied to the Helichrysums. Normally the species need wall protection and even in this position they may be badly damaged during the winter. An attempt to improve a damaged or straggly specimen may be made by pruning hard in the spring, just as growth is about to commence. *O. ledifolius* Hook. often responds better than many to this treatment if it is considered necessary.

Paeonia

The shrubby species normally require very little pruning. After the fruits have ripened, the old flower stalks die back to the terminal bud on the new shoot. The shrub has a tidier appearance if these old stalks are cut off after the leaves have fallen. At the same time, any old and worn growths may be removed at ground level. The summer is also a good time to search for dead wood, as it is sometimes difficult to pick out during the winter.

Paliurus

P. spina-Christi Mill. As a shrub this has a spreading habit, the main branches often spring from ground level. In this form, the lower branches are often weighed down to a horizontal position and even lie on the surface as more and more growth is put on laterally. It is also an untidy grower with many crossing branches, but it is not worth while attempting to correct this fault in any way, as it does not appear to affect the health of the shrub.

This subject may also be trained as a small tree with a 0·9 to 1·5 m. (3 to 5 ft.) clear stem, by retaining the lead and by cutting out the rivals at the nursery stage. When grown either as a tree or a shrub, this subject can be restricted in size by careful pruning hiding the cuts and retaining an informal effect. If very overgrown, a specimen may be cut hard back, even close to ground level, when it will respond by breaking out strongly. Pruning should be carried out during the dormant season.

Parrotia

The only species in the genus is *P. persica* C. A. Mey. It is usually classed as a small tree and is capable of growing 9·0 to 12·0 m. (30 to 40 ft.) in height. However, once branching commences, even on a nursery specimen, the head quickly opens up and the lead is lost. As a result, the specimen becomes a large bush without any trunk, even when mature. In most cases the best form for planting is a standard on a definite leg of at least 1·8 m. (6 ft.), which has been selected and trained in the nursery. A dense canopy of foliage is formed, making a perfect spot for a garden seat set in the shade against the beautifully mottled trunk and main branches.

The branches have a spreading habit and many are horizontal and even pendulous, growing along the ground as they reach it. In order to retain the full beauty of this plant, these growths should be left to grow unrestricted. A grass foreground is ideal, but care must be taken when mowing on the perimeter of the branch system, for injury to the growths will spoil the effect (see Plate 64). There should be no attempt to thin the branching, however much this appears to be crowded, for the overlapping and often crossing system is the natural habit of this tree and is also one of its beauties. Often a deep shade is cast on the lower branches of this canopy, but usually they retain a full covering of foliage. This ability to survive in shady conditions is again displayed when branches develop under neighbouring trees with quite a dense canopy. However, full sun is preferred.

Parrotiopsis

P. jacquemontiana (Dcne.) Rehd. forms quite a dense, twiggy head, developing into a large shrub, rarely a tree. In the nursery, the head may be formed on a short leg 0·3 to 0·6 m. (1 to 2 ft.) in length. Branching is very extensive and the head forms very quickly. The beauty of this shrub is in the branching, and this should be encouraged to develop, even on to the ground. Once the head is formed, any suckers which appear, as they sometimes do from the region of the trunk should be removed.

Parthenocissus

One characteristic of this climbing genus is that the tendrils usually flatten upon contact with solid objects and form discs or pads which cling very tightly to the surface.

P. quinquefolia (L.) Planch. is one of the strongest species and it is typical of the majority, which are suitable for growing over trees, sheds or other buildings, walls or fences. Pruning is unnecessary when they are grown in the wilder parts of the garden, although a careful watch should be kept to see that nearby shrubs are not smothered unintentionally.

These self-clinging vines are sometimes planted against buildings, but this can lead to damage if they are allowed to grow beyond the eaves and among the tiles. The thickening stems disturb these, while the annual leaf fall can lead to blocked gutters and the surface of rough-cast walls can be torn away and damaged by the weight. It is certainly advisable to keep the growths below the eaves and guttering by pruning annually in the autumn.

Pergolas may also be used as supports, the pruning being carried out annually. The young growths are taken back to the rods which are trained onto the uprights and cross-pieces. The point of pruning being just above the lowest bud. The period for this is in December, when there is no danger of bleeding. Under this system, spurs build up on the vine, while the growths hang down to form a curtain of attractive foliage, *see* Fig. 20 (6).

Passiflora

P. coerulea L. is commonly grown in the south of the country, particularly on walls where it may be trained up a trellis or wire system. It is best when taken up to a height of 2·4 to 3·0 m. (8 to 10 ft.). The available space is covered by a framework of main branches which are trained hard up against the structure. This is not difficult, as this subject climbs naturally, using tendrils for support. The main stems are spaced approximately 150 to 250 mm. apart, but it may become necessary to thin these later.

The laterals from these are allowed to hang down at full length and are pruned back to a good bud at the base. This is carried out annually in the spring; it is in fact a type of spur pruning. The subject flowers on the long growths which are produced during the summer.

Paulownia

The three species most commonly grown are *P. fargesi* Franch, *P. lilacina*

Sprague and *P. tomentosa* (Thunb.) Steud., although the latter is the best known. Some authorities are of the opinion that *P. fargesi* is more suited to the climate of the British Isles but this certainly does not always hold good and, so far as the arboriculturist is concerned, there appears to be little difference in their training and pruning. The following details will therefore hold good for these three species.

They are all fast growers and are especially tender when young. Often, they will reach a height of 1·8 to 2·4 m. (6 to 8 ft.) after two years from seed. They prefer a rich soil, but the large, sappy growth which is produced is often unripe at the tip when the winter sets in and is thus damaged or killed. This does not matter a great deal, for the dead growth may be cut back to a strong developing shoot; in fact, it is seldom that a terminal bud is produced on the tip of the shoot and an axillary bud beneath invariably takes over in the spring. It is important to build up a single lead for as long as possible and the first main branch should be formed with a clear stem of at least 1·8 m. (6 ft.).

Occasionally, after a wet year, a shoot is thrown up through the tree which may eventually rival the leader. Normally, this should be pruned at an early stage, but such a growth ought to be left on a weakly specimen as it may eventually prove to be the tree's means of survival and development. It is difficult to grow shapely trees on wet, cold soils. Under these conditions, un-controllable cavities form in the soft wood, while whole branches often die back. Paulownias do not do well in shade, for a sunny position is required to ripen the wood.

Formerly, Paulownias were frequently grown for their tropical foliage effect. The way to produce this is to cut the stems down to within 50 to 80 mm. of ground level in the spring each year before growth begins. The resultant shoots are then thinned out to one. Feeding and watering, if this is necessary, ensures rich, luxuriant growth.

Periploca

P. graeca L. This is a vigorous twining shrub which may reach a height of 6·0 to 9·0 m. (20 to 30 ft.). It branches freely from ground level. When grown against a wall, vertical wires are necessary in addition to the horizontal strands to give support in the initial stages. However, this subject is more suitable for pergolas and similar structures, though it will also climb small trees which are weakly or dying.

Little pruning is required and it is difficult to keep this shrub tidy. However, some of the weakest growths may be cut out in the spring.

Pernettya

The habits of growth of the species and forms are all very similar. Many spread by means of suckers and form a dense thicket. Normally, very little pruning is necessary unless it be to prevent the overgrowing of neighbouring shrubs. *P. mucronata* (L.) Gaud. will often grow in close association with *Gaultheria shallon* Pursh. to form a pleasing cover. It will also grow well with *Erica carnea* L. 'Springwood White'.

Growths which are dying back should be cut off at ground level in the spring. When it becomes necessary to restrict the size of a clump, perhaps along one edge, the growths should be cut off at ground level, carefully removing any roots or suckers, but ensuring that a natural form and habit is retained and not a straight, clipped edge.

Perowskia

The most commonly grown species in this small genus is *P. atriplicifolia* Benth. This late-flowering, semi-woody member of the Family Labiatae, produces long flower spikes terminating the growths which develop rapidly during the spring and early summer from the woody rootstock. During the winter these are killed back severely, often to within 50 to 80 mm. of their bases, but in the spring buds break freely from the living portion.

There is a definite advantage in hard pruning annually in the spring, just as the buds break, for the dead wood which has served as a protection during the winter is then removed to allow the new growths to develop unrestrictedly, and the plant is left tidier. Also, with the buds breaking the severity of the pruning may be adjusted with accuracy, cutting hard back to the base of each shoot, leaving only one or two developing buds on each. This is really a form of thinning and results in few shoots but better spikes.

The remaining Perowskias may be dealt with in the same way.

Pertya

P. sinensis Oliv. Provided that this interesting shrub is well positioned in an open situation, it is a neat grower and very little pruning is necessary.

Petteria

P. ramentacea (Sieber) Presl. This shrub should be left to grow and branch naturally, when it will develop into a sturdy bush. Normally no pruning is required.

Phellodendron

These trees are fast growing and thrive best on a well drained but rich soil. They have rather a stiff, sparsely branched habit and providing that good growth is encouraged in the nursery they train very readily. A good lead should be maintained throughout the stages, until the crown has been formed when, with the main branches taking much of the vigour, it will quickly be lost. Late frosts may damage the young growths.

P. sachalinense (Fr. Schmidt.) Sarg. is the most outstanding, forming a good lead from which a clear trunk of 1·8 to 2·4 m. (6 to 8 ft.) may be trained. The lower branches develop sparsely, even down to eye-level. The foliage is attractive, especially in the autumn, the leaflets turning bright yellow and dropping later to reveal the bright yellow midrib which eventually falls as well. The remaining species have a similar habit but they are not as large growing in cultivation. *P. amurense* Rupr. and *P. chinense* Schneid. seem to be more prone

Q

to damage from late frosts than the others and, as a result, the branching is not so clean and definite, but is twiggy with a covering of dwarf shoots over the system. Due allowance must be made for this development. *P. lavallei* Dode produces a beautiful canopy of foliage and when viewed from beneath against the light, the mosaic effect is perfect.

Philadelphus

Most of the shrubs in this genus grow freely from ground level and form a stool. They flower on laterals produced on growths made in the previous year. This stool habit may be encouraged by planting slightly deeper, after a bushy habit has been developed by close pruning in the nursery.

A good soil and sufficient moisture, with feeding and mulching, provide the conditions necessary if these plants are to remain healthy and flower well year after year. Their general condition can be judged by the amount of new growth, which should develop rapidly during and after flowering.

In most cases some annual pruning immediately after flowering is necessary. The wood which has flowered may then be cut away to a suitable growth. Sometimes an entire branch may be cut out to ground level, but there should be a new growth from this region for replacement. In this way annual pruning should be seen as a necessary operation to regulate growth and flowering, keeping a good supply of young wood coming up from the base. As a general rule most of the wood above ground level should be no older than five years.

In the case of really old bushes which are spent and overgrown, most of the top growth may be cut down to ground level during the winter and early spring, or after flowering. However, it is often a better policy to replace such plants with young ones

It is important to take the natural habit of growth and vigour of the species or variety into account, for there is a considerable variation in this respect. As an example, *P. coronarius* L. is a strong grower, reaching up to 3·7 m. (12 ft.), while 'Argenteo-Variegatus' is much smaller, producing thin almost wiry stems. Many other instances of variation could be quoted among the named *P.* × *lemoinei*, 'Lemoine Hybrids' yet the general method of pruning is common to all, provided that habit is taken into account.

P. microphyllus Gray, is a low-growing shrub with fine growths and small leaves. With this species it is necessary to carefully prune back any branches which trail and overhang other plants but generally an informal shape should be retained.

P. c. 'Argenteo-Variegatus' has already been mentioned. Both this and *P. c.* 'Aureus' are grown mainly for their foliage. The best colour is found on the younger growths and it is therefore important to maintain a good proportion of these on the bushes.

Aphis is a serious pest of *Philadelphus* and the young growths which are so important often suffer badly. A control using a derris or pyrethrum preparation should therefore be applied in good time, before the damage is extensive.

Phillyrea

One reaction which is common to all the species and cultivars in this genus is that they regenerate freely and produce a plentiful supply of new growths from the region of pruning cuts, even if they are made on the old wood. They also produce substantial branches from ground level, eventually becoming large shrubs or small trees.

P. decora Boiss. & Bal., with large leaves, is spreading and rounded in outline. The branching is very rigid, even to the extremities of the system. The spread may be restricted, if necessary, by pruning in May after flowering, the longest growths being pruned back to suitable points well inside the bush. With a badly overgrown specimen the pruning may be spread over several years, selecting the growths carefully so that the process is a gradual one and the whole surface is kept well furnished.

P. angustifolia L. has a closer habit, but with the variety *P. a.* var. *rosmarini-folia* Ait. the density of individual branches is such that there is a considerable build up of dead twig growth inside the bush. This in turn increases the weight to such an extent that the upper branches are bent down onto the lower ones. Also, the inside branches are deprived of light and thus there are few living growths in this region of the bush. Owing to the dense habit it is difficult to prune with the aim of restricting size, and it is better to give this subject a grass foreground where its natural habit can develop. Should very severe damage occur as a result of a gale or a heavy snowfall, hard pruning to near ground level is often the best policy.

P. latifolia L. has a similar habit.

Phlomis

Although these are classed as shrubs and consist of a woody branch system, the leafy shoot tips are soft and are liable to injury in a severe winter. However, one characteristic which is common to all the species is that new growths break freely from the old wood, provided that this is in a healthy condition. Thus, after a severe winter the injured growths may be cut back as the young shoots break out in the spring. Very old and woody specimens may not break freely and should be replaced.

Over-grown specimens also respond to hard cutting back, again choosing the spring period. It is possible, however, to keep these shrubs in good condition for many years by pruning back a selected number of growths each spring, for example, cutting back any which have become weak and woody or have over-grown into neighbouring plants. *P. chrysophylla* Boiss. becomes very heavy with growths which are eventually weighed down to the ground. These will even root and form fresh plants well away from the parent. *P. italica* L. has a woody habit and develops a very ragged appearance unless this is controlled by an occasional pruning. *P. viscosa* Poiret, has a loose habit which is kept more compact by a limited amount of cutting back each year, again in the spring.

Photinia

P. villosa (Thunb.) DC. is a large, deciduous shrub or small tree which often consists of several upright branches. Normally, this subject needs little regular pruning, but strong young growths are often thrown up from ground level.

These can be thinned and trained to eventually replace old branches if this is considered necessary. As they become old, the top growth often does not produce much young wood and thus the shrub loses strength.

P. davidsoniae Rehd. & Wils. is an evergreen for a sheltered position. It should be trained to form a lead, but should be allowed to branch from ground level. It may be cut back by severe weather, but it will break freely from living wood despite the fact that this may be old. *P. serrulata* Lindl. is similar in this respect. This latter species and *P. beauverdiana* Schneid. are really at their best when grown in the shelter of a wall. One or two main stems should be trained up and tied loosely to the wall but otherwise they are self supporting. The side growths may need pruning back carefully from time to time as they grow extensively. This should be carried out in April, taking the cuts back into the bush to a suitable point so that they are hidden and leaving a furnished appearance.

Phygelius

P. capensis Mey. 'Coccineus' is the most popular form of this plant. It is often grown as an herbaceous plant in the open border, being killed down to ground level each winter. It spreads extensively by stoloniferous growths which develop just beneath the soil surface.

This is also a good subject for a wall with a southerly aspect. The wood is retained from year to year up to a height of 1·5 to 1·8 m. (5 to 6 ft.). Pruning is carried out in the spring, back to the main stems which are secured loosely to the wires. In very mild districts it will survive as a woody shrub in the open. Pruning is carried out in the spring back to the living wood.

Phyllodoce

Normally, very little pruning is needed on these small shrubs which are rather exacting in their cultural requirements. A bushy habit should be encouraged in the nursery and in the permanent position and, as a result, plenty of strong growths will be thrown up from the base of the plant each year. Any dead growths which do occur should be cut out, but often there is a wholesale browning over the whole of the plant which is a sign that it is dying. Often, one or two branches in a clump extend well beyond the remainder and these may be layered down with pins, when they will serve a useful purpose in forming fresh plants and increasing the size of the clump.

Phyllostachys – *See* Bamboos.

Physocarpus

P. opulifolius (L.) Maxim. This shrub adopts a stool-like habit and it throws up many young growths among the older branches at ground level. Pruning consists of cutting out a proportion of the older wood after flowering. The extent of this pruning must depend upon growth and condition, but the shrub should be left well furnished. The older branches are quite attractive with peeling bark during the winter and this should also be considered. The pruning policy may consist of cutting out the oldest wood at ground level taking away whole branches, of cutting out some of the old wood on the remaining mature growths to a suitable point and of thinning out the young canes which originate at ground level. When cutting back part of a branch system it is often better to take the cut back to an outward growing young shoot, as the bush then assumes a more natural appearance.

P. capitatus (Pursh) Ktze. is even stronger growing, and with a large number of young canes springing from the base it may need a more drastic thinning. This species also suckers extensively and it is more suitable for the more natural parts of the garden. *P. monogynus* (Torr.) Coult. has a small stool head with a spreading but stiff branch system and it should be given sufficient space for a 1·8 to 2·4 m. (6 to 8 ft.) spread. A greater proportion of the older wood will need to be left on this and on *P. malvaceus* (Greene) Ktze. *P. stellatus* (Rydb.) Rehd. throws up plenty of new growths and the old ones may be cut out quite severely after flowering. The natural arching habit should be retained.

Picea

As with many other conifers, the spruces have a strong central lead which is built up from the seedling stage in the nursery. Most of the species will only thrive well with at least some shelter and a sufficiently moist soil. A free and adequate branch spread down to ground level is to be desired, but for this, adequate light should reach the whole tree and the immediate surround must be kept free of shrub growth, etc. It is important to grow them well from the seedling stage for the best results.

Picrasma

P. quassioides (D. Don) Benn. is a small tree or shrub grown for its foliage effect. The branches are ascending and preferably it should be trained with a short leg 0·6 m. (2 ft.) high. Even the lower and outer branches on a mature tree are horizontal and seldom droop. Cuts heal very well, but in a mature tree the long branches with little furnishing except at the ends sometimes split at the narrow crotches and bracing may eventually be needed.

Pieris

There is quite a variety of growth within this genus, but all the species have one or two requirements and characteristics in common. Growth is more likely to be healthy and typical in a sheltered position and, provided the plants are strong and healthy, they will respond well to hard pruning although it should not be resorted to more often than is necessary. Free natural growth is ideal and it is often necessary to cut back neighbouring shrubs in order to ensure this. Low overhanging branches or difficult positions where the light comes only from one side may bring about unequal growth and a poor shape. *P. floribunda* (Pursh) Benth. & Hook. and *P. japonica* (Thunb.) D. Don seem in particular to suffer in such conditions, and the heavy one-sided growth which follows may pull the whole bush out of shape. Under such circumstances, in addition to correcting the cause of this unnatural growth, the excessively heavy branches may often be cut back to suitable upright branches, but if the latter are not available they will normally break out in response to pruning. Another justifiable reason for hard pruning is when it is necessary to cut off growths which have been severely damaged during the winter. Often these shrubs will break forth, even when they have been cut hard back close to ground level. *P. formosa* (Wall.) D. Don and its forms perhaps show a more ready response than the others. Concerning the species generally, a good bush should be well furnished to ground level and the aim should be to keep this surface intact by good culture. If it is necessary to prune, do this in the spring.

Pileostegia

The species commonly grown is *P. viburnoides* Hook. f. & Thoms. It is self-clinging, producing long extension growths which become attached to a support by means of masses of roots, *see* Fig. 39. Thus it is a suitable subject for rambling over an old tree-stump or a wall. If the latter, it is advisable to allow the growths to develop on the top as this gives additional support to the mature flowering wood which is built up. A wire system is also necessary for supporting ties as the heavier branch system develops.

Fig. 39. A young growth of *Pileostegia viburnoides* showing the free production of adventitious roots along the stem which enable this subject to cling to a suitable surface.

Pruning consists of cutting back any surplus extension growths which develop once the allotted space has been covered. The flowering branches also need shortening if they become heavy and in danger of breaking, or grow too far from the wall. This should be carried out in the spring, although the extension growths may be stopped as they develop during the summer months.

Pinus

As with most of the Conifers, the retention of a lead is important to the form and well-being of the vast majority of this large group, but their habits vary considerably. It is important to have some knowledge of the species under consideration, especially when the final position is being selected, for little pruning or training is possible without spoiling the trees completely.

Following up the point that it is important to retain the lead in a healthy condition, this is only possible if the tree is growing vigorously. The radial branches produced round the central stem must be healthy and vigorous to give support and shelter to the main extension shoot, *see* Plate 75.

Should the main lead be lost for any reason, a vigorous tree will often produce several growths which will grow up in its place. These should be thinned down to one in the following spring, retaining the strongest and bearing in mind the desirability of selecting a growth which is in direct line with the main axis. The best time for pruning is in the spring when the new growths are 50 to 80 mm. (2 to 3 in.) long. Once a flat-topped effect has developed and the tree has reached its ultimate height, there is no point in trying to select a leader as it is seldom successful.

A group of the Pines, mostly the larger and more vigorous growers and including *P. nigra* Arnold and *P. sylvestris* L., appear to have two distinct phases of growth, but the transition from one to the other is a very gradual process. The first phase is an extension in height within the limits set by the environment and exposure generally. It is during this period, which lasts until the ultimate height for the tree is reached, that the preservation and well-being of the leading growth is important. In the second phase many or all of the lower branches die, partly through lack of light and also because the vigour is taken into the upper system. Often in the higher portions a definite crown forms as a number of the branches thicken, as a result of which the smaller ones usually die out completely. The extent to which the thickening occurs and the crown develops varies, even within a species, but a crowded specimen is less likely to form an extensive head. The amount of all-round light is the most important deciding factor.

This may appear confusing, for there is no definite advice to give upon the species or varieties which develop this habit, but the general rule to follow is to keep the specimen growing healthily and to cut any dying branches back hard to the trunk. Thickening and extension into main branches will soon become evident when it occurs. The arboriculturist may often welcome the ultimate development of a head, in contrast to the forester who does not look kindly upon heavy branching.

It should, of course, be remembered that a number of species have an attractive bark which is shown to full effect on a long straight trunk, clear of branches. Examples are *P. nigra*, *P. sylvestris* and *P. bungeana* Zuzz. ex Endl.

The many other forms of growth among the various species are often quite distinctive; for example *P. muricata* D. Don, *P. pinea* L. and *P. radiata* D. Don may branch heavily from low down to form a wide crown with little or no trunk, especially if planted in the open. *P. mugo* Turra is also variable, being either a shrub or a small tree, but it is low branching.

P. wallichiana A. B. Jacks., the Bhutan Pine, retains and builds on the lower branch system if it is in an isolated position and receives sufficient light. These branches often spread horizontally and even lie on the ground. A mature specimen with this habit needs special care, for during periods of extreme drought or impoverishment the topmost branches tend to die back and this spoils the general shape of the tree.

P. rigida Mill. is quite distinctive in that even a mature tree will freely produce adventitious shoots. This is a characteristic of this species and there should be no attempt to remove them. *P. serotina* Michx., a related species, also produces these growths.

Piptanthus

P. laburnifolius (D. Don) Stapf is the hardiest and most widely grown species, but wall protection is often necessary. The shrub has a stool-like habit, producing strong growths from the base, a habit which in time results in overcrowding and this may spoil the effect.

As this shrub may suffer during severe winters, pruning should be left until the spring so that the young growths have maximum protection. At this period, when the danger of severe frost has passed, the old and worn growths are cut out completely down to ground level, but sufficient mature shoots should be left for furnishing. The laterals on the main upright and healthy branches are only tipped back if they have been injured.

This shrub should be left to grow freely as a bush, and not be trained on the wall's surface.

Pistacia

P. chinensis Bge. This is the most reliable species for growing in the open but sometimes it is not altogether happy. The main stem should, if possible, be trained up to form a trunk 1·5 to 1·8 m. (5 to 6 ft.) in height before the branch system is formed. The lead should be maintained for as long as possible but this species does not often form a large tree in this country. There is often a considerable amount of dead wood to cut out, and it may be desirable to leave the epicormic growths to balance up this loss of wood. Prune in July if this is necessary.

P. terebinthus L. is slow-growing and is not altogether satisfactory in the open as it really needs wall protection. It should be trained up with a single lead and apart from one or two loose ties to the wall it is capable of self-support. The laterals are pendulous and become untidy.

Pittosporum

Normally, even the hardiest species require the protection of a wall in all but the warmer localities. They are not trained hard against the surface but are grown as bushes, being planted 0·6 to 0·9 m. (2 to 3 ft.) from the base. The habit of growth varies not only with the species but also with local climatic conditions. The well-drained, open and sunny position tends to produce a more compact and well-ripened growth which is more typical of many species, and such plants have a better chance of wintering successfully.

Those species, such as *P. ralphii* T. Kirk, which produce a bush with a spreading habit, may be pruned in the spring if this is considered necessary, in order to encourage a more compact habit. The cuts should be taken to a suitable point inside the bush in order to maintain an informal surface. By contrast, *P. patulum* Hook. f. has ascending branches and is more upright in growth.

P. tenuifolium Banks & Soland. is a tender species which reaches the proportions of a small tree. It should be left to form a single stem but will branch very thickly, both from this and on growths which are sent up from ground level. It is used for hedging in mild districts.

Pittosporums regenerate freely from the old wood and therefore respond to hard pruning in the spring. So often, however, a severe winter will kill the tenderer species outright.

Plagianthus

P. betulinus A. Cunn. is very like a birch in general appearance, especially in the early stages when it has a straight leading trunk with thin, intertwining, semi-pendulous laterals. More definite side branches appear as the shrub matures. *P. divaricatus* Forst. produces masses of thin growths. Both subjects normally need wall protection. No regular pruning is necessary.

Platanus

The Planes are strong-growing, majestic trees which are much prized by arboriculturists as they respond well to good, early training and develop into shapely specimens.

P. × *hispanica* Muenchh. retains a lead very readily and young trees are often shapely. However, rival leads often develop and these should be dealt with at an early stage. It is considered good practice to grow a 1·8 to 2·4 m. (6 to 8 ft.) clear stem in the nursery, although at a later stage, as the crown extends, the length of clear trunk may be increased to 4·6 to 6·0 m. (15 to 20 ft.). The clean growth and bark effects of the main trunk and branches are the great attractions of this hybrid. When the tree reaches the mature stage the ends of the lower branches are pendulous, and although this habit cannot be encouraged in a thoroughfare where it would impede traffic, it produces a fine effect in the garden, *see* Plate 65. These growths may be 6·0 m. (20 ft.) or more in length and reach the ground. The base of the trunk thickens considerably in a large mature tree and a low mound of soil develops beneath this, but seldom do the individual buttress roots develop to the surface. 'Pyramidalis' does not develop the same pendulous habit in its lower branches.

P. orientalis L. develops a more rounded head with heavier branches and a shorter trunk. It is a strong tree, but there is some evidence that older wood on specimens beyond their prime produces cavities, which might in time result in the loss of a large limb. The main branches of very old trees should therefore be braced as a precaution and a thorough overhaul and shortening is often advisable.

P. occidentalis L. is not a satisfactory tree in this country, as the young growths suffer severe damage from the late spring frosts.

Platanus species regenerate very freely from the tissues surrounding cut surfaces. This amazing response to frequent cutting is proved beyond all doubt when it is used as a street tree and is cut back year after year to form a dense crown of young growths. This practice is not advocated as a long term policy and the reader in need of advice is referred to Chapter Two.

Platycarya

P. strobilacea Sieb. & Zucc. This is a slender tree or even a large shrub. It needs great care and attention when young, with shelter and protection, for it is subject to damage by late frosts. Trained properly, it will retain its lead well and a clear trunk of 1·5 to 1·8 m. (5 to 6 ft.) can be formed. The slender branches are naturally well spaced round the lead while the crown is fairly dense.

Pleioblastus – *See* Bamboos.

Podocarpus

Many of the species are grown successfully in milder climates than ours, although a few are suitable for the more favourable counties of the south and west. *P. andinus* Poepp. is hardy in many districts provided that it is sheltered from the north and east. Typically, this species forms a very low but dense and spreading crown. At the best it will normally only form a very short trunk before splitting up into a number of upright stems, but often these spring directly from ground level. The branches grow out from these horizontally, but the lowest ones will sweep to the ground over a lawn or open space adding greatly to the attraction of this beautiful tree.

This species may also be used as a low, formal hedge, approximately 0·9 m. (3 ft.) high. For this purpose they should be planted about 300 mm. apart, and should be encouraged to branch low near the base by hard pruning. The very young growths, especially those on the top surface, are susceptible to frost damage and it is not advisable to clip later than July in order to allow sufficient time for subsequent growths to harden. It may be necessary to clip twice during one season, in which case the best months are May and July.

P. alpinus R. Br. ex. Mirbel and *P. nivalis* Hook. f. require no training and need only sufficient space and light for development. *P. salignus* D. Don normally develops into a large shrub in all but the most sheltered areas. It should be allowed to break freely from ground level if it shows a tendency to do this.

Poliothyrsis

P. sinensis Oliv. This interesting, late-flowering subject forms a small, slender tree with a very bushy crown. It should be trained to a single lead, eventually forming a clear trunk of 1·2 to 1·8 m. (4 to 6 ft.). However, once branching has become strongly established, it is difficult to retain a lead. Stopping is therefore important in order to build up height and length of stem while young. The flowers terminate the short, twiggy growths of the current season. No regular pruning is needed.

Polygonum

P. baldschuanicum Reg. This rapid growing deciduous subject climbs by twining. It does this so freely that seldom is training needed, even when young, provided that there is a wire or branch support. It is difficult to restrict it to a confined space, but if it is necessary, pruning may be carried out during the dormant season. The ideal support for this subject is an old tree where it has almost unlimited space for development. Eventually long, trailing growths hang down to give a completely natural effect. Under this condition a considerable amount of dead wood builds up in the centre, as more and more trailing growths are produced which deprive the older ones of light. With care some of this can be cut out.

Poncirus

There is only one species in this genus, *P. trifoliata* (L.) Raf., the Japanese Bitter Orange. It does in fact bear 'orange blossom' flowers in May on the growths produced during the previous year. The shrub forms a very thick bush when it is growing freely and in the early stages strong shoots are thrown up from near the base. A bushy habit should be encouraged in the nursery stage by at least one pruning. At a later stage in its growth a maturing bush thickens up considerably, often with crossing branches. There should be no attempt to thin the bush or to cut out the offending branches, for this dense growth is one of its attractions. In the same way, any small furnishing branches near the base should be left and the lower and outer ones will almost reach ground level.

This shrub loves the sun and a shaded branch sometimes dies back, especially in a severe winter. Any such dead wood may be cut out in an annual inspection each spring.

It is sometimes grown as a formal or informal hedge. Under close clipping, which is carried out in June, a very dense surface is produced. Often, growths are produced later in the season, particularly on the sunny side, so that a second light pruning may be necessary.

Populus

Many of the species and hybrids are rapid growers which will quickly develop into quite large trees and are much favoured for this reason by the timber industry. Mostly too, they respond well to training and will rapidly form a lead and trunk.

For ornamental purposes they are often grown with a clear length of trunk, but the branches should not be trimmed back for a greater height than 6·0 to 9·0 m. (20 to 30 ft.) unless it becomes absolutely necessary through die-back. Epicormic growths develop freely, even on mature trunks once they have been trimmed up, and this involves considerable work if it is to be carried out to any height. The epicormic growths which do develop on the trunk must really be trimmed annually during the winter, as otherwise if they are left for some years the problem becomes an even greater one.

Poplars generally hold their limbs remarkably well and are seldom ruined by gales in the same way that Ash trees are, for example. They do suffer minor twig damage but this does not seem to matter a great deal.

Any trimming which is to be carried out should be completed by January as bleeding can be troublesome. The wood itself is soft but tough and does not saw easily unless the teeth are widely set.

Many Poplars produce main roots close to the surface. As they thicken, these may be on or even above the ground. This often leads to difficulty when mowing and the only remedy is to raise the soil level carefully to cover such obstructions. With really large trees a mound often builds up round the base of the trunk as the buttress roots thicken and push the surface soil up.

Among the diseases which are most serious is the bacterial organism which causes the condition termed Poplar Canker. It may be so serious that even large branches are killed. Varying degrees of resistance are shown by some species and hybrids. The appropriate Forestry Commission Leaflets give an account of these.

Poplars are grouped in sections botanically and it is convenient to deal with the pruning according to this system.

Sect. 1. Leuce. White Poplars, Aspens.

The tendency of this group to sucker is more marked in some species and forms than in others. *P. alba* L. is effective when planted on the edge of a clump of trees as the white under-surface of the leaf is often exposed even in a light breeze and makes an attractive feature. For the same reason a good furnishing should be encouraged as low down as possible. This species suckers freely. *P. canescens* (Ait.) Sm. also suckers and will thus form large clumps if allowed to grow freely. With both species the suckers must be regularly removed unless a clump effect is required. Both species are good on the coast and in exposed places and are most effective if in natural clumps in such a situation. In this way the smaller, suckerous stems give protection to the larger ones. The lower branches of *P. canescens* often have a semi-pendulous habit and the tree will furnish up with an attractive growth which shades most of the trunk. *P. tremula* L. is definitely at its best when grown as a natural suckering clump.

Sect. 2. Leucoides

One of the most ornamental of Poplars is in this group, *P. lasiocarpa* Oliv. It forms a round-headed tree and has a stiff, branching habit. The individual branches are mainly either ascending or horizontal. Poplars generally are light demanding, but normally this species is so shapely that a poor, badly-shaped specimen is very evident by contrast. A tiered effect is often produced by strong development of the terminal bud and those immediately below it, *see* Plate 15.

Sect. 3. Tacamahaca. Balsam Poplars.

P. tacamahaca Mill. and *P. candicans* Ait. sucker freely and these must be kept down if ornamental specimens are desired. *P. trichocarpa* Hook. and the hybrid *P. × generosa* Henry are strong, large growers and it is important to maintain a lead for as long as possible.

Sect. 4. Aegeiros. Black Poplars.

The above is also true for the strong-growing species and hybrids in this group. Failure to retain a lead results in very heavy and unnatural branching. The ability to retain one varies considerably with the species and variety; for example, *P. × canadensis* Moench var. *eugenei* (Simon-Louis) Schelle forms a long, straight trunk quite easily with comparatively light branching, whereas *P. × marilandica* Bosc. will often produce very heavy branching and a wide head. These various branching habits should be taken into account by the arboriculturist responsible for their care and maintenance, who should be acquainted with the habit of trees in his charge.

The arboriculturist who is looking for ornamental poplars rather than large and vigorous hybrids may prefer the smaller growers such as *P.* × *berolinensis* Dipp. This has an attractive, burred trunk, the branchlets often being pendulous with the growing points turned up. As with *P. nigra* L., the burrs should be trimmed over annually in order to remove any dwarf shoots which may arise. *P.* × *canadensis serotina* (Hartig.) Rehd. Moench var. has the interesting habit of turning the lead away from the direction of the prevailing wind, although this habit is also displayed to some extent by others. This hybrid comes into leaf late and thus escapes the late April and May frosts. The danger of spring frost damage must be taken into account when making a selection of Poplars to plant up.

Such fastigiate forms as *P. nigra* 'Italica'. require very little pruning, being most effective when furnished down to ground level.

Potentilla

P. fruticosa L. There are numerous varieties of this popular shrub grown in our gardens but the type species forms a dense shrub about 0·9 m. (3 ft.) in height. The main branches are upright or ascending, increasing in size to form a permanent branch system. Many of the forms, hybrids and varieties follow this habit, e.g. *P.* × *friedrichsenii* (Spaeth) Rehd. Left unpruned, they develop a mat of growth, the older and weaker branches being weighed down by the younger. Fallen leaves collect in the fine mass of branches, making the bush very untidy.

Pruning should be carried out in the spring and consists of cutting out the weaker wood and smaller growths to stronger wood or to the base. The strong, young growths, often sent up from the base or from older wood in the centre, should be shortened to half or two-thirds of their length. It is the laterals from these which flower the most and over the longest period. The old, small and twiggy growths do not flower extensively, nor for so long a period.

However there are a number of low, dwarf forms which are very popular. A modified form of this type of pruning should be adopted, for it is still a good policy to cut out the weakest wood and at the same time cut back the strong, young growths.

This subject may also be grown to form an informal hedge and it is pruned in the same way in the spring.

Prinsepia

P. sinensis (Oliv.) Oliv. This forms a dense thorny bush with a large number of young growths originating from the older wood, particularly from the more upright portions of branches which, as a result, become weighed down to and below the horizontal. Very little pruning is possible, apart from the removal of dead wood in the summer; indeed, the natural habit can easily be lost by unnecessary thinning. The larger branches have scaling bark which is attractive. *P. uniflora* Batal. is even more disorderly in growth. *P. utilis* Royle needs wall protection, where it should be grown as a bush. It has a graceful, arching habit. These shrubs must have sufficient space for free and full development.

Prostanthera

Even the hardier species require the protection of a wall, and may be tried in this situation in the warmest districts of the South-west. They do not conform to a rigid training and should be planted 0·3 m. (1 ft.) away from the base and grown as bushes. Their normal habit is to break low down at or near ground level and produce upright growths which branch very freely, forming a thick and bushy shrub.

Any pruning which is necessary, either to restrict size or to prevent over-growth onto neighbouring specimens, is carried out after the flowers have dropped in the spring. However some attention may be necessary after a severe winter when much dead growth may have to be cut back. This should be left until the new growth is breaking.

Prunus

In this genus are various subgenera which are based on well-known groups:– Subgenus I. Prunophora, Plums and Apricots; Subgenus II. Amygdalus, Almonds and Peaches; Subgenus III. Cerasus, Cherries; Subgenus IV. Padus, Bird Cherries and Subgenus V. Laurocerasus, Cherry Laurels.

Very few of the prunus need annual pruning. In fact, the majority seldom need attention once the tree or bush has been formed in the nursery, apart from the removal of dead or diseased pieces. It is difficult to over-stress the importance of sound propagation and good training, for a bad start through the choice of a poor or incompatible stock cannot be corrected by culture and pruning in later years. Again, should the grafting be set at the wrong height on the stock no form of training will hide this. It is therefore preferable with ornamental trees generally, for the union to be made near ground level, so that if an unsightly bulge forms in later years it can be hidden by grass or suitable plantings.

While it is true that most prunus do not need annual pruning, many horticul-turists believe that even an occasional pruning when needed is definitely harm-ful. It is difficult to produce any direct evidence that this is so, but there is a danger of certain diseases entering a wound, e.g. Silver Leaf, especially during the winter when the trees are dormant. The best period for large prunings to be removed is before mid-July, *see* Chapter Two.

In order to reduce the need for pruning to a definite size and shape, it is important to select the species or variety most carefully before the planting is made. Among the prunus there is a great variety of form and size to choose from and thus with the ideal selection, perfectly natural and unrestricted growth can be left to develop.

Subgenus I. Prunophora, Plums and Apricots

Prunus spinosa L., the Blackthorn, a spiny shrub or small tree, is usually found in thickets on waste ground. It spreads rapidly by means of suckers and eventu-ally each clump will colonise extensive areas. If trained to a single stem and grown in grass which is mown short, the sucker development is kept in check and a small, slow-growing tree may be formed. The other forms may also be trained in the same way. This species will colonise extensive areas even on poor soils in exposed districts and near the coast, but if it is necessary to keep to a definite line of demarcation, there should be an annual cut-back of the suckers.

This species could be used extensively to give shelter and protection to young trees in the early years for it is difficult to imagine that vandals and hooligans would risk being torn and scratched just to damage a tree. The competition would also induce the specimen to grow up to the light and thus produce a good stem. The clearance of the Blackthorn would take place after 10 to 15 years.

P. insititia L., Bullace, has a similar habit.

P. cerasifera Ehrh., Myrobalan, forms a small tree with a dense crown. Often during good growing seasons very strong branches are thrown directly up through the centre of the crown. This is a natural habit and it is difficult to maintain a neat and tidy crown. If they are cut out the resultant proliferation of growths requires the 'clean-up' to be carried out annually. This is a good subject for hedging and screening purposes. The forms and varieties have a similar habit.

There are many other species in this Subgenus but their habits vary, some becoming tree-like and similar to *P. domestica* L., the Garden Plum, others forming thickets like *P. spinosa*; but it is important to have some knowledge of their natural growth at planting time.

The Apricots are also in this section and include *P. armeniaca* L., which on a well-drained soil is hardy, but needs a wall to ripen its fruit. *P. mume* (Sieb.) Sieb. & Zucc., the Japanese Apricot and its cultivars may be trained to form a 1 to 2 m. standard, but it needs shelter and usually a stake for a longer period.

Subgenus II. Amygdalus, Almonds and Peaches

The Common Almond, *P. amygdalus* Batsch and several of the cultivars all make shapely trees, the exception being 'Macrocarpa', which has very large flowers but is often a tall straggly grower, especially in a shaded position. These, with the coloured varieties of Peach, *P. persica* (L.) Batsch, are often grown as half-standards. With peaches some of the oldest, twiggy branchlets may be cut back to suitable growths after flowering, thus letting light and air into the bush to encourage a better display in the following spring. The hybrid *P.* × *amygdalo-persica* (West.) Rehd. 'Pollardii' and *P. davidiana* (Carr.) Franch. also display this characteristic habit of growth. For the best effect, balance is important and secure staking and shelter is very necessary for this, especially in the early years.

On their own roots, peaches and almonds often die back by whole branches at a time, especially on a heavy soil, or after a very wet winter. The shape is quickly spoilt, and regenerating growths tend to spring from the main trunk and these are out of character with the remainder of the tree, being strong and upright. In many such cases it is better to grub up such a tree and replace it with one which has been grafted onto a plum stock.

P. triloba Lindl. 'Multiplex' may be grown as a bush, but it looks very fine against a south-facing wall. In this position the branches are trained fanwise to provide a framework over the allotted space. After this, the growths which are produced at right-angles to the surface of the wall are cut back hard to one or two buds immediately after flowering. Even during the formative period, growths not required for the framework are cut hard back in like manner. As this subject flowers freely from the previous season's wood, a good annual display is given each spring, provided that growth and vigour are maintained. By this method the shrub is kept hard against the wall, but the temptation to dig over and to plant bedding plants up to the foot of the wall must be resisted, as the roots will be disturbed with disastrous results. It is sometimes grown as a half-standard and pruned annually in the same way.

P. tenella Batsch., the Dwarf Russian Almond, is also in this group, but this and the cultivar forms need no pruning.

Many peaches and almonds are attacked by the fungus which causes 'Peach Leaf Curl' and this will seriously impair growth, especially in a bad season. The necessary spraying to combat this should be carried out in the early spring.

Subgenus III. Cerasus, Cherries

The species and varieties display great variation in growth and size and this is seen even among the Japanese Cherries, most of which are forms or varieties of *P. serrulata* Lindl. The beauty of these trees is in their natural spread and this is shown to full effect with 'Fugenzo', which forms a flat head with spreading branches, or with 'Tai Haku' whose pendant branches will reach the ground as the tree matures. With the latter variety these branches often appear untidy, but much of the flowering beauty will be lost if they are cut off. As a contrast to these varieties, the well known 'Kanzan' has ascending branches, while 'Amanogawa' has an erect, almost fastigiate growth. A neat appearance with this latter variety is maintained by using single strands of wire at intervals to keep in offending growths which break from the general outline. The size of the tree will depend to some extent upon the length of the trunk, and the height at which the head is formed. The type of tree which branches low from close to ground level is useful for planting on the edges of groups or in an exposed position.

With the species, too, it is a matter of allowing free growth after the initial training has been carried out in the nursery and if need be continued during the first year or so after planting. The aim must be to maintain health by good culture, for if growth is produced most cherries will flower.

Cherries are usually trained as open-headed specimens, but the large tree-like species such as *P. avium* L. may be trained with a central lead running up to 6·0 to 9·0 m. (20 to 30 ft.). This is likely to occur naturally where the tree is in light woodland competing with others. *P. serrula* Franch., grown for its beautiful bark, should be trained as a half-standard, the lower part of the branches and the trunk being kept clear to show this beauty to the full. Thus the branchlets should be cut off during training and soon after planting, choosing midsummer for this pruning. In this way the size of the wounds is kept small and they heal more readily than large ones which seldom close completely. *P. incisa* Thunb. is almost alone among the cherries in that it does not produce gum in the region of wounds and thus reacts better to pruning.

P. glandulosa Thunb. forms an attractive, small bush if planted at the foot of a south wall and pruned hard back immediately after flowering, taking away all the old wood to the stool at the base. Die-back occurs during the winter if the growths do not ripen properly.

Subgenus IV. Padus, Bird Cherries

It is advisable to train *P. serotina* Ehrh. with a central lead which will develop through the greater part of the tree, the length of clear trunk being from 1·8 to 2·4 m. (6 to 8 ft.). In this way it will grow into a fairly large tree 18 m. (60 ft.) or more in height. If rival leads are allowed too early, the branch systems which develop from them will have a very narrow angle, and will thus be weak. The same is true of other large growers in this group, e.g. *P. padus* L. One habit of this species is that strong, upright growths are often thrown up by mature specimens from horizontal branches, through the centre of the tree. On no account, if this occurs, should thinning be attempted for this will check the tree and may even cause its death. *P. maackii* Rupr. has a finely coloured bark and stem, and the main branches should be cleared of twiggy growths before these become too large.

Subgenus V. Laurocerasus, Cherry Laurels

The Common Laurel, *P. laurocerasus* L., is frequently used to provide a formal surface, but clipping results in the disfigurement of a high proportion of the large leaves which remain on the surface. The alternative is to remove individual shoots and leaves one by one, using the secateurs, but this is very time-consuming. This subject is better as a screen plant when, if it is left unpruned, it will develop into a large specimen of considerable height and spread. Grown this way, any pruning which is necessary to restrict size should be carried out with the aim of retaining an informal effect. Brambles and other woody plants often grow on the edges of these clumps and these should be checked before they get out of hand. Laurel regenerates and grows very strongly and, if cut hard back and coppiced periodically, will make an excellent cover shrub, even in a dry situation. The best period for this hard cutting back is in the spring or early summer.

P. lusitanica L., The Portugal Laurel. This is similar in many respects to *P. laurocerasus* and it is at its best if left to grow freely when it will develop into a small tree. It does, however, respond to formal clipping and may be used in colder districts to provide a Bay Laurel effect in suitable settings.

Pests and Diseases

Those which commonly attack the various species when they are planted on a commercial scale are fortunately not as troublesome in the ornamental garden. This is undoubtedly the result of the better balance which exists in this community and all possible means should be taken to conserve this happy state of affairs. Neglect of feeding and mulching for the maintenance of good healthy growth is one of the commonest causes of trouble, but the too free use of a

R

drastic insecticide may be equally disastrous. If growth is impaired by insect attack, derris or pyrethrum sprays are usually effective if applied in the early stages and until the balance is restored. Diseases can in most cases be contained by cutting out affected branches as soon as they are noticed during inspections making sure that the cut is made sufficiently low down to remove all the infected wood. Diseased wood should be burnt at once, and the wound sealed with a suitable dressing.

Disease and die-back is more prevalent in badly drained or unsuitable soils, and the requirements of individual species and varieties should be studied before a selection is made.

Pseudolarix

P. amabilis (Nels.) Rehd. This beautiful tree will respond well to training, provided that the environment and growing conditions are suitable. A good, central lead is desirable and the horizontal branches which spring from it should be allowed a full spread in open surroundings. In this way the beauty of this conifer can be fully appreciated, as the lower branches, perhaps laden with cones, sweep down almost to ground level.

Often, after transplanting from the nursery into their final position, the young trees remain stunted for a few years, perhaps even losing vigour in the lead. However, provided that the planting site was adequately prepared and every attention is given to watering and feeding when necessary, such young trees usually grow away strongly, even to the extent of forming a new lead which often springs from beneath the older and perhaps weaker one. The secret of success is, therefore, to maintain good growth, thus enabling the tree to overcome any disaster which may befall the all-important leading shoot.

Pseudopanax

This small genus can only be grown in very mild localities, but it may survive against a wall in many parts of the South. The species appear to exhibit four distinct stages of growth. *P. ferox* T. Kirk in the second stage is occasionally met with. In this form it grows up to a height of 1 or 2 metres (3 or 6 ft.), but is usually completely unbranched. It is noticeable that the parent plant will branch if cuttings are taken off the top. Regular pruning is, however, out of the question. It is necessary to see that the shrub is firmly staked, as it becomes top-heavy with increased height. Mature bushes of *P. lessonii* Koch throw strong, young growths from the base and branch system. It may therefore be pruned in order to restrict size or spread by carefully cutting to the most promising of these growths.

Pseudosasa – *See* Bamboos.

Pseudotsuga

P. menziesii (Mirbel) Franco is capable of rapid growth and reaches a considerable height provided conditions are suitable. Growing well, it can be a delight to the arboriculturist, but on a poor dry soil it will cause him to despair. A healthy young tree will develop its lead and produce tiers of branches which should be encouraged to spread to their full extent. The tree is naturally irregular in growth and outline and no attempt should be made to trim it into shape by cutting back individual branches. Generally, if any cutting back needs to be done, it means that the cut is made right back to the main trunk, that is, apart from the removal of small, dead twiggy material.

Psoralea

P. glandulosa L. This is a half-hardy shrub with slender, upright and almost cane-like growths. It should be grown as a bush in the shelter of a sunny wall. The flowers are produced from the previous year's wood and from the young growths late in the season. This shrub has the curious habit of retaining clusters of buds in a living condition on the old wood. It is capable of breaking out quite strongly if cut down, even to ground level, by a severe winter. If it is necessary to confine the bush, this may be done in April, taking care to preserve as many growths at full length as possible.

Ptelea

This genus of small trees or shrubs is made up of only a few species. Apart from training in the nursery, very little pruning is necessary. *P. trifoliata* L. is the most common representative. It has a spreading habit and in the early stages of crown formation the branching is upright. Later, with a generally slender branch system this effect may be lost. One of the most important features of this species is the fruiting display which is quite conspicuous during the autumn and early winter months. The petioles which remain attached to the parent stems for a short time also add to the attraction. This display can be better appreciated when the specimen is well balanced against a background of deciduous trees. Some pruning on neighbouring trees may be necessary to retain this balance.

In training, a short leg 0·6 to 0·9 m. (2 to 3 ft.) is to be preferred. Staking is necessary, often for many years after planting, for this and other *Ptelea* species sometimes adopt a leaning posture, perhaps as a result of a weak root system. The powers of regeneration are good and should a tree be cut down to ground level, growth may be expected to break out freely to form a new head of branches.

The habits of growth and treatment of the remaining species are very similar.

Pterocarya

These trees are strong-growing when young and should be raised in the nursery under good conditions but in a sheltered position, as the young shoots in particular suffer in a severe winter or in a late spring frost. Damaged growths should be carefully cut back to living tissue as the buds break. A sunny position ensures that the growths are ripened and will winter better. It is important to retain the lead and to develop a 1·5 to 1·8 m. (5 to 6 ft.) leg. The reason for this is that the young trees show a tendency to branch low and for the crown to develop without a lead. The branching, however, is strong.

P. × *rehderiana* Schneid. This is the most common representative of this genus. As with the species, this hybrid will produce a furnished effect down to ground level, even with a 1·5 to 1·8 m. (5 to 6 ft.) trunk. Planted by the waterside, the branches spread out 0·3 m. (1 ft.) or so over the surface and the large, pinnate foliage produces a tropical effect. Eventually the branches dip beneath the water as the extending growth makes them heavier. Under these conditions even the more mature parts of the branch system form massive bunches of roots on the portions which are submerged and the whole surface becomes a jungle. This can be remedied by cutting back to remove such growths and at the same time to lighten the weight, leaving a fully furnished and natural effect. This hybrid suckers extensively, and unless an absolute thicket is desired, they should be cut down annually. Owing to the extensive and shallow root system which this subject produces, it is ideal for retaining banks by the waterside, *see* Plate 57.

Epicormic shoots are sometimes produced on the more horizontal branches, but these should be left unless they are very thick, as their removal will result in the production of a heavier crop in a year or so.

The species have similar habits, although normally they do not sucker as extensively. Even mature trees are prone to frost damage in the late spring. Owing to the danger of bleeding, large pruning cuts should be made in the late summer.

Pterostyrax

P. hispida Sieb. & Zucc. The form which this subject takes depends to a large extent upon the nursery training in the initial years. It may be trained to a single stem, when it will definitely form a small tree. On the other hand, the more common and perhaps better form is achieved by allowing the natural development of a few main stems which grow upright from ground level. With this habit it gains height more slowly, but will eventually reach 4·6 to 6·0 m. (15 to 20 ft.).

A healthy specimen may freely produce young growths from the main branches and from ground level. These may be thinned out and the strongest trained as replacements or as additions to the branch system. No regular pruning is needed to the main head of branches.

Punica

P. granatum L. This is normally a shrub for a warm, sunny wall. It may be trained up to the support or grown as a bush. The latter method is the better one, although it will have considerable spread, perhaps 1·8 to 2·4 m. (6 to 8 ft.) from the wall, and is also low-branching. It will respond to pruning and some of the older and weaker wood may be cut out during the late spring or summer. Wood should not be cut out during the winter as it is then difficult to distinguish living from dead. In severe winters this shrub may be cut back into the old wood which if alive will break out strongly.

When trained up close to a wall the main branches are tied out fanwise. Growths coming away from the wall are pruned short as the buds break in the spring. The free production of strong, young growths along the branch systems allows for some replacement of the old wood.

Pyracantha

The natural habit of the species is to form a system of closely knit branches, and they are very effective when grown as specimen shrubs in the border and in the more natural parts of the garden. Under these conditions they require very little pruning. If any is carried out for any reason, the cuts should be taken back into the centre so that the wound and the effects of the pruning are hidden. The stiff, rigid ends of cut and mauled branches look very unsightly and the effect of free growth is spoilt.

Pyracanthas conform well to extensive wall training, for the flowers and fruits are freely produced from spurs on the old wood. Thus the main branches may be trained fan-wise to cover the support, although it will be found that they conform well to any system of training. There are several methods of pruning as the structure is covered. A free form of bush is obtained by very little pruning at all. The main branches are loosely tied to the wiring system, and if necessary invasive branches are cut back in the spring after flowering to points hidden within the bush.

A closer system of training consists of cutting back all the growths which are not tied in for furnishing or replacement. This is done after flowering. Another system of rigid control is to clip over the whole surface annually in the spring or even two or three times during the growing season. Under this system the surface is given a very close covering, but the actual flowering may suffer.

Pyrus

This is a genus of small or medium-sized trees, one of the largest growers being *P. communis* L., the Common Pear, which may reach a height of 15·0 to 18·0 m. (50 to 60 ft.).

The species are normally propagated from seed or by grafting onto seedling stocks, usually *P. communis*. They are mostly strong-growing and it is important in the early years to train carefully, the best form of tree being a 2·4 to 3·0 m. (8 to 10 ft.) standard with a central lead. Often they grow so strongly that rival leads are easily formed and these need to be spotted and dealt with at an early stage. When the growth is free after the final planting it is difficult to avoid crossing branches. The natural growth of many of the species is very thick indeed. When the head finally matures the outer and lower branches have a pendulous habit. *P. ussuriensis* Maxim. is typical of the larger growers with a dense head and pendulous outer branches. Some knowledge of the growth and final habit is necessary, for example, *P. amygdaliformis* Vill. has a spreading shrub-like habit while *P. salicifolia* Pall 'Pendula' forms a small tree with a branching which is distinctly pendulous. For this habit to develop and be appreciated to full effect the foreground should be clear of any but dwarf shrubs.

Many of the species are susceptible to Fire Blight, (*Erwinia amylovora*), and a careful look out should be kept for this, especially after flowering, *see* Chapter Five.

Quercus

This great genus of trees contains species which vary enormously in size and, while a few of the hardier species are evergreen or, semi-evergreen, the majority are deciduous. From the arboriculturist's point of view their culture is very rewarding, for on good soils the hardy species grow well and, provided that a good lead and shape is formed in the nursery and the situation is not too exposed, fine trees are quite easily produced. It is more difficult to grow shapely trees in exposed sites but a few such as *Q. petraea* (Mattuschka) Lieblein, the Durmast Oak and *Q. ilex* L., the Holm Oak, will succeed well even on the coast, although the latter does not prove to be hardy in the colder districts.

Generally the oaks are safe trees to work on and they hold their framework well, even during severe gales. During such weather it is more likely to be the odd small branch which is twisted off than a large one, provided the tree has been well trained. Even dead branches are retained for a long period as the inner core of wood does not rot quickly. These often fall in considerable quantities from neglected oaks during severe gales.

Most of the oaks heal well, but even large wounds made on really old specimens which may never cover over completely, remain healthy, provided that the surface of the exposed wood is firm and intact and a protective dressing is applied immediately and renewed as necessary from time to time.

Many of the oaks produce epicormic growths, often on an extensive scale. These commonly occur on the branch systems and provided they do not become too large and out of proportion, they may be left. Usually their removal is quickly followed by a more vigorous outcrop. They should, however, be removed from the trunk unless the specimen has been cut hard back to the extent that there is little growth left other than in this region.

The oaks are classified botanically in a number of sub-genera and the following notes deal with those most commonly met with in this country.

Subgenus II, **Erithrobalanus,** the North American species.

These vary considerably in their reaction to our climate. *Q. borealis* Michx. f. *maxima* (Marsh.) Ashe is one of the best growers. The lead is retained very well, although the tendency for the ascending branches to rival this at a later stage demonstrates the importance of raising trees which have been formed well in the early years. *Q. b.* 'Aurea' is much slower in growth and requires shelter. However, the background should not be too close otherwise the tree develops a poor leaning shape. A distance of 15 m. (50 ft.) is suitable. Other rapid growers in this section include *Q. palustris* Muenchh., but the pendulous branches which often develop on mature specimens, although desirable in the garden, lead to increased work if used for roadside plantings. *Q. phellos* L. will grow to a large size, often with very heavy branching and it is important to keep the lead running up through the head in a young tree.

Generally the species in this group which come from the Southern United States are not completely at home in this country. This may not be due so much to the severity of our winters as to the rather indefinite seasons and a lack of sufficient sun to ripen the wood. *Q. agrifolia* Née may be quoted as an example. It comes from California, is evergreen and is often shrubby. Yet in the warmer and more southerly parts of this country, if carefully looked after when young, it will form a lead from which a trunk may finally develop. It is therefore wrong for the nurseryman and the planter to be too set in their methods and, with trees and shrubs which are on the borderline of hardiness, some modification of the original plan may be desirable. A mature tree will often lose a considerable amount of small growth after a severe winter and an annual check in the spring is advisable. The bark on the trunk often lifts in blocks and large patches and this needs attention before cavities form. The healing powers of this species are usually very strong. *Q. wislizeni* A. DC., a related species, is also found in California. It produces dense, twiggy growth and there is often considerable die-back to attend to after a severe winter.

Subgenus III, **Lepidobalanus**

This is divided into six sections which are also quite distinct from the arboriculturist's point of view.

Section 1, **Cerris**

Two species which will often grow into giants if given the position are *Q. castaneaefolia* C. A. Mey and *Q. cerris* L., the Turkey Oak. Both should be trained with good trunks and leads. The latter species produces outer and lower branches which are almost pendulous. The result of this is that the inside branches are likely to die-off through lack of sufficient light and will then need to be removed.

Q. variabilis Bl. is worthy of special mention as it shows how the good arboriculturist is able to bring out the best in a tree by correct training. The species is slender and light branching, but the main attraction is in the bark of the main trunk which is flaked in a beautiful diamond pattern. To show this to full effect the trunk should be run up as straight as possible and should be cleared of lower branches up to 3·0 m. (10 ft.), before these get too large.

Section 2, **Suber**

The species in this section are evergreen and many suffer severely during a hard winter. *Q. suber* L., the Cork Oak, to some extent provides an example for the remainder, for if the climate and conditions are not ideal, it seems impossible to grow anything but a miserable specimen. *Q. alnifolia* Poech and *Q. coccifera* L. are usually shrubby and unless nursery specimens show a definite tendency to form a lead they should be left to grow freely.

The one distinctive tree in this section is the hybrid *Q.* × *hispanica* Lam. var. *lucombeana* (Sweet) Rehd., the Lucombe Oak, and it should be trained to form a large tree.

Section 3, **Ilex**

This is a section of evergreens of which *Q. ilex* L., the Holm Oak, is the most important. In earlier days it was much used in formal designs and very large specimens were often clipped annually in the late summer to maintain a dense, rigid outline. Even as a hedge the Holm Oak will maintain a good surface.

However, the beauty of this tree is shown to perfection in free growth and heavy branching. The outer growths and branches should be left to grow down to ground level, when they will look particularly fine with the light green growths set against the dark foliage. A trunk of 1·8 to 2·4 m. (6 to 8 ft.) is preferable, but the shade which is cast is very dense, and there should be no attempt to have a border beneath or near a large specimen. It is better to use grass as a foreground, running this up to the base of the tree or, if the growths are already touching the ground, up to the outer perimeter of foliage. It will also take many years for this subject to reach the ground again once the lower branches have been removed and therefore this should not be done lightly without serious consideration. Where large formally clipped specimens still exist under conditions where there is insufficient labour to attend to the annual trimming which is so necessary, they will quickly develop a free, natural growth with very little attention. As free growth develops after two or three years the trunk can, if necessary, be cleared and formed, while at a later stage some of the smaller growths may be thinned out in the centre as the stronger branches become more evident.

Q. phillyraeoides Gray should be left to grow freely in the nursery as it is more often shrub-like.

Section 5, Robur

Most of the species in this group are strong growers and will develop into large trees. *Q. frainetto* Ten., *Q. canariensis* Willd., *Q. macranthera* Fisch. & Mey., *Q. pyrenaica* Willd., *Q. petraea* (Mattuschka) Lieblein, the Durmast Oak, and *Q. robur* L., the English Oak, all form good leads and with training will branch well to form a good length of clear trunk with a large head. *Q. pubescens* Willd. is a smaller tree, but it is usually possible to retain a lead of 4·6 m. (15 ft.) or more through the tree before it is left to open out. *Q. pontica* K. Koch branches low on a short trunk and is, in nature, often shrubby. It should therefore be left to form a head even though the leg may only be 0·6 to 0·9 m. (2 to 3 ft.) in length. *Q. robur* in particular suffers from die-back on the topmost and outer branches, a condition which is referred to as 'stag-headed'. A tree which has this does not necessarily show a general decline in health, for much depends upon the causes of this condition. Often the primary cause is a lowering of the water table, and the fact that the living part of the tree may remain in reasonably good condition is an indication that, with encouragement, the effect can be delayed or even offset for many years. Eventually, of course, rot and decay gain a foothold on the cut ends formed by the removal of the dead wood, but at least a number of years usually elapse before such trees die completely, and this gives time for new plantings to mature. Impoverishment or a check to the root system may be another cause of die-back. There are many forms of *Q. robur* and their habits of growth must be recognised during the training stage. 'Cristata', for example, forms a small crowded head and it is usually difficult to retain the lead for long. 'Purpurascens' is found in several forms, but in one it produces a dwarf stunted tree whose branches are covered with epicormic growths. These should be left as it is a characteristic of this variety and an attraction.'Filicifolia' Hartw. & Rumpl., which tends to produce a branch system in layers, has most beautiful foliage and should be allowed to branch low in an open space for this to be seen to best effect. The fastigiate form, 'Fastigiata' must be allowed to grow freely unpruned.

Section 6, Prinus

So many of this group do not succeed well in this country that there is a temptation for arboriculturists to dismiss them completely. However, at least one, *Q. bicolor* Willd., is worthy of consideration, for it produces a good lead and the trunk, if it is kept clear of branches, will display a shaggy bark to full effect. *Q. prinus* L. produces thin, wiry branchlets and the general effect of the foliage is seen to best advantage if there is full light on at least one side, for the branching to come down to eye level. *Q. dentata* Thunb. tests the skill of the arboriculturist to the full, for it has the reputation of being short lived in this country. Die-back often occurs on the younger wood during the winter, causing bushy growths on the tips of the branches as a result of regeneration.

Raphiolepis

These are slow-growing, stiff shrubs with leathery leaves. *R. umbellata* (Thunb.) Mak. forms a fairly compact and rounded bush in full sun, but under even slightly shaded conditions it tends to be more spreading with an untidy habit. There also seems to be a greater tendency for the shrub, when under these conditions, to produce long growths, often at random, which throw it completely out of shape. If desired, some pruning to shape may be carried out in April by taking off such growths to a suitable point well inside the bush. Dead branches which appear from time to time should also be cut out. Otherwise, no regular pruning is needed.

  R. indica Lindl. is less hardy and needs wall protection in all but the milder localities. The same is true to some extent of *R.* × *delacourii* Andre.

  Wall protection is best afforded these shrubs by allowing them to grow as a bush rather than by training them rigidly to the wall face. They should be planted about 0·5 m. from the base of a south wall.

Rehderodendron

R. macrocarpum Hu. This rare tree eventually reaches a height of approximately 6·0 m. (20 ft.). It should, if possible, be kept to a single lead, but should be allowed to furnish as fully and as close to ground level as possible. Little pruning is needed.

  This is a subject for a sheltered part of a woodland garden but nearby trees and shrubs should if necessary, be pruned, rather than that the growth of this choice tree should be impaired in any way, *see* Fig. 26.

Rhamnus

Although the species within this genus are grouped botanically there is not suffi- cient difference in the pruning to warrant an elaboration of this classification.

It is however essential to be acquainted with the final habit and form while the young plants are in the nursery stage.

Many of the larger growers will develop into small trees, particularly if a short leg of 0·9 to 1·2 m. (3 to 4 ft.) is kept clear of branches as the head is being built up. *R. purshiana* DC. will even grow to a height of 9·0 to 12·0 m. (30 to 40 ft.), but if allowed to develop low branching from ground level, it will be much shorter. The species which develop into large shrubs or small trees are most attractive when growing on the edge of a clump, when the pendulous habit of the ends of the branchlets can be seen to best effect. With this habit dead wood is formed on the undersides of such branch systems and this must be cut away cleanly.

R. alaternus L. is quite a distinct grower. It has an attractive evergreen shoot and leaf system which is seen at its best when the shrub is grown in the front of a border, and allowed to furnish right down to ground level. By careful pruning a perfect informal surface may be maintained, as this subject branches very freely. 'Argenteo-variegata' is somewhat tender and needs a sheltered position.

It is worth noting that there are dwarf species such as *R. pumila* L., which is procumbent and suitable for the rock garden.

R. frangula L., a slender-growing shrub or small tree, is suitable as a support for such climbers as *Lonicera caprifolium* L.

Rhododendron

Normally this large genus requires very little pruning, the main essential being to maintain healthy growth by the provision of correct growing conditions. Not only is it necessary to study and provide for their soil and moisture requirements, but some will tolerate quite exposed and sunny positions, while others require shade and shelter. These factors are of course directly connected with cultural conditions, but it is most likely that failure to provide a suitable environment will result in ill-health and die-back, which in turn will necessitate pruning. This cutting-out of dead branches which should in fact be living, can be very disheartening, for almost invariably the whole plant is unhealthy and it is just a question of time before the poor specimen is cut away completely. The rule should be to follow the use of the secateurs or saw with improved culture.

From time to time it becomes necessary to cut out dead wood which has developed inside the bush as a result of the loss of light. This is most likely to occur on crowded specimens, when the result is often a mass of trunks and branches, perhaps near the path or on the edge of the border, with the foliage and flowers well above head level. This is a difficult position to correct, the best method with the larger leaved species being to slowly reduce selected specimens by pruning in order to give the remaining ones more light. This should be carried out over a period of at least 3 to 4 years, when a final decision to clear any undesirable specimens may be taken. It is possible that the bushes which have been cut back will have regenerated and be in better condition than the unpruned ones. The one danger of thinning and clearing in one operation without any preparatory pruning, is that the remaining bushes will be unduly exposed and more likely to be blown out during a gale. It is sometimes possible, by replanning the beds and paths, to avoid cutting back altogether, in which case this may be the more desirable course.

It should be noted that many species and varieties of Rhododendron will regenerate with young growth after being cut hard back, but it is difficult to be more precise than this, as it then becomes a matter of trial and error with experience playing a big part. *R. augustinii* Hemsl., *R. davidsonianum* Rehd. & Wils., *R. yunnanense* Franch. and *R. concinnum* Hemsl. are very responsive indeed and they will break out freely even after being cut back to the old wood or to near ground level. It should be noted that those mentioned above are in the Series Triflorum, a group which, among others, responds readily to hard pruning. It is possible that the response would be far greater than is generally realised, but it is a sounder policy to cut back the commoner subjects, leaving the rarer and more choice ones intact with sufficient space for development. Who would think of cutting back a large specimen in the Series Grande, such as *R. macabeanum* Balf. f. when the overcrowding could be relieved by reducing thick and towering clumps of *R. ponticum* L. Often such a surround, although reduced, is needed for shelter and thus there is need of balanced pruning in relation to microclimate, *see* Fig. 26.

Rhododendrons are sometimes used for informal hedging and screening; *R. ponticum*, in particular is planted for this purpose. Pruning to restrict size, if necessary, should take the form of regular, annual pruning after flowering. The cuts may be made well into the bushes on growths which extend beyond the limits, thus concealing the fact that they have been cut at all. It is emphasised that, if this controlled and systematic pruning is carried out regularly, there is no need for the drastic cut-back, which, although effective, is rather unsightly for a time. However, should this hard cutting back be necessary, perhaps as a result of overgrowth through years of neglect, it should be carried out directly after flowering and before the new growth is put on.

Clumps of *R. ponticum* in a natural setting have a habit which can be divided into two distinct phases. Firstly, new growths extend and arch up from near ground level, often creating the effect of a low border round a clump. This is the stage at which pruning should take place, for these quickly send up new and extensive growths, which gain height quickly to enlarge the clump considerably.

It is a common practice to remove the old flower heads as the blossoms fade and before energy is spent in useless seed production. This is a form of pruning and it is very effective in helping the new growth, particularly if a dry spell sets in. It is done quite easily by holding the old flower truss firmly in the hand with the fingers and thumb on the lower part of the main stalk but above the developing growth. Sometimes it is necessary to use the free hand to steady the growth and to assist generally. Provided that sufficient care is taken, the heads come away cleanly without damaging the remaining growths and foliage.

It is important to watch for suckers with grafted plants, and these should be cut off as soon as they appear, as close to the root as possible.

Rhodotypos

R. scandens (Thunb.) Mak. This shrub is allied to *Kerria japonica* and has a similar habit of growth. Wood is thrown up from the base of the shrub so freely that it is advisable to cut a proportion of the older wood down to ground level. The shrub flowers on short laterals from the previous year's wood and therefore young canes produced in one season will flower in the next. The intensity of the pruning should depend upon condition, growth and flowering. Sometimes the cuts are made to suitable growths on the old wood, at other times at ground level. Pruning is best carried out after flowering but as a second best it may be done in the winter.

Rhus

The species within this genus vary considerably in their habit and mode of growth but, apart from specialised systems of culture, very little pruning is necessary. The tree species need training to a single lead in the early stages of their formation. *R. verniciflua* Stokes forms a large, wide-branching tree and is similar from the arboriculturist's point of view to *R. pontanini* Maxim. Both callus and heal well if cuts have to be made, although it is better to do this just before leaf fall in order to minimise the risk of bleeding. Both may have a 1·2 to 1·8 m. (4 to 6 ft.) length of clear trunk. *R. punjabensis* Stew. var. *sinica* (Diels) Rehd. & Wils. and *R. vernix* L. are also in this group, the sap of the latter being reputed to have toxic properties. Some of the other species, *R. toxicodendron* L. for example, may on contact also cause irritation and rashes, some people being more susceptible than others, and it is advisable to work on any suspected tree or shrub for two or three short, trial periods before any major task is undertaken. Rubber gloves should also be used for protection.

A number of species may be looked upon as forming trees or shrubs, for example *R. typhina* L. often develops into a small tree, particularly if it is trained with a short, clear stem when it is young. *R. trichocarpa* Miq. with stiff upright branches is another example and no pruning other than training is needed. *R. glabra* L. is similar to *R. typhina*, but is smaller. To be seen at their best these three latter species should have an open foreground, when the furnished effect to ground level will be particularly attractive with autumn foliage tints.

Those species which are definitely shrubby, for example, *R. trilobata* Nutt. and *R. aromatica* Ait., should be allowed to branch freely from ground level. Often a number of young growths are thrown up from the base and these may be used for replacement purposes.

The lower, shrubby species such as *R. toxicodendron* L. sucker freely, forming spreading clumps and are thus more suitable for the more natural parts of the garden, but never where children are likely to play.

R. glabra 'Laciniata' and *R. typhina* 'Laciniata' may be grown purely for foliage effect. Under this system the young growths are cut back to within approximately 100 mm. (4 in.) of the old wood. Thus a low framework is gradually built up. Shrubs so treated should be heavily mulched and fed each year. If the growths are considered to be too crowded, they should be thinned as they shoot up in the spring.

Ribes

Within this genus are three subgenera; I. Berisia, mostly unarmed, II. Ribesia, the Currants, which are unarmed and III. Grossularioides, the Gooseberries, which are armed. All have a stool mode of growth, freely producing shoots and branches just beneath ground level. Most are alike too in requiring a sunny position in which to develop and ripen their wood. The most ornamental forms flower freely from almost the whole length of the shoots made during the previous season. A number of the less decorative forms, for example *R. rubrum* L., flower near the base of the previous season's wood and also from spurs on the older branches.

However, this minor difference matters very little, for their general habit does allow whole branches to be cut down, even to ground level, thus giving light and air to the new growths springing from the base. By this means a balance is maintained between old and young wood.

Many of the Currants, for example *R. sanguineum* Pursh., are best pruned immediately after flowering, taking away the older branches and cutting them down to a bud or growth as close to the ground as possible. It may be necessary to remove from a quarter to one-third of a mature bush each year, aiming to leave no wood above ground level which is older than five years.

With the Gooseberry section the framework is more permanent, but some pruning must be carried out to remove old branches and to restrict growth within reasonable bounds. They should be looked over for any pruning which may be needed at least twice during the year, in the dormant season and again at the height of growth. The latter period is particularly useful, for when in foliage their full size and effect can best be judged. Also it does ensure that neighbouring shrubs are prevented from being overgrown if growth is heavy.

Most members of this genus respond well to hard pruning when they are neglected and overgrown. This may be carried out during the summer or winter and all but the youngest shoots or branches may be removed. If all top growth is to be removed completely this should only be done during the dormant season in order to give them the best chance of recovery. Often the growths which are produced as a response to this treatment are lush and soft for the first season, and are liable to be broken by severe winds. They should therefore be staked in time to avoid this, while some thinning may also be necessary.

The natural habit of growth must also be taken into account and the method varied accordingly. For example, most of the *R. sanguineum* varieties produce a strong and fairly rigid framework and are a complete contrast in growth to *R. odoratum* Wendl. which has a loose habit and whose supple branches may even lean over on to neighbouring plants. Again, *R. alpinum* L., 'Pumilum' is dwarf growing, and pruning, unless dead branches occur, is not necessary. *R. sanguineum* 'Brocklebankii' is not a strong grower and slight shade with good cultural conditions are more essential than pruning.

R. speciosum Pursh. is sometimes treated as a wall shrub and in this position it often reaches 3·0 m. (10 ft.) in height. Full account must be taken of its habit of growth. The young shoots produced from the base should be used for the replacement of the older ones, otherwise over the years the vigour of the specimen may diminish. This replacement pruning may be done during the late summer after the new growths have been produced. The growths must be tied hard against the surface of the wall and trained fanwise.

The *R. sanguineum* varieties make good hedge plants. By pruning after flowering, using secateurs to cut out the older wood, the dimensions are restricted, but the whole effect is informal. If the outline is cut rigidly to a definite height and width, a build up of old wood reduces the amount of young growth, which in turn affects flowering. Also the secateurs are selective and the strongest and most forward growths can be saved, whereas with the shears these are often cut off and the shrubs are forced to develop weaker and retarded buds. This species has a good reputation for wind resistance and even thrives near the coast despite periodic scorching from sea gales.

Many of the Ribes genus suffer badly from attacks by aphis in the spring and early summer. The tips of the young growths are badly distorted and thus the health of the bushes as a whole is affected. Corrective sprays must be applied in the early stages of an attack. The Gooseberry Sawfly will also attack many species.

Robinia

This genus of leguminous trees and shrubs is distinctive by reason of the very light and attractive foliage canopy, in addition to the branch system which is beautiful at all times of the year. The wood has a reputation for being brittle and large limbs are sometimes torn off during gales at the junctions with the main stems or branches, leaving bad tears which often extend for considerable distances. This is more likely to happen with an old tree which is declining in health. Trees which are suspected of being dangerous should have their limbs shortened, or more drastic action taken if this is considered advisable.

Owing to the danger of bleeding all pruning should, if possible, be carried out during the mid to late summer period. Dead wood should also be cut out at this time.

Robinias in general are healthier after a sunny summer when the young wood is well ripened, and a tree in this condition winters better than one which is poorly ripened. The wood will also be healthier on a well drained soil. Sometimes the young growths are damaged by the late spring frosts and it is therefore better to avoid frost pockets when choosing a site.

In the nursery the tree forms and species should be trained up with a single lead and this should be retained through the crown. A clear stem of 1·8 to 2·4 m. (6 to 8 ft.) is advisable. Rival leads produce a forked or divided main trunk, and in later life these trees in particular are very weak at such points. Old trees which have this weakness should be braced for safety.

R. pseudoacacia L. is the most common species. It is a rapid grower and suckers freely, especially from roots left in situ after the parent tree has been cut down. This species also regenerates and throws out very strongly after being pruned or cut back. Upright growths will even develop inside the cavities of old stems if they extend for some considerable distance to the light.

It is grown in many forms. 'Inermis' forms a very close and compact head and is termed the 'Mop-head Acacia'. This close habit is normally maintained without pruning, but a careful watch should be kept for strong growths from the stock which sometimes break out at the graft-line normally situated just below the head. If they are left the whole mop-headed nature will be destroyed as they develop and extend. 'Pyramidalis' has a habit which is very similar in form to that of the 'Lombardy Poplar'. It is most effective when it has a clear foreground with low branching, even close to ground level. With an old specimen some form of bracing between the main branches may be necessary. 'Tortuosa' is slow growing, but despite this a lead should if possible be retained as the crown forms. 'Rehderii' is not grafted, but is grown on its own roots and is normally allowed to branch from ground level. There are a number of other well-known forms, but the main point to remember is to take the habit of growth into account when training and pruning. 'Frisia' is so conspicuous by reason of its yellow foliage that any malformation will detract from the overall beauty.

The remaining species also display variations of growth and habit. R. × *ambigua* Poir. 'Bella-rosea' forms a small tree with upright branching and a twiggy shoot system. R. × *hillieri* also forms a small tree. R. *luxurians* Schneid. will often form a large shrub unless a lead is selected and trained.

The definitely shrubby species seem to be more difficult to grow well and they demand better conditions with a warm, sunny position on a well-drained soil. Shelter from strong winds is also desirable, for the growths and branches are brittle. This is also a difficulty when they are grown as standards, for the branch system is then more exposed.

Robinia pseudoacacia wood is very durable, and the trunk of a tree which is condemned will serve as a useful support for such a climber as *Celastrus* or *Lonicera*, and will last for many years. It should be cut down to 3·0 to 4·6 m. (10 to 15 ft.), leaving the remainder of the trunk and the root system intact.

Romneya

These thrive best in a sunny, warm, well-drained position. They spread by means of buds on thick fleshy horizontal roots. The extent to which the stems are killed back is dependent upon the severity of the winter. The growth above ground is often killed right down to ground level, but the stems should be left until growth commences in the spring, when the cuts can be made to living wood, or taken down completely. In either case the subject will flower, as the blossoms terminate the current season's wood. Wood which is growing hard up against a wall is more likely to be retained and a greater height may then be built up. Even so it is advisable to renew the wood by cutting out old stems and retaining young growths from the base.

Rosa

This vast genus, including many species and related hybrids, displays three distinct habits of growth and flowering. They are:

(i) those which flower best on the growths made during the previous year. Long growths are thrown up, often from the base of the plant each year. R. *wichuraiana* Crep. and the Rambler Hybrids are examples.

(ii) those which flower on laterals which are produced from growths made during the previous season. However, all the growths are part of a framework which is retained in a vigorous condition for many years. New growths are also sent up from the base. Many of the species and allied hybrids are in this group, for example, *R. moyesii* Hemsl. & Wils. The framework is retained but is invigorated by strong growths from ground level, while there is usually a definite period for flowering, followed by fruiting. It should, however, be noted that summer pruning, or an extended period of mild weather in the autumn, sometimes results in flower production on the new growths soon after their development is completed.

(iii) those which flower from laterals produced from the previous years wood, but also directly from growths made during the current season. Thus there is a continuous flowering from about June until the first frosts in the autumn, starting with the growths produced on the last season's wood and continuing with the young shoots which are produced often from near the base. Those in the Indicae Section, which includes *R. odorata* Sweet, the Tea Rose, have this habit.

Pruning related to Growth and Flowering

It will be seen at a glance that the group which flowers best on laterals, which are produced by the young shoots made during the previous year may have much of the old wood cut out after flowering, provided there is sufficient of the new. With the two remaining groups, on the other hand, to cut this older wood out would be wrong when it supports a good flower display, and when there is not sufficient replacement wood. However, this is perhaps an over-simplification, and it may be dangerous to apply these rules generally. It should, however, be looked upon as an attempt to give the reader an over-all understanding of the subject. Most roses grow naturally by a system of replacement of the older flowering branches by young ones. The nature of the pruning depends in many cases upon the vigour of the plant and the extent of this ability to replace old wood. With this understanding an intelligent pruner, using his powers of observation to the full, will adjust the pruning according to the vigour and type of wood of each bush in turn, in order to obtain the maximum display the following season.

The rose species are divided botanically into subgenera and sections, each of which displays a typical habit of growth and has its own pruning requirements.

Subgenus Hulthemia

R. persica Michx. This is a very rare shrub indeed, which is normally grown under glass or in a very warm and sheltered border. It spreads by means of suckers and these should be left to develop as they produce the strongest growth and are more likely to succeed. There is little actual pruning apart from cutting out the dead wood.

Subgenus Eurosa

Section 1. **Pimpinellifoliae.** *R. spinosissima* L. is a species which normally suckers, especially in a light, sandy soil where it is very much at home. For this reason it is difficult to restrict this species and many of the varieties to a given area, and the suckers need constant attention during the summer months. Occasionally, some of the older wood can be cut out of the larger growers such as *R. s.* var. *altaica* (Willd.) Rehd. The form *R. s.* 'Andrewsii' Willm., makes an attractive, informal hedge about 1·2 m. (4 ft.) high. Of the stronger-growing species in this section, some have graceful, arching branches such as *R. hugonis* Hemsl., but they may become untidy as they grow older, for as extension growths are produced on the older wood these too arch over and thus the shape is spoilt and a bare stem exposed. By looking over the bushes after flowering, this habit may be checked, cutting out the oldest wood low down and near ground level. The remainder of the branches and the laterals are left intact, many of the latter having a definite horizontal habit and with the foliage being almost fern-like an attractive effect is produced.

The following species may be treated in a similar manner: *R. primula* Boulenger, *R. ecae* Aitch., *R. farreri* Stapf, *R. xanthina* Lindl. and *R. omeiensis* Rolfe. A study of the growth which these make will serve as a guide for others. *R. xanthina* f. *spontanea* Rehd. (Syn. 'Canary Bird') is sometimes grown as a standard on rugosa stock. Pruning is much the same, but staking needs to be very rigid, for a heavy head of foliage is produced. A wire frame or cross-piece secured to the stake may be concealed and yet hold the head rigid, thus preventing wind sway which would otherwise occur. *R. foetida* Herrm. itself, with some of the stronger forms, produces strong, arching growths which readily extend over neighbouring shrubs and become a nuisance. This can be corrected by thinning out the older wood which weighs the new growth down and encourages this habit.

Section 2. **Gallicanae.** The Moss Roses and many of the other old fashioned hybrids belong to this group.

R. gallica L. The varieties in this group vary in growth and habit. Most need good growing soil and conditions but the branches often become thick and crowded, especially as the new growth is put on during and after flowering. Some thinning is therefore necessary, taking out the older shoots after flowering down to good healthy growths or buds, often to ground level. Final adjustment may be made in March before the new growth commences, taking out more of the thinner and older wood, and even shortening a number of the young growths if this is considered necessary. Hard pruning will not, however, help these roses to make good if the growing conditions are not suitable.

R. centifolia L., the Cabbage Rose, is also related to many of the old hybrids including the Moss Rose. If it is considered necessary some of the weaker and older wood may be thinned after flowering and a final look over the shrubs made before growth commences in the spring. Vigour must be taken into account, for example, the variety 'William Lobb' reaches up to 3·0 m. (10 ft) and needs the support of a pillar or wall. *R. damascena* Mill., the Damask Rose, has similar pruning requirements, but again the importance of taking vigour into account is stressed.

R. × *alba* L. is quite a strong-growing shrub, and the branches are often so

s

heavy with fruit that they spoil the general shape of the bush. These may be pruned back to suitable upright growths after the fruiting display is over.

Section 3. **Caninae.** In growth the species in this section vary considerably, some being sturdy, others producing long, arching branches. Those with a sturdy habit are suitable for border culture, but the scrambling species are difficult to control and satisfy in such a situation and need a small tree or artificial structure for support.

R. glutinosa Sibth. & Sm. is dwarf and compact and spreads by means of suckers. It should be planted in a group in the front of the border. There is little pruning with this beyond the removal of the obviously dead wood. *R. pomifera* Herrm. and *R. mollis* Smith have a fairly erect and sturdy habit and are suitable for border culture. After the fruiting display is over, the older wood may be thinned out before the new starts. *R. tomentosa* Smith has an arching habit and will rest on neighbouring shrubs. It is therefore better suited to the more natural parts of the garden. *R. rubrifolia* Vill. is suitable for the border or a coloured foliage feature. There is little pruning, except to thin out the oldest wood after the fruits have vanished.

R. corymbifera Borkh., *R. micrantha* Sm., *R. stylosa* Desv. and *R. canina* L. have arching growths and if growing strongly they are a nuisance in the border unless a stake or support is given. They are better in the wilder parts of the garden, for it is difficult to prune them on a restrictive policy and yet do them justice. Growths can be looped over and around stakes, but unless some pruning is carried out before the season's growth commences each year, the bushes develop into an impossible tangle of shoots, which will in the end prove difficult to control. The early spring period is selected for this pruning operation as many of these species have an attractive fruiting display. *R. eglanteria* L., the Sweet Briar, has an erect habit with arching branches, but it is easier to keep under control. It is also grown as a hedge plant, being tied down to the fence or supporting wire system. Pruning takes place in the late winter or early spring when the fruit display is over. Some of the older wood is then cut out and the new growths tied in.

Section 4. **Carolinae.** *R. carolina* L. and *R. virginiana* Mill. are somewhat similar in habit as they both form dense clumps of erect stems, the former spreading by means of suckers. Both species are more suitable for the more natural parts of the garden, for the branches arch over as they become laden with fruit. In the border, unless they are surrounded by shrubs which are of equal size, they need staking, as otherwise this habit spoils their effect. Pruning consists of cutting out the oldest branches after the fruits have disappeared, but the stems tend to support each other and they should not be over-thinned. *R. foliolosa* Nutt. has the same habit although it is only 0·9 m. (3 ft.) in height. Its branches are thin, it spreads by means of suckers and in the border needs quite a large and sheltered area. *R. nitida* Willd. has similar requirements although it is not as invasive or untidy in its habits. With both species, just the oldest wood should be cut out after the fruiting display is over.

Section 1. **Cinnamomeae.** This section shows considerable variation in habit and size, but the general rule is again to cut and thin out the older wood after the fruiting display has finished, remembering the all-important essential that the natural habit of growth must be taken into account. The habit of *R. rugosa* Thunb. need only be compared with that of *R. davidii* Crep. for one to realise how wide this variation is – wider in fact than in any other section. However, pruning to confine these strong growers spoils their free and vigorous habit. This is also true of other strong growers such as *R. moyesii* Hemsl. & Wils. and *R. willmottiae* Hemsl.

Section 6. **Synstylae.** These are strong growers and many of the species and hybrids in this group may reach considerable heights, provided that a suitable support is available. They will even climb 9·0 to 12·0 m. (30 to 40 ft.) over large trees. *R. multiflora* Thunb. and *R. moschata* Herrm. are good examples. Both, with others, have been used for hybridisation purposes, the Rambler Roses having been derived partly from the former species. Little pruning is necessary if these are growing unrestrictedly unless its purpose is to invigorate, when old wood may be cut out after flowering back to suitable young wood. Normally, if the plant is strong the old wood should be left for the fruit display. *R. wichuraiana* Crep. has long, prostrate or trailing growths which are ideal for covering banks. Again, pruning is unnecessary provided growth is strong.

Many, even the most vigorous in this group will also trail well over banks when no support is available. As an example, *R. multiflora* Thunb. will, under these conditions, form a large, dense clump which would defy all efforts to produce a tidy bush by pruning; indeed, under natural or semi-wild conditions it would be wrong to try. It is only when they are grown in a confined space, perhaps tied to a single stake in a border or a pergola in a formal setting, that annual pruning becomes necessary. By cutting out lengths of the old wood after flowering the development of young wood is encouraged, that which originates from near the base being especially valuable. The amount of old wood to be cut out depends entirely upon the condition of the young, developing growths. The long, arching growths which are left may also be looped over and tied in, a good method of containing large climbers in a small space.

It is an advantage to hard-prune a young plant intended for this restricted training and habit for the first season or two after planting, for this ensures the production of sufficient young growth from the base. Flowering does not matter at this early stage and pruning can therefore be carried out in the spring back to growths or buds near the base of the plant.

Section 7. **Indicae.** The species and hybrids in this section flower over a long period during the early summer on growths from the old wood, and later in the year from shoots produced during the current season, often from near the base of the plant. *R. odorata* Sweet, the Tea Rose, and *R. chinensis* Jacq., the China Rose, both have this habit. Pruning in February or March should consist of cutting out some of the oldest and weakest growths and branch systems, often close to ground level. In this way the bushes are thinned out, allowing less crowded conditions for the growth and flowers which are produced later. Some of the previous year's growths are left on the more promising branch systems.

These laterals are shortened back by a third or more, thus removing the old heads and the unripened portions.

R. × *noisettiana* Thory has a climbing or spreading habit and thus much of the framework is retained from year to year. The laterals are pruned back in the spring together with the oldest and weakest branches, provided there is new growth coming up from the base which can be used for replacement.

R. × *borboniana* Desp. is a strong, upright grower. The oldest and weakest wood is cut out in the spring. The unripened and flowered tips of the laterals which remain are cut back.

Section 8. **Banksianae.**   The most important rose in this section is R. *banksiae* Ait. It is a climber and may reach a height of 12·0 m. (40 ft.). It is not likely to be successful in the open garden, even with a suitable support, for it is not sufficiently hardy. A South or West facing wall is necessary, using the ordinary strained wire method of support in order that the plant may be tied in as close to the wall as possible.

As maturity is reached some annual pruning is advisable, otherwise the plant becomes very untidy with long trailing growths which extend for 1 or 2 metres (3 or 6 ft.) from the protective surface of the wall. It is also necessary to keep the young growths close to the wall for protection during the winter, as otherwise they may suffer considerable damage.

The main pruning period is after flowering when some of the very old wood may be cut out and the young growths tied in as replacements, thereby preventing overcrowding. Much of the main framework, however, remains for the life of the plant, although sometimes strong growths several feet in length are produced from the base in one season, and there need be no hesitation in cutting out even the main branch systems if they are considered to be old and weak. In the late autumn, before the winter sets in, any growths which have developed away from the wall should be tied in. Spring pruning in April consists of cutting out any wood or shoot tips which may have been frosted during the winter.

The method of pruning by spurring back all the young growth after the petals fall results in a loss of flowering potential in the following season. The forms R. *b.* var. *albo-plena* Rehd. and R. *b.* var. *lutea* Lindl. are more common than the type R. *b.* var. *normalis* Reg.

Section 9. **Laevigatae.**   R. *laevigata* Michx., the strong tender grower in this section, is more suited to wall culture, except in the mildest parts of the country where it may be grown in the open with a tree for support. Trained on a wall, the young growths should be tied in to replace some of the older wood after flowering. The same method of pruning may be applied to the hybrids in which this species is involved such as R. × *anemonoides* Rehd. and 'Silver Moon'.

Section 10. **Bracteatae.**   R. *bracteata* Wendl. is not fully hardy and must be given wall protection. Even with this safeguard it is only suitable for the warmer localities. In the nursery it should be encouraged to form laterals low down on the plant, by stopping if necessary. These are trained out fanwise to form the permanent branch system. As these branch, the space allocated to the plant is covered.

At a later stage the laterals produced from the framework grow out from the wall and flower. Pruning should be carried out annually in the spring, the aim being to keep the plant tidy and as close to the wall as possible for maximum protection. Also, the extent of the winter's damage is then evident, and any dead pieces may be cut back to living tissue. The laterals which have flowered during the previous season may be shortened to strong, healthy growths which should be developing near their bases. Some of the older branch systems may be cut out entirely, provided that there are young growths which have wintered and are suitable as replacements. These young growths are more certain to winter well if tied in against the wall as they develop during the summer and autumn. The old branches which they will replace are not cut out until the spring, as they will protect the young growths which are more likely to be killed by severe weather.

The hybrid, 'Mermaid' is hardier and may be grown in colder areas, provided that a wall is selected. In the milder districts a stake or pergola is suitable. This hybrid is often budded onto one of the rose stocks, but it may be grown successfully on its own roots, and has even been known to sucker strongly from these. Pruning is similar to that carried out on the species, *R. bracteata*. A low branching should be encouraged in the nursery. By having the lower part of the shrub shaded, perhaps by suitable shrubs, the wood is prevented from hardening, and is thus more likely to throw strong, young, basal shoots which can be used for replacement purposes.

Subgenus Hesperhodos

R. stellata Woot. is in this small group. It is difficult to grow, liking a well-drained, sunny position. *R. minutifolia* Engelm. has similar requirements and is even more difficult. Both species are better suited to warmer and sunnier climates than ours.

R. s. var. *mirifica* (Greene) Cockerell is a stronger grower but also prefers a sunny, well-drained position. It has a suckerous habit and flowers better on this younger and stronger wood from laterals produced in the second season. Pruning consists of cutting out the old and dead wood in the spring and looking over the plants again after flowering, when the new season's growth may be taken into account in deciding just how much of the old should finally be removed. The suckers often appear among neighbouring plants as the clump becomes established and, if these are valued, must be removed at an early stage, tracing the root back to the parent plant if possible. A shrub with this habit is better in an isolated bed surrounded by grass or among taller shrubs which will not suffer in any way. This rose should not be grown closer than 0·6 to 0·9 m. (2 to 3 ft.) from a path, as the thorny branches will be weighed down over the edge as they extend and become older, and will thus be a nuisance.

THE PRUNING OF THE HYBRID ROSES

Hybrid Tea Roses

This is a very large group of mixed origin, and one which in recent years has absorbed many of the older hybrids such as the Tea, Hybrid Tea, Hybrid

Perpetual and Pernetiana groups. Hybridisation for colour, scent, disease resistance, vigour and continuity of flowering has taken place to such an extent that it is impossible to define or to classify many of the modern roses. At first sight this seems very confusing to the pruner but there is one safe guide. This is continuity of flowering during the growing season which may even extend into late autumn or early winter. This characteristic has been handed down from at least one parent which is common to most – *R. odorata* in the Indicae Section. The reader is referred to this section and the pruning advised for this species and for *R. chinensis*. The early crop of flowers is produced on laterals from the old wood, while a later display is provided by the young growths during their first season, these often being long and originating from low down near the base.

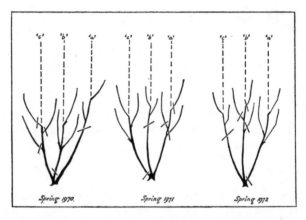

Fig. 40. Diagrammatic representation of pruning a modern hybrid tea rose.
A bush with three branches 'a' 'b' and 'c' is shown, each branch being at a different stage of a three-year cycle of growth and pruning. The cycle for branch 'a' is as follows:
(1) SPRING 1970. The branch is almost all new wood produced in 1969 and will probably have flowered late that summer. It should be lightly pruned in spring 1970 as shown.
(2) SPRING 1971. The new laterals produced in 1970 will flower early that year and should be cut back to two or three buds in spring 1971 as shown.
(3) SPRING 1972. More laterals will be produced in 1971 and will flower early that year. But now, the lower part of this branch is three years old and it should be cut hard back to near ground level in spring 1972 as shown.
BRANCH 'b' has reached the third stage described above by the spring of 1970 and therefore must be cut hard back then to near ground level as shown. In 1970 a new shoot will be produced which may flower late that year. In spring 1971 this is cut back lightly and in spring 1972 the new laterals are cut back more severely to two or three buds.
BRANCH 'c' has reached the second stage by the spring of 1970 and consists of one and two-year-old wood. The laterals are therefore pruned to two or three buds and in the following spring of 1971 the whole branch is severely cut back as shown. In spring 1972 only light pruning will be required.
It is emphasised that this is a very much oversimplified example, its purpose being to illustrate the three-stage cycle of pruning.
This method of pruning can equally well be applied to a modern Floribunda Rose.

If left to grow on from year to year the bushes will become large and congested, with a mass of growths which often form an impenetrable thicket. By contrast, a well-managed plant is healthier and more balanced and the flowers, although fewer, are better shaped and more typical. The annual pruning, which is advised for most if not all of the Hybrid Tea types old and new, is designed to control growth and bush formation, and is based upon the cutting out of the old, weak and dead shoots and the preservation of the new wood.

It is helpful, especially for the beginner, to carry out the annual pruning of this type of rose in stages, which are well defined. These are described below.

Stage I. *The cutting out of dead, diseased and frosted wood.* Sometimes dead or dying snags from previous prunings are found. These should be removed together with any other dead material. Frosted wood is likely to be found on the tips of the unripened, young wood produced late in the season. These should be cut back hard into sound wood. With practice, the work entailed at this stage may be reduced, for there is no point in removing the dead wood from a growth which is to be pruned back at a later stage.

Stage II. *The removal of the older branch systems.* This is an important, if not the most important, stage of the pruning. A healthy bush produces a crop of new growths annually, often from the lower portions of the bush or even from the base. By cutting out the branch systems which are made up partly of old wood perhaps three or more years old the young growths are encouraged. The beginner would do well to examine these older branch systems after they have been removed. Living branches will, of course, be made up of some young wood, but, when this is compared with the younger shoots coming from the base, it will be found to be much weaker. In some cases only a portion of such an old system can be cut out, but often it is possible to make a complete removal at or near ground level. The pruner must decide just what proportion of the older systems should be removed, taking the cuts back either to good dormant buds or to younger and more promising growths. In other words, a balance must be maintained which can be adjusted from year to year, taking response and the previous season's growth into consideration at the time of pruning. No hard and fast rule can be laid down, for behaviour varies both with the soil and with different varieties. The weaker the bush the greater the care needed in cutting back the old branch systems to a suitable point, for some of the older and weaker wood may need to be retained in order to keep an adequate furnishing.

It is emphasised that the cutting out of the old wood merely takes the place of a natural process whereby hybrids of this nature, which have the *R. odorata* habit and origin, eventually shed their older branch systems. By the process of replacement already described, these older branch systems would be naturally crowded out and, deprived of food, would eventually die. The rose grower, however, cannot afford to allow this process to occur naturally for poor and crowded growth often means an increase in pest and disease troubles. Also, many of the hybrids would never survive or bloom well without specialised and intensive methods of culture, which include pruning.

Stage III. *The shortening of the previous year's wood which is to remain on the bush.* The growths of the previous season which are to remain should be shortened, as a general rule, to half their length. Thus the number of buds which remain and possibly develop is reduced, as the cuts are made into stouter wood. It must be clearly understood that this shortening takes place after the weakest wood has been cut back to a suitable bud, or to the base as described in the previous section.

At this stage it should be noted that the height of the bush is to some extent controlled by the measure of the pruning, but no attempt should be made to keep a large and strong grower down by severely cutting back. In fact, the strongest growers need only light pruning, taking the young growths back by a quarter or less. The weaker growers are pruned harder, leaving only a third or less of the young wood, *see* Fig. 40.

Choice of bud or growth above which the cut is made. It is important to select the position of the cut very carefully. This has already been mentioned in the opening chapter of this book, and to some extent in earlier paragraphs in this section on roses. The bud or growth left just beneath the cut is, by virtue of its position, the leading growing point. It must be healthy and strong enough to take the lead. In addition, in order to keep the centre of the bush open as a means of countering congestion, it is advisable to prune to an outward-pointing bud. Ideally, the cuts should be sloping and made just above the buds, in order to avoid dead snags which are not only unsightly but may encourage diseases to gain a foothold and spread later into healthy wood, *see* Plates 80 and 83.

No plant will grow to order but if necessary the annual pruning may be corrective. A bud which grows in towards the centre of the bush, for example, may result in crossing branches. This position may be corrected during the winter's pruning which follows for, if left, other branches may eventually be weighed down and broken, spoiling the shape and general effect.

Period for pruning Hybrid Tea types. Normally these are pruned in the spring just before growth commences. If left till later when growth is actively under way much of this is wasted, as the shoots most forward and active are those on the topmost portions which are cut away. Many rose growers prune in the autumn after the leaves fall or during the winter but this should not be attempted by the beginner. Experience is necessary for the selection of suitable buds when they are dormant.

Summer Pruning and Dead-heading. This operation, which entails looking over the bushes at regular, perhaps at weekly, intervals during the growing and flowering season, improves the appearance and display and, if carried out carefully, it is also a partial growth regulator.

Dead-heading is often referred to as entailing the removal of withered blossom. This prevents seed production and thus conserves energy in addition to giving the plant a tidier appearance. When the withered blossoms are on the head it should be carried out very carefully, ensuring that the remainder, which may be fresh or even unopened, are left intact.

When the whole head, or in some cases the single blossom, has withered, it may be shortened back to a suitable bud or growth. Often this means removing several inches of flower stalk with some leaves attached. This may be referred to as summer pruning although in part it overlaps dead-heading. It should not be carried to the extent that there is a considerable loss of foliage and branch growth otherwise the health of the bush may suffer, *see* Plate 79.

Pruning after planting and before the first season's growth. This operation is very important, for if the bushes are left unpruned before the first season's growth they become straggly with few if any low breaks. In order to carry out the subsequent pruning properly the breaks must be low down or at ground level. To encourage this the stems are cut back to approximately six inches, choosing outside buds. This may be carried out any time after planting and before the new seaon's growth begins.

Floribunda Roses

As with Hybrid Teas, extensive hybridisation has taken place within recent years. The modern varieties are mostly vigorous growers and throw up strong shoots, often from near the base. If left unattended, the bushes become very congested with wood which is old and has lost much of its vigour.

Firstly, the dead and diseased wood is cut out. The removal of a proportion of the older wood follows, if possible making the cuts low down to a suitable bud near the base. This in fact means that branch systems based on three or four year old wood are removed to make way for the younger wood. Growths which remain are also cut back and, as with Hybrid Teas, the extent of this depends upon age and condition. When the growth is very strong the pruning is light, the harder pruning being reserved for the weaker growers when as much as two-thirds or even more is removed. With moderate pruning the growths may be cut back by one-third or a half. Young growths, which are based upon any older wood which remains, are cut back harder than new shoots which spring directly from the base. Under this system the older wood supporting the weaker, exhausted or close-growing laterals is thinned and pruned, the cuts being made above a promising shoot or buds. Thus more light and air is left for the younger material which remains, this being pruned according to vigour. Thus each branch and growth is judged upon its age and vigour, and it is only when the bushes concerned are of one variety either in a group or bed that uniformity is considered. Great care is needed even in this situation, for a uniform level and appearance at the time of pruning does not mean that the bushes will grow uniformly. Careful and selective pruning is a means of encouraging weaker bushes so that the planting as a whole is uniform.

Summer pruning is of great benefit to the bushes and to their appearance. It is carried out on the same principle and by the same method as for Hybrid Teas.

Rambler Roses

The reader is referred to the opening paragraphs on the flowering habits of the genus *Rosa*, *see* page 247, and in particular to the account of the growth and flowering of the Synstylae Section, *see* page 251. The habit of growth of the majority of the species in this section is to throw up a strong crop of shoots annually, but the new canes produced are much stronger in some species than others and it is the same with the varieties and hybrids of this section. However, it is possible to establish two definite groups:

(i) This group is made up of those varieties which throw up long growths abundantly each year from the base. These are the true Ramblers being hybrids of *R. wichuraiana*, for example, 'Dorothy Perkins'. These young growths produce their best crop of flowers in their second year. The pruning, which is carried out annually, is based on this habit of growth and flowering. The complete lengths of old growths over two years old are cut out at ground level immediately after flowering and the new ones tied in. It is an example of replacement pruning, *see* Fig. 41.

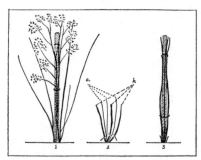

Fig. 41. The pruning of Rambler Roses which send up a sufficient crop of canes each year to allow the old ones to be cut out.
(1) Before pruning, just as flowering has finished.
(2) A close-up of the base, showing (a) the young growths and (b) the old canes with the positions of pruning cuts made after flowering.
(3) After pruning, the new growths tied in.

(ii) In this group are the varieties which do not make a sufficient number of young growths in any one year to allow the old wood to be cut out completely. Often too, the strong growths spring from high up on the old wood. The aim in pruning must be to keep the bush, which is usually tied to a support, well furnished with young wood. Sufficient of the old wood is cut out to allow this. Occasionally, to prevent the base of the plant from becoming bare, an old growth is cut down hard to a dormant growth or bud at ground level. The pruning is carried out after flowering.

The pruning of these two groups after planting is based upon the need to encourage breaks from low down. The canes are therefore cut down to approximately 200 to 250 mm. (8 to 10 ins.), *see* Fig. 42.

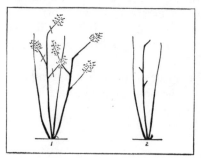

Fig. 42. The pruning of a Rambler Rose type which does not make a sufficient number of new growths in one year to allow the old wood to be cut out completely.
(1) This shows the position of the oldest growth, while the laterals which have also just flowered on the younger cane are cut back to near their bases.
(2) The same bush after pruning.

Climbers

In this group are the types of climbing roses not already mentioned. Among these are the climbing sports and hybrids, all producing a similar growth which makes them suitable for training over a support such as a fence or pergola or on a wire system against a wall surface. The framework or branch system is tied out and is often kept for a number of years, *see* Plate 82. Flowering laterals are produced from this and these are cut back to the lower buds in the spring before the new growth commences. From time to time young growths are produced which may be used for extension. These should be carefully tied in and later, as they grow, used as replacements for older and spent branch systems.

Unlike most of the other types of roses, the varieties and hybrids in this group should not be pruned after planting or during the first season's growth, unless it be to cut out any dead wood. This is an important rule to observe with the climbing sports in particular, for there is a danger of reversion to a bush habit if pruned back too hard.

Standards

Usually these are made up of hybrid tea varieties which have been budded onto stems of *R. canina* stocks, although other stocks are also used. Apart from the removal of suckers and the need to keep the stem clean and free from stock growths, pruning follows the same principles as for the Hybrid Teas.

Weeping Standards

These are often formed from Rambler varieties, the stems being trained over a hood or umbrella framework. The new growths are tied in after old stems have been cut off when the blossom display is over.

Forms other than Ramblers trained in this way are treated according to the methods advocated for their own group.

Hedges

Roses grown in this way are treated informally, the pruning following the lines already described for each species. With many of the hybrids and varieties which flower throughout the summer, the withered heads may be cut back as they form in a series of weekly operations. The cut is always made above a suitable bud. In this way and by feeding and watering if necessary, a continuous display is assured.

Rosmarinus

R. officinalis L. This shrub is not fully hardy and it may be damaged in severe winters, especially in a damp area. It will however regenerate very freely if there is living wood to which it should be cut down. This strong and ready response to cutting back is more certain with a young and vigorous plant, and there need be no hesitation in cutting back a straggly overgrown specimen. The spring is the best time for this. When the shrub is very old it is often advisable to replace it with a younger one, choosing the spring as the planting time. It is less likely to become overgrown and worn out if a sunny, open position is selected.

Bushy plants should be encouraged by stopping at least once in the nursery and once again at the start of the growing season after planting.

Some pruning after flowering may be undertaken with advantage when long branches may be cut to suitable growths. These are plentiful on a vigorously growing bush and by this means it is kept more compact. A Rosemary hedge is trimmed after flowering.

There are a number of cultivars and their individual habits must be taken into account when deciding upon a pruning policy, for example, the cultivar 'Pyramidalis' has a very erect growth.

Rubus

These flower on laterals which are produced from the previous season's wood, but many species will retain their long canes for three or four years, producing new laterals from buds at the base of the flowering growth. As a general rule, however, the practice is to cut out all or much of the old wood, as a characteristic of the genus is to throw up a plentiful supply of young growths from the base during the summer. It is important to study growth and behaviour, both from the point of view of pruning and of training.

The white-stemmed species are most distinct. As an example we may quote *R. cockburnianus* Hemsl. The young growths are very attractive during their first winter, but they lose this pure white colouring as they ripen in the second season after the flowering period. However, by this time a fresh crop of canes has been produced from ground level, and the old ones may be cut out completely. If they were left they would spoil the effect of the young growths. Most of the young canes are vigorous and should reach full height, provided the shrub is healthy and is well fed and mulched, but the smaller growths may also be left, as they provide furnishing and thus contribute toward a more natural appearance. The natural arching habit of the long growths should also be retained. Other species with a similar habit and effect may also be treated in this way, for example, *R. biflorus* Buch.-Ham. var. *quinqueflorus* Focke, and *R. thibetanus* Franch. Staking may be necessary but the natural habit should be preserved as far as possible.

R. odoratus L. belongs to another distinct group. It is upright in growth and the flowers, which are borne by the canes in their second season, are attractive. Immediately the display is over the old canes should be cut out. Thus the young growths are given more light and air for ripening and the flaking bark, which is quite attractive, is displayed to full effect during the first winter.

R. deliciosus Torr. may be quoted as an example of a species which does not produce enough young growth from the base to allow all the old wood to be cut out each season after flowering. Sufficient of the old wood must therefore be left to form a framework. Young growths for replacement should be encouraged from ground level. 'Tridel' needs similar treatment, cutting away the flowering growths and some of the older wood if possible.

Many species have a scandent habit and produce long growths which need staking if grown in a restricted space or border. The stake may take the form of a stout pole, although a tripod support is more secure. Pruning consists of cutting the old growths down to ground level, usually in the autumn, after the fruits have been gathered. The new shoots are then tied in. If insufficient new wood is produced, some of the older canes may be left after the flowering laterals have been cut back. This group is grown more for its fruit than for its ornamental value.

Ruscus

These require very little pruning, apart from the dead and discoloured 'foliage' and stems, which need cutting off when the shrubs are looked over each spring. A proportion of the large 'leaves' of *R. hypoglossum* L. in particular, may be discoloured during the winter and appear very unsightly. The whole stem should be cut away at ground level.

Some adopt the practice of cutting established clumps of this species right down to ground level each spring just before the new growth commences, but such drastic treatment is not always successful, especially on the drier and poorer soils. Normally, with this species and *R. aculeatus* L., it is not necessary to cut out healthy stems even to thin the growths as they have a naturally close and tufted habit.

Ruta

These are referred to as herbs or subshrubs, but although some wood is produced it is seldom sufficiently strong to reach more than three feet. The pruning, which should be rather hard, is carried out in April, cutting back to good growths and taking out weaker wood altogether. The flowers are interesting, but the corymbs are often cut off with the stalk down to the leaves with the object of keeping the plants tidy as they are grown mainly for their foliage effect. A compact form of *R. graveolens* L. is named 'Jackman's Blue'.

Salix

This is a large and botanically a confusing genus, but as far as the arboriculturist and horticulturist are concerned there are three distinct groups;
(a) strong growing species and varieties suitable as trees.
(b) medium growers taking the form of bushes, the height and form varying with the species.
(c) strong or medium growers which are cut down annually for stem effect.

Most species are adaptable and will throw growths freely even after being cut back hard. This characteristic is a great advantage in training.

Strong growing species and varieties suitable as trees

These can be subdivided into (i) those forming upright trees; and (ii) those with a weeping habit.

In the first category, *S. alba calva* G. F. W. Mey. is typical. It is a large upright grower often pyramidal in outline and it is quite a simple matter to retain a central lead. *S. alba* L. also produces ascending branches and again a lead can easily be retained. *S. fragilis* L. forms a spreading head with wide-angled branching, a habit which makes it difficult to retain a lead. The lower and main limbs quickly reach a girth equal to or even exceeding that of the central and leading system, which may then quickly lose its dominance. Such a spreading and heavy framework is sometimes prone to damage during gales as the tree becomes old and declines in health. Cavities also have a weakening effect, and in this respect it should be remembered that the wood is soft and the rot is therefore likely to spread rapidly. Cavities must always be promptly dealt with whatever the species, but it is a matter of even greater urgency with the softer wooded subjects such as willow.

Among the smaller trees is *S. matsudana* Koidz. and the cultivar 'Tortuosa'. During the formation of the framework both in the nursery and after planting, it is important to select and train the leading growth most carefully, as otherwise there will be a tendency for rival leads to develop. This applies in particular to 'Tortuosa'. *S. pentandra* L. is often quite a small tree, but there is a natural tendency for low branching and a clear stem must be trained if a good height is required. The same is true of *S. daphnoides* Vill. Both are effective either as a large, bushy shrub or a small tree with a clear stem. This latter species is mentioned again in Groups (b) and (c) below.

In the second category, *S. babylonica* L., *S. alba* L. 'Tristis', *S.* × *sepulcralis* Simonk. all have a weeping habit; the latter is considered the best of the group. Weeping Willows often produce a few main branches which are large and heavy. Once branching is left to develop on a length of clear stem, the lead is quickly lost as more and more vigour is diverted into this extending system. The habit of growth is such that the main branches arch over, additional height being built up by strong, upright shoots which in turn droop over and so the process is repeated. The main danger is with a very old and large tree which may lean, often with considerable weight, perhaps over water, when one or more of its heavy limbs may be torn away from the trunk by a severe gale. Bracing will help to alleviate this danger, but it is also advisable to check any tendency for a tree in this position to develop in one direction where there is more light, thus throwing the crown out of balance. It is often possible to anticipate trouble and take corrective action even on an old tree, although it is better carried out while the tree is young.

S. purpurea L. 'Pendula' forms a small but spreading head of fine thin growths. Usually this is grafted on to *S. purpurea* stocks at a height of 2·4 to 3·0 m. (8 to 10 ft.) In the early stages particularly, it is important to keep the stem and crown clear of growths from the stock, rubbing these out while they are young and undeveloped.

Medium growers which take the form of bushes, although on occasion they grow into tree form

One common species in this group is *S. caprea* L. The natural form of growth is for the branching to be low, often from ground-level. Little pruning is required. *S. daphnoides* Vill., a species with attractive young growths, may also be grown as a bush. After pruning to encourage a bushy habit in the nursery, the subject is left unpruned for a number of years. Ultimately as the young growths become more numerous they are shorter and less conspicuous. When this happens the younger growths may be encouraged by cutting out a proportion of the older wood. It is usually advisable to continue this on an annual basis in the early spring, maintaining a natural form by carefully positioning the pruning cuts. In no way must it be confused with the method of pruning this and other willows hard back to a main stump for a completely young stem effect.

The need to retain vigour in the young wood is also important with *S. medemii* Boiss. This subject is grown for the decorative effect of the catkins, which are freely produced on strong, young growths of the previous season. A vigorously growing bush or tree will therefore be the most effective. Pruning should be devoted to cutting out any weak or dead branches remembering the need for a shapely bush, an essential for a subject which is to provide a display in the dormant season, when every branch shows up in relief against other subjects. Feeding is also necessary to retain vigour.

Much could be written about many of the other bushy species, but they can be covered briefly by the advice to study and retain the natural habit of growth. Each species and variety varies in this respect. Many of the species have the habit of layering naturally and this may not be desirable, as it is often difficult to keep the ground thus occupied free from strong-growing weeds and saplings such as bramble or ash. It may therefore be the better policy to correct this habit.

Strong or medium growers which are cut down annually for stem effect

A number of species and varieties are grown for the colour and decorative effect of the young shoots as they ripen after their first season's growth. The method is to cut the growths hard back in the spring of each year, which results in a crop of young shoots which extend during the season to provide a display of stems the following winter.

Fig. 43. A *Salix* stool which is cut back hard each spring, being grown for the decorative stem effects. The broken lines indicate the growths which are cut back.

The species and varieties which are grown for this effect are pruned to a definite height of 0·6 to 0·9 m. (2 to 3 ft.) each year and this in time results in the building up of spurs which increase in size until a large number of coloured stems are produced. It is often found desirable to keep the short leg clear of growths, although some prefer one or two small spurs to be left on the lower part to increase the decorative effect, *see* Fig. 43. The intensity of the colouring is more pronounced in the late winter and early spring and the stems are therefore left as long as possible until the buds break to commence the new season's growth. They are then pruned back to within one inch of the old wood or spur. The following are among those which respond well to this system of culture: *S. alba* L. 'Chermesina', 'Chrysostella' and 'Vitellina', *S. daphnoides* Vill. and *S. irrorata* Anders.

The stools may be over-vigorous in the early years, in which case a root pruning operation is advisable.

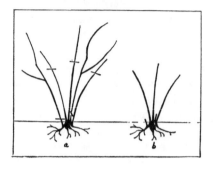

Fig. 44. The method of pruning foliage forms of *Sambucus* which do not send up sufficient growths each year, to provide an adequate furnishing when cut hard to near ground level. The one-year-old canes are left after being pruned back while the older growths are cut down hard to near ground level.

Salvia

S. officinalis L., the common Sage, described as a subshrub, is the only really hardy species which is definitely woody. When young, it forms an attractive plant, but as it becomes older patches of bare wood are exposed at the base leaving the plant straggly and unsightly. However, in this condition when it is old and woody, the shrub responds to hard cutting back in the spring, for even in the older wood buds remain alive and develop very quickly if called upon to do so. An alternative is to discard such specimens, replacing them with young material. The need for such drastic treatment may be delayed by cutting back after flowering almost to the base of the younger wood. This advice also holds for the variegated forms.

The remainder of the woody species need the protection of a South or West wall. Examples are *S. grahamii* Benth., *S. neurepia* Fern. and *S. rutilans* Carr. Often, especially with *S. rutilans*, a woody system may be built up over the years reaching a height of 0·3 to 0·6 m. (1 to 2 ft.). Species in this group should be pruned back to the older wood in the spring just as growth is about to break out. In severe weather the growths may be killed back to near ground level. Left unpruned, these shrubs become weak and untidy. Some form of staking will also keep them in a tidier condition, but no attempt should be made to train them to a wall as they are more successful when planted a foot or so away from the base and allowed to develop a bushy growth. Often sucker-like growths are produced as the shrub spreads. A covering of bracken round the bases in the winter is advisable.

Sambucus

These are often short-lived shrubs and thus periodic propagation is necessary in order to replace the old, weak specimens. The pruning consists of cutting out the older wood and branches, a task which may be carried out during the dormant season. A healthy bush has sufficient young wood to cut to, but a weak and overgrown specimen may be taken hard back to near ground level, when a supply of young shoots will spring from the base.

Some of the foliage forms such as *S. nigra* L. 'Albo-variegata' may be trained as small standards on a 1·5 to 1·8 m. (5 to 6 ft.) leg. The suckers, which tend to spring from the base in particular, should be cut off as they appear. Other species include *S. sieboldiana* Graebn. which is strong growing and, if kept well supplied with young growths by cutting out the oldest branches the strong shoots which are left spread out to give a tropical foliage effect. These shrubs are sometimes grown purely for foliage effect, in which case they are cut down hard each year. One method is to prune down to near ground level each winter, but this does not always result in a full and well furnished plant. By leaving the one year old canes pruned down to half their length, and, at the same time cutting down to ground level those which have been treated in this manner the previous year, a larger and more spreading plant is obtained, *see* Fig. 44. The coloured forms of *S. nigra* L. may be treated in this manner, but vigour is all the more important when these shrubs are grown for colour and foliage effect. Mulching and feeding are an important part of their culture. *C. canadensis* L. f. *maxima* (Hesse) Schwer., benefits from hard pruning down to near ground level each spring, and the strong canes resulting from this produce large heads of flower in the late summer.

S. nigra is a very good shrub in exposed coastal areas where it will help to form the first line of defence against the wind.

Santolina

These small shrubs, when young, form close masses of leafy shoots. As they grow older, however, the heavy branches are weighed down and the whole appearance and shape is spoilt. If left unattended the upright growths produced on the now horizontal branches are in their turn weighed down, until the whole becomes a mass of stems, dead growths and fallen leaves. In a wet winter this may cause the plants to die.

Occasional hard pruning will prevent this unhappy condition occurring. The regular annual pruning should be carried out in the autumn and consists of cutting off the old flower heads and stalks, at the same time cutting back any tall and straggly growths to prevent them from being weighed down by snow and rain, thus spoiling the remainder of the shrub during the winter.

Eventually however, despite this attention, the general condition of the plant appears overgrown and worn. It is then that it should be cut hard back into the old wood in the spring. The recovery from this harsh treatment is very rapid and it may be necessary to repeat this every two or three years. Often however, it becomes necessary to replace old plants every two or three years.

Growth tends to be shorter and more compact in a rather dry and sunny position.

This advice applies generally to the two or three species which are normally grown in gardens.

T

Sarcococca

These useful shrubs require very little pruning, apart from the removal of dead or worn out growths. Usually these should be taken off at ground level, but sometimes it is better to cut back to a strong growth inside the bush. It is not desirable to thin, because the growths are crowded as this is the natural habit.

S. hookeriana Baill. often throws strong growths well above the remainder and these may lose their leaves during the winter and appear dead. Cutting back is, therefore, best left until the spring, when the dead wood can be readily distinguished from the living. The habit of a mature bush of this species is often very spreading, as the branches extend and bend over with the extra weight. This is a natural habit and should not be spoilt by pruning. *S. confusa*. Sealy often develops one or two ragged growths which spoil the general appearance. These may be cut back in the spring to a growth which originates well down inside the bush or at ground level.

Sasa – *See* Bamboos.

Sassafras

S. albidum (Nutt.) Nees. The best form in which to grow this species is to a single stem, retaining the lead through the crown for as long as possible. The branches often have an ascending habit as they arise from the trunk, while the individual branches form close heads of twig growth and foliage, which gives the crown an unusual but pleasant appearance. As the specimen develops, the trunk should be cleared of branches to a height of 1·8 to 2·4 m. (6 to 8 ft.), for the furrowed bark is also of beauty. Grown as a lawn specimen the lower branches tend to sweep down in a pleasant manner and these should be retained.

Often this species suckers in neighbouring borders and at the bases of nearby trees should these be in grass. These form a ready means of propagation if potted up singly and placed under a mist unit. They may however be left to form a colony.

Schima

The only species which are to any degree hardy are stiff-branching, evergreen shrubs. In addition, the whole framework and twig system are covered with dwarf shoots which are spine tipped. *S. dependens* Ortega may be grown in a sheltered position while *S. bonplandianus* Marchand really needs wall protection. The latter can either be grown as a bush within the shelter of the structure, or be trained up close to the wall with the main branches and laterals spreading out fanwise. Growth is kept hard up against the wall by careful pruning in the spring. Shoots which extend too far from the surface are pruned back to suitable points where the cuts are concealed.

These two shrubs show a remarkable response to hard cutting back, and there need be no hesitation in doing this with an overgrown shrub or with one which has been damaged by severe weather.

Schisandra

This is a genus of twining shrubs, which are suitable for growing against a shaded wall. In the early years after planting, some form of training is necessary in order to cover the available space adequately with the main branch system. Usually this entails tying out five to eight growths fanwise from the shrub at ground level. The laterals and extension growths from this system should be left to hang down, when short spurs which form the flowering growths will develop. The topmost growths are very vigorous, especially if the height of the wall is limited to 1·5 to 1·8 m. (5 or 6 ft.). It is therefore important that they should not hide those which spring from lower down on the branch systems, as if they are deprived of light they will die. Pruning consists of thinning out the older and weaker of these pendulous growths during the winter before the buds break out. Some of the young wood, the extension growths which it naturally produces as a climber, may need to be cut away completely. A limited number, however, will be needed for replacement purposes.

Although they are climbers, the branch system will need tying, as the main means of support are the young twining growths which under wall culture cannot be left in quantity to develop.

These shrubs may also be grown on poles or tripods for supports. The stub ends of the branches should be left on the poles as these form a good support and a hold for the twining stems without which, as the weight increases, the mass would slip down to form a tangle at the base, *see* Fig. 20 (1 and 2). A pendulous habit from the top of the stake should be encouraged. Pruning with this system of culture consists of cutting out the older wood in the winter, using the young growths as replacements. The young growths which are not needed may be cut out.

Certain species are stronger and are more suitable for culture under normal conditions, *S. grandiflora* (Wall.) Hook. & Thoms. var. *rubrifolia* (Rehd. & Wils.) Schneid., for example, is able to reach 3·0 to 3·6 m. (10 to 20 ft.) in height while *S. chinensis* (Turez.) Baill. is much weaker by contrast.

Schizophragma

S. integrifolium (Franch.) Oliv. is the species commonly found in gardens. It may be grown against a wall for support and it is self-clinging by means of the adventitious roots which are freely produced, like Ivy, from the young growths. However, some additional support by means of ties to a wire system is often necessary. The main framework is trained out to cover the available space, but the habit is often somewhat ungainly, and it is not often possible to space the branches out neatly.

Two types of growth are produced: (i) extension shoots which are long and self-clinging. These often grow many feet in the one season with short laterals on their basal portion and (ii) branched laterals which grow from the main framework and have a semi-pendulous habit. These are the flowering growths and during the winter the blossom buds may be found terminating the short spur systems.

Pruning may be needed during the dormant season to remove any long extension growths which may be surplus. The cut should be made just above a lateral, which may also need shortening. It may also be wise to remove weak growths.

This species is sometimes grown over a low stump, where it will form an attractive bed or informal drift. Under this system flowering branches should be encouraged, but there must be a number of extension growths to allow older branches and dead wood to be cut out if need be.

S. hydrangeoides Sieb. & Zucc. has a similar habit.

Sciadopitys

S. verticillata Sieb. & Zucc. This is a slow-growing tree which in its best form has a central lead from which the smaller branch systems spring directly. They have a crowded appearance and may be semi-pendulous. However, many specimens show a tendency to throw out strong branches, which first grow out at an angle from the main stem and then assume an upright position. In time this habit may result in the production of one or more rival leads. A number of specimens produce leads freely from ground level, a habit which develops during the nursery stage. Early training and selection are therefore important if a single lead is desired. Timely corrective training is important even with an established specimen, for once rival leads have developed and are perhaps 2 to 3 metres in height, it would be unwise to remove them. A good specimen is often clothed with a dense branching down to ground level. While it may prefer light, partial shade, especially when young, this does not seem to be essential, while over-shading may quickly cause loss of foliage.

Securinega

S. suffruticosa (Pall.) Rehd. Either of two methods of pruning can be adopted with this shrub. One is to cut down almost to ground level in the spring of each year. The growths which are sent up during the summer flower in August and September. Treated in this way it becomes an ideal subject for positioning near the front of the border.

The other method is to allow the subject to grow more naturally, thinning the weakest branches only by cutting them down to ground level.

Semiarundinaria – *See* Bamboos.

Senecio

These are sun-loving shrubs which are not completely hardy and thus prove more difficult in the colder districts. In many parts of the country the shelter of a sunny wall is desirable. They are very happy in coastal districts where the growth tends to be more compact and typical.

Most of the species are better for an occasional hard pruning, for example, once every four or five years, in the spring just as the new growth is about to commence. The shrubs, if healthy and vigorous, break out freely. This will also occur if a hard pruning is given by cutting away wood which has been severely damaged during the winter, provided of course that healthy wood remains. Left unpruned, these shrubs often present an untidy appearance, as the older branches become heavy with extensive shoot development and thus grow over edges and other plants. Heavy falls of snow also weigh the branches down and they may never return to their former position. However, it must be stressed that by a little careful, corrective pruning each spring the need for this periodic drastic pruning may never arise. These observations apply, among other species, to *S. greyi* Hook. f., *S. laxifolius* Buch. and *S. monroi* Hook. f., the latter tending to have thinner growths which are weighed down more readily. *S. rotundifolius* Hook f. has a stiff habit and does not need pruning unless it is necessary to cut out dead wood.

S. cineraria DC. is a leafy subshrub which flowers terminally on growths made during the previous season. Growths are also produced along the lengths of these shoots and at their bases. Pruning consists of cutting off old flower heads in the autumn and at the same time very long straggly growths should be removed. This prevents the plants from being blown about excessively, although limited staking may be necessary. A heavier cutting back may be carried out in the spring if necessary.

Sequoia

S. sempervirens (D. Don) Endl. This is a tall species and will, under suitable conditions, reach considerable heights. It prefers shelter and in exposed positions the tree is ragged and the growth stunted. There is considerable variation in the growth of the branch systems, some producing sub-branches which trail down for many feet, often reaching the ground. This habit, if it develops, should be encouraged and the extremities safeguarded when mowing or carrying out other work round the tree, for the effect is most desirable. Trees of this species often produce suckerous growths which usually spring from round the base of the trunk. These should be removed at least annually during the autumn or winter, both as a means of improving appearance and for the benefit of the tree, as they will take nourishment away from the crown if they are allowed to develop.

Young trees, both in the nursery and for a few years after planting, need exceptionally well-sheltered conditions. The leading growth is also susceptible to frost damage.

Sequoiadendron

S. giganteum (Lindl.) Buchholz. This is a large and tall grower, provided the soil and situation are suitable, and the natural habit is to retain the lead until the ultimate height is reached. This may, in sheltered positions, be well over 30 m. (100 ft.). The height to which this species grows is directly related to the degree of exposure to strong winds. Once the general height of the surrounding trees is reached, unless there is some other form of effective shelter such as a hillside, the top-most growing point often loses vigour and further extension is reduced or stops altogether.

When in good condition, the trunk is often furnished with branches for almost its entire height. However, any of the lower branches which show signs of serious and extensive die-back should be sawn off to the main trunk. If there are only a few dead ends on the branches these may be cleaned up, making these branches and the tree look much tidier. This is a difficult task on a large tree.

It is desirable to provide exceptionally well sheltered positions for young trees both in the nursery and in the years immediately after planting.

Shepherdia

S. argentea Nutt. is a slow-growing shrub which has a spiny, twiggy growth. In the nursery it should be trained with a single stem and this is retained for the life of the shrub. The growth coming away from this consists of small branches, giving the shrub, as it matures, a miniature tree-like appearance, growing up to 3·7 m. (12 ft.) in height. No pruning is needed beyond the removal of dead wood. Occasionally, multi-stemmed specimens are grown and these are quite attractive if allowed to develop from ground level.

S. canadensis Nutt. is, by contrast, a spreading shrub.

Shibataea – *See* Bamboos.

Sibiraea

S. laevigata (L.) Maxim. This shrub is closely related to the Spiraeas and it produces terminal panicles of blossom in the late spring or early summer.

Pruning consists of cutting out the weaker wood after flowering, making the cuts as low down on the bush as possible. Two or three years of experimental pruning are needed, for it is dangerous to cut out more than the shrub can make up with young growth in one year.

Sinarundinaria – *See* Bamboos.

Sinofranchetia

S. chinensis (Franch.) Hemsl. is a vigorous, hardy subject which climbs by means of long, twining stems. Grown where it can climb a small tree, which is perhaps declining in health, or a trunk left after a large specimen has been cut back, it is no problem and requires little or no pruning. When it is grown in a restricted space, for example on a single stake or a tripod some pruning of the long, climbing growths is needed once the support has been covered. They can be cut back to the lowest two or three buds in the spring. A better alternative is to stop the developing extension growths at 6 to 8 leaves in July, cutting these back to two buds in the spring. Under this system short, spur-like growths build up and these should be encouraged.

For wall culture the same system can be adopted. It is advisable to have vertical wires tied to the horizontal strands as these are a considerable help to the developing shrub in the first instance. Ideally, the young shrub should have two main branches which can be secured to the lowest horizontal wire. In this way the twining growths quickly take to the vertical wires, which may be set at 0·3 m. (1 ft.) apart.

Sinojackia

S. rehderiana Hu. This forms a small tree or a large bush, usually with many branches springing from ground level. Also a considerable number of young branches are often thrown up from the older wood and these can be used for renewal purposes. The two-year-old wood, has the curious habit of shedding bark in strips during the winter, giving the bush a ragged appearance.

There is little need for pruning unless there is dead wood to cut out, for it is difficult or impossible to produce a shapely bush as there are so many crossing branches. The lower branches should be left to provide furnishing, as they will do almost to ground level.

S. xylocarpa Hu has a similar habit of growth.

Sinomenium

S. acutum (Thunb.) Rehd. & Wils. This is a vigorous, twining shrub which is better when grown up a small tree for support, for it is too strong and rampant for the average pergola or stake system. Masses of twining stems form long chords to the climber's topmost growths. Little pruning is required, in fact it is risky to remove the dead vines as, twined with the living, they help to support the shrub generally.

Skimmia

These compact, bushy evergreens rarely need pruning, for informality is their character and beauty. Provided that there is sufficient room, they are effective when planted in a group with the bushes growing together to form one large clump. Such a clump is even more effective when it is made up of a mixed planting of the forms of *S. japonica* Thunb.

When these shrubs are established, taller growths are thrown up well beyond the general height and canopy of foliage. These should be left intact, as their development is a sign of vigour and well-being.

Sometimes long, bare and bent branches appear which should be cut back well into the shrub leaving a well-furnished, informal surface. When these shrubs are grown too close to an edge they often require a periodic cutting back, but it is difficult to do this without spoiling the surface. If it is necessary, pruning should be carried out in the spring.

Smilax

These climb by means of tendrils which occur as modified stipules, but they also scramble over neighbouring bushes gaining advantage from the extensive growths often produced from the base in one season. The thorny stems undoubtedly helped in this connection.

Tall posts are suitable for training and it is better that the short 0·3 to 0·6 m. (1 to 2 ft.) stub ends of the side branches are left on them as more support is gained in this way, *see* Fig. 20 (2). In the early stages it may be necessary to tie growths in. Some species such as *S. rotundifolia* L. are very vigorous indeed and should be given positions where they can ramble over neighbouring shrubs with perfect freedom. Such strong subjects are therefore more suited to the natural parts of the garden.

It is possible to restrict growth and size by pruning, but this must be very carefully carried out, otherwise the shortened canes can appear very unsightly. The cuts should be made where they are hidden and it is often better to cut out complete lengths rather than shorten every one to the same level. Some thinning of the weaker growths is also advantageous in the spring. There may be dead growths to cut back after a severe winter.

Solanum

S. crispum Ruiz. & Pav. This has an arching habit and will ramble over low supports such as tree trunks or the roofs of low buildings. It may be trained as a bush, a suitable form in which to grow this plant in a sheltered place. However, in this form it is an untidy grower. Grown either way, some pruning may be carried out although considerable patience will be needed. It consists of cutting out the weak wood in the spring, taking this back to promising young growths. It should not be carried out after flowering as the subject is tender and liable to suffer during a severe winter. The mature wood is more likely to survive than the younger growths.

When trained against a wall the framework should be tied out fan-wise. The young growths are tied in loosely in the autumn and the final pruning and tidying up left until the spring. This consists of cutting out lengths of the weaker wood and tying in the best of the young shoots as replacements, before the surplus ones are cut off.

In the nursery a bushy habit is encouraged by pruning at least once before planting out.

S. jasminoides Paxt. is definitely tender and can only be grown outside in the mildest districts. The thin shoots grow rapidly and are thus adapted for rambling over supports, when a mass of shoot growth will result. Grown on a large wall, the aim should be to cover the area with the main branches and both horizontal and vertical wires are necessary for this. At a later stage some of the thinner and weaker wood should be cut out in order to relieve the congestion, doing this before the new growths develop in the spring.

Sophora

The various species and cultivars are at their best in the south and south-west of this country in sunny positions. Under these conditions the wood is ripened more thoroughly and the tree or shrub is better able to withstand the winter.

S. japonica L. forms a large tree with a spreading crown. There is a tendency for the lowest branches to put on a larger proportion of growth in comparison to the remainder of the tree and as a result they become unduly heavy which may cause weakness at a later stage. It is important therefore to retain the lead for as long as possible, and for a nursery trained tree a clear stem of 1·8 to 2·4 m. (6 to 8 ft.) is preferable. The lower branchlets often have a semi–pendulous habit and sweep low to ground level making it a very beautiful tree which is ideal as an isolated lawn specimen. A mature specimen may be in need of bracing, as large limbs sometimes rip off at the main junctions during gales. Pruning should be carried out during the late summer and never in the spring, as there is a risk of bleeding from the cut surfaces, which makes it impossible to dress the wounds properly.

S. tetraptera Ait. and its various forms are not really hardy, but they will often survive in the warmer parts of the country when planted against a south-facing wall. The shrub must have plenty of head room where it may grow up to 6·0 to 9·0 m. (20 to 30 ft.). It does not conform well to pruning. If left unpruned to form a bush it is self-supporting. It flowers heavily in the spring on the strong growths, the flower buds being formed in terminal clusters in the autumn.

S. davidii Kom. is hardy and forms a large shrub with a woody trunk and main branch system. One of the beauties of this species is in its stiff branching, many of the smaller ones having a naturally arching habit. Pruning may destroy this habit, but should it be necessary to sever or clean up a torn limb, the shrub often responds by throwing a quantity of young shoots.

Sorbaria

The species within this genus were formerly included under *Spiraea*. However, the leaves are pinnate and they are very strong in growth, suckering and flowering on the current season's wood in large, terminal panicles. Provided they have sufficient nourishment they respond well to annual pruning, for growth and vigour is directed into the production of fewer shoots, the result being better and more luxuriant foliage with an increased flower display. The species are alike in producing new flowering growths both from the crown and from the base. Often, the strongest growths of all originate as suckers from below ground level.

A general pruning policy can be based on the principle that much of the young wood must be shortened to reduce the number of buds which grow out to flower. This pruning should be carried out in December and January. Once the framework for the bush has been formed the previous season's wood is cut back to 150 to 230 mm. (6 to 9 ins.) according to vigour. The very strong growths, especially those springing from the older branches or at ground level, should be

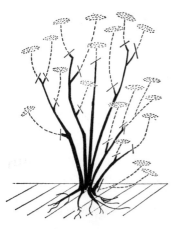

Fig. 45. A mature bush of *Sorbaria arborea*, showing the pruning which is carried out in December to January. The broken lines and discs represent the previous summer inflorescences and these, as indicated, are cut back severely close to their point of origin on the main framework. Unless it is desired, notice how the spread beneath ground level may be prevented by making a cut hard back to the main stool.

left longer, perhaps 0·6 to 0·9 m. (2 to 3 ft.). These can be used to replace older wood and branches, see Fig. 45.

The species vary in growth. For example, S. arborea Schneid., one of the tallest, suckers very freely, and these suckers must be removed unless the shrub is growing in the more natural parts of the garden where extensive colonisation might be welcomed. S. assurgens Vilm. & Bois. and S. sorbifolia (L.) A. Br. are shorter and more erect in habit, the latter suckering very freely. S. tomentosa (Lindl.) Rehd. is less hardy than the others. S. aitchisonii Hemsl., the most popular, also suckers extensively.

× Sorbaronia

This group of bigeneric hybrids are classed either as small trees or shrubs. To a large extent the ultimate size and form is dependent upon the initial training in the nursery. They may be taken up with a single lead to form a clear stem; × S. alpina (Willd.) Schneid. 'Superaria' is an example. With a clear trunk the lower branches, having a semi-pendulous habit, sweep down, and the whole head forms a close network of twigs and branches. Thus a perfect umbrella of foliage is produced, and the only pruning necessary is to cut out the dead wood which develops on the underside. This should be done during the summer months.

× Sorbopyrus

× S. auricularis (Knoop) Schneid. This interesting, bigeneric hybrid should be propagated by grafting. Normally, growth is run up to form a clear stem and a definite head with a central lead. However, as the crown forms, this lead will often quickly break up to become part of the branch system. A watch should be kept for the stock suckering and for dead wood, which may form beneath the dense crown as it develops.

Sorbus

There are four botanical sections in this genus and it is useful to use them as a basis for studying their cultural, pruning and training methods.

Section I. Sorbus

S. aucuparia L., the native Mountain Ash, typifies this section which has pinnate foliage. The species and varieties are fast-growing and are thus popular, especially in smaller gardens. They should be well trained with a good central lead, for there is considerable strain on the framework when the tree is fully laden with fruit. Some damage is also likely on young trees freshly planted in an exposed position after being raised in a sheltered nursery. There is a good case for specially raising trees which are to be planted in these exposed positions in nurseries on the poorer, dryer soils, where the rainfall is light and the situation somewhat exposed. Such conditions encourage a short-jointed, strong branch structure. Further evidence of this is provided by the well-formed specimens of *S. aucuparia* which are often found in the higher and more exposed parts of this country. They are perfect in shape and are able to withstand such conditions because they have grown in the situation from the very start.

When planting in the final position, good growth should be encouraged by careful planting and adequate staking. The species in this section reach maturity so quickly that a fault in training in the early years is difficult to overcome. This applies particularly to the ill effects of stunting in the early years. The most desirable form of tree depends largely upon the position and role for which it is intended. In a completely informal setting the many-stemmed tree, which branches low from ground level, is attractive and lends itself to the situation. Furthermore the species in this group seldom grow sufficiently large to be dangerous.

There is considerable variation in habit, and the intending planter should take this into consideration before making the final choice. No amount of subsequent pruning and training will alter a habit which is thought, after trial, to be undesirable. As examples of the variation, *S. aucuparia* 'Asplenifolia' K. Koch forms a graceful tree, but has an upright habit, *S. aucuparia* 'Sheerwater Seedling' has a fairly compact, cone-shaped head, while the type species is rather open, especially when old and after having borne several heavy crops of fruit. *S. aucuparia* 'Asplenifolia' spreads out at a later stage, but often produces a quantity of epicormic growths on the more horizontal parts of the branch system. These cannot be seen unless the centre of the tree is studied and there is little point in cutting them out, indeed, the increased number which break out during the following and succeeding years will only add to the problem. *S.* 'Joseph Rock' has an upright habit.

Section II. Cormus

S. domestica L. is in this group. It is a large grower living to a great age. The best type of tree to plant is a 1·8 to 2·4 m. (6 to 8 ft.) standard with a clear stem and a central lead. At maturity the lower and outer branches trail down near to ground level.

Section I × III. (Aucuparia × Aria)

S. × *hybrida* L. has an erect habit, but the central lead should be retained for as long as possible.

Section III. Aria

S. torminalis (L.) Crantz., forms a wide and spreading head often with little or no leader. It should be trained in the nursery with a 1·8 to 2·4 (6 to 8 ft.) clear trunk. This is a species which is only seen to full effect when able to develop its head unrestricted and without being hemmed in by neighbouring trees.

S. latifolia (Lam.) Pers. forms a tall tree and will retain a central lead quite easily with a clear trunk of 2·4 to 3·0 m. (8 to 10 ft.). *S.* × *magnifica* Hillier produces magnificent foliage, which is only seen at its best when the branches come down unimpeded to at least eye level. *S. intermedia* (Ehrh.) Pers. will, unless encouraged to form and retain a lead both in the nursery and after planting, form a shrub, especially on the dryer and thinner soils. *S. aria* (L.) Crantz will form a shapely but close, often ovoid, head with an erect branching system. The closely related species, *S. cuspidata* (Spach) Hedl. has rather sparse branching, but the large leaves are its chief attraction. For this reason the lowest branches should be left to develop into the foreground, which should be kept clear to allow for their growth.

Section IV. Micromeles

S. alnifolia (Sieb. & Zucc.) K. Koch is a fairly upright grower, but the lower branches should be encouraged, for the richly coloured autumn foliage and bunches of small red and yellow berries are very attractive.

Spartium

S. junceum L. benefits from annual pruning in the early spring, as by this means the growth is more compact and rigid and is better suited to the border. Left unpruned, the main branches build up a mass of top growth, which eventually becomes so heavy that despite staking to prevent them bending over and exposing bare lengths and patches, the whole effect is one of neglect and untidiness.

In the nursery a bushy habit of growth is obtained by pruning hard back in the spring, just before the one-year-old plant breaks into growth. After this subject has been planted out, the main branches are left to gain height, but are still pruned to at least half their length to encourage a bushy growth. Later, as the bush matures, the previous year's growths are cut back to within 25 mm. of the older wood just as growth is commencing in the spring. It is tedious work to prune each shoot individually and the growths should be gathered together in bundles, using a knife. The new shoots break out very quickly and the clipped effect is soon lost. A very straggly and neglected bush will regenerate even if it is cut down to ground level. This should be carried out in the spring.

This is a fine subject when grown with an informal stretch of Laurel hedging and the Spartium should be planted about 300 mm. (12 ins.) inside the outer edge. No pruning is made in the initial years and thus the growths which are staked on the edge of the hedge to begin with tend to grow straight up, unbranched. Later, when the Spartium is well beyond the height for the hedge, the whole bush is pushed into the centre just leaving the flowering head to develop above the general line. This is pruned annually and the hedge kept within bounds informally using the secateurs.

Sphaeralcea

S. fendleri Gr. is a small, semi-woody shrub which requires a sheltered position at the foot of a sunny wall. Thin but bushy growths are produced from a woody rootstock which develops 50 to 100 mm. above soil level. It is these growths, which have finished flowering, that are most likely to be killed back during the winter. Also at times, stronger and thicker growths are produced as extensions to the woody branch system. Pruning consists of cutting back to developing growths in the spring. In most cases this means a rather drastic cut-back. This subject flowers on the current season's wood.

Spiraea

The shrubby members of this large genus fall broadly into two groups: (i) those which flower from wood made during the previous season and (ii) those which flower on the current season's wood, that is, extensive shoot growth is produced which flowers in the same year.

It is important to relate pruning to the habit of growth and flowering and the two groups will therefore be dealt with individually.

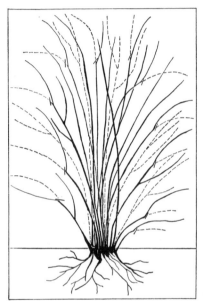

Fig. 46. This represents a *Spiraea* which flowers on the previous year's wood. The broken lines indicate growths which would be pruned out after flowering. Notice that a number of old growths are taken out entirely to ground level.

Those which flower from wood made during the previous season

Most of the species in this group produce short, leafy twigs from growths made during the previous season and these terminate in a flat head or cluster of flowers, usually by early summer. However, a number flower directly from last season's wood, examples being *S.* × *arguta* Zab., *S. gemmata* Zab., *S. hypericifolia* L. and *S. thunbergii* Sieb.

Despite this difference, the general pruning policy for the whole of this group consists of cutting out a proportion of the older wood after flowering to make way for the young growths which provide the next season's display. In some cases the cuts are made just above a suitable growth on the general framework, but occasionally an older branch may be cut out completely to ground level. With this policy in mind, the habit of growth of each individual species must also be taken into account. Some produce an arching growth and as an example we may choose *S. thunbergii* Sieb. A quantity of strong, upright growths are produced from the centre and crown of the shrub but, in addition, new wood is also formed on the older branch system. The extra weight, in addition to the flowers and fruits, causes these to arch over. After this occurs there is an increased tendency for the upright or horizontal portion of the bent branches to throw new growth. This is repeated over and over again, until a considerable amount of dead wood builds up under the bush as it is deprived of light. Thus some of the weaker as well as the older wood should be cut out after flowering, always ensuring a plentiful supply of new growths without leaving any snags or dead wood, *see* Fig. 46. If the bush is near the front of a border or grown as an isolated specimen, it should be left furnished down to ground level, but it may also be important to keep young growth to the centre of the bush to prevent undue spread. Other examples of this habit are *S. canescens* D. Don, *S. gemmata*, *S. mollifolia* Rehd., *S. prunifolia* Sieb. & Zucc., *S. sargentiana* Rehd. and *S.* × *vanhouttei* (Briot) Zab.

S. veitchii Hemsl. is a tall, graceful grower with strong, arching growths. Any pruning must retain this attractive habit. *S.* × *brachybotrys* Lange. produces cascades of growth, the foliage remaining green until very late in the year. The bush is very dense and it is difficult to restrict the size without spoiling the effect. It flowers on long laterals of the previous season and some of the oldest wood may be pruned out after flowering.

As a contrast the following have a more erect habit, often with a very bushy top. They are *S. alpina* Pall., *S. cana* Waldst. & Kit., *S. chamaedryfolia* L., *S. longigemmis* Maxim. and *S. media* Schmidt. *S. henryi* Hemsl., however, has a very spreading habit.

Many species and hybrids in this group which also flower from the past season's wood have not been mentioned. The fact that many have a suckering habit must also be taken into account. Such growths which spread beyond the intended limits should be removed with care. These suckering species and hybrids are ideal for the wild garden or places where it is unnecessary to confine them.

S. nipponica Maxim. needs very careful attention, it being advisable to prune after flowering to a few shoots, leaving only the strongest. At the same time vigour should be encouraged by liberal feeding.

S. chinensis Maxim. may be killed down to ground level in winter as it is not fully hardy. Alternatively, it may be reduced to a few arching branches. This lack of hardiness is shared by *S. cantoniensis* Lour. and both species are better grown in the shelter of a wall.

Those which flower on the current season's wood

As explained earlier, these put on extensive shoot growth during the summer, which produces flower in the same season. Often the growth originates at or a little above ground level. Most of the species and hybrids within this group are suckerous and spread to form a thicket of growths which, without attention, deteriorate in vigour and thus in flowering. By pruning this group hard in the spring, cutting out the weaker growths completely, vigour is concentrated into fewer shoots and therefore flowering and general appearance are improved. The extent of this pruning depends upon vigour, but much of the oldest wood, even though it may support young growth, is cut out completely to ground level, while the young canes which have flowered during the previous summer are shortened by one third or less. They are thinned out if spaced closer than 150 mm. (6 ins.) or so apart, *see* Fig. 47. In addition, as the site becomes exhausted after a few years, perhaps with a heavy infestation of perennial weed, the whole clump may be dug up in the spring. After cultivation and enrichment, selected young canes with roots and a piece of the old connecting growth attached are planted from 230 to 460 mm. (9 to 18 ins.) apart, dependent upon the vigour of the subject. The young growths are cut down to 150 mm. (6 ins.) immediately after planting. Some of the species and hybrids which respond to this method are *S. amoena* Spae, *S. corymbosa* Raf., *S. douglasii* Hook., *S. japonica* L. f. and cultivars, *S. × margaritae* Zab., *S. menziesii* Hook., *S. salicifolia* L. and *S. × sanssouciana* K. Koch.

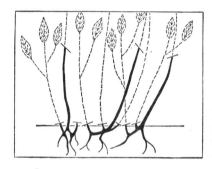

Fig. 47. *Spiraea douglasii* showing how the young growths are thinned and pruned in the spring, at which time the old flowering stems are also cut out.

Some variation must be made in pruning dwarf species and forms which have this flowering habit. *S. × bumalda* Burven. 'Anthony Waterer' is pruned just before growth commences in the spring, cutting down to within 100 to 130 mm. (4 to 5 ins.) of ground level. Thus a short length of the previous year's wood is left, though very old and dead wood should be cut right down to ground level. *S. bullata* Maxim. is a close compact grower. Pruning consists of cutting over the clump or shrub in the spring with a pair of shears taking care to avoid cutting into the old framework. Small compact growths spring up from ground level to flower later in the season, thus extending the display, *see* Fig. 48.

A number of those in this group give a succession of blooms, if the old heads are removed as soon as they have faded.

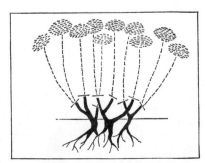

Fig. 48. *Spiraea × bumalda* 'Anthony Waterer', showing the severe cutting back which is carried out before growth commences in the spring.

Stachyurus

The two species, *S. praecox* Sieb. & Zucc. and *S. chinensis* Franch have a natural arching habit, and nearby plantings and general cultivation should allow for free and unrestricted development. This includes furnishing right down to ground level. Both species have a stool-like habit and freely produce young, strong growths from the base. Thus some of the old and thin wood may be cut out low down, or at the base if necessary. This should be carried out after flowering in the spring, but regular annual pruning is not required.

Both species may be grown as wall subjects in colder districts, when they should be trained hard against the surface on the supporting wires. The branches are trained fanwise. The older branches are replaced by the young growths from the base after flowering, which means that they must be carefully tied in for the autumn and winter before they can be placed permanently after pruning. This cutting away, however, may not be needed annually, and in some cases it is even desirable to remove the young growths at a very early stage by rubbing them out, thus conserving the energy of the shrub.

Staphylea

S. colchica Stev. is one of the most vigorous species. It is an upright grower and spreads by means of naturally layered branches and by suckerous growths, which often appear at some distance from the plant. An overgrown bush may be cut back to suitable growths, or the old wood may be taken down to ground level. The young growths which spring up may be thinned and the best used for replacement purposes. Normally suckers are taken up cleanly. While the main pruning may be carried out during the winter, the removal of an odd stray branch or light thinning of the old wood is better done immediately after flowering.

The slender branching and neat habit of *S. bumalda* DC., the compact, thick and upright growth of *S. pinnata* L. and the suckerous spread of *S. trifolia* L. are characteristics which should be taken into account when pruning. With the latter species, the strongest and most centrally placed suckers may be trained for renewal purposes, removing the remainder. *S. holocarpa* Hemsl. has a permanent stem system and may develop into a large shrub or small tree.

Stauntonia

S. hexaphylla Dcne. A vigorous, twining shrub which is similar in many respects to the *Holboellia spp*. It is a tender subject and needs a wall in all but the most favoured localities. With horizontal wiring, vertical strands should be added to assist the young growths to cover the available space in the early years. Branching should be encouraged as close to ground level as possible.

Once the full height of the wall is reached, the growths may be allowed to hang down. Treatment after this should involve thinning out the weaker growths in the spring, wherever possible cutting out complete lengths rather than shortening, thus avoiding a congestion of poor material.

Stephanandra

These shrubs are grown for their foliage and for the coloured stems, which are quite bright during the winter when the leaves have fallen. The flower display is not at all spectacular and pruning is aimed at maintaining vigour, thus ensuring healthy foliage and strong growth for winter colour. After flowering, the old growths are cut back annually, either to healthy side branches springing from lower down on this old wood, or to ground level. Enough old, flowered wood is cut out to leave the shrub well furnished. These shrubs have a stool-like habit and, with good culture and plenty of mulching, strong, young canes are thrown up from the base each year. Often, established clumps have a suckerous habit. The reason for pruning after flowering is to encourage the young growths while letting in sun and air for ripening, which in turn means good colouring. For this latter effect *S. tanakae* Franch is the best species.

When pruning, the natural habit should be preserved. *S. incisa* (Thunb.) Zab., is very graceful indeed with long arching branches and this habit should be retained as far as possible.

Stranvaesia

S. davidiana Dcne. is commonly grown. It has a stiff, erect branching habit and appears to be rather an ungainly grower when compared with many other shrubs. However, this is a natural habit and there should be no attempt to correct it by pruning. In fact, this subject and its varieties need little pruning beyond the removal of dead wood. Like so many Rosaceous shrubs it will break freely from cuts, even on the older wood. It is also quite attractive when trained fairly close to a wall with the main branches tied fanwise to wire supports. In this position pruning should consist of cutting away the oldest wood and branches, if they are worn and spent, provided that healthy young shoots remain which can be trained as replacements. Otherwise it may be necessary to wait for the old wood to break after cutting them out. The young growths not required for tying in may be stopped during the summer to 6 to 8 leaves, pruning these back hard to near their base during the winter.

S. nussia Dcne. develops into a small tree, but is only suitable for mild localities.

Stuartia

These grow best in a fairly sheltered position and a clearing among evergreen or small deciduous trees is ideal. A grass foreground is suggested, for the natural spread of their branch systems is attractive during the winter. There should be no attempt to restrict their size, for these are such choice subjects that it is better to prune back neighbouring trees and screening plants if more space is needed for good and free growth. A grass foreground also allows a natural spread on the lower branches, enabling the flowers and bark effects to be seen at close quarters without difficulty.

Some of the larger growers under ideal conditions often develop small trunks, but these form naturally as the strong, extending branches develop in

U

the upper crown of the young tree. Thus the smaller branches springing from the trunk near ground level may be removed in order to show the bark to good effect. Never should the lower part of the main branches be cleared of twig growth at too early a stage. The timing for this becomes evident when lack of light causes die-back.

The species exhibit varied habits, some being stronger and more tree-like than others. *S. malacodendron* L., for example, is a shrub with a slender branching system. *S. pseudo-camellia* Maxim., on the other hand, is a stout grower with upright branches.

The young plants should not be pruned in the nursery, rather it is important to encourage good growth and strong leads then develop naturally. A young plant which is checked seldom makes good later.

Styrax

This genus of trees and shrubs contains a few choice species which are hardy enough to be grown in many parts of the country. However, they do need care and shelter, especially when young. In the nursery, the larger growers, which are really small trees, need to be trained to form a single lead. *S. japonica* Sieb. & Zucc. forms an interesting, small tree with almost horizontal branching and fine, twiggy growth. Unless it is for the removal of dead wood or intensive competition for light with nearby subjects, pruning might quite easily spoil this natural beauty. *S. dasyantha* Perk. is an example where training can produce a lead of 4·6 to 6·0 m. (15 to 20 ft.), resulting in the formation of a small tree. In such cases the lower branches up to a height of 0·9 to 1·2 m. (3 to 4 ft.) may eventually die back and need to be cut off. *S. hemsleyana* Diels. often branches low at ground level and will form ascending branches with a more rigid, twig system. However, a lead can be trained up. *S. wilsonii* Rehd. is also distinct, being a shrub with quite a dense habit.

Habit of growth must, therefore, be taken into account during training in the nursery. Many of the species break readily, even from older wood, if cuts need to be made. The young growths are prone to damage from late frosts.

Sycopsis

S. sinensis Oliv. is an evergreen shrub or small tree. It branches very freely from the base. A clear foreground encourages growth to develop on the lower branches, thus allowing the small flowers to be examined without difficulty. The thick, bushy habit is natural and no pruning is necessary, apart from the removal of dead twig growth which forms inside the bush.

Heavy snow may cause extensive damage and the growths should be freed at the first opportunity. If damage requiring some hard cutting back is suffered, regeneration occurs quite freely, even from the main branches.

Symphoricarpos

These are strong growing shrubs which quickly produce a thicket, even when they are growing in poor and shaded conditions. However, certain species have distinct habits and these need to be taken into consideration at planting time. By exercising care in the selection of position the need for pruning will be reduced, for these are plants which spread extensively and are difficult to control.

S. albus Blake, the Snowberry, is an upright grower with slender lateral branches which droop heavily, especially when laden with fruit. Dead pieces should be cut out, but there is little need for regular pruning. It is a difficult shrub to control owing to the free production of suckers from the roots. As a hedge therefore it invades neighbouring ground and is thus difficult to confine. This suckering habit is restricted if a hard edge, for example a road, is alongside the length of the hedge. *S. occidentalis* Hook. has a similar habit, but *S. orbiculatus* Moench. produces arching growths when it gains height, and these overgrow shorter branches causing them to die. If this plant is grown on a large scale it is difficult to cut this dead wood out, and it is better to allow the plants to form a thicket.

Syringa

There are two distinct growing habits. The varieties of *Syringa vulgaris* L. and a few other species build up a permanent framework of twiggy, compact growth, while the majority of the species throw strong shoots, often from low down in the bush, which eventually replace the older ones as they become weaker.

Subgenus I. Eusyringa

Section 2. **Vulgares.** *Syringa vulgaris* L. and varieties. These flower from large buds which have formed on the previous season's wood. Generally, as the flowers open, the growth buds directly beneath them develop and extend rapidly, so that by the time the blossoms fade they are often several inches long. This habit can be directly related to the pruning. It is beneficial to remove the old flower heads to prevent wasted energy in seed production, but it is important in doing this to cut them off without injury to the developing growths. If these are injured, or if the growths are cut hard back, the plant will have to open up the season again with dormant buds. Valuable time will be lost and, in this country, it is seldom that such late shoots are sufficiently mature to flower in the following season. However, the pruning of misshapen specimens may be necessary, in which case it should be carried out after flowering. If the loss of bloom is unimportant, pruning or even a hard cutting back to invigorate may be done during the winter.

It is a mistake to plant lilacs too closely. As an example, strongly growing varieties will meet after a few years even if they are planted at 4·5 m. (15 ft.) apart. Under crowded conditions most of the blossom is produced on the top of the bush where there is more light. With sufficient light even the low branches produce a few blossoms though the best flowering heads are in the crown.

When used for hedging purposes, pruning should be carried out by cutting each shoot away individually, aiming to remove a portion each year back to a general line. A hard pruning over the entire surface will result in no flower the following year.

In former days Lilac varieties were frequently grafted on to *S. vulgaris*, but the practice is a bad one owing to the free production of suckers. These should be removed as they appear. The use of Privet as a stock may lead to difficulty, unless the shrubs are planted with the union well below the soil level to encourage scion rooting. Planting with the union above ground level leads to poor growth, and cutting back as a means of invigoration will only aggravate the position.

In habits and vigour the varieties vary considerably and the ultimate height and form is as important when making a choice as flower colour. 'Clarke's Giant' is a very strong grower which may sometimes develop cracks in the bark about 0·3 m. (1 ft.) in length. These may be caused by sun scorch or excessive growth and a protective dressing should be applied.

The species in this section include *S. persica* L., which is a small shrub producing slender growths, which may even trail on the ground as they become longer and heavier over the years. Occasional shaping is therefore necessary, cutting back to upright growths or even down to ground level, provided that there are plenty of replacement shoots. *S. oblata* Lindl. forms weak branches which bend over as they extend and branch. These should be cut back to upright growths after flowering.

Section 1. **Villosae.** This group flowers on terminal buds, but the growth is often distinctive, and the free production of young shoots allows some of the older wood to be cut out as the blossoms fade. *S. emodi* G. Don 'Aurea-variegata' should be grown in full sunlight with an encouragement of the lower branches to bring the variegations down to eye level.

Subgenus II. Ligustrina

S. pekinensis Rupr. is definitely tree-like, having the form of a sizeable apple tree, but new shoots will break out readily from old wood if it needs to be cut back. *S. amurensis* (Rupr.) Rupr. is an upright grower, but crowded clusters of weak young wood in the centre should be thinned out.

Tamarix

These shrubs or small trees are often found growing naturally in coastal regions. Thus almost constant winds, poor soils and intensive sun produce a sturdy and often shortened habit. Under garden conditions, which are usually sheltered with a fairly rich soil, growth often tends to be longer and stronger, with the result that a straggly bush is produced. Extensive top growth, unless it is accompanied by an increase of the spread, results in the production of a dome-shaped bush and eventually leads to a loss of stability, when the shrub may be weighed down by snow or blown loose in the soil by the wind. It is worth noting that in nature extra stability may also be gained from the accumulation of wind-blown sand which often builds up round the shrubs to form a protective mound.

In the garden, pruning and if need be staking help to give stability. In the nursery, and for a year or so after planting, a bunched and sturdy framework should be built up by hard pruning. The species which flower in late summer or autumn do so on the young shoots which are produced during the spring and summer. Thus a sturdy growth may be maintained by pruning annually in the spring, before the new growth commences. These growths are then pruned back to within 50 to 80 mm. (2 to 3 in.) of the old wood. The species which flower late in the season make ideal subjects for an informal hedge, for trimming hard back may be carried out each year in the spring. However rigid and formal the outline after trimming, the effect as the growths are produced is quite the opposite and is very pleasing.

The spring-flowering species, *T. tetrandra* Pall. and *T. parviflora* DC. are pruned after the blossoms fade when long and straggly growths may be shortened. These species flower on growths made during the previous season. Very weak growths may be cut right back and an overgrown bush may be pruned hard, taking away much of the old wood. Flowering may, however, be missed for a year or two afterwards.

T. juniperina Bge. seldom flowers, but it has beautiful foliage. It needs a warm position. Pruning to keep the subject sturdy should be carried out in late May, for flowering, should it occur, is during that month.

Taxodium

T. distichum (L.) Rich., the Swamp Cypress, is the most common species. Its habit is to form a strong leading growth and to maintain this until a considerable height has been reached. Young trees for planting should be single stemmed with a strong lead, and if the site is well prepared, a suitable height is very quickly gained, giving a typical 'church spire' effect.

At a later stage, often when a specimen is near to maximum height, strong, upright branches are thrown out, usually from the upper half of the trunk system. This is a natural habit of growth, for a mature tree has a flat-topped look and no attempt should be made to correct this.

The two other species, *T. ascendens* Brongn. and *T. mucronatum* Ten., both much less common, are treated in the same way.

Taxus

T. baccata L., the Common Yew, is better known in gardens as a hedge plant, but fine though it is when grown and trained for this purpose, it is also very good as a single specimen or for screening purposes on the edge of a garden or enclosed feature. In less formal settings a free lateral growth and spread is desirable, provided of course that there is sufficient space. Many of the varieties have distinctive habits, which will only develop to perfection if allowed to grow freely.

Should it become necessary to restrict spread by pruning and yet retain an informal effect, it must be carried out very carefully. The Yew responds so well to pruning that a flat, hedge-like surface is quickly built up if the cuts are all made on a definite line and in the one operation. An informal effect is only obtained by varying the position of the cut, taking some into the centre when whole branches are removed. It is emphasised that the process, which may be carried out in the early summer, should be a gradual one spread out over a period of three or four years, *see* Plates 43 and 44. The alternative is a really drastic pruning, when the cuts are made right back into the main branches and over the whole bush or tree, but this is only necessary when the specimen is badly overgrown. Such drastic pruning should be made in May.

As the habits of growth among the varieties are so variable many form no distinct leader. Extreme cases are 'Horizontalis' and the other prostrate forms. With these it is often necessary to dig out bramble and other growth, which would otherwise swamp them or spoil their effect.

The nursery training of forms which naturally produce a leader is quite straightforward. For single-stemmed specimens, any rival leaders which appear are reduced to one and this is run up as far as possible through the centre, as the crown is formed. The stem is cleared of lateral growths to give a clean trunk if this is desired and the crown is formed by strong branch systems. When trained for hedging purposes the leads are retained until the ultimate height intended for the particular feature is reached. A Yew hedge is trimmed during August or September, but if overgrown and in need of a hard pruning this should be carried out during May.

The fastigiate forms are sometimes used and these, if desired, can be tied and trained to a very tight, columnar shape. The naturally erect branches may be held together by plastic-coated wiring which is bound tightly round the cylinder of growth at intervals. The subsequent growth quickly hides the binding but these should be pruned during August, otherwise the appearance will quickly become ragged. Being a fastigiate form, most of these growths are naturally upright and it is necessary to take these out individually with secateurs, as otherwise they will not be cut back cleanly. It may be desirable to tuck a proportion of these behind the wiring rather than remove them. In an exposed setting, staking of these tightly clipped fastigiate forms may also be necessary and tubular steel piping is most suitable for this purpose. It should run up the entire height and be hidden in the centre, as otherwise it may be unsightly, *see* Plates 77 and 81.

Tecomaria

T. capensis Spach is a tender climber which will succeed only on sunny walls in warmer parts of the country. The rods should be trained to cover the available space and growths will be plentifully produced from these. The main pruning should be carried out in the spring, cutting the weaker and older growths back to the main rods. It may also be necessary to thin out some of the remaining growths if they are thickly placed, or have developed behind the wires. Some pruning of surplus wood may also be necessary during the summer.

In time, a spur system builds up on the main rods, from which the young growths develop.

Tetracentron

T. sinense Oliv. Under good conditions this subject will develop with little or no training into a small or medium-sized tree. An open foreground is desirable to allow for low branching. Late spring frosts may be damaging, especially to young growths on small trees.

Teucrium

T. fruticans L. is normally grown against a sunny wall as it is not fully hardy. It is trained fanwise and usually bamboo canes are required to assist in this, first tying these to the wire system. Long growths which are not required for extension should be pruned back to suitable shoots in the spring, but not before the new growth commences, when it can be seen just how much wood has been killed during the winter.

T. chamaedrys L. is a low, procumbent subject which is used for ground cover. In time, it forms an untidy mass of growths with erect heads of flowers. It will, however, respond to cutting back in the spring. On a large scale a pair of shears may be used. If it needs to be cut back to prevent overlapping of an edge, this should be done carefully to leave an informal effect rather than a straight-clipped line.

Thamnocalamus – *See* Bamboos.

Thuja

Probably the most satisfactory species from the arboriculturist's point of view is *T. plicata* D. Don, as it is the strongest grower and produces a definite lead which runs up through the centre of the tree. Given sufficient space, the lower branches will spread extensively, providing adequate furnishing to ground level. Good, strong growths should be encouraged both in the nursery and after planting out. *T. standishii* (Gord.) Carr. is also a spreading tree in addition to forming a definite lead. No attempt should be made to form a lead with *T. orientalis* L., for with many forms of this species the trunk naturally splits up almost at ground level. *T. occidentalis* L., on the other hand, has a columnar habit built up with a central lead and normally the lower branches do not spread extensively. *T. koraiensis* Nakai varies from being a shrub with an untidy habit to a small tree with a lead. Often among a batch of seedlings, a number show a tendency to produce a definite lead and, if a tree form is desired, these should be selected and encouraged.

Thuya is sometimes grown for hedging purposes and *T. plicata* in particular is ideal for this purpose. The lead should be retained and allowed to grow 150 to 300 mm. (6 to 12 in.) above the height intended for the hedge, before being pruned back to about 150 mm. (6 in.) below this height. The laterals are then pruned at the intended height, and as a result a much better top surface is procured than if the main stems were cut on this line. The lower branches quickly grow into each other to form a dense base as height is gained. *T. occidentalis* is also used for hedging.

Thujopsis

T. dolobrata (L. f.) Sieb. & Zucc., when raised from seed, shows a considerable variation in habit. While a number will eventually form a definite lead, others remain as rather untidy, spreading shrubs. Of those which grow out of this shrubby habit, a number produce rival leads and the result is a small tree made up of slender upright trunks with their supporting branches. To be certain of a form with a strong central growth which will enable a lead to be trained, it is advisable to propagate by cuttings taken from growths at the top of strong leading shoots.

Tilia

The Common Lime, *T.* × *vulgaris* Hayne is frequently found in tree collections and was quite often used as an avenue tree in former days. One of the reasons for this widespread planting may be connected with the fact that it is so easily propagated by layering. Limes generally do not like too dry a soil and given good conditions this hybrid will develop into a lofty tree. The lead should be retained up through the crown but, as the tree matures, the upper branches may rival the main lead. This appears to be a natural habit. The main lower branches are often nearly horizontal in character, but occasionally a strong upright growth develops along their length, often as a response to extra light on this part of the tree. A careful watch should be kept on any such growths and if need be, they should be checked or removed at an early stage. Old and mature trees having large, upright branches which have developed on a mature branch system also need regular inspection, and it may become necessary to remove such pieces in order to reduce excessive weight. Normally the tree should be raised as a standard with a 1·8 to 2·4 m. (6 to 8 ft.) leg, but it may be planted as a feathered tree, to be trained as the specimen develops. Large burrs often occur on the trunk and these develop masses of epicormic growths which should be pruned back hard each winter, *see* Plate 29. These unsightly burrs and the extra work they involve, coupled with the fact that infestations of aphis frequently occur during the summer months and cause heavy deposits of honey-dew, has made this hybrid an unpopular one to plant. Certainly there are better alternatives.

T. × *euchlora* K. Koch has a thick crown and the outer branches are semi-pendulous, forming a dense canopy. This may be allowed to develop down to ground level when planted as a lawn specimen. Often there is a considerable amount of wood to cut out from the underside of the crown, caused by die-back through lack of light. It is planted extensively as an avenue or street tree and with a good lead and a dense crown with well-spaced branches, it is rightly considered to be a safe tree.

Many other species and forms of Tilia have distinctive but characteristic habits of growth. *T. americana* L., although it has fine, large leaves, often forms a stunted crown with die-back which needs attention. *T. cordata* Mill. is slow-growing and has a fine twig and branch system. *T. oliveri* Szyszy forms a small tree with a branch system which is semi-pendulous and these branches should be allowed to develop to ground level.

The dense branching and habit of *T. platyphylla* Scop. 'Laciniata' is also very distinctive and produces an effect which is rare among Limes. But sometimes this variety has a tendency to form bark wounds and cavities. One of the most distinctive trees for the arboriculturist to plant and train is *T. tomentosa* Moench. The crown is very thick, being formed of long, upright branches which are heavy and impressive.

In the nursery, young plants often grow rapidly and produce a heavy head of foliage. Thus the central lead should be staked and tied when necessary. Frequently, side growths which have been stopped produce sub-laterals very readily a week or so later. These should also be stopped at two leaves.

Of limes generally, many form cavities very readily and exposed wood must be protected, renewing the dressings as and when necessary. Large pruning work should be carried out in late July and August in order to reduce the danger of bleeding and to promote rapid healing.

These trees seem to lose large quantities of small, dead twigs and branches during gales.

Torreya

T. californica Torr. is better suited to the milder parts of the country. It should form a definite lead, producing a straight trunk, and the branches, which occur in whorls, are often slightly pendulous at the extremities. It is important to train and nurse the lead from the seedling stage and a sheltered position should be selected for the young plants in the nursery, avoiding frost pockets. The leading growth, if it weakens or is killed, is quickly overtaken by the vigour of the laterals, and the shape is spoilt. *T. grandis* Fortune can be expected to form a definite lead. *T. nucifera* (L.) Sieb. & Zucc. forms a large shrub in this country, for it usually branches strongly from ground level. Normally, very little pruning is needed.

Trachelospermum

In all but the mildest parts of the country these need wall protection. *T. jasminoides* Lem. is an example. It produces twining extension growths and climbs in nature by this means, *see* Fig. 49. Once the space allotted is covered, the growths keep hard up against the wall and eventually this is furnished by a close mass of stem and foliage. Any growths which do extend out from the wall may be tucked behind the horizontal supporting wires. The flowers are produced on small laterals from the old wood.

Pruning consists of cutting back the small, dead pieces and the weaker growths as the stronger ones take their place. Any extension shoots which go

Fig. 49. A short compact branch taken from the masses of growth produced by a mature specimen of *Trachelospermum jasminoides*. Extension growths like the one on the left are produced on the outer edges.

beyond the wall or the space allocated, and which are surplus, may be cut back to a point just above a shorter, flowering growth. *T. asiaticum* (Sieb. & Zucc.) Nakai also forms a close mat of growth. It is treated in the same way.

Tripetaleia

These rather rare Ericaceous shrubs require very little pruning and the only attention normally necessary is the removal of dead or weak wood.

Trochodendron

T. aralioides Sieb. & Zucc. forms a large shrub or even a small tree. Usually it branches freely from the base, but the main growths are upright, and it retains a lead quite readily. Even the laterals have an ascending habit, but the branchlets on the lower part of the tree are pendulous and may reach the ground giving a fully furnished effect.

There is no need for any pruning. In fact, the head of foliage which terminates each branchlet is quite large, making it very difficult to do so effectively, even if it is necessary to reduce size. The leading growths should never be pruned.

Tsuga

T. heterophylla (Raf.) Sarg. is the most common species. It is a rapid grower on good soils and a typical tree has a sound and definite lead with a spire-like form. It must have sufficient space and a clear foreground to be fully appreciated. As many of the lower branches as possible should be retained and kept in good health, in order that the shapely outline may be continued down to ground level. Should the lead be lost in the early stages, rival ones quickly develop. These should be reduced to one, certainly before their second season of growth. *T. canadensis* (L.) Carr. shows a tendency to produce a number of upright stems from near ground level and is often more irregular in outline than the former species. It also is only seen to advantage if the furnishing is complete to ground level.

Many of the other species are smaller growers and may be no more than large shrubs. Included among these are *T. caroliniana* Engelm., *T. chinensis* (Franch.) Pritz and *T. diversifolia* (Maxim.) Mast. Although small, they should be given sufficient space to form a lead and spread out their branch systems which are often horizontal, with very adequate and attractive furnishing.

T. heterophylla may be used for hedging purposes, for which it will be found quite effective. The plants are set out at 0·9 m. (3 ft.) intervals and the leads are retained until they are approximately 150 to 300 mm. (6 to 12 in.) above the desired height. The cut is then made to the first branches about 150 mm. (6 in.) below this line. The result is that rival leads develop which in due course are also cut, thus forming a top surface at the required height. The sides are later formed by clipping along the line decided on, and it is surprising how the surface develops as the laterals extend after the leading growths have been cut on the branch systems. In turn these laterals are also pruned and thus a compact surface is built up. Clipping should take place in August although a young hedge may also require a late April or May pruning.

Ulex

The species are similar in their habit with the exception of *U. minor* Roth, which is dwarf and compact. The young plants should be encouraged to bush out at an early stage, and if necessary pruning may be resorted to in the early spring before growth commences. As the shrubs develop they will also respond to cutting back. This should be done every two or three years after flowering in May. Provided the growth is reasonably compact and the bush shapely, there is no need to go hard back into the old wood. However, growths will break out freely from the older parts of the plant and there should be no hesitation in cutting straggly, bare-stemmed shrubs back really hard, almost down to ground level. This is carried out in the spring just as growth is about to commence and within a year or so the shrubs quickly make good.

Ulmus

Elms have the reputation of being troublesome trees, but this is rather a pity for it is not entirely justified and our English landscape would be considerably poorer without them.

They are found, with one or the other species predominating, over most of the country, and it is for this reason that they frequently occur as large specimens in our parks and gardens. Naturally these trees have been incorporated in development schemes, but concrete, tarmac and busy roads offer an entirely different and unkindly environment compared to the quiet country lane. No tree takes kindly to such treatment, but in addition, Elms, have suffered badly from Elm Disease and Elm Bark Beetle. As a result their numbers have been reduced and the vigour of many of the remaining ones has suffered. There is another factor which has contributed to the unsafe condition of many Elms, particularly those in our towns and cities. Elms respond well to lopping or severe heading back and this practice has been indulged in, not only in cases of doubt about their safety, but because this was generally accepted as the correct thing to do. As explained in the section on lopping, *see* page 34, trees which have been mauled in this way eventually become unsafe and further drastic action is necessary.

U. procera Salisb., the English Elm, has suffered most from the bad practice of lopping, mainly because it has a widespread distribution over much of southern England. Some of the blame for this may be due to the fact that this species has the reputation of suddenly dropping large limbs, which may snap when the tree is in full leaf, often in the evening after a hot, still day. From a height of 24 m. (80 ft.) or more this can be frightening and the possibility of this happening to a large tree over a public thoroughfare cannot be ignored. It is more likely to happen to a large English Elm than a Sycamore or Oak. However, trees which drop limbs in this manner cannot be healthy. Old age, root disturbance, or bad cultural conditions may be the cause of this, and all possible steps should be taken to keep the root system in a healthy condition, if necessary by aeration, drainage, feeding or watering. Thinning and a reduction in the crown may be all that is required to make the tree safe but a careful inspection is necessary before any decision is made. This species is a tall grower and, as the natural habit is to develop the lead to a considerable height, this should be encouraged. One feature which this species has, in common with a number of other species and hybrids is the suckering habit. This can be so extensive that the whole area occupied by the root system of a large tree quickly becomes covered with a thicket, which changes the character of the site and in time impoverishes the specimen. It may, in certain circumstances, be an advantage to retain the thicket of Elm suckers. For example, as a hedge or a clump it may act as a wind-break in an otherwise exposed situation, perhaps with the parent tree already dead or in a bad condition. In a nature reserve also the thicket may give shelter to bird life and thus serve a useful purpose.

The varieties and forms vary; for example, U. p. 'Viminalis' Rehd. is a smaller tree with pendulous branchlets. It appears to be prone to damage by gales and is therefore better in a sheltered position.

U. glabra Huds., the Wych Elm, in its typical form has some very large branches. The lead should be retained for as long as possible in order to spread the branches and the weight evenly. This species is non-suckering and is there-fore a contrast to U. × hollandica Mill. and its forms and varieties, which are suckering but also form large trees. U. × h. 'Major' forms a very wide, spread-ing crown on a trunk which is often short and the aboriculturist can only retain the lead for as long as possible. The ascending branches, as the tree reaches maturity, thicken to form a round head and almost appear to be rival leads. At this stage the branching is rather open and even large old specimens withstand gale-force winds without damage, whereas with a failing specimen, a hot, still day is more likely to be disastrous because of the danger of falling limbs. It is often possible to keep people from such danger areas by the erection of neat 'shin' rails.

U. carpinifolia Gleditsch. F. sarniensis Loud.) Rehd. forms a dense, conical head with a natural tendency to retain the lead to the complete height. In its typical form, U. americana L. makes a large tree with a wide-spreading, graceful habit and pendulous branchlets.

U. villosa Brandis has a most distinctive habit and the process of twig shed-ding is more deliberate than with most trees. Callused and healed scars are formed where the twigs have been shed as a definite habit of growth. The tree and its bark are best appreciated if a central lead is retained. This species is quite attractive in flower and it is worth allowing the branchlets to sweep down to the ground or at least eye level, so that they can be seen easily. The habit which this species has of producing large roots at or near the surface of the soil can be a nuisance, for as they enlarge they protrude well above ground level thus inhibiting the use of the mower. However, the way to overcome this is either to raise the level or to plant up the area beneath and around the tree with ground cover.

There is a specimen at Kew of the rare U. bergmanniana Schneid. which is many-stemmed from ground level. This may be a characteristic habit of growth.

Umbellularia

U. californica (Hook. & Arn.) Nutt. requires a sheltered spot, where it may be grown into quite a medium sized tree. It should be trained to a single stem in the nursery, for if allowed it will break up into several rival leads, which have a very upright habit. Thus the narrow angles between them at the point of junction may prove to be a weakness in later years, especially during periods of heavy snow. The slightest crack in the wood and outer bark lets in air and water and this will quickly set up rot, especially with a tree whose natural habitat is a sunnier climate.

With a single lead, the laterals are usually quite slender and well placed. The inside furnishing growths which are often found, even on the main lead, should be left.

The lower branches should be left to sweep down to eye level, for the buds are quite interesting, even during the winter.

Vaccinium

The members of this genus vary considerably in growth, but they have much in common. Normally they require very little pruning, apart from the removal of dead and weak growths. If cuts are to be made there is no difficulty in deciding just where they should be. There are often strong growths springing directly from the older wood, but a number of species such as *V. vitis-idaea* L. have creeping rhizomes and constantly send up renewing shoots from below ground. It is more likely that the larger, deciduous growers such as *V. corymbosum* L. will need pruning than, for example, *V. angustifolium* Ait., which is dwarf and compact. The larger shrubs eventually acquire a predominance of unproductive wood and benefit from some thinning.

If it is required, the pruning of the deciduous species may be carried out during the winter, but the evergreen species are better left until the spring. The main reason for this delay, apart from the general undesirability of pruning evergreens during the winter, is that much of the foliage may be lost during a severe spell and as a result there may be difficulty in distinguishing between the living and dead wood.

Viburnum

In general Viburnums have a very characteristic growth, being mostly stool-like in habit and often throwing young shoots freely from the base or from the lower and older branches. Thus there is an opportunity to cut out some of the older wood if it becomes necessary. Many species will regenerate freely if pruned hard, despite the fact that there may not be any young wood at the time of cutting.

The cutting out of the older wood may be often undertaken after flowering if it is needed, but the fruiting display of many species is quite attractive and should be left until the winter period. It is emphasised however that, if the shrub is healthy, there is little need for frequent pruning.

Sometimes specimens become large and woody with bare branching near the base and with the flowers and foliage well above eye level, where they cannot be appreciated. This is often due to close planting and the desired effect is gained

by shortening the branch systems to suitable points and thinning the neighbouring shrubs. This encourages the lower parts of the shrub to furnish up and
develop.

Viburnums are divided into at least nine botanical groups or sections, but
there is little difference between these where pruning is considered. It is important, however, to take into account the habit of growth of the individual species
or variety before any pruning is attempted. *V. plicatum* Thunb. 'Tomentosum'
is an example of this, for the horizontal growths from the main upright branches
are tiered, and the effect is quite distinctive. Little pruning is required, although
the strong canes, which often grow up through the centre of the bush from the
base, may either be cut out at an early stage of their development or used for
replacement. If the mature branch system is healthy, there seems to be little
point in cutting such wood out just to use the younger growths. It is emphasised
that the age and condition of the shrub must always be taken into account when
deciding whether or not to retain these young central growths. They are essential to the young plant in order that it may gain height and stature. Fewer, if
any, of such growths are produced by a mature shrub.

V. farreri Stern has a growth habit which is characteristic of many viburnums.
The branching is stool-like, with abundant young wood produced from ground
level. They grow to a height of $1 \cdot 2$ to $1 \cdot 8$ m. (4 to 6 ft.) are erect and their
general outline, especially with a young plant, is vase shaped opening out to a
rounded head. The oldest branches, if they become too old and weak for good
flowering, may be cut out, often at ground level, to make way for younger
growths. The lower and shorter branches near the base should be left for
furnishing. Rooted branches which have layered naturally may be dug out, for
the resultant growth from them produces an untidy, suckerous effect which may
be considered out of place in the ornamental parts of the garden. Under more
natural conditions this habit may be considered an advantage. When pruning
does become necessary, whole branches should be taken, for a general 'tipping'
of the bush would produce too formal an effect and might impede subsequent
flowering. It should be undertaken immediately after flowering. The same
methods may be adopted with many other species and varieties which are
similar in growth, even though they may flower in the early or mid-summer
period. Thus, for pruning purposes, *V. rhytidophyllum* Hemsl. is much the
same, for although it is a larger and coarser grower than *V. farreri* and is an
evergreen, it will, under a good system of culture, send up plenty of renewal
shoots from the base and respond in much the same way.

V. betulifolium Batal. is one of the better known fruiting forms. It should be
allowed plenty of space and a clear foreground, in order that the heads of flower
and the heavy bunches of fruit may be displayed to the full as they bend over
under their own weight. When this shrub is really established, the long centrally
placed branches may even grow through and onto neighbouring trees and
shrubs for support.

V. tinus L. is distinctive with quite a dense habit. This species responds
vigorously to hard pruning and will break out freely, even when cut down to
the oldest wood near ground level. This treatment is ideal for specimens which
have grown too large for their position or which have become old and worn.

It should be carried out in May. Shrubs which have been injured by a severe winter may be cut back hard in the same way.

V. odoratissimum Ker.-Gawl. requires the protection of a wall in many parts of the country. It is better when grown as a standing bush with an odd tie if necessary to keep it close to the wall. *V. atrocyanum* C. B. Clarke is also grown against a wall for protection. Pruning consists of cutting out the older wood after flowering, tying in the new growths hard against the surface.

Vinca

V. major L. is described as a semi-procumbent shrub. The stems are upright at first when they spring from the parent plant. Later they loop over and root at the tips, continually producing new vegetative growing points by this means. Growth quickly becomes matted and forms excellent cover against annual and perennial weeds. Some woody seedlings such as Ash or Elder may become established and an occasional hard cutting back, for example every other year, will enable a good general clean-up to be undertaken. This should be carried out in the spring before new growth commences. When restricting size along an edge, it is better to leave an informal rather than straight clipped line.

V. minor L. is a smaller grower with a more prostrate habit which cannot be pruned in the same way. However, the whole area may be cut over to remove unwanted growth and weeds without extensive damage to the Vinca.

Vitex

V. agnus-castus L. This shrub is tender and needs the protection of a wall in all but the warmest parts of the country. The terminal inflorescence is produced in the late summer on wood of the current season. Thus it conforms well to annual pruning during early March. The growths are pruned hard back to within an 25 to 50 mm. of their bases once a general framework has been built up. This framework may be trained fanwise hard up against the surface of the wall and a system of spurs gradually builds up along the entire length of the branches to give a complete furnishing, *see* Fig. 50. Occasionally, worn branches may be replaced by the plentiful growths which appear from the base.

Alternatively, the shrub may be trained as a free growing bush within the shelter of a wall. To begin with, as the shrub builds up, very little pruning is necessary, but in maturity some reduction of the previous year's wood will help to maintain the quality of the growth and flowers. Regular pruning to definite

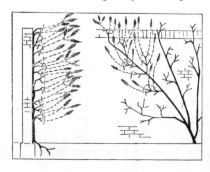

Fig. 50. *Vitex agnus-castus* trained to a wall. The previous year's growth with the old flower heads is pruned back to a spur system which is based on the main framework.

levels and spurs may in time produce a rather unsightly habit. Care must therefore be taken to preserve the natural habit if it is grown as a bush. The free production of young growths from the base and on the branch system should be encouraged, so that older pieces or whole lengths may be cut out entirely on occasion.

V. negundo L. has a similar habit but is larger.

Vitis

Under the pergola system, some of the stronger vines produce growths which are at least 1·8 m. in length. The species which are vigorous growers, such *V. coignetiae* Planch., are thus ideal for climbing over old stumps or even up large trees. In such a situation, after the first pruning which immediately follows planting, little attention is necessary. If pruning is attempted, it must be done very carefully in order to avoid cutting living stems which may appear dead. One mistake of this nature might sever a large portion of the crown.

Vines which are grown in a restricted space may be pruned back each winter to a framework, which is trained to cover a given area of wall or pergola. The pruning should be carried out in December or early January, for once they become active there is danger of bleeding from the cut surfaces, which is undesirable. The young wood which has just completed its growth is cut back to one or two buds. This results in the build up of spurs which are twisted and gnarled and quite attractive. So is the bark which becomes flaked as the age of the rod increases.

Grown over a pergola, the stiffer growths do not hang down so freely as *Ampelopsis* or *Parthenocissus*, but are nevertheless, very attractive. However some stopping may be necessary when they are grown in a restricted space, as the strong shoots, which often grow out extensively become a nuisance. This stopping or summer pruning is carried out in July as the growths begin to ripen on the basal half. The cut is made just above a node at 5 to 6 leaves. Sub-laterals are often quickly produced, but these have a pleasing effect against the older foliage. As an example, the young growths of *V. coignetiae* are greyish-white and make a good contrast to the mature foliage. The shortened growths are cut back hard in the winter, *see* Fig. 50.

Weigela

This genus must not be confused with *Diervilla*, as the habits of growth and flowering, and therefore the pruning needs, are quite different.

The dozen or so species of *Weigela*, all from East Asia, flower on laterals from the previous year's wood, whereas *Diervilla*, consisting of three species from North America, flowers on the current season's wood.

Weigela species may be pruned, if necessary, after flowering in June or July and in this way the shrub is spared from wasting energy in seed production. Mature bushes which are trained properly with a good balance of old and young wood may need thinning as growth extends and thickens and a proportion of the old wood is cut out often near or at ground level. The rule should be to leave the shrub well furnished and if this is applied, it will not be difficult to decide just where the cuts should be made. Often the branches arch over from the point of flowering and the new canes are produced on the more upright part of the growth below the portion which bends over.

Should a stool be overgrown and weak it may be cut hard back in the spring, for it will regenerate very readily. The crop of shoots which arise is often so thick that it must be thinned. This should be done in June or July, for if it is done too early, secondary growth will develop which will be soft.

It is important to encourage good growth with the coloured forms. 'Looymansii Aurea' produces the best foliage and stem effects from young wood and therefore a considerable amount of the older wood should be cut out in the late summer. *W. florida* (Sieb. & Zucc.) A. DC. 'Variegata' should be kept growing freely, although it is more compact in growth than many others. Occasionally a growth of pure green, without any variegation, will break out. This should be removed at an early stage, cutting away a portion of the older wood to which it is attached.

Wisteria

Essentially all the species and forms have similar requirements and with their natural climbing habit they lend themselves to training over pillars or pergolas, up trees or against walls. They may also be trained in bush form to be grown as lawn specimens.

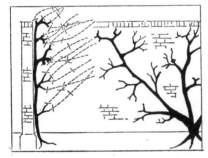

Fig. 51. *Wisteria* trained to a wall. The shrub consists mainly of large branches which are well furnished with a spur system. This is shown in the diagrams but on the left is a sectional drawing with the crop of extension growths which are produced annually. These are shown in broken outline with the positions of the summer and winter pruning.

For pillar, pergola or wall training, the main growths are tied or placed to cover the allotted space. Initially these growths may be trained to approximately 230 mm. (9 in.) apart, but as compound spurs build up under a summer and winter pruning system on the laterals, some thinning may eventually be required. It is desirable to control the growths which are to form the framework in order to prevent them becoming twisted together, as it is impossible to correct this later.

The lateral growths from the main stems are spur-pruned annually, but in order to promote freer and better flower bud formation, this should be carried out in two stages. First by summer pruning the laterals, which take the form of long, trailing growths, back to 150 mm. (6 in.) in July; and secondly, during December or January, to shorten these to two buds. The summer pruning may be carried out in one operation, or extended over a period of several weeks, taking back the growths as they begin to harden and ripen at the base, *see* Fig. 51.

It will be recognised that this system of pruning is similar to that carried out on cordon apples. In the same way, in addition to maintaining a satisfactory balance of growth and flowers, it does keep the climbers neat and enables one to restrict their size. At the same time it must be borne in mind that a considerable amount of ladder work is involved at least twice a year on a large specimen, which may well be 9·0 m. (30 ft.) high against the wall of a house.

The fact that it is possible to restrict size with a spur system of pruning without impairing flowering, enables these climbers to be grown as specimens in bush form, as already mentioned. However, the branches, although thickened, are not capable of supporting their own weight and thus, as they radiate out, they should be tied to upright stakes. Under this system they may reach a height of 1·8 to 2·4 m. (6 to 8 ft.). This can be done quite neatly with strong ties which allow for expansion. It should be pointed out that the branching will have a twisted or crooked and almost deformed appearance, but this is a natural habit and no attempt should be made to correct it, so long as the branches generally radiate from the centre. The summer and winter pruning is carried out on this framework in the way described above, *see* Plate 54.

Xanthoceras

X. sorbifolium Bge. forms either a large shrub or a small tree. In the nursery stage it is encouraged to develop 4 to 6 main branches perhaps on a very short leg of 0·3 m. (1 ft.) or so. With older specimens the extending branches often bend down with their increasing weight, especially in an exposed position. This tendency may be checked if necessary by carefully reducing the weight on the branch ends and by bracing if required, using wire instead of cable, to make it less obvious.

This subject throws young growths very freely from old wood should there be any need for hard pruning. It is, however, a mistake to thin the central growths as this is a natural habit. Sometimes this shrub is grown on walls where the main branches are secured and the extension wood is tied in each year. The growths coming away from the wall are pruned back in the autumn.

Xanthorrhiza

X. simplicissima Marsh. Although to some extent this low-growing shrub is an untidy grower, this is a natural habit which cannot be corrected by pruning. It spreads slowly by suckering, while as growth extends on the older branches they are weighed to the ground. No regular pruning is needed.

Zanthoxylum

This is a genus of stoutly branched shrubs or small trees which retain very broad spines on even the oldest wood. Normally they require little pruning, but the crowns often develop considerable quantities of dead wood, as the build-up of extensive growths deprive others of light. This should be cut out and it is worth noting that the dead wood often seems to be prone to Coral Spot (*Nectria cinnabarina*).

The main beauty of these interesting shrubs is in their habit of growth and heavy branching when they reach maturity and they should not be pruned to restrict their size if it can be avoided. The habit of growth does vary with the genus; for example, Z. *americanum* Mill. has an upright habit compared with Z. *alatum* Roxb. var. *planispinum* (Sieb & Zucc.) Rehd. & Wils., which is weaker in the branching and is inclined to spread along at ground level.

The members of this genus will often respond to hard cutting back by breaking out from the old wood, but it should if possible be avoided.

Zelkova

This genus is of great interest to the arboriculturist, as the few species have distinctive and yet contrasting habits of growth and outline. Z. *carpinifolia* (Pall.) K. Koch forms a head with a large number of ascending branches which originate at one level as soon as laterals develop from the main lead. It is important to train a lead up to form a clear stem of 1·8 to 2·4 m. (6 to 8 ft.) as this enables the trunk and main branching to be seen to the best effect as the tree reaches maturity. Without training, this species will branch low, even at ground level. Should the removal of a limb be needed, it is often difficult to make a clean, flush cut owing to the density and positioning of the branches.

Z. *serrata* (Thunb.) Mak. forms heavy, spreading but semi-erect branches. The lead should be maintained for as long as possible and a clear trunk of 1·8 to 2·4 m. (6 to 8 ft.) is preferable. The outer branches sweep down nicely to produce graceful branching. Z. *sinica* Schneid. also has an attractive trunk. Z. *davidii* Hemsl. forms a small tree with twiggy and thorny branching. Both this latter species and Z. *verschaffeltii* Nichols., a very graceful tree, should have a clear 6 ft. trunk. Z. *cretica* Spach. is a shrubby species.

No regular pruning is desirable beyond that required for corrective training.

Zenobia

Z. *pulverulenta* (Bartr.) Pollard. This shrub and the form *nuda* Rehd. develop into bushy, vigorous shrubs. New extension growths are freely produced each season, both from the base and along the length of many of the branches. The energies may be directed into better and more vigorous growth and thus to give improved flowering during the following season, by pruning as the blossoms fade. The old flowered pieces and small weak branches are then cut off just above suitable growths. Occasionally a whole branch may be cut out completely from ground level. However, care should be taken not to cut away so much that the natural habit is spoilt. The rootstock has a suckering habit.

Should growth be very poor and weak the shrub will respond to most of the old wood being cut out, provided that the roots are encouraged by mulching and the growing conditions improved generally.

Appendix I

A List of the more Common Synonyms

Sometimes two or more names have been applied to the same plant. These are known as synonyms. This list is intended to be a help and guide if information is sought upon a subject which appears in the alphabetical list under a synonym which is not recognised. No claim is made that this list is exhaustive.

Acanthopanax ricinifolius Seem. *see* Kalopanax pictus
Acer creticum L. *see* Acer orientale
Acer dasycarpum Ehrh. *see* Acer saccharinum
Aegle sepiaria DC. *see* Poncirus trifoliata
Ailanthus glandulosa Desf. *see* Ailanthus altissima
Alnus cordifolia Ten. *see* Alnus cordata
Aloysia citriodora Orteg. *see* Lippia citriodora
Althaea frutex Hort. *see* Hibiscus syriacus
Ampelopsis heterophylla var. **amurensis** Planch. *see* Ampelopsis brevipedunculata
Ampelopsis quinquefolia Michx. *see* Parthenocissus quinquefolia
Ampelopsis virginiana Hort. *see* Parthenocissus quinquefolia
Amygdalus communis L. *see* Prunus amygdalus
Amygdalus nana L. *see* Prunus tenella
Amygdalus persica L. *see* Prunus persica
Andromeda arborea L. *see* Oxydendrum arboreum
Andromeda floribunda Pursh. *see* Pieris floribunda
Andromeda formosa Wall. *see* Pieris formosa
Andromeda japonica Thunb. *see* Pieris japonica
Aralia japonica Thunb. *see* Fatsia japonica
Aralia sieboldii Hort. *see* Fatsia japonica

Araucaria imbricata Pavon. *see* Araucaria araucana
Aristolochia sipho L'Herit. *see* Aristolochia durior
Armeniaca vulgaris Lam. *see* Prunus armeniaca
Atraphaxis lanceolata Meissn. *see* Atraphaxis frutescens
Austrocedrus *see* Libocedrus
Azara gilliesii Hook & Arn. *see* Azara petiolaris
Benthamia fragifera Lindl. *see* Cornus capitata
Benthamia japonica Sieb. & Zucc. *see* Cornus kousa
Benzoin aestivale Nees *see* Lindera benzoin
Benzoin grandifolium Rehd. *see* Lindera megaphylla
Bignonia radicans L. *see* Campsis radicans
Biota orientalis Endl. *see* Thuja orientalis
Bridgesia spicata Hook. & Arn. *see* Ercilla volubilis
Buddleia variabilis Hemsl. *see* Buddleia davidii
Calampelis scabra Don. *see* Eccremocarpus scaber
Callicarpa giraldiana Schneid. *see* Callicarpa bodinieri var. giraldii
Callicarpa koreana Hort. *see* Callicarpa dichotoma
Callicarpa purpurea Juss. *see* Callicarpa dichotoma
Calocedrus decurrens (Torrey) Florin *see* Libocedrus decurrens
Calycanthus glaucus Willd. *see* Calycanthus fertilis

Calycanthus macrophyllus Hort.
  see Calycanthus occidentalis
Carpinus americana Michx. *see*
  Carpinus caroliniana
Carya illinoensis (Wanger.)
  K. Koch *see* Carya pecan
Castanea fargesii Dode *see*
  Castanea henryi
Castanea vilmoriniana Dode *see*
  Castanea henryi
Castanopsis henryi Skan *see*
  Castanea henryi
Catalpa syringaefolia Sims. *see*
  Catalpa bignonioides
Cephalotaxus drupacea Sieb. &
  Zucc. *see* Cephalotaxus
  harringtonia var. drupacea
Cephalotaxus pedunculata Sieb.
  & Zucc. var. fastigiata Carr. *see*
  Cephalotaxus harringtonia
  'Fastigiata'
Chaenomeles lagenaria (Loisel.)
  Koidz *see* Chaenomeles
  speciosa
Chimonanthus fragrans Lindl. *see*
  Chimonanthus praecox
Chrysolepis chrysophylla (Hook.)
  Hjelmqvist *see* Castanopsis
  chrysophylla
Citrus trifoliata L. *see* Poncirus
  trifoliata
Cladrastis amurensis K. Koch *see*
  Maackia amurensis
Cladrastis tinctoria Raf. *see*
  Cladrastis lutea
Clematis calycina Ait. *see* Clematis
  balearica
Clematis graveolens Lindl. *see*
  Clematis orientalis
Clematis nutans Hort. *see*
  Clematis rehderiana
Cornus paniculata L'Herit. *see*
  Cornus racemosa
Corylus maxima Mill. var.
  atropurpurea Bean. *see* Corylus
  maxima 'Purpurea'
Cotoneaster humifusus Duthie.
  see Cotoneaster dammeri
Cotoneaster microphyllus var.
  glacialis Hook. *see* Cotoneaster
  congestus

Cotoneaster nummularius Lindl.
  see Cotoneaster lindleyi
Cotoneaster pyrenaicus Hort. *see*
  Cotoneaster congestus
Crinodendron dependens Schneid.
  see Crinodendron patagua
Cunninghamia sinensis R. Br.
  ex Rich. *see* Cunninghamia
  lanceolata
Cupressus lawsoniana A. Murr. *see*
  Chamaecyparis lawsoniana
Cupressus nootkatensis D. Don.
  see Chamaecyparis nootkatensis
Cupressus pisifera (Sieb. & Zucc.)
  K. Koch *see* Chamaecyparis
  pisifera
Cydonia japonica (Thunb.) Pers.
  see Chaenomeles japonica
Cydonia lagenaria Loisel. *see*
  Chaenomeles speciosa
Cydonia maulei T. Moore *see*
  Chaenomeles japonica
Doxantha capreolata Miers. *see*
  Bignonia capreolata
Daphniphyllum glaucescens.
  Hort. *see* Daphniphyllum
  macropodum
Desfontainea hookeri Dun. *see*
  Desfontainea spinosa
Deutzia crenata Sieb. & Zucc. *see*
  Deutzia scabra
Diervilla canadensis Willd. *see*
  Diervilla lonicera
Diospyros chinensis Bl. *see*
  Diospyros kaki
Diplopappus chrysophyllus
  Koehne *see* Cassinia fulvida
Ehretia acuminata Hemsl. *see*
  Ehretia thyrsiflora
Ehretia macrophylla Hemsl. *see*
  Ehretia dicksoni
Ehretia serrata Fr. & Sav. *see*
  Ehretia thyrsiflora
Elaeagnus argentea Pursh. *see*
  Elaeagnus commutata
Elaeagnus edulis Carr. *see*
  Elaeagnus multiflora
Elaeagnus longipes Gray *see*
  Elaeagnus multiflora
Ercilla spicata Hook. & Arn. *see*
  Ercilla volubilis

Euonymus radicans var. acuta
Rehd. *see* Euonymus fortunei

Euonymus radicans var.
argenteo-marginata Rehd. *see*
Euonymus fortunei f. gracilis

Euonymus radicans var. kewensis
Bean. *see* Euonymus fortunei f.
minima 'Kewensis'

Euonymus radicans pictus
J. Makoy *see* Euonymus fortunei
f. gracilis

Euonymus radicans var. rosea-
marginata Rehd. *see* Euonymus
fortunei f. gracilis

Euonymus radicans var. vegeta
Rehd. *see* Euonymus fortunei var.
vegeta

Eupatorium weinmannianum
Reg. *see* Eupatorium micranthum

Exochorda alberti Reg. *see*
Exochorda korolkowii

Exochorda grandiflora Hook. *see*
Exochorda racemosa

Fagus americana Sweet. *see* Fagus
Fagus grandifolia

Fagus ferruginea Ait. *see* Fagus
grandifolia

Fagus sylvatica var. purpurea Ait.
see Fagus sylvatica 'Atropunicea'

Firmiana platanifolia R. Br. *see*
Firmiana simplex

Fitzroya patagonica Hook. f. *see*
Fitzroya cupressoides

Fortunaea chinensis Lindl. *see*
Platycarya strobilacea

Frangula alnus Mill. *see* Rhamnus
frangula

Fraxinus alba Marsh. *see* Fraxinus
americana

Fraxinus pubescens Lam. *see*
Fraxinus pennsylvanica

Gaya lyallii var. ribifolia Kirk.
see Hoheria lyallii

Gleditsia horrida Mak. *see*
Gleditsia japonica

Gordonia altamaha Sarg. *see*
Franklinia altamaha

Gordonia pubescens L'Herit *see*
Franklinia altamaha

Gymnocladus canadensis Lam.
see Gymnocladus dioicus

Halesia tetraptera Ellis *see*
Halesia carolina

Helianthemum alyssoides Vent.
see Halimium alyssoides

Helianthemum halimifolium
Wild. *see* Halimium halimifolium

Helianthemum umbellatum Mill.
see Halimium umbellatum

Helichrysum ledifolius Benth. *see*
Ozothamnus ledifolius

Hesperhodos stellatus Boulenger.
see Rosa stellata

Hydrangea altissima Wall. *see*
Hydrangea anomala

Hydrangea vestita var. pubescens
Maxim. *see* Hydrangea
bretschneideri

Illicium religiosum Sieb. & Zucc.
see Illicium anisatum

Kalopanax ricinifolium Miq. *see*
Kalopanax pictus

Kerria japonica var. variegata
T. Moore *see* Kerria japonica 'Picta'

Laburnum vulgare Bercht. & Prsl.
see Laburnum anagyroides

Larix amabilis Nelson *see*
Pseudolarix amabilis

Larix europaea DC. *see* Larix
decidua

Larix japonica Carr. *see* Larix
leptolepis

Larix kaempferi Sarg. *see* Larix
leptolepis

Ligustrina pekinensis Reg. *see*
Syringa pekinensis

Ligustrum coriaceum Carr. *see*
Ligustrum japonicum
'Rotundifolium'

Liriodendron tulipifera L. var.
pyramidale Lav. *see* Liriodendron
tulipifera 'Fastigiatum'

Lithospermum prostratum
Loisel. *see* Lithospermum diffusum

Magnolia fuscata Andr. *see*
Michelia figo

Michelia fuscata Bl. *see* Michelia
figo

Neillia malvacea Greene *see*
Physocarpus malvaceus

Neillia opulifolia Brew. & Wats.
see Physocarpus opulifolius

Nemopanthus canadensis DC.
see Nemopanthus mucronatus

Nuttallia cerasiformis Torr. &
Gray *see* Osmaronia cerasiformis

Opulaster alabamensis (Rydb.)
Rehd. *see* Physocarpus stellatus

Osmanthus aquifolium Benth. &
Hook. *see* Osmanthus ilicifolius

Ostrya vulgaris Willd. *see* Ostrya
carpinifolia

Padus racemosa Lam. *see* Prunus
padus

Padus serotina Agardh. *see* Prunus
serotina

Paulownia imperialis Sieb. &
Zucc. *see* Paulownia tomentosa

Persica vulgaris Mill. *see* Prunus
persica

Phillyrea vilmoriniana Boiss. &
Bal. *see* Phillyrea decora

Photinia variabilis Hemsl. *see*
Photinia villosa

Physocarpus ferrugineus Daniels.
see Physocarpus stellatus

Physocarpus pauciflorus Piper
see Physocarpus malvaceus

Picrasma ailanthoides Planch. *see*
Picrasma quassioides

Pinus austriaca Hoess *see* Pinus
nigra

Pinus griffithii McClell. not Parl.
see Pinus wallichiana

Pinus insignis Doug. ex Loud. *see*
Pinus radiata

Pinus montana Mill. *see* Pinus
mugo

Piptanthus nepalensis D. Don *see*
Piptanthus laburnifolius

Plagianthus lyallii Gray. *see*
Hoheria lyallii

Plagianthus lyallii Gray (in part)
see Hoheria glabrata

Platanus × acerifolia (Ait.)
Willd. *see* Platanus × hispanica

Podocarpus chilinus Rich. *see*
Podocarpus salignus

Populus balsamifera Du Roi not
L. *see* Populus tacamahaca

Populus balsamifera var.
candicans Gr. *see* Populus
candicans

Pourthiaea variabilis Dcne. *see*
Photinia villosa

Prunnopitys elegans Phil. *see*
Podocarpus andinus

Prunus nana Stokes not Du Roi
see Prunus tenella

Prunus serrula var. tibetica
Koehne *see* Prunus serrula

Pseudolarix fortunei Mayr *see*
Pseudolarix amabilis

Pseudolarix kaempferi Gord. *see*
Pseudolarix amabilis

Pseudotsuga douglasii (Lindley)
Carr *see* Pseudotsuga menziesii

Pseudotsuga taxifolia (Poir.)
Britt. ex Sudw. *see* Pseudotsuga
menziesii

Quercus bungeana Forb. *see*
Quercus variabilis

Quercus conferta Kit. *see* Quercus
frainetto

Quercus mirbeckii Durieu *see*
Quercus canariensis

Quercus pedunculata Ehrh. *see*
Quercus robur

Quercus rubra Du Roi not. L. *see*
Quercus borealis maxima

Quercus sessiliflora Salisb. *see*
Quercus petraea

Quercus toza DC. *see* Quercus
pyrenaica

Raphiolepis japonica Sieb. &
Zucc. *see* Raphiolepis umbellata

Rhodotypos kerrioides Sieb. &
Zucc. *see* Rhodotypos scandens

Rhus americana Nutt. *see* Cotinus
americanus

Rhus cotinus L. *see* Cotinus
coggygria

Rhus cotinoides Nutt. *see* Cotinus
americanus

Rhus vernicifera DC. *see* Rhus
verniciflua

Rhus venenata DC. *see* Rhus
vernix

Ribes aureum Lindl. not Pursh. *see*
Ribes odoratum

Ribes fuchsioidea Moc. & Sess.
see Ribes speciosum

Rosa chinensis var. fragrans
(Thory) Rehd. *see* Rosa odorata

Rosa dumetorum Thuill. *see* Rosa corymbifera

Rosa indica var. fragrans Thory *see* Rosa odorata

Rosa indica var. odoratissima Lindl. *see* Rosa odorata

Rosa luciae Hook. f. *see* Rosa wichuraiana

Rosa lutea Mill. *see* Rosa foetida

Rosa pimpinellifolia L. *see* Rosa spinosissima

Rosa polyantha Sieb. & Zucc. *see* Rosa multiflora

Rubus giraldianus Focke *see* Rubus cockburnianus

Rubus veitchii Rolfe. *see* Rubus thibetanus

Salix aegyptiaca *see* Salix medemii

Salix laurifolia Wesm. *see* Salix pentandra

Schizophragma viburnoides Stapf. *see* Pileostegia viburnoides

Sequoia gigantea (Lindl.) Dcne *see* Sequoiadendron giganteum

Sequoia wellingtonia Seem. *see* Sequoiadendron giganteum

Sophora viciifolia Hance *see* Sophora davidii

Sorbaria lindleyana Maxim. *see* Sorbaria tomentosa

Spiraea aitchisonii Hemsl. *see* Sorbaria aitchisonii

Spiraea arborea Bean *see* Sorbaria arborea

Spiraea assurgens Rehd. *see* Sorbaria assurgens

Spiraea bracteata Zabel. *see* Spiraea nipponica

Spiraea callosa Thunb. *see* Spiraea japonica

Spiraea capitata Pursh. *see* Physocarpus opulifolius

Spiraea confusa Koern. *see* Spiraea media

Spiraea crispifolia Hort. *see* Spiraea bullata

Spiraea flagelliformis Hort. *see* Spiraea canescens

Spiraea laevigata L. *see* Sibiraea laevigata

Spiraea lindleyana Wall. *see* Sorbaria tomentosa

Spiraea opulifolia L. *see* Physocarpus opulifolius

Spiraea pubescens Lindl. *see* Spiraea chinensis

Spiraea reevesiana Lindl. *see* Spiraea cantoniensis

Spiraea sorbifolia L. *see* Sorbaria sorbifolia

Stephanandra flexuosa Sieb. & Zucc. *see* Stephanandra incisa

Sterculia platanifolia L.f. *see* Firmiana simplex

Tamarix japonica Hort. *see* Tamarix juniperina

Tamarix tetrandra var. purpurea Hort. *see* Tamarix parviflora

Tamarix plumosa Hort. *see* Tamarix juniperina

Taxodium sempervirens D. Don *see* Sequoia sempervirens

Tecoma radicans Juss. *see* Campsis radicans

Teucrium latifolium L. *see* Teucrium fruticans

Thermopsis laburnifolia Don. *see* Piptanthus laburnifolius

Thuja dolabrata L.f. *see* Thujopsis dolabrata

Thuja gigantea Nutt. *see* Thuja plicata

Thuja japonica Maxim. *see* Thuja standishii

Thuja lobbii Hort. ex Gord. *see* Thuja plicata

Tilia alba Ait. *see* Tilia tomentosa

Tilia argentia DC. *see* Tilia tomentosa

Tilia glabra Vent. *see* Tilia americana

Tilia grandifolia Ehrh. *see* Tilia platyphylla

Torreya myristica Hook. *see* Torreya californica

Trachelospermum divaricatum Kanitz *see* Trachelospermum asiaticum

Tricuspidaria lanceolata Miq. *see* Crinodendron hookerianum

Tricuspidaria dependens Ruiz & Pav. *see* Crinodendron patagua

Tricuspidaria patagua Miers. *see* Crinodendron patagua

Tsuga albertiana (A. Murr.) Seneclauze *see* Tsuga heterophylla

Tsuga sieboldii Carr. var. nana Carr. *see* Tsuga diversifolia

Ulmus campestris Mill. *see* Ulmus procera

Ulmus montana Stokes *see* Ulmus glabra

Viburnum fragrans Bge. *see* Viburnum farreri

Vitis arborea L. *see* Ampelopsis arborea

Vitis brevipedunculata Dipp. *see* Ampelopsis brevipedunculata

Vitis hederacea Ehrh. *see* Parthenocissus quinquefolia

Vitis quinquefolia Lam. *see* Parthenocissus quinquefolia

Weigela amabilis Hort. *see* Weigela florida

Weigela rosea Lindl. *see* Weigela florida

Xanthorrhiza apiifolia L'Herit. *see* Xanthorrhiza simplicissima

Zelkova acuminata Planch. *see* Zelkova serrata

Zenobia speciosa D. Don. *see* Zenobia pulverulenta

Appendix II

Some Common English Names with their Botanical Equivalents

Acacia, False, Robinia pseudoacacia
Alder, Alnus
Alder, Grey, Alnus incana
Alder, Italian, Alnus cordata
Almond, Common, Prunus amygdalus
Almond, Dwarf Flowering, Prunus glandulosa
Almond, Dwarf Russian, Prunus tenella
Angelica Tree, Chinese, Aralia chinensis
Apricot, Prunus armeniaca
Arbor-vitae, Thuja spp.
Ash, Common, Fraxinus excelsior
Ash, Manna, Fraxinus ornus
Ash, Red, Fraxinus pennsylvanica
Ash, White, Fraxinus americana
Aspen, Populus tremula
Beech, Antarctic, Nothofagus antarctica
Beech, Common, Fagus sylvatica
Beech, Dawyck, Fagus sylvatica 'Fastigiata'
Beech, Fern-leaf, Fagus sylvatica 'Laciniata'
Beech, Oriental, Fagus orientalis
Beech, Purple, Fagus sylvatica 'Atropunicea'
Beech, Weeping, Fagus sylvatica 'Pendula'
Big Tree, Sequoiadendron giganteum
Birch, Betula spp.
Birch, River, Betula nigra
Blackthorn, Prunus spinosa
Bladder Nut, Staphylea spp.
Bladder Senna, Colutea spp.
Bog Myrtle, Myrica gale.
Bottle Brush, Callistemon spp.
Box, Common, Buxus sempervirens
Box, Elder, Acer negundo
Broom, Common Yellow, Cytisus scoparius

Broom, Montpelier, Cytisus monspessulanus
Buttonbush, Cephalanthus occidentalis
Buttonwood, Platanus occidentalis
Californian Poppy, Romneya coulteri
Californian Redwood, Sequoia sempervirens
Cape Figwort, Phygelius capensis 'Coccineus'
Cedar, Atlas, Cedrus atlantica
Cedar, Cyprian, Cedrus brevifolia
Cedar, Deodar, Cedrus deodara
Cedar, Incense, Libocedrus decurrens
Cedar, Lebanon, Cedrus libani
Cherry, Bird, Prunus padus
Cherry, Japanese, Prunus serrulata cultivars
Chestnut, Golden-leaved, Castanopsis chrysophylla
Chestnut, Spanish, Castanea sativa
Chestnut, Sweet, Castanea sativa
Chilean Fire-Bush, Embothrium coccineum
Chinese Gooseberry, Actinidia chinensis
Chinese Persimmon, Diospyros kaki
Christ-thorn, Paliurus spina-Christi
Cobnut, Corylus avellana
Cowberry, Vaccinium vitis-idaea
Crab, Malus spp.
Cranberry, Vaccinium vitis-idaea
Crowberry, Empetrum nigrum
Currant, Flowering, Ribes sanguineum
Currant, Golden, Ribes odoratum
Cydonia, Chaenomeles speciosa
Cypress, Italian, Cupressus sempervirens

Cypress, Lawson, Chamaecyparis lawsoniana

Cypress, Leyland, × Cupressocyparis leylandii

Cypress, Monterey, Cupressus macrocarpa

Cypress, Swamp, Taxodium distichum

Daisy Bush, Olearia gunniana

Date Plum, Diospyros lotus

Dawn Redwood, Metasequoia glyptostroboides

Devil's Walking-stick, Aralia spinosa

Dogwood, Red-barked, Cornus alba

Dogwood, Yellow-barked, Cornus stolonifera 'Flaviramea'

Douglas Fir, Pseudotsuga menziesii

Dove Tree, Davidia involucrata

Elder, Sambucus spp.

Elm, English, Ulmus procera

Elm, Smooth-leaved, Ulmus carpinifolia

Elm, Wych, Ulmus glabra

Fig, Ficus carica

Filbert, Purple-leaf, Corylus maxima 'Purpurea'

Firs, Silver, Abies spp.

Firethorn, Pyracantha spp.

Fringe-tree, Chionanthus spp.

Ghost-tree, Davidia involucrata

Goldenrain-tree, Koelreuteria paniculata

Golden Larch, Pseudolarix amabilis

Gorse, Ulex spp.

Hawthorn, Crataegus monogyna

Hazel, Chinese, Corylus chinensis

Hazel, Common, Corylus avellana

Hazel, Turkish, Corylus colurna

Heath, Besom, Erica scoparia

Heath, Cornish, Erica vagans

Heath, Corsican, Erica terminalis

Heath, Cross-leaved, Erica tetralix

Heath, Dorset, Erica ciliaris

Heath, Grey, Erica cinerea

Heath, Irish, Daboecia cantabrica

Heath, Spanish, Erica australis

Heath, Tree, Erica arborea

Heather, Calluna vulgaris

Hemlock Spruce, Tsuga spp.

Hercules Club, Aralia spinosa

Hickory, Carya spp.

Holly, Ilex aquifolium

Honeysuckle, Lonicera periclymenum

Hop Hornbeam, Ostrya carpinifolia

Hop-tree, Ptelea trifoliata

Hornbeam, Common, Carpinus betulus

Horse-chestnut, Common, Aesculus hippocastanum

Horse-chestnut, Indian, Aesculus indica

Horse-chestnut, Pink, Aesculus × carnea

Indian Bean-Tree, Catalpa bignonioides

Ivy, Common, Hedera helix

Japonica, Chaenomeles speciosa

Judas-Tree, Cercis siliquastrum

Laburnum, Common, Laburnum anagyroides

Larch, European, Larix decidua

Larch, Japanese, Larix leptolepis

Lemon Plant, Lippia citriodora

Laurel, Bay, Laurus nobilis

Laurel, Cherry, Prunus laurocerasus

Laurel, Portugal, Prunus lusitanica

Laurustinus, Viburnum tinus

Lavender, Old English, Lavandula spica

Lilac, Common, Syringa vulgaris

Lime, Common, Tilia × europaea

Lime, Silver, Tilia tomentosa

Lime, Small-leaved, Tilia cordata

Ling, Calluna vulgaris

Lobster Claw, Clianthus puniceus

Locust, Caspian, Gleditsia caspica

Locust, Honey, Gleditsia triacanthos

Loquat, Eriobotrya japonica

Maidenhair Tree, Gingko biloba

Maple, Common, Acer campestre

Maple, Cretan, Acer orientale

Maple, David's, Acer davidii

Maple, Italian, Acer opalus

Maple, Japanese, Acer palmatum

Maple, Montpelier, Acer
monspessulanum
Maple, Norway, Acer platanoides
Maple, Oregon, Acer macrophyllum
Maple, Paperbark, Acer griseum
Maple, Silver, Acer saccharinum
Maple, Snake-bark, Acer
pennsylvanicum
Maple, Sugar, Acer saccharum
May, Crataegus monogyna
Medlar, Mespilus germanica
Mexican Orange, Choisya ternata
Mock-Orange, Philadelphus spp.
Monkey Puzzle, Araucaria araucana
Mountain Ash, Sorbus aucuparia
Myrtle, Common, Myrtus
communis
Mulberry, Black, Morus nigra
Mulberry, White, Morus alba
Nettle Tree, Celtis spp.
Oak, Algerian, Quercus
canariensis
Oak, Armenium, Quercus pontica
Oak, Common, Quercus robur
Oak, Cork, Quercus suber
Oak, Durmast, Quercus petraea
Oak, Chestnut-leaved, Quercus
castaneaefolia
Oak, Holm, Quercus ilex
Oak, Kermes, Quercus coccifera
Oak, Lucombe, Quercus ×
hispanica 'Lucombeana'
Oak, Pin, Quercus palustris
Oak, Pyrenan, Quercus pyrenaica
Oak, Red, Quercus borealis var.
maxima
Oak, Turkey, Quercus cerris
Oak, Willow, Quercus phellos
Olive, Olea europaea
Palm Willow, Salix caprea
Paper Mulberry, Broussonetia
papyrifera
Passion, Flower (Blue), Passiflora
caerulea
Peach, Prunus persica
Pear, Pyrus spp.
Periwinkle, Vinca spp.
Pine, Bhutan, Pinus wallichiana
Pine, Bishop, Pinus muricata
Pine, Monterey, Pinus radiata
Pine, Mountain, Pinus mugo

Pine, Northern, Pinus rigida
Pine, Scots, Pinus sylvestris
Pine, Stone, Pinus pinea
Pine, Umbrella, Sciadopitys
verticillata
Plane, American, Platanus
occidentalis
Plane, London, Platanus ×
hispanica
Plane, Oriental, Platanus orientalis
Plum, Bullace, Prunus institia
Plum, Myrobalan, Prunus
cerasifera
Pomegranate, Punica granatum
Pocket-handkerchief Tree,
Davidia involucrata
Poison Ivy, Rhus toxicodendron
Poplar, Balsam, Populus tacamaha
Poplar, Black, Populus nigra
Poplar, Grey, Populus canescens
Poplar, Ontario, Populus candicans
Poplar, Western Balsam, Populus
trichocarpa
Poplar, White, Populus alba
Poppy Bush, Dendromecon
rigidum
Privet, Common, Ligustrum
vulgare
Privet, Oval-leaved, Ligustrum
ovalifolium
Quick, Crataegus monogyna
Quince, Common, Cydonia oblonga
Rose, Anemone, Rosa
anemonoides
Rose, Austrian Briar, Rosa foetida
Rose, Banks, Rosa banksiae
Rose, Burnett, Rosa spinosissima
Rose, Cherokee, Rosa laevigata
Rose, China, Rosa chinensis
Rose, Cabbage, Rosa centifolia
Rose, Damask, Rosa damascena
Rose, Dog, Rosa canina
Rose, French, Rosa gallica
Rose, Macartney, Rosa bracteata
Rose, Memorial, Rosa wichuraiana
Rose, Musk, Rosa moschata
Rose, Sweet Briar, Rosa eglanteria
Rose, Tea, Rosa odorata
Rosemary, Rosmarinus officinalis
Rowan, Sorbus aucuparia
Rue, Ruta graveolens

Sage, Salvia officinalis
Sea Buckthorn, Hippophae
  rhamnoides
Service-tree, Sorbus domestica
Service-tree (Wild), Sorbus
  torminalis
Silk Vine, Periploca graeca
Smoke-tree, Cotinus coggygria
Snowberry, Symphoricarpos spp.
Snowdrop-tree, Halesia carolina
Snowy Mespilus, Amelanchier spp.
Sorrel-tree, Oxydendrum arboreum
Southernwood, Artemisia
  abrotanum
Spanish Broom, Spartium junceum
Spanish Gorse, Genista hispanica
Spruce, Picea spp.
Strawberry-tree, Arbutus unedo
Sumach, Stag's Horn, Rhus typhina
Sweet Fern, Comptonia peregrina
  var. asplenifolia
Sweet Gale, Myrica gale
Sweet Pepper Bush, Clethra
  alnifolia
Sycamore, Acer pseudoplatanus
Tree of Heaven, Ailanthus
  altitissima
Tulepo, Nyssa sylvatica

Tulip-Tree, Liriodendron tulipifera
Virginia Creeper, Parthenocissus
  quinquefolia
Vine, Vitis spp.
Walnut, Black, Juglans nigra
Walnut, Common, Juglans regia
Wayfaring-tree, Viburnum tinus
Whitebeam, Sorbus aria
Willow, Bay, Salix pentandra
Willow, Crack, Salix fragilis
Willow, Goat, Salix caprea
Willow, Golden, Salix alba var.
  vitellina
Willow, Violet, Salix daphnoides
Willow, Weeping, Salix babylonica
Willow, White, Salix alba
Wing-nut, Pterocarya spp.
Winter Sweet, Chimonanthus
  praecox
Wire-netting Bush, Corokia
  cotoneaster
Witch Hazel, Hamamelis spp.
Woodbine, Lonicera periclymenum
Yellow Root, Xanthorrhiza
  simplicissima
Yellow Wood, Cladrastis spp.
Yew, Common or English, Taxus
  · baccata

Appendix III

TOOLS AND EQUIPMENT

As explained in the Preface, it is difficult to define the limits which must exist, for the purposes of this book at least, between the operations and work connected with the pruning of trees and shrubs and actual tree work, which is mainly concerned with heavier and more specialised equipment as used on large trees and often at considerable heights.

The following list is intended to give the reader some idea of the different tools and equipment required for these two classes of work. No claim is made that it is a complete list, and most people would agree that the choice of tools and equipment is very much a matter of personal preference.

SAWS

Design

A saw should be comfortable to use with a well-shaped, securely-fitted handle. These are often made of beech wood, but they are now being replaced, to some extent at least, by plastic grips which are similar in design. The blade should be of high quality, flexible steel, which will retain an effective cutting edge for a reasonable period, at the same time allowing the teeth to be reset during sharpening, without snapping off completely. The British Standard, 3159:1959 Woodworking Saws for Hand Use (Part 1. Hand Saws), although essentially a manufacturers' publication, contains details and information which are of use to all saw users, arboriculturists included.

Cutting Action

The principle of the saw is that a groove or kerf is made of sufficient width to allow the blade to pass through as the cut is being made. The teeth, which are 'set' or bent alternately to one side or the other to form the groove, are essentially a series of cutting edges which tear at the fibres and other tissues. The broken pieces form the dust which collects in the gaps between the teeth and is carried to the ends of the groove where it falls away. The width of the groove should vary according to the nature and condition of the wood. Green, soft or wet wood will need a comparatively wide groove, for the teeth do not cut through such material cleanly. Without sufficient width the blade may jam, and if it is then forced through there is a danger of the saw buckling. A good saw blade is tensioned during manufacture and it is for this reason that buckling should be corrected by an expert at an early stage before the tool becomes completely useless. Once jamming occurs, it is better to make a fresh start with a saw better suited for the purpose, than to push ahead with the risk of this happening again.

Large teeth, fewer in number, may be set wider and they bite more deeply than the saws designed for use on hard and dry wood. With the latter type the teeth are smaller and more numerous but the set, and therefore the groove, is correspondingly smaller. As a guide, the number of teeth to the inch is taken as a measure of their size. Thus a saw with 10 points to 25 mm. (1 in.) has small teeth and produces a fine cut. With a decrease in the number of teeth to the inch they become progressively larger, the set wider, and the cut coarser. A rip saw may have only 5 teeth to 25 mm. (1 in.). For tree work, the 650 mm. (26 in.) saw with 6 to 7 points to 25 mm. (1 in.) is preferred by many.

Use

Some knowledge and skill is required to use a saw properly. With a good saw it is possible to gain a strong but comfortable grip on the well-fashioned handle. Most operators prefer to place the index finger so that it rests outside and in line with the blade, claiming that this ensures a stronger and more comfortable grip. The position of the cut is established by opening a small groove with a few backward strokes of the saw, or by using the set of small teeth which are often provided especially for this purpose on the first 80 to 100 mm. of the cutting edge. It is also helpful to use the thumb of the free hand against the blade as a guide for accurate position.

When about to make a cut it is important to take up a good comfortable position, and it may be necessary to use a pair of steps or a ladder and safety harness for this. Also, when a large branch is being sawn it is often advisable to consider a means of retreat should the sawn end split and spring up suddenly toward the operator. This is important even when working on the ground, which should be clear of all obstacles. In all pruning one should always guard against the unexpected. Wind direction also needs consideration, for even a small piece of sawdust in the eye can be very painful and cause injury. Sometimes a pair of goggles is essential for protection.

Once the cut is under way, the strokes should settle into a rhythmic action, using the full length of the blade and working from the elbow without bending the wrist. Actual pressure is not needed, only the power to drive the saw through the cut.

At this stage is it important to differentiate between the two main classes of saw. *Cross-cut saws* are normally used for tree work. They are designed to cut across the grain, the teeth being shaped and sharpened for this purpose. *Rippers saws* are designed to cut with or down the grain and the teeth are shaped and sharpened to cut on the forward stroke with chisel edges which sever the fibres. More power is needed for this than for the backward stroke, when the tool is merely drawn into position to repeat the process.

In tree work, it is wrong to change the angle of the blade frequently or to travel round the circumference of the stem or branch for ease of cutting. The temptation to do this is greater with a poor saw. A change of angle also presents an abrupt corner, and until this has worn down a greater strain is put on the edge to the teeth. There is also a danger of the cut closing, thus wedging the tool and perhaps spoiling the set and, if the saw is forced through, causing buckling. Conifer wood, for example Larch, is very resinous, and this may impede the free passage of the blade, thus making the work difficult. In these circumstances it is an advantage to oil the blade frequently, at the same time using a cloth to produce a polished surface. Avoid using vegetable oils for saw cleaning, for they tend to gum as they dry.

Types of Saws

There are a number of types or designs, some of them having specialised uses.

Hand Saw.   This pattern is used frequently in tree work, both for the actual pruning and for the cutting up afterwards. The length varies, but it is approximately 600 to 650 mm. (24 to 26 in.).

Tubular Frame Saw.   This has a replaceable blade. It cuts easily and quickly, but being coarse-toothed the finish is rough. There are many uses for this saw, for example cutting up fallen prunings. It has a limited use in actual tree pruning, but it can be used for branch shortening if desired and where space allows. The final cut on the main trunk or branch is often made with a hand saw or a pruning saw as the frame prevents a close cut against the main stem or branch.

Pruning Saws.   With this type of saw the blade, which usually varies from 350 to 450 mm. in length, is pointed and quite small by comparison with many hand saws. The handle is also small so that it does not protrude to any extent to impede the free use of the tool. Occasionally the open type of handle is fitted to this type of saw when the hold is similar to that of a pistol grip. This saw is designed for use in narrow angles and small gaps between branches such as frequently occur, and where a larger saw would be too big and clumsy. It is also a light and convenient saw to carry from tree to tree, particularly if they are small and need little attention.

The double-edged pruning saw has a set of coarse double teeth on one side, with fine peg teeth on the other. The coarser are used for the larger branches or with the softer wood, when a wide cut is needed. This tool is useful in straightforward pruning where a variety of thicknesses and types of wood have to be dealt with and there is no danger of damaging wood which is to remain. The single-edged saw, however, is preferred by many, for with the double-edged type there is a danger that upper branches will be damaged when the tool is used in a narrow angle. It is often necessary to watch the whole length of blade in addition to the attention which is needed on the actual cut being made, and this may be difficult at times.

Grecian Pruning Saw.   The blade, which is tapered to a point, is approximately 350 to 400 mm. long, while the short handle is shaped to enable it to be gripped firmly, this being referred to as a pistol grip. The teeth are so shaped that the cutting stroke is made as the tool is drawn towards the operator, i.e. the teeth point toward the handle. The pointed and slightly curved blade allows it to be used with full effect in a narrow angle without injury to other branches. The pointed tip allows this portion to be used if the space between the branches is very small until the saw has penetrated sufficiently for the full length of the tool to be operated. The short blade gives great manoeuvrability and accuracy, and it is a very useful tool indeed which should be more commonly and frequently used.

Long-arm Saw. This has a curved blade similar in design to that of the Grecian Saw. The blade, which may be 450 to 500 mm. (18 to 20 in.) in length, is fitted on the end of a long handle by two straps held in position by screws. The handle varies in length from 1·8 to 3·0 m. (6 to 10 ft.) and is made of light but strong batten, 50 × 25 mm. (2 × 1 in.). The teeth are identical with those of the Grecian Saw with the cutting stroke as the tool is drawn towards the operator. The long-arm saw is designed for use on branches which are well out of reach of the ordinary saw. It may be used from the ground or from a ladder or steps.

There are a number of disadvantages with this type of saw, despite the fact that it is a useful tool. It is important that the operator is aware of these.

(1) It is difficult to maintain full control of the blade because of the weight and length of the cumbersome handle. Care must be taken to make the cut accurate. If used from a ladder or a tree, careful positioning and the use of a safety harness are essential precautions to prevent over-balancing and perhaps a bad fall.

(2) It is not possible to undercut, and thus the branch may rip back from the parent stem if it falls away before the cut is completed. This will not of course happen with dead wood, and it is often used for this purpose.

(3) It is difficult and often impossible to pare or dress the wound after the cut has been made. Admittedly this is not so important when small twiggy growths are removed from large and rapidly developing trunks or branches, when the natural processes of healing can be expected to take place rapidly.

(4) Sawdust often falls straight down onto the operator and in this case the use of a pair of goggles is advisable to prevent injury to the eyes. With the introduction of the modern safety harness most parts of the tree are accessible and the need to use this type of saw on large scale work has been reduced.

One-man and Two-men Cross-Cut Saws. These are larger saws designed for cutting up fallen logs and other tasks connected with larger timber. The length varies from 0·9 to 1·5 m. (3 to 5 ft.) with the former, and 1·8 to 2·4 m. (6 to 8 ft.) with the latter. The individual teeth are large, giving a wide set but a quick cut, though a coarse finish. The teeth are often set in groups with large recesses or gullets between each group to allow the bulky accumulations of sawdust to be conducted away from the cut. The one-man cross-cuts often have a detachable handle allowing conversion into a two-man saw if desired.

This type of saw has been superseded by the mechanical chain-saw which can cut through wood much faster and thus more economically. However, it is a useful tool for the small estate where the amount of cutting is so limited that the purchase of a mechanised saw is not justified. It is also a useful standby on larger establishments, for use in an emergency in the event of a breakdown with the chain-saw.

Generally the cutting edge is slightly convex to allow for the blade to rock or see-saw as it is pulled to and fro by the operators. It should be noted that the action is for each operator to pull the saw in turn in a rhythmic movement which involves the complete length of the blade with each stroke. With the feet set firmly and widely apart, the whole body is used in a steady pull followed by a swing forward to gain position for the next pull. (*See also* Appendix IV, 'Saw Sharpening and Maintenance.').

CUTTING TOOLS

Secateurs

This tool has been developed quite extensively within recent years with the result that the more advanced types and patterns are precision-made, with bearings which enable the scientifically designed cutters to make a nearly perfect severance. With most of the modern ones the parts are replaceable, *see* Plate 84.

Many of the older models were of the 'parrot' type, with two curved cutting blades of strong metal and, provided they were used properly without being strained, they lasted for a very long time. One type which has become popular within recent years has clearly been developed from these earlier models. One blade has been designed as a cutter and this closes on the shaped anvil block so accurately that the cut is made without tearing. Another pattern has a cutting blade which closes on to a soft metal anvil. As with the other types it is important that the blade should be properly sharpened and the tool well maintained.

A good pair of secateurs is comfortable to hold and use. It is essential, therefore, that the handles should be well shaped, and controlled by a spring mechanism which is only sufficiently strong to open the secateurs once the cut has been completed. A spring which is stronger than necessary places a greater strain on the hands and may cause blistering. One pattern is produced with a cylindrical handle which turns with the fingers as the handles are opened and closed, thus reducing friction and the chance of blistering, *see* Plate 39.

The need for good maintenance has already been mentioned. It is very necessary, for a blunt tool in poor condition will produce inferior cuts which may be jagged or split, often with torn or damaged bark. At best, the healing will be slow, while the danger of dead and diseased snags is increased. At the same time it must be remembered that the mechanism will be strained by forcing a blunt cutter through the wood and thus the performance will deteriorate still further.

Even a good sharp pair of secateurs can quite easily be misused and spoilt. For example, the blade, or blades, should be taken straight through the wood. By twisting the tool the blades are often strained. It is also wrong to cut through too large a piece, for the cut is likely to be a poor and jagged one with extensive bark injury, while the tool itself may be damaged, never to cut properly again. For safety, when the tool is not in use, the catch to hold the cutters in a closed position should be sound and trustworthy, otherwise an accident is likely to occur. A badly worn blade may not close properly and with a sharp exposed edge it may be dangerous even when not in use.

Long Arm or Standard Pruners

This tool is used for pruning smaller branches which are out of reach of the secateurs, either from the ground or from a pair of steps or a ladder.

The cutting unit consists of a swivelling blade which turns in a half circle onto the anvil through the operation of a lever at the lower end of the handle or arm. The lever and blade are connected by a stout wire which runs through eyeholes positioned at intervals along the arm. When closed, the blade is positioned between the two flat plates which form the hook-shaped anvil. A spring is often fitted to the lever so that the blade is pulled back into position for the next cut. This description applies to the standard tool, but from time to time various manufacturers produce modified versions. One pattern has a light alloy tubular handle which can be extended or even fitted with a saw blade instead of a pruner if required. The general principles of their use and movement, however, remain the same.

The tool is used quite simply by hooking the anvil over the branch, which is then cut off by operating the lever. Although the diameter of the branch which may be removed is limited by the size of the hook, some discretion is necessary in order to avoid making poor cuts and perhaps straining the tool. There is also the danger that if the blade jams in the cut an attempt to free this by reversing the lever may strain the wire.

It is important to position the tool carefully and hold it firmly each time a cut is made, but one of the greatest disadvantages of this tool is that the cut is made a considerable distance from the operator. Accuracy must therefore be sacrificed, and in this respect it is inferior to the secateurs. However, the disadvantages related to a poor cut and a possible snag are not so serious on a rapidly growing limb or trunk. One good use for this tool is on small dead twig growth which is often found at the extremities of a mass of dense branching, as for example on the Holm Oak.

Maintenance. It is important to keep the tool in good condition, with the blade clean and well sharpened. The blade and lever should move freely and close properly, and be strongly and securely attached, while the gap in the anvil should be kept clear of wood pieces, etc. The attachment wire and handle should also be inspected periodically to ensure that they are working correctly.

Long-handled Pruners or Lopping Shears

There are various patterns, but in principle they are much stronger than hand secateurs and are thus suitable for tougher work and for cutting through large branches. The long handles ensure a good leverage or purchase but, in addition, the cut can be made well inside a tree or bush at some distance from the operator. This is an advantage in cases of congested or thorny growth such as one gets with Berberis, *see* Plates 85 and 86. It is not a tool to use where accuracy and neatness are required, or where the cut is accessible and of a suitable size for secateurs. Many uses, however, can be found for it in clearing operations and for rough pruning prior to felling, *see* Plates 43 and 44.

Patterns are also available which can be described as a pair of long-handled secateurs. These handles may vary between 400 and 500 mm. (15 and 20 in.) in length and the cutting action is therefore quite powerful. They can be used for quite accurate work and are suitable for pruning among thorny subjects and long twig growths.

Pruning Knife

There is considerable variation in the quality of knives, of which there are many types and patterns. Here are some of the more essential points.

Fig. 52. The 'Tina' 635 in use for snagging. This model has a strong curved blade and a comfortable handle which makes it an ideal tool for nursery work.
(Drawn from an illustration in the 'Tina' catalogue.)

The handle should be substantial and properly shaped to enable a good grip to be gained. This is most necessary when comparatively large pieces are to be cut, for example, when 'snagging' (the removal of the snag end which is left above the union after budding).

The blade should be of hardened steel which is likely to retain a good edge, during use. Inferior blades can be sharpened up very speedily, but they will not retain a cutting edge for long. The shape of the blade is largely a matter of taste but the curved pattern is generally preferred for pruning for this facilitates a more extensive penetration as the cutting edge passes through the tissues. The point of attachment to the handle should be strong and secure, and without rock. The spring action must hold the blade securely in the open or closed position. A knife with a blade which turns back or closes too freely will be dangerous to use or to carry about.

One of the main uses is for paring the surface edges of saw cuts and other wounds before applying the dressing in order to leave them smooth, thus facilitating healing. However, the knife is commonly used for pruning, especially on young trees under training, for in the hands of a skilled person the cut may often be positioned accurately with an absence of bruising. The operation of snagging has already been mentioned and this must be carried out neatly and accurately, otherwise an unsightly union may result which would be evident for many years, possibly for the life of the tree, *see* Fig. 52.

A comparison is often made between the cut made by a pair of secateurs and that made with a pruning knife; indeed this is a point of great argument among gardeners, of all classes. The case put forward for the secateurs is that the cut may be made easily even by an amateur and that the exposed surface is small. The knife cannot cut straight across the stem, but the increase in area which is exposed is negligible while in the hands of a skilled person no bruising occurs. Also a greater area of cambium is exposed for quick healing, *see* Fig. 53.

It is largely a matter of practice, for the efficient use of the knife requires considerable skill and unless care is taken serious injury from deep cuts may be caused to the hands and arms. On these grounds alone, it is advisable for the

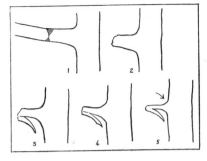

Fig. 53. This set of diagrams shows how a branch of some thickness can if necessary be cut off flush with a suitable and sharp knife.
(1) The main part of the branch is removed by making wedge-shaped cuts which are enlarged until the portion is severed, leaving a short stub as in (2).
(3) and (4) show how shavings are removed until only a thin portion is left.
(5) Lastly, a downward cut is made in the direction of the arrow.

majority to use a good pair of secateurs. It should be noted, however, that the knife is one of the best tools to use for pruning *Cytisus* or *Spartium*, where the method is to cut a collection of growths which have been bundled together with the free hand. The severance of the shoots individually would be very time-consuming.

AXES AND HATCHETS

These are often used for tree work, the axes for felling, perhaps to a larger extent in copse clearing, but also for cutting the roots when the butts are taken out completely. Hatchets, on the other hand, are used for a variety of tasks, including chopping up and cleaning the smaller and thinner wood which has been removed from the tree and is lying on the ground. Another important use for a hatchet is when it becomes necessary to chip or take out a wedge-shaped section before a saw-cut is made on the opposite side. This is often necessary when sections of the trunk or nearly vertical branches have to be removed, or when the wood pinches the saw on the undercut, making a sufficient penetration impossible.

The British Standards publication, 294:1958, Axes and Hatchets, gives the specifications and tests to be applied to bring these tools within the scope of the standards described. Furthermore, the publication defines the main types and gives the dimensions, weight, quality and performance of each. It is clearly stated that for the purposes of the standard, tools of any type which have head weight of up to and including 1 k. (2 lb.) are hatchets; over this they are classed as axes.

Axes

For this tool to be used properly, not only is a considerable amount of skill and confidence necessary, but the tool must be kept well sharpened and in good condition. The good axe-man deals heavy, accurate blows on either side of the intended line of severance, so that the chips are cut through and fly away completely. Never should a blow be made on a branch, stem or root which is free at one end and is liable to spring back. If this is done there is a real danger of the tool rebounding out of control, perhaps hitting the face or head and causing considerable injury. Another important safeguard, especially for the beginner, is to keep the handle down as the blow is made, thus ensuring that the tool does not swing onto the feet or legs if the stem or branch is missed completely.

Hatchets

To a large extent the above advice also applies to this tool. Both must be kept in good condition if they are to be used effectively.

LADDERS AND STEPS

In the interests of efficiency and safety it is important to use only the best models. A careful selection is also necessary for there are various patterns and lengths, each being suited to a particular use and purpose.

A good ladder made by a reliable firm will have been manufactured according to specifications laid down by the British Standard Institution. There are at least two publications produced by this authority which are of interest to the arboriculturist, B.S. 2037:1964, 'Specifications for Aluminium Ladders, Steps and Trestles' and B.S. 1129:1966, 'Specifications for Timber Ladders, Steps, Trestles and Lightweight Stagings for industrial use.'

The arboriculturist and student would do well to read through these publications so that he may realise the amount of skill, thought and care which has been put into the subject, and into the manufacture of the ladders and steps which he can purchase.

Two materials are in common use:

Timber

Wooden ladders are made from timber which is selected for weight and strength. One advantage with these is that the sag is less pronounced than with most of the metal types, and there is less tendency for them to spring up and down when in use. They should definitely be used in preference to metal ladders if work is to be carried out near high powered electrical installations.

Aluminium Alloy

Ladders made from this material are comparatively light in weight and do not deteriorate with age. Also they will not rust.

Metal ladders are naturally good conductors of electricity and they should not be used in proximity to any electric cables.

The main types of ladders and steps may be classified as follows:

Single-section ladder

This is a complete unit in itself. There are two types—
    (i) *Standing ladder*. This type has rungs.
    (ii) *Step ladder*. This has wide treads which are laid in at an angle so that they are horizontal when the ladder is in a leaning position.

Extending Ladder

This is made up of two or three sections which, by a sliding action, may be adjusted to give varying heights. Usually this action is operated by a rope and pulley system, *see* Plate 60. With some patterns it is possible to use the sections individually as a single stage ladder.

Steps

These vary considerably in design but the back or legs are hinged and when opened out the steps are self-supporting. Patterns are also available which have a hinged platform at the top which rests in a horizontal position when the legs are open.

Inspection and Maintenance

Both ladders and steps must be kept in a perfect state of repair, and thus regular inspections are necessary to ensure that no fault has passed unnoticed. Accidents frequently occur through the use of ladders which are defective either from lack of maintenance or because they are beyond repair. Once a defect is discovered, even though it is a minor one, it should be repaired as soon as possible by an expert. In a large establishment it is wise to have at least one spare of each pattern to allow for repairs without disruption of work.

The frequency of these inspections depends upon the amount of use the ladders are put to. If they are in use every day inspections should be on a weekly basis. The main points to look for are as follows:

1. Check to see that the stiles are secure and cannot be pulled or pushed out of position. The wooden ladder of good quality is fitted with metal tie rods, or the rungs are arranged in such a way that the whole unit is rigid. (The stiles are the sides to which the rungs are attached).

2. With timber ladders, the grain should run lengthways which makes a split less likely. A close inspection should be made to ensure that there are no cracks or splits present.

3. Test the firmness of each rung in turn to ensure that there is no movement. It is important that there are no missing rungs.

4. The ropes on extension ladders should be replaced at regular intervals.

5. The working parts should move freely and they must, if necessary be oiled. The guide brackets and stops must be firmly secured.

6. In the case of steps, the back should be securely fixed with hinges which function properly and are sufficiently strong. The extent to which the legs open should be limited to prevent them from spreading and causing the whole to collapse.

7. Ladders or steps which have been accidently dropped or hit in any way, perhaps by a falling limb, should be inspected immediately. Should there be any damage it must be repaired before they are used again.

In connection with safety, it should be remembered that regulations have been made under the Agriculture (Safety, Health and Welfare Provisions) Act, 1956. Ladders are covered by these regulations and both employers and workers have responsibilities. Faulty ladders must not be used.

Storage when not in Use

The best method is to lay the ladders horizontally across bars 100 × 100 mm. (4 × 4 in.) placed at a true level and no more than 3·0 m. (10 ft.) apart. These should be under cover, *see* Fig. 54. It is better to use this method of storage than to hang them on pegs which are sometimes fixed to a wall for this purpose. With the latter method the stiles are strained and the rungs loosened.

It is wrong to lean a ladder against a wall for storage, as other articles may in turn be laid or piled against it, and the extra weight may cause sagging which in time could cause weakening or straining of the stiles.

It is a good plan to secure ladders and steps with a padlock as a safeguard against use by unauthorised persons.

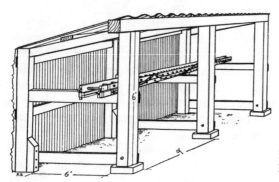

Fig. 54. The best method of ladder storage.

Use

It is important that ladders should be raised carefully and according to a set procedure. Normally this is a two-man task. First, the ladder should be laid near the intended position but clear of any branches which would impede its erection. One man should then stand on the lowest rung, while the other lifts the top above his head. The latter then walks toward the lower end, which remains firmly on the ground through the weight of the first man, raising the ladder by moving his hands steadily forward. The anchor man holds onto a rung as long as possible as the ladder is raised in order to prevent overbalancing. As the ladder is raised the weight on the arms is gradually reduced until it is perfectly vertical, when the first man steps down and both are able to steady the top as the ladder is lifted and moved into position. The first man may be needed again for anchoring while the ladder is being finally positioned. The same procedure in reverse is necessary for lowering.

Sectional ladders are extended after being raised and held in an approximate position against the tree or structure. Often it is better to run an extension ladder up the main trunk in the first place, especially if this is straight and clear of low branches.

It is important to stand both ladders and steps on firm ground, and safe placement should be tested by standing on the lower rung and throwing the weight on the feet by a jolting action. Particular care should be taken if the ladder is placed on a border against a wall, for soil which has been disturbed by cultivation is likely to be loose and will not offer a sufficiently firm surface to carry all the weight, especially when the ladder is in use. A sudden jolt caused by one or both of the legs sinking can easily cause an accident. A wall planting should be planned to allow for such operations to be undertaken with safety. If there is doubt, it is never wise to take a chance, and it is wrong to to climb up a ladder which has been insecurely placed, hoping to control any movement by holding on to the branches or wires, for these can easily break or swing out of control.

The top of the ladder should be firmly rested on the main trunk or on the base of a sound branch or in the case of a wall, on the actual surface. It is also advisable to lean the ladder into the tree so that if the branch does give way there is less likelihood of it falling completely without being stopped by other branches. If the support is a branch there should be sufficient overlap of the top of the ladder above the point of contact with the branch so that if the tree or branch should sway, or the limb becomes lighter through shortening, the ladder will still remain supported. The top should rest firmly so that there is no rock when the position is tested. Once a ladder is erected and positioned securely it is worthwhile roping the top to the branch, but this must only be done when up and down movement is unlikely, *see* Plate 60. In this connection, it is most un-wise to work on trees during periods of strong wind or during wet or frosty weather. While the ladder is in use, the anchoring man should always be standing on the lowest rung, attentive to every movement made by the climber.

Ladder moving, from one part of the tree to another, may become necessary but a limited amount of movement is possible with the ladder in a leaning position for, by first moving the base round, a new and suitable place may be found. However, when the move involves taking an extended ladder to a completely new position, even if it is on the same tree, it should first be returned to the vertical position by taking the base in towards the tree, when by means of the ropes and pulleys, the sections should be allowed to slide back under control. The move is then made, but it may even be necessary to lower the ladder to the ground completely.

Safety Precautions

An erected ladder should not be left unattended unless precautions are taken to see that it is not interfered with in any way. A wide plank, at least 3·6 m. (12 ft.) in length, laid flat on the rungs is an effective and useful deterrent to the would-be unlawful climber. It should be chained and locked in position and the top of the ladder must always be tied to prevent dislodgement. However, it is much safer to take a ladder down completely, if it is to be left unattended for any length of time.

List of Tools and Equipment

Category	Required for Tree and Shrub Pruning	Additional items for large tree work
SAWS	Hand Pruning Grecian Tubular, frame Two-man crosscut Longarm	Power or Chain

ROPES	45 m. (150 ft.) length
	44 mm. (1¾ in.) circum.
	  Sisal or Manilla
	45 to 60 m. (150 to 200 ft.) length
	  strong weighted cord
		A variety of stronger
		45 to 60 m. (150 or
		200 ft.) lengths

LADDERS	Steps Single, 6 to 8 m. (20 to 25 ft.)	Two-stage Three-stage
MISCELLANEOUS	Secateurs Lond-handled pruners Longarm or Standard pruners Pruning knives Shears Sledge hammers up to 6·3 k. (14 lb.) Wedges Spades Digging forks Mattocks Axes and Hatchets	
LIFTING EQUIPMENT		Hand winches Jacks
SAFETY EQUIPMENT		Safety harness Helmets Barriers Notices
TOOLS FOR CAVITY WORK		Augers 25 mm. (1 in.) and 50 mm. (2 in.) Chisels Gouges Mallets Hammers Blowlamps

Appendix IV

SAW SHARPENING AND MAINTENANCE

An extract from the publication 'Concerning Handsaws'
by kind permission of Messrs. Spear and Jackson, Aetna Works, Sheffield, 4

HOW TO MAINTAIN YOUR SAW IN PERFECT WORKING ORDER

A saw in really bad condition will need the following operations, *in this order:*

    1. Topping.
    2. Shaping.
    3. Setting.
    4. Sharpening.

But, just as a chisel may be honed many times before regrinding becomes necessary, so a saw can be re-sharpened several times before the set is worn away. A good rule when sharpening a saw is 'little and often'.

Topping

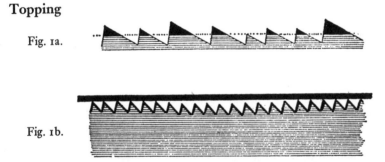

Fig. 1a.

Fig. 1b.

When the teeth of a saw are of different heights (fig. 1a), or when the edge has worn hollow (fig. 1b), the saw must be 'topped' to level off any unevenness. Use a second-cut mill file, 10 in. long, or any well worn flat file. Fix the saw in a saw-vice, hold the file quite flat and run it along the whole length of the saw. Should the saw have a very uneven edge it is unwise to top it completely before beginning the shaping, as, with more than about a third removed from the tops

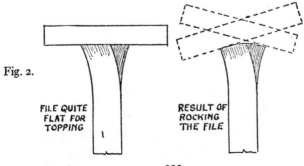

Fig. 2.

FILE QUITE
FLAT FOR
TOPPING

RESULT OF
ROCKING
THE FILE

of the most prominent teeth, it becomes difficult to retain the original spacing when performing the next operation of shaping (*described on pages* 324 *and* 325). When the edge is badly out of true, top lightly so as to file only the highest teeth. Shape these and top again, and continue shaping and topping alternately until all the teeth are reached.

When topping, care should be taken to keep the file quite flat (fig. 2), otherwise the edges of the teeth will become rounded and thus difficult to sharpen correctly. If holding the file quite flat and square with the saw blade is difficult, make a 'topping clamp' (fig. 3).

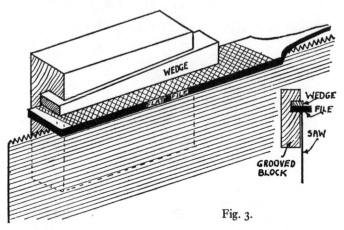

Fig. 3.

Shaping

In shaping, the teeth of your saw are all filed to a uniform shape and size with a taper or slim taper saw file, using these sizes:

Saw, points per inch	Rip 6	7–8	10–12	
Taper, saw-file, length	8″	7″	6″	6″ (slim taper)

For best results the width of the file face should be just over twice the depth of the saw teeth (A, fig. 4). If the file is too narrow (B, fig. 4), two of its faces may become completely worn, so that when the file is turned over only one new face is brought into action, the other being already worn.

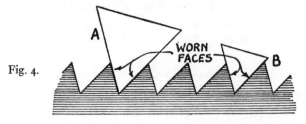

Fig. 4.

Fix the saw in the saw-vice so that not more than $\frac{1}{4}$ in. of the saw projects above the cheeks of the vice. Place the file in a gullet between two teeth and press it down firmly with the left hand so that it assumes the correct pitch of the teeth. Grip the file handle in the right hand with the thumb on top and finger alongside and maintain this grip until the shape is complete.

The same *pitch* will then be given to each tooth. *Pitch* is the angle at which the leading edge of the tooth leans forward, as much as 14° for a cross-cut saw, but a much lesser angle for the rip-saw (fig. 5).

Fig. 5.

The teeth are shaped by filing straight across the saw at right angles, and with the file held horizontally (fig. 6).

File each gullet carefully and accurately with slow steady strokes of the file.

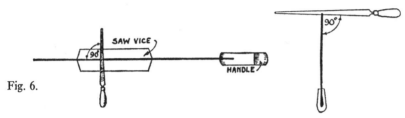

Fig. 6.

When shaping is completed, all flats formed on the tips of teeth during topping will have just been removed and each tooth brought to a point. The teeth should now all be quite even in height, all of the same shape, and the front and back of each tooth should be sloping at the correct angle (fig. 5). *Do nothing to bevel the teeth. This is done during the final sharpening process after the teeth have been 'set'.* Teeth should be shaped as uniformly as possible so that each tooth will play its proper part in the cutting action. This uniform shaping of each tooth is a vital factor in the ease with which a saw does its work.

Setting

The most common mistake made in reconditioning of saws is to give the teeth too much 'set'. Teeth well set will cut a kerf wide enough to give clearance for the blade; the *least* amount of set to give this clearance is the *right* amount. Rarely will the kerf need to be more than $1\frac{1}{2}$ times the thickness of the blade. Greater set than this makes the saw less efficient because more effort has to be expended in producing an unnecessarily wide kerf and also more wood is wasted as saw-dust.

The nature of the wood to be cut will affect the amount of set. If the wood is wet the saw does not cut so cleanly and so the teeth must be set more widely than for dry wood.

Teeth should not be set for more than half their depth (fig. 7). Any attempt to set them deeper may cause distortion of the blade at the roots of the teeth, cracking the blade at the bottom of the gullets, or even the breaking out of some teeth.

Undoubtedly the best method of setting is that used by the manufacturers. They use a fine cross pean hammer and saw anvil consisting of a piece of steel with a rounded edge and some form of guide or stop so that the teeth overhang the bevel by the correct amount (fig. 8a). The saw blade rests on the anvil. The guides are adjusted so that *no more than half* the depth of the tooth projects

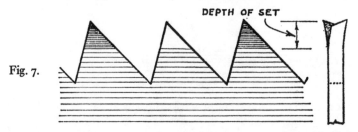

DEPTH OF SET

Fig. 7.

over the bevel on the anvil. The first tooth is set with two or three light blows with the hammer rather than with one heavy one. Alternate teeth along the whole length of the saw are then set in the same way. The blade is then turned over to set the intermediate teeth. Take care to set the teeth to their original sides. Bending teeth first one way and then the other may break them.

Fig. 8a.

The plier type of saw set, such as the 'Eclipse' (fig. 8b), will also set saws satisfactorily. The pliers are operated by placing them over a tooth and compressing the handles. A plunger pushes the tooth over against an anvil. To suit each particular saw the amount and the depth of set are both automatically controlled by the adjustment of the anvil and depth stop. The old type of saw-set – a steel blade with a number of slots cut in it – will not usually produce an even set and is not recommended. It may, however, be employed successfully for setting saws used for very coarse work.

Fig. 8b.

Whatever the method, a uniform set must be produced along the whole length of the blade, each tooth being bent by exactly the same amount. A saw will not work true to a line unless the teeth on both sides do the same amount of work. Slight irregularities of set are removed by side dressing. Lay the saw flat on the bench and then run an oilstone slip slightly over the teeth to reduce any that are too prominent. Turn the saw over and repeat on the other side.

A saw that consistently wanders away from the line of cut most probably has more set on one side than on the other. A careful side-dressing with the oilstone slip will cure the trouble.

Sharpening

The final sharpening of the saw teeth is done in one of two ways according to whether the saw is to be used for cutting across or along the grain.

Cross-cut Saws. The teeth must be bevelled with a file to produce knife-edges to sever the fibres of the wood.

If this bevel is made too long a very thin edge is produced on the tooth (A, fig. 9). Though this cuts excellently it will very quickly be worn away — particularly on hardwoods — so a shorter bevel is better for general use (B, fig 9).

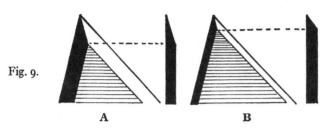

Fig. 9.

A   B

Fix the saw so that not more than ¼ inch of the blade projects above the cheeks of the saw vice. In figs. 10 and 11 the handle of the saw is assumed to be on the *right* of the vice.

Fig. 10.

Next, 'top' the saw very lightly. This makes certain that all the teeth are the same height and puts a 'shiner' on the tips of the teeth to help in the sharpening process.

Place the file to work on the front edge of the first tooth set towards you (A1, fig. 11). It will then also be working on the back edge of the tooth on the left of the file, this tooth being set away from you.

Move the file handle over to the left until the file makes an angle of 65° to 75° with the line of the saw blade, (fig. 10). This angle *must* be maintained throughout. Keeping the file perfectly horizontal, give each tooth two or three slow steady strokes of the file. When half of the 'shiner' is filed away the file is transferred to *the next gullet but one*. The front edge of the tooth set towards you is being filed each time, (A2, fig. 11). Continue to the end of the saw, filing in each *alternate* gullet.

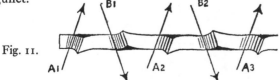

Fig. 11.

B1   B2

A1   A2   A3

When you reach the end of the saw, reverse it in the saw-vice. The handle is now on the *left* of the vice (fig. 12). Repeat the filing on the front edge of the teeth set towards you, i.e., in the gullets which were missed the first time (B1, B2, in fig. 11). The file handle must be swung round to the right so that the filing is again done towards the saw handle. Maintain the original angle of 65° to 75° (fig. 12), and keep the file perfectly horizontal. The filing is completed when the other half of the 'shiner' on each tooth just disappears. The teeth should then be sharp.

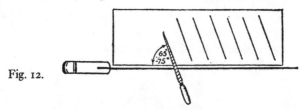

Fig. 12.

Rip Saws. The teeth of a rip saw must be filed to produce the chisel edges which sever the fibres of the wood, (fig. 13).

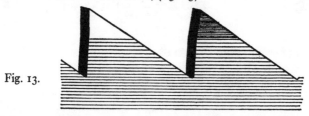

Fig. 13.

Fix the saw in the saw-vice (see *Sharpening Cross-cut Saws*, page 327), with the handle to the right. Give the teeth a very light topping to produce the shiners. The sharpening procedure is the same as for the cross-cut saw *except* that in this case the filing *must* be done at *right angles* across the saw (fig. 14).

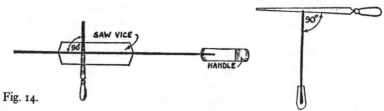

Fig. 14.

File each alternate gullet, A1, A2, etc. (fig. 15), then reverse the saw in the vice so that the handle is now to the left. Then file the intermediate teeth which were missed on the first filing (the file will now be at B1, B2, etc. in fig. 15). The file *must* be quite horizontal at all times (fig. 14).

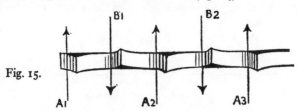

Fig. 15.

After sharpening, side-dress the saw very lightly with an oilstone slip to remove any burr caused by the file.

Appendix V

SLINGING

Introduction

It is frequently necessary to remove limbs or sections of limbs, and to lower them carefully by means of ropes, in order to avoid damage to a structure or feature beneath, for example, a building, a path or plants. It is emphasised that this is a skilled operation, and that it can be very dangerous with heavy limbs if carried out by workers who have insufficient knowledge, or if it is attempted with poor or inadequate equipment. The operation really comes under the heading of Tree Surgery, and the following is intended to serve only as a brief guide. The subject should be studied in greater detail before it is attempted, even in practice form.

The Main or Supporting Ropes

The length of each rope used to support the weight should be twice the height of the tree. The reason for this is that some of the spare length which is on the ground is taken up as the branch is lowered. There must also be enough left on the ground to allow a good hold and control until the operation is complete. It is very important for reasons of safety that the ropes used for this purpose are sufficiently strong, and the choice of rope for a particular task is a matter of knowledge and experience.

Normally it is considered advisable to use two ropes for adequate control and safety, each rope being taken over a strong crotch, preferably in line with and above the branch to be removed. It is not advisable to use the same crotch for both ropes. One rope is tied near the base of the limb to be removed, the other at about two-thirds along the length, provided the wood is sufficiently strong and able to carry the weight. A strong reliable knot is used, such as a timber hitch.

From the crotches, the ropes are run down the trunk and are wound twice round it at the base, but at working height (three or four feet above ground level). The ropes are tightened and held while the spare is laid out across the ground free of obstacles. A guide rope (approx. $1\frac{1}{2}$ in. in circumference) is attached to the outer end of the branch as a means of steadying and steering it during lowering.

Cutting

Whether a branch is severed and lowered in portions or as a whole, an undercut should first be made to prevent tearing. In some cases it may be necessary to cut out a wedge-shaped section before attempting the main cut. This enables the supported branch to be lowered slightly if the saw is pinched in the cut. (*See also* page 5 where the method of removing a limb in sections is described.)

Lowering

Throughout the operation helpers on the ground should remain on the alert, holding the rope ends and ready to follow the directions of the climber in charge. Once it has been severed, the branch is lowered by gradually allowing more rope to pass up the tree, but always under full control.

As the limb nears the ground it is usually possible, by use of the guide rope and by actual handling, to choose the most convenient position for it to lie. If the limb is over a border, many of the branchlets may be sawn off and either thrown or handed on to the edge, thus avoiding damage by lowering it onto the plants. A good tree-craftsman takes a pride in the neatness of his work, causing the minimum of damage both to the tree being worked on and to the neighbouring trees, shrubs, plants or turf.

The removal of a limb or portion of a trunk without the aid of a strong, higher crotch involves techniques which come under the heading of specialised tree work.

Appendix VI

ACCIDENT PREVENTION and FIRST AID
in pruning and allied tasks

by

GRACE M. WEBBER, S.R.N., O.N.D.

Introduction

It is not the aim in this Appendix to provide a complete First Aid Manual. There are already many excellent publications available, and courses in First Aid are held by the St. John Ambulance Association and the British Red Cross in towns and villages throughout the country.

The average person, however, does not think about first aid until it is needed, and this section has, therefore, been included in order to provide some of the essential knowledge required in emergencies, and in the hope that the reader will be prompted to seek further instruction in the subject.

Prevention of Accidents

Accidents can largely be prevented by proper care of machinery, tools, and equipment, the use of protective clothing when appropriate, and common sense in the organization of the work and the working area.

Tools should be kept clean and sharp, and the sharp edges protected when not in use. Equipment, e.g. ladders, safety harness, etc., should be frequently inspected and kept in good repair.

Machinery. Machinery must be well-maintained, and at all times kept in good working order. If guards are provided, they are there to protect the operator, and must on no account be removed.

The Factories Act gives very clear instructions about protective measures, and it behoves every employer and employee to familiarize himself with the Act, as published and revised.

Protective Clothing. Clothing should be adequate and comfortable. Tight sleeves hamper movement, but, conversely, loose sleeves may catch on tools or on the branches and are thus a source of danger. Shirt sleeves should be rolled up over the elbows, or fastened securely at the wrists.

Stout shoes should be worn, and the laces tied securely.

Hair can become entangled in machinery, so hair styles should be sensible.

The use of safety helmets is a wise precaution for workers beneath trees as a protection against falling branches which have been sawn off by the pruner. But their use does not relieve the pruner of the responsibility of giving ample warning of impending danger from falling limbs.

Anti-tetanus injections.   Tetanus, or, as it is commonly called, 'lockjaw' can be a very distressing and crippling disease. It is caused by an organism entering a wound at the time of injury, and is most likely to occur in cases of road accidents and in agricultural and horticultural occupations. A wound can become infected when working in one's own garden.

Immunization against tetanus is a simple procedure. The course of three injections can be given by your own doctor. After completion of the course, a booster dose should be given every five years.

Nowadays, children are usually immunized against Tetanus at school, but it is important that the 'booster doses' are kept up throughout adult life.

First Aid Box

Every household and every employer should have a portable First Aid Box. The following is a suggested list of contents:

		Quantity
1.	Sterilized wound dressing	
	(a) finger dressings (containing either absorbent or boric acid lint)	3
	(b) small plain wound dressings	2
	(c) medium plain wound dressings	2
2.	Triangular bandages of which the base should not be less than 1300 mm. (51 in.) and each of the other two sides not less than 900 mm (36 in.)	2
3.	Adhesive wound dressings (not the waterproof variety unless aerated)	
	30 by 50 mm. (1½ by 2 in.)	3
	50 by 75 mm. (2 by 3 in.)	3
4.	Absorbent cotton wool, half-ounce packet	1
5.	Cotton bandages	
	25 mm. (1 in.), 50 mm. (2 in.) and 75 mm. (3 in.)	1 of each
6.	Crepe bandages	
	75 mm. (3 in.) and 100 mm. (4 in.)	1 of each
7.	Roll zinc oxide plaster 25 mm. (1 in.)	1
8.	Large pieces of clean, old linen or cotton (remains of old sheets are most useful)	
9.	Paper tissues	
10.	A bottle of mild antiseptic lotion	
11.	Witch hazel (useful for sprains)	
12.	Glucose sweets	
13.	Common salt	
14.	Bicarbonate of soda and vinegar if there is a likelihood of bee and wasp stings	
15.	1 pair scissors (blunt-ended, or with one blunt and one sharp end)	
16.	1 pair tweezers	
17.	Safety pins (assorted, rust-proof in box)	

Definition of First Aid

The purpose of First Aid is to save life, help recovery and prevent the casualty's condition becoming worse, until medical aid can be obtained.

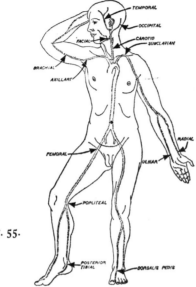

Fig. 55.

General Procedure

1. Take steps to prevent further injury occurring.
2. Treat the obvious injuries such as failure of breathing, severe bleeding, severe shock.
3. Organize help.
4. Avoid all unnecessary movement. (If spinal injury is suspected, the casualty must not be moved).
5. Continue care and treatment for as long as necessary.

Shock

All accidents involve a certain degree of shock, the signs varying from slight faintness to complete collapse.

To treat for shock:

1. Reassure the casualty, and do not leave him alone unless it is unavoidable.
2. Loosen constricting clothing.
3. Lay him on his back. Keep the head low and turned sideways.
4. Keep him warm but not overheated, and as comfortable as possible.
5. Do NOT give alcohol or apply hot water bottles.
6. If thirst is complained of give small quantities of water or sweet tea, unless internal injury is suspected, in which case give no liquids. The mouth, however, may be washed out.

7. If there is a tendency to vomit, or breathing is noisy and bubbling, turn him three-quarters over with one knee drawn up and one arm bent, and support him there with the head turned sideways.

Artificial Respiration – mouth to mouth method

If the casualty is not breathing, lay him flat on his back on the ground or any flat surface such as a table. Working from the side, hold the head firmly with both hands, one hand on the forehead pressing the head backwards and at the same time pinching the nostrils shut with finger and thumb, the other pressing the lower jaw upwards and forwards. This ensures that the tongue will not block the air passage.

Take a deep breath and, opening your mouth wide, place your lips closely round the casualty's mouth. Blow into his lungs until his chest rises, then remove your mouth. Repeat four times as quickly as possible, and thereafter at the rate of ten times per minute. Shallow and more frequent breaths will be required in the case of a child. If, however, the lungs will not inflate, try cleaning out the mouth with your finger covered by a handkerchief. Also make sure the head is tipped right back with the neck extended, and that you have closed the nostrils properly.

Continue the inflations until medical help arrives or the casualty is breathing normally. Do not give up if there appears to be no early response, as cases have been known of success after several hours. Even after normal breathing is resumed, the casualty should be watched in case of a relapse.

Heart Resuscitation

If the heart beat has stopped, it is essential to restart the circulation of the blood if artificial respiration is to be of any use. But this First Aid method has its dangers and should not be attempted unless one is sure the heart is not working.

If there is no pulse in the neck (carotid artery) and ten or a dozen inflations have produced no apparent improvement in the colour of skin, lips etc., another helper should kneel at one side, place his hands one on top of the other over the middle of the casualty's chest, and, after each inflation of the lungs, press firmly about six times with the arms straight, at a rate of one per second.

If no second person is available, the First Aider should attempt to carry out such chest massage pausing every ten or twelve seconds to inflate the lungs.

Wounds and Bleeding (Haemorrhage)

(a) *Severe bleeding* must be stopped at once. The simplest method is to apply a pad and pressure over the wound. The pad may be a piece of linen or gauze, or even a clean, folded handkerchief, surmounted by a thick wad of cotton wool. This pad must be kept pressed over the wound until bleeding stops. Unless there are signs of fracture, raise the bleeding part. If bleeding persists, pressure may be applied at certain 'Pressure Points', *see* Fig. 55, but this should not be attempted unless the rescuer has had some instruction. Tourniquets should never be applied.

In all cases of severe bleeding which cannot be quickly stopped, medical aid must be sought.

Do Not Disturb a Clot.

(b) *Slight bleeding*. Where the wound is slight and bleeding is not severe, the First Aider should wash his hands thoroughly before washing the wound in clean water, preferably under a running cold tap. Cleanse with antiseptic lotion and apply a dressing plaster or else a clean gauze dressing with cotton wool and bandage. Any foreign body, e.g. splinter, thorn, grit, etc., should, if possible be removed before applying the dressing.

A long, deep cut may require stitching and should be seen by a doctor. A doctor should also see any wound which is badly lacerated, or in which a foreign body or dirt are still embedded.

Blood blisters should not be pricked.

(c) *Nose bleed*. Do not lay the casualty flat. Put him in a sitting position and gently squeeze just below the bridge of the nose. A cold compress, or ice may also be applied at this point. If bleeding persists, however, seek the advice of a doctor.

Fractures

If a broken bone is suspected, the affected part must not be moved. The casualty should be made comfortable and treated for shock. Then send for an ambulance. Do not attempt to fix a splint or give any other treatment unless you are properly trained.

Dislocations

A dislocation is a displacement of the bones at a joint, characterised by severe pain. The joint cannot be moved and looks misshapen and swollen.

Do not attempt to manipulate the bones back into position. Support the part with pillows or cushions in the position most comfortable for the casualty, and obtain medical aid.

Sprains – e.g. of wrist and ankle

Where it is certain there are no broken bones, cover with a cold compress held in place by a crepe bandage, to reduce the swelling. The casualty should then be encouraged to use the joint normally as soon as possible, though not, of course, so as to risk another accident.

Burns and Scalds

First remove the cause, e.g. smother flaming clothing with a blanket or rug or roll the victim over and over on the ground if a blanket is not available, switch off electricity, wash off chemicals by thorough flooding with cold water. Then:

1. Make sure your hands are as clean as possible.
2. Do not pull off burnt clothing, which may have stuck to the skin.
3. Do not break or prick blisters.
4. Do not apply lotions of any sort, but plunge the burnt limb into cold water or hold it under a running tap.

5. Cover the area with a clean, and preferably sterile, dressing of lint or linen.
6. Bandage firmly (lightly where there are blisters).
7. Prevent movement of the injured part.
8. Treat the casualty for shock.

No burns, however small, must be neglected, and severe burns require hospital treatment as soon as possible.

Sunburn

In general, the above rules apply, but when the skin is unbroken, calamine lotion may be dabbed lightly on to relieve discomfort.

Eye Injuries

Goggles must always be worn when there is a danger of sawdust moving or blowing into the eyes.

Foreign body in the eye. Particles of grit, sawdust, etc., may lodge in the eyes and can usually be removed with the corner of a clean handkerchief soaked in a little water. Alternatively, get the casualty to blink the eye under water.

Use no force, and do not attempt to remove anything actually embedded. In such a case, cover the eye lightly with a pad or handkerchief, and take the casualty to hospital immediately. Do not allow him to rub the eye. If a cotton wool pad is used it must be covered with gauze or soft linen, otherwise a corneal abrasion may be caused if the patient opens his eye under the pad.

Irritant liquid in the eye. Wash out thoroughly under a cold tap, or sluice the eye with a jug of cold water. Do not let him rub the eye. Cover as above, and, if irritation persists, send him to hospital.

Miscellaneous

Poisons. Many substances used nowadays in agriculture and horticulture are toxic or irritant, and can do serious harm if swallowed or allowed to come in contact with the skin. The manufacturers' instructions should always be rigidly observed.

Where a poisonous substance has been swallowed, give large quantities of water or milk as quickly as possible. In the case of a skin irritant, flood the area with cold water. In both cases, get medical aid without delay, stating, if possible, the actual substances involved.

Toxic plants. Many plants, such as those in the Rhus group, Primulas, and even Daffodils, may cause a skin rash in some people. Seek medical advice, and, if you can, produce a specimen of the plant.

Insect stings. If a bee-sting is present, remove it with forceps and apply weak ammonia, or bicarbonate of soda dissolved in water. If the sting is inside the mouth, or in the ear passage, seek medical advice.

If the victim has been stung by a wasp, vinegar or lemon juice is beneficial.

Any bite may be soothed by the application of a strong solution of common salt.

Glossary

Some of the less common botanical and technical terms.

BIGENERIC HYBRID
A sexual hybrid between two species of different genera. The name is preceded by the sign ×. For example, × *Osmarea burkwoodi* is a hybrid between *Osmanthus delavayi* and *Phillyrea decora.*

CHIMAERA
A plant which is made up of two tissues growing together but remaining distinct. They may occur as graft hybrids or as the result of bud mutations.

CLONE
A plant which has been propagated vegetatively and not by normal sexual reproduction. This method is used for many cultivars in order to perpetuate some desirable characteristic.

COPPICE
Certain trees such as Sweet Chestnut and Hazel are grown for the production of brushwood and stakes for various purposes. As the crop is collected they are cut down to within 0·3 m. (1 ft.) or so of ground level, a process which is repeated at intervals of 5 to 7 years. Such a planting is referred to as a coppice.

CULTIVAR
The term now officially recognised to distinguish a cultivated form from a botanical variety. Cultivars are distinguished in this book by using capitals for the initial letters of their distinctive names and by putting these names in single inverted commas, e.g. *Euonymus fortunei* 'Silver Queen.'

DECUMBENT
A prostrate or semi-prostrate growth, the ends of the shoots being turned up to a vertical position.

DIOECIOUS
The male and female flowers occur on different plants.

EPICORMIC SHOOT
A shoot system growing on a mature portion of the main stem, trunk or branch. Often these shoots are in clusters in the region of wounds or burrs, having originated from adventitious shoots or dormant buds.

FASTIGIATE
A variety or form with erect and often clustered growths.

FRUCTIFICATION
A fruiting body.

GRAFT-HYBRID
A plant made up of two distinct tissues. The plant must be propagated vegetatively, having originated in the first place from a graft union made up of stock and scion tissues. The name of a graft-hybrid is preceded by the sign +, an example being +*Laburnocytisus adami* which is made up of *Laburnum anagyroides* + *Cytisus purpureus*.

HYBRID
Generally taken to refer to a sexual hybrid or cross between two species in the same genus, e.g. *Berberis* × *stenophylla* which is a hybrid between *B. darwinii* and *B. empetrifolia*.

INFLORESCENCE
The flowering portion.

INTERNODES
The section of stem between two nodes.

LACINIATE
A leaf which is fragmented or cut into narrow and often pointed lobes.

LATERALS
Distinct from the leading shoot, these are the side growths which develop at an angle from the main axis. As growth extends each lateral often produces a complex branch system, but the leading shoot(s) on these should not be as vigorous as the main leader.

LEADING SHOOT
Generally the top-most growth on the framework of a young or mature tree. It should be the dominant growth and thus stronger than the remainder. One or more leading shoots may also be found on the laterals.

MERISTEMATIC CELLS
These make up a tissue which increases rapidly by cell division, provided that conditions are suitable. The cambium which develops as a healing tissue in the region of wounds is largely made up of meristematic cells.

MONOECIOUS
The flowers are either male or female with both types occurring on the same plant.

PETIOLE
A leaf stalk.

PROCUMBENT
Growth on or very close to the soil surface.

SCANDENT
A plant, generally woody, which gains height by the production of long growths which clamber over the host plants. Often they are held in position by recurved thorns.

SPUR
A slow-growing and usually dwarf shoot system with rosetted leaves. Frequently this type of growth is specialised for flowering and fruiting.

STOLONIFEROUS
A plant with a creeping stem system developing at or just beneath ground level, from which vertical growths develop to give height.

STOOL
A plant with many shoots which originate at or just beneath the soil surface. Often new cane-like growths are produced annually.

STRATIFICATION
Certain seeds will not germinate immediately upon sowing and require a period of 'rest' before germination. One method of ensuring that the seed is given ideal conditions during this period is to place the required number in single layers alternating with peat or sand. This practice is referred to as stratification.

SUBSHRUB
A plant which produces soft wood which is often lost completely during the winter. Such plants generally survive by the production of new growths from the older wood at the base.

Index

Nomenclatural Update

George E. Brown's classic *The Pruning of Trees, Shrubs and Conifers* is as useful to the arborist and gardener today as it was when it was first published. The Latin names accorded to plants do change, however, and readers will find that a small number of names in the text have been superseded. Readers are advised to consult this update in case of any confusion. The list of older synonyms provided in Appendix I dates from the original edition and should be consulted only as a last resort. Names, most at the level of species, have been brought into accordance with the New Royal Horticultural Society Dictionary *Index of Garden Plants* (1994).

Acca sellowiana *see* Feijoa sellowiana
Actinidia deliciosa *see* Actinidia chinensis
Ageratina ligustrina *see* Eupatorium micranthum
Aloysia triphylla *see* Lippia citriodora
Amelanchier canadensis *see* Amelanchier oblongifolia
Amelanchier sanguinea *see* Amelanchier amabilis
Argyrocytisus battandieri *see* Cytisus battandieri
Aristolochia macrophylla *see* Aristolochia durior
Aristotelia chilensis *see* Aristotelia macqui
Aster albescens *see* Microglossa albescens
Berberis aristata *see* Berberis chitria
Betula fontinalis *see* Betula occidentalis
Brachyglottis greyi *see* Senecio greyi
Caesalpinia decapetala *see* Caesalpinia japonica
Calocedrus decurrens *see* Libocedrus decurrens
Carya illinoiensis *see* Carya pecan
Caryopteris incana *see* Caryopteris mastacanthus
Celtis occidentalis *see* Celtis pumila
Cephalotaxus harringtonia *see* Cephalotaxus drupacea
Cionura erecta *see* Marsdenia erecta
Cocculus orbiculatus *see* Cocculus trilobus
Colletia hystrix *see* Colletia armata
Colletia paradoxa *see* Colletia cruciata
Coronilla valentina *see* Coronilla glauca
Cotinus obovatus *see* Cotinus americanus
Crataegus ×prunifolia *see* Crataegus prunifolia
Docynia indica *see* Docynia rufifolia

Ehretia acuminata *see* Ehretia thyrsiflora
Ercilla spicata *see* Ercilla volubilis
Erica carnea *see* Erica mediterranea L. non hort.
Erica ×darleyensis *see* Erica mediterranea var. hybrida
Erica erigena *see* Erica mediterranea auct. non L.
Escallonia rubra *see* Escallonia macrantha
Euphorbia characias *see* Euphorbia wulfenii
Fothergilla major *see* Fothergilla monticola
Fraxinus angustifolia 'Raywood' *see* Fraxinus oxycarpa
Fraxinus angustifolia subsp. **syriaca** *see* Fraxinus syriaca
Fraxinus latifolia *see* Fraxinus oregona
Fraxinus ornus *see* Fraxinus rotundifolia
Garrya laurifolia *see* Garrya macrophylla
Gaultheria mucronata *see* Pernettya mucronata
Genista monspessulana *see* Cytisus monspessulanus
Halesia tetraptera *see* Halesia carolina
Hebe odora *see* Hebe anomala
Hemiptelea davidii *see* Zelkova davidii
Hydrangea heteromalla *see* Hydrangea ×anthoneura
Hydrangea serratifolia *see* Hydrangea integerrima
Jasminum mesnyi *see* Jasminum primulinum
Kalopanax septemlobus *see* Kalopanax pictus
Larix kaempferi *see* Larix leptolepis
Laurus azorica *see* Laurus canariensis
Lavandula angustifolia *see* Lavandula spica
Lithodora diffusa *see* Lithospermum diffusum
Luma chequen *see* Eugenia cheken
Mandevilla laxa *see* Mandevilla suaveolens
Meliosma alba *see* Meliosma beaniana
Meliosma dilleniifolia subsp. **cuneifolia** *see* Meliosma cuneifolia
Meliosma dilleniifolia subsp. **flexuosa** *see* Meliosma pendens
Meliosma pinnata *see* Meliosma oldhamii
Metrosideros umbellata *see* Metrosideros lucida
Mimulus aurantiacus *see* Mimulus glutinosus
Neillia sinensis *see* Neillia ribesioides
Oemleria cerasiformis *see* Osmaronia cerasiformis
Olearia phlogopappa *see* Olearia gunniana
Osmanthus decorus *see* Phillyrea decora
Osmanthus heterophyllus *see* Osmanthus ilicifolius
Ozothamnus scutellifolius *see* Helichrysum scutellifolium
Paulownia tomentosa 'Lilacina' *see* Paulownia lilacina
Perovskia *see* Perowskia

Photinia davidiana *see* Stransvaesia davidiana
Physocarpus opulifolius *see* Physocarpus stellatus
Picrasma ailanthoides *see* Picrasma quassioides
Piptanthus nepalensis *see* Piptanthus laburnifolius
Plagianthus regius *see* Plagianthus betulinus
Platanus ×acerifolia *see* Platanus ×hispanica
Platycladus orientalis *see* Thuja orientalis
Populus balsamifera *see* Populus tacamahaca
Populus ×jackii 'Gileadensis' *see* Populus candicans
Prumnopitys andina *see* Podocarpus andinus
Prunus ×domestica *see* Prunus insititia
Prunus dulcis *see* Prunus amygdalus
Quercus rubra *see* Quercus borealis
Rhaphiolepis *see* Raphiolepis
Rosa elegantula *see* Rosa farreri
Rosa pimpinellifolia *see* Rosa spinosissima
Rosa sericea *see* Rosa omiensis
Rosa xanthina *see* Rosa hugonis
Salix aegyptiaca *see* Salix medemii
Senna *see* Cassia
Sibiraea altaiensis *see* Sibiraea laevigata
Sorbaria kirilowii *see* Sorbaria arborea, S. assurgens
Sorbaria tomentosa *see* Sorbaria aitchisonii
Sorbus vestita *see* Sorbus cuspidata
Spiraea betulifolia *see* Spiraea corymbosa
Spiraea douglasii *see* Spiraea menziesii
Spiraea japonica *see* Spiraea bullata
Spiraea nervosa *see* Spiraea chinensis
Stewartia *see* Stuartia
Syringa reticulata *see* Syringa amurensis
Tetradium daniellii *see* Evodia henryi, E. hupehensis
Toona sinensis *see* Cedrela sinensis
Toxicodendron radicans *see* Rhus toxicodendron
Toxicodendron vernicifluum *see* Rhus verniciflua
Zelkova abelicea *see* Zelkova cretica
Zelkova carpinifolia *see* Zelkova verschaffeltii